STOCKHOLDERS' EQUITY

ACCOUNTING
RESEARCH
STUDY NO. 15

STOCKHOLDERS' EQUITY

By Beatrice Melcher, CPA
Accounting Research Staff

Published by the
American Institute of Certified Public Accountants, Inc.
666 Fifth Avenue   New York, N.Y. 10019

Copyright © 1973
American Institute of Certified Public Accountants, Inc.
666 Fifth Avenue, New York, N. Y. 10019

Notice to Readers

The activities of the Accounting Principles Board and its research arm, the Accounting Research Division, which was created in 1959, terminated June 1973. The series of accounting research studies, the first of which was published in 1961, terminates in 1973 with the publication of the fifteenth study. Research studies authorized and assigned to authors prior to 1973 and not published in the accounting research series have been transferred to the AICPA's newly created Technical Research Division. This division was created by the AICPA to continue research on financial and reporting matters to support its positions before the new Financial Accounting Standards Board. All technical research activities of the Institute are consolidated in the new division.

D. R. Carmichael, Director
Technical Research

Publication of this study by the American Institute of Certified Public Accountants does not in any way constitute official endorsement or approval of the conclusions reached or the opinions expressed.

Contents

Page

DIRECTOR'S STATEMENT xiii

AUTHOR'S PREFACE xv

Chapter

1. REPORTING STOCKHOLDERS' EQUITY 1

   Meaning of Equity, 1
   Recommendations for Changes, 2
      Presentation of Equity, 2
      Equity Transactions, 3
   Scope of Study, 6
      Recurring Transactions, 6
      Legal Regulation of Corporate Equity, 8
      Decisions of Management, 9
      Changes in Equity Not Studied, 9
   Organization of Study, 11

Part I
Status of Accounting for Stockholders' Equity

2. ISSUING STOCK 17

   Consideration for Stock Issued, 17
   Legal Regulation, 17
      Capital Stock, 17
      Corporate Statutes, 18
      Corporate Charters, 20
      Changes in Legal Capital, 20
      Accounting Requirements in the Law, 21
   Stock Issued for Cash, 22
      Recording Proceeds of Sales, 22
      Costs of Issuing Stock, 23

Chapter	Page

    Stock Issued for Property or Services, 23
        Acquired Assets at Cost, 23
    Stock Rights and Warrants, 24
        Characteristics of Securities, 24
        Alternative Accounting Practices, 25
    Conversions of Securities, 26
        Conversion of Debt, 27
        Conversion of Preferred Stock, 27
    Stock Options, 28
        Stock Option and Purchase Plans, 28
        AICPA Pronouncements on Options, 29
        Date To Measure Compensation, 31
        Recognized Compensation, 34
        Stock Issued for Exercised Options, 35
        Disclosure of Plans in Financial Statements, 35
    Business Combinations, 36
        Two Methods of Accounting, 36
        Pooling of Interests Method, 36
        Purchase Method, 37
    Stock Dividends and Stock Splits, 38
        Distinctions Between Distributions, 39
        Terminology, 40
        Accounting for Stock Dividends, 41
        Accounting for Stock Splits, 44

3. DECREASES IN STOCKHOLDERS' EQUITY 45

    Types of Decreases, 45
        Reacquisitions of Stock, 45
        Recapitalizations, 45
        Distributions of Dividends, 46
    Reacquired Shares of Stock, 46
        Reacquired or Treasury Stock, 46
        Treasury Stock as Asset or Equity, 46
        Legal Restrictions on Reacquiring Stock, 46
        Basic Views of Reacquiring Stock, 49
        Accounting for Preferred Stock Reacquired, 52
        Accounting for Common Stock Reacquired, 52
    Retirement of Stock, 52
        Differing Views of Retirement Accounting, 52
        Accounting for Preferred Stock Retired, 55
        Accounting for Common Stock Retired, 57

Chapter *Page*

    Other Dispositions of Treasury Stock, 57
        Legal Restrictions, 57
        Accounting for Dispositions of Treasury Stock, 58
        Differences in Methods, 61
        Prevalent Accounting Practices, 64

4. ADJUSTING COMPONENTS OF STOCKHOLDERS' EQUITY . . 67

    Changes in Par or Stated Value of Stock, 67
    Other Transfers Between Components, 67
    Recapitalizations and Exchanges, 68
    Quasi-Reorganizations, 68
        Adjustment of Carrying Amounts, 68
        Accepted Accounting Procedures, 69

5. COMPARISONS OF VARYING PRACTICES 72

    Features of Present Practices, 72
    Contrasts in Prevailing Practices, 73
        Timing of Transactions, 73
        Consideration for Stock, 74
        Relative Interests of Stockholders, 77
    Influences on Accounting Practices, 81
        Factors That Determine Accounting, 81
        Authoritative Pronouncements, 81
        Regulation of Equity Transactions, 81
        Existing Equity Components as Decisive Factor, 84
        Purpose of Transaction, 85
    Results of Varying Practices, 86

6. PRESENTATION OF COMPONENTS OF STOCKHOLDERS' EQUITY 87

    Traditional Presentation, 87
        Components in Financial Statements, 87
        Influences on Presentation, 88
        Terminology in Financial Statements, 89
        Presentation of Treasury Stock, 90
        Disclosure of Rights and Restrictions, 91
    Status of Current Presentation, 93
        Customary Equity Components, 93
        Alternatives Possible, 94

Chapter	Page

Part II
Solving the Presentation Problem

7. RECOMMENDED COMPONENTS OF EQUITY 97

    Purposes of Equity Accounting, 97
        Useful Reporting, 97
        Appraisal of Influencing Factors, 97
        Selection of Presentation, 98
    Impact of Corporate Equity, 98
        Distinctive Features of a Corporation, 98
        Accounting for Corporate Proprietorship, 99
    Alternative Presentations of Equity, 100
        Sources of Equity, 100
        Invested Capital, 103
        Total Equity, 104
    Selection of Most Informative Presentation, 108
        Present Practice Relies on Legal Concepts, 108
        Invested Capital Derived From Legal Status, 112
        Total Equity Restricts Information, 113
        Sources of Equity Recommended, 115
    Recommended Presentation, 116
        Components of Equity, 116
        Customary Disclosures, 120
        Contingent Equity Financing, 123
        Advantages of Sources of Equity, 127

Part III
Solving the Accounting Problem

8. RECOMMENDED ACCOUNTING FOR EQUITY TRANSACTIONS. . 133

    Selecting Principles for Transactions, 133
        Influencing Factors, 133
        Need for Uniform Treatment, 134
        Features of Sources of Equity, 134
        Factors To Determine Accounting, 136
    Recommended Principles, 136
        Transactions in Equity Securities, 137
        Consideration Other Than Cash, 139
        Fair Value of Security, 143

Chapter	Page

    Costs of Financing, 144
    Maintaining Sources of Equity, 146
    Pooling of Interests Method, 148
  Application of Principles, 149

9. INCREASES IN EQUITY SECURITIES—
    INDIVIDUAL INTERESTS REDUCED 151

  Types of Transactions, 151
  Sales and Original Issues, 152
    Consideration of Cash or Property, 152
    Services as Consideration, 153
    Distributions To Satisfy Liabilities, 154
    Common Stock Issued at a Discount, 154
  Stock Purchase Warrants, 157
    Nature of Warrant Transactions, 157
    Issuance and Elimination of Warrants, 157
    Exercise of Warrants Sold Separately, 158
    Exercise of Warrants Issued for Other Than Cash, 163
    Exercise of Marketable Warrants Sold in a Unit, 163
    Exercise of Nonmarketable Warrants, 165
    Exercise Price Below Market at Date Issued, 166
    Distributions in Business Combinations, 168
    Lapse of Warrants, 168
    Cancellation of Warrants, 169
  Stock Options, 169
    Similarities of Options and Warrants, 170
    Consideration for Stock Issued Under Options, 170
    Value of Services, 172
    Contingent Consideration for Services, 173
    Contingent Plans Acceptable, 175
    Reasonable Compensation, 176
    Fair Value of Stock Issued, 178
    Dilution of Stockholders' Interests, 181
    Recognizing Compensation for Services, 182
  Convertible Securities, 188
    Comparison of Convertible Debt and Equity Securities, 188
    Outstanding Convertible Debt, 190
    Conversion of Debt Securities, 192
    Warrants Attached to Debentures, 195
    Results of Recommendations, 195
    Conversion of Preferred Stock, 196

Chapter	Page

Acquisition of a Business, 197
   Accounting by the Purchase Method, 197
   Delayed Determination, 199
   Illustration of Recommended Accounting, 205

10. INCREASES IN EQUITY SECURITIES—
    INDIVIDUAL INTERESTS UNCHANGED 210

   Stock Issued for Consideration, 210
      Stock Subscription Rights, 210
      Warrants Distributed Pro Rata, 212
   Stock Issued Without Consideration, 213
      Stock Splits and Stock Dividends, 213
      Defects of Present Accounting, 218
      Recommended Accounting, 219

11. DECREASES IN EQUITY SECURITIES 221

   Factors To Determine Accounting, 221
      Characteristics of Equity Securities, 222
      Purpose and Nature of Transactions, 222
      Legal Requirements To Be Recognized, 224
   Preferred Stock Retired, 225
      Status of Preferred Stock, 225
      Accounting for Costs of Preferred Stock Retired, 227
   Common Stock Retired, 232
      Status of Common Stock, 232
      Accounting for Costs of Common Stock Retired, 233
   Stock Reacquired for Financing Purposes, 237
      Financing Purposes of Transactions, 237
      Results of Transactions, 240
      Dispositions of Treasury Stock for Financing Purposes, 246
   Stock Reacquired for Operating Purposes, 250
      Operating Purposes of Transactions, 250
      Results of Transactions, 251
      Dispositions of Treasury Stock for Operating Purposes, 255
   Results of Recommended Accounting, 263

Chapter	Page
12. ADJUSTMENTS OF EQUITY	264

    Major Adjustments of Capital Structure, 264
        Changes in Outstanding Securities, 264
        Proportionate Equity Interests Unchanged, 265
    Recapitalizations and Reorganizations, 265
        Equity Interests Adjusted, 265
    Exchange of Outstanding Securities, 267
        Rank of Equity Interests Unchanged, 267
        Partition of Interests, 268
        Common Stock Interests Adjusted, 268
        Common Stock Interests Eliminated, 270
    Distribution of Additional Securities, 271
        Distributions to Holders of Debt Securities, 271
        Distributions to Holders of Preferred Stock, 272
        Distributions to Holders of Common Stock, 274
    Quasi-Reorganization, 275
        Accompanying Conditions, 276
        Procedure Endorsed, 277
    Transactions With Nonstockholders, 280
        Governmental Units, 280
        Creditors, 282
        Other Business Entities, 282
        Absence of Donations, 283

Part IV
Implementation

13. ADOPTING RECOMMENDED PRESENTATION AND ACCOUNTING	287

    Results of Adopting Recommendations, 287
        Uniform Accounting Practices, 287
    Practical Aspects of Restating Equity, 289
        Available Details of Components of Equity, 289
        Results of Accounting for Past Transactions, 289

Chapter	Page

    Possible Restatements of Equity, 290
        Complete Restatement, 291
        Restatement After Arbitrary Date, 291
        Estimates of Effects of Transactions, 291
        Recorded Components Restated by Source, 292
        Combined Capital Stock and Additional Capital, 292
        Selected Procedure, 293
    Recommended Restatement, 293
        Aims in Classification, 293
        Revision of Total Stockholders' Equity, 293
        Classification of Remaining Equity, 294
        Recognition of Legal Capital, 297
        Revised Equity, 297
    Future Transactions, 297

COMMENTS BY MEMBERS OF PROJECT ADVISORY COMMITTEE 298
    Comments of William P. Hackney, 298
    Comments of Merle S. Wick, 316

COMMENTS OF DIRECTOR OF ACCOUNTING RESEARCH 318

SELECTED REFERENCES 327

    Reporting Equity, 327
    Business Combinations, 332
    Conversion of Securities, 333
    Reacquired and Retired Stock, 334
    Reorganizations and Adjustments of Equity, 336
    Restricted Securities, 337
    Stock Dividends and Stock Splits, 338
    Stock Options and Stock Purchase Warrants, 339

INDEX 343

Director's Statement

Perhaps no major part of accounting is so subject to piecemeal study as stockholders' equity. Accountants have rarely considered stockholders' equity as a whole. Rather, they have attempted to solve problems in accounting for treasury stock at one time, stock dividends at another, stock options at still another, and so on. It is small wonder that present accounting for stockholders' equity does not exactly constitute a unified whole.

Studying stockholders' equity comprehensively is a major project, as the length of this study indicates. Miss Melcher has studied the subject comprehensively and thoroughly. I believe that all of the major, and all or most of the minor, problems in accounting for and reporting stockholders' equity are included in the study and that the accounting and reporting of each generally fits consistently into the overall pattern developed in the study. I express my appreciation to Miss Melcher specifically for the study and generally for the opportunity of being her colleague on the accounting research staff for almost nine years.

I also wish to express my appreciation to members of the project advisory committee for valuable assistance and for reviewing several drafts of the study. All members of the committee favor publication of the study. Two members have contributed comments which are published following the study (pages 298 to 317). The fact that a committee member approves publication, omits comments, or restricts comments to specific parts or aspects should not be interpreted as concurrence with the contents, conclusions, or recommendations of the study. I have also appended comments on one aspect of the study (pages 318 to 326).

Due to changes in Institute organization, described in Notice to Readers, this study will be the last in the series of Accounting Research Studies. However, I invite interested individuals and groups to read the study carefully and submit comments on it to

> D. R. Carmichael, Director
> Technical Research
> American Institute of CPAs
> 666 Fifth Avenue
> New York, New York 10019

Comments submitted will be most useful if they cover not only the conclusions but also the analyses, premises, and arguments and if they include supporting reasons. The study and all comments received will be sent to the Financial Accounting Standards Board.

New York, N.Y. REED K. STOREY
March 1973 *Director of Accounting Research*

Author's Preface

Accounting for stockholders' equity has often stressed traditional practices, and many procedures have been adopted to agree with precedent. But I found that investigation of the reasons for existing practices was sometimes scanty and thus the accounting accepted for some transactions was not defensible.

This study attempts to coordinate all aspects of accounting for and reporting of stockholders' equity and to support recommendations for changes in present practices.

A good way to judge each recommended practice is to answer the question: Do I as a stockholder want this information? If accountants assumed a stockholder's role, they might less readily reject recommendations that differ from established notions of acceptable practices. The recommendations do not change the historical cost basis of accounting but do change some accepted principles.

The heart of the study is the selection of principles to account for all equity transactions regardless of titles. However, the study includes discussions of many typical transactions by their customary titles to help a reader understand applications of the principles.

I sincerely appreciate the criticism and suggestions of members of the project advisory committee who read and commented on several drafts of the study. Present members of the committee are: Marshall S. Armstrong, chairman, William P. Hackney, Louis H. Rappaport, Abraham M. Stanger, William J. Vatter, and Merle S. Wick. Former members who participated at the beginning of the study were: A. L. Boschen, Ray Garrett (deceased), Thomas G. Higgins, and Howard O. Wagner.

Reed K. Storey, Director of Accounting Research of the AICPA, and Roland L. Laing of the AICPA staff assisted me greatly with their comments on content and presentation. I am also grateful to Eileen T. Corcoran, John L. Fox, Eldon S. Hendriksen, and Willis A. Leonhardi who read and criticized early drafts of the study.

New York, N. Y., March 1973   BEATRICE MELCHER

1

Reporting Stockholders' Equity

Meaning of Equity

Images of stockholders' equity are often unlike in the minds of various economists, brokers, lawyers, and accountants. The term is broad and covers an amount that some individuals and groups refer to as capital, some mean to be book amount of corporate equity, and others call investment. All of them no doubt picture the same financial component of a corporation but they focus on selected aspects or characteristics. For example, most accountants view as the foremost features of stockholders' equity the financial significance and the amount of owners' interests in a corporation. Accountants emphasize that the term refers to the interests of stockholders recorded under the historical cost basis of accounting. Therefore, the amount is not synonymous with the estimated value of the owners' interests.

The attention today on corporate earnings has led to some referring to stockholders' equity as claims on earnings of the holders of outstanding securities, including some nonequity securities. That expression may be convenient but is inaccurate because stockholders' equity in accounting today is an amount—the interests in recorded net resources. The total amount represents the cumulative net contributions by stockholders plus recorded earnings that a corporation has retained.

Total stockholders' equity changes for many reasons and ordinarily many transactions determine its components. The accepted methods of accounting for changes and reporting the results have been revised over the years. The various methods that have been accepted are among the possible alternatives that are considered in this study to determine adequate reporting of transactions and status of stockholders' equity.

The aim in this study is to investigate the nature of stockholders' equity and equity transactions and the effects of the transactions to find the best methods of recording and reporting the financial and economic facts. Accounting cannot alter facts; accounting can detract from or enhance the disclosure of the facts.

Recommendations for Changes

The recommendations in this study follow detailed analyses of existing and alternative methods of accounting for transactions that affect stockholders' equity and presenting the results. A brief summary of the major changes recommended without the supporting reasons is given in this chapter merely to show most of the areas explored.

Presentation of Equity. Stockholders' equity need not be shown in financial statements in a new manner just for the sake of a change. Nor is status quo desirable if another presentation will furnish better information—improvement should not be postponed simply to cling to the traditional format of financial statements. A preferable presentation is recommended in the study.

Two sources of equity. A major conclusion in this study is that the sources of stockholders' equity are the most useful information and those components should be shown in financial statements. The primary sources from which equity is derived are contributions by stockholders and earnings retained by a corporation, and each corporation should account for and present those two components. Since the interests of different classes of stock vary and the same transactions do not necessarily affect each class, the amounts contributed for each class or series of outstanding stock should be reported separately.

Although legal aspects of capital stock may be disclosed, legal requirements should not be the accounting basis for classifying and reporting the components of equity. The par or stated value of outstanding shares of stock sometimes exceeds the contributions by stockholders. If so, the directors of the corporation should appropriate retained earnings to the extent of the excess, and the corporation should present both the appropriated and unappropriated segments of retained earnings in financial statements.

Conclusions on presentation in this study must answer those who seek to retain the traditional components of equity in financial statements as well as those who recommend adopting other alternatives, for instance a single amount of stockholders' equity. In addition, the study needs to show that reporting the separate sources of equity helps readers to understand the financial status of a corporation and is useful to investors and others. The reasons supporting the recommended presentation are explained in Chapter 7 and practical methods of restating the traditional components of equity are described in Chapter 13.

Contingent equity financing. The greater variety and complexity of some corporate securities that are now issued increase the need for clear reporting of the status of and the changes in stockholders' equity. Investors and potential investors wish to understand and appraise readily the rights and potential claims of holders of unorthodox securities, some with overlapping debt and equity characteristics. The presentation recommended in this study provides that a separate category of contingent equity financing should include obligations and nonequity securities that carry a right to obtain equity interests in exchange. Stockholders' equity should exclude consideration received that does not apply to shares of stock.

Equity Transactions. Changes in accounting for many transactions in stockholders' equity are a sequel to revisions in presenting equity to show its sources. The effects of transactions need to be analyzed to determine whether they change one or both of the two primary sources of equity. Some current accounting procedures should be modified so that reported results fit with the nature of the transactions and the recommended presentation of equity. Thus the separation of contributions by stockholders and retained earnings is continued and the two sources of equity are not commingled.

Uniform principles. This study is based on a presumption that the present historical cost basis of accounting is retained and proposes neither fundamental changes in accepted principles of accounting for assets and liabilities nor a new overall system.

A few basic principles that apply to all types of equity transactions are developed and supported in Chapter 8. The principles that are enumerated relate to the

> date a corporation recognizes a transaction,
> consideration that a corporation receives or distributes,

measure of consideration—both cash and other assets, nature of a transaction, and costs of equity financing.

Applying the recommended principles to all types of transactions will result in consistent treatment of transactions of a similar nature and replace the current diversity and conflict in accounting and reporting practices. The analyses of various kinds of transactions emphasize the nature of a transaction rather than the name of a security.

The major recommendations for changes in present accounting practices are needed because corporations do not now always recognize the entire consideration received for stock issued, and they sometimes modify the traditional components of equity for transactions that do not affect sources of equity. Several of the treatments recommended in the study would change net income otherwise reported under present practices although total stockholders' equity would not differ.

The principles recommended should be applied to all types of equity transactions except a business combination accounted for by the pooling of interests method. The unique nature of that transaction is explained in Chapter 8 and no changes are recommended in the accounting procedures now accepted except that the components of stockholders' equity should be classified by sources.

Changes recommended. The more significant changes in accounting for stockholders' equity transactions that are recommended in this study are, in brief:

Increases in outstanding equity securities that reduce stockholders' proportionate interests (Chapter 9):

Recognize the entire consideration received for restricted stock issued at a large discount measured by the fair value of unregistered stock at the date issued. Deduct related financing costs from retained earnings.

Recognize the entire consideration received for stock issued on exercise of purchase warrants measured by the fair value of the stock at the date issued. Deduct related financing costs from net income or retained earnings according to the nature of the transaction in which the stock purchase warrants are issued.

Recognize the entire consideration received for stock

issued on exercise of employee stock options measured by the fair value of the stock at the date issued. Deduct related compensation expenses from net income.

Recognize the entire consideration received for stock issued on conversion of other securities measured by the fair value of the stock at the date issued. Deduct related financing expenses from net income for debt securities converted and deduct related financing costs from retained earnings for equity securities converted.

Distinguish between arrangements for contingent consideration that result from the unresolved measure of (1) the fair value of the consideration received and (2) the fair value of the stock issued for that consideration. Recognize consideration received for stock issued under condition 1 measured by the fair value of the stock at the date issued and allocate the amount between the assets acquired and costs of financing. Recognize no additional consideration received for the shares of stock issued under condition 2.

Increases in outstanding equity securities that do not change stockholders' proportionate interests (Chapter 10):

Recognize the additional number of shares of stock issued for a stock split and a stock dividend without changing equity components.

Decreases in outstanding equity securities (Chapter 11):

Allocate an expenditure to acquire stock for retirement between the two sources of equity: reduce contributed equity by the pro rata portion applicable to the number of shares retired and reduce or increase retained earnings by the difference between that portion and the expenditure.

Account for capital stock reacquired for financing purposes and held as treasury stock as retired shares.

Account for capital stock required to be reacquired for operating purposes and held as treasury stock as an asset and include in net income the difference between the purchase price and consideration received on distribution of the stock.

All of the practices for which changes are recommended in the study have been topics of controversy for years. Undoubtedly, some recommendations will not be popular, but they should be judged on the analyses of the transactions and justifications for those treatments which are explained in the chapters of the study indicated parenthetically.

Consolidated financial statements. The study is written in terms of a single corporation and does not refer specifically to presenting consolidated financial statements. The presentation and accounting principles that are recommended in this study apply equally to a parent corporation and the financial statements presented for a consolidated entity. Generally, the problems of presenting stockholders' equity in consolidated financial statements relate to the amount of retained earnings of subsidiaries to be recognized in determining consolidated retained earnings.

Scope of Study

Every transaction of a corporation, except exchanges of one asset or liability for another equal one, ultimately affects stockholders' equity. Obviously, this single study is not intended to encompass accounting for all transactions that relate to corporate equity. The study is first limited to items associated directly with stockholders' equity and thus omits individual income transactions. Even then, covering all items and transactions directly associated with stockholders' equity is impractical. The areas included in the study and those not discussed are described briefly in this section on scope.

Recurring Transactions. Many types of equity transactions recur often for many corporations and they in turn often pose recurring accounting problems. This study is devoted to those frequent problems. If the preferable accounting for recurring transactions can be agreed on, many isolated transactions will easily follow the same pattern.

Prevailing practices. Those practices that now prevail in accounting for stockholders' equity as well as other minority practices are summarized and compared in the study to serve as a basis for appraising desirable practices and further analysis. The related presentation of accounting results also needs to be known to judge the informativeness of possible disclosures.

The existing practices described in this study and their development were determined from several sources. Articles in periodicals summarize various studies of practice at different times. Some areas of accounting for and presentation of stockholders' equity are included in statistics published annually by the American Institute of Certified Public Accountants (AICPA) in *Accounting Trends & Techniques*. Several hundred recently published annual reports of publicly held corporations were inspected as a part of the study to determine the variations and prevalence of practices. Accounting practices disclosed in published reports are described, summarized, and compared with those supported by authoritative pronouncements. The primary purpose of the summaries is to display both the customary and unusual practices, without citing sources or statistics.

Official pronouncements. The development of official pronouncements that support prevailing or alternative practices is described in the study to complete the background of present accounting. Recommendations and requirements related to some areas of stockholders' equity have been changed over the years and a few have been revised drastically. Authoritative pronouncements cover the accounting procedures for some items and transactions but no one or all of the pronouncements together are comprehensive. Pronouncements of the American Institute of Certified Public Accountants, Securities and Exchange Commission, and New York Stock Exchange and tax and state corporate laws and regulations have influenced practices the most. Statements of the American Accounting Association also pertain to stockholders' equity and probably influence practices, although the effects are perhaps indirect.

Accounting Principles Board (APB) Statement No. 4, "Basic Concepts and Accounting Principles Underlying Financial Statements of Business Enterprises," was issued in 1970 and summarized the general principles underlying the present accounting for owners' equity. Chapter 5 of *Accounting Research Study No. 7*, "Inventory of Generally Accepted Accounting Principles for Business Enterprises," by Paul Grady, published in 1965, which was one of the bases of *APB Statement 4*, described the present broad objectives in accounting for equity and acceptable practices in general terms. Since the descriptions of practices in Part I of this study are more detailed than in either *APB Statement 4* or *ARS No. 7*, excerpts from the documents are not repeated.

Nature of transactions. Customary equity transactions may be placed in basic groups of the same nature since their effects on results of operations and equity are similar. To help analyze the nature of the changes in stockholders' equity, transactions are grouped in this study as increases in outstanding equity securities, decreases in outstanding equity securities, and changes in components of stockholders' equity. Desirable accounting principles are selected for a type of transaction; the procedures then follow naturally for many essentially similar transactions even though the titles differ.

Legal Regulation of Corporate Equity. Individual corporations are subject to the business laws of their respective states of incorporation (including the District of Columbia) and in some respects to the laws of the states in which they operate. General aspects of statutory regulation of corporations in the area of stockholders' equity are discussed in this study because the laws of a state of incorporation may control many transactions in stockholders' equity and legal requirements cannot always be ignored in accounting. State laws usually prescribe requirements for issuing stock, treatment of proceeds of issued stock, permitted distributions to stockholders, effects of retiring stock, regulations for and restrictions on acquiring treasury stock, and other procedures and restrictions.

Diversity of laws. The importance of the diverse laws and regulations are evaluated in this study. The development of the corporate form of business organization and the status of existing laws are summarized to furnish background. Many states have adopted in their corporation laws the principles contained in the Model Business Corporation Act (Model Act) prepared in 1959 by the Committee on Corporate Laws of the American Bar Association; the resulting laws are often similar although not uniform. Other states have enacted corporate legislation with contrary features, often elaborate and rare provisions.

The state laws are complex and vary not only in their provisions but also in their definitions of the same terms. At least some statutory definitions are ambiguous. Some laws fail to define technical terms and those terms often mean one thing in one state and another in a different state. Confusion increases if the terms that restrict equity transactions are defined using a phrase such as "in accordance with generally accepted principles of sound accounting practice" (North Carolina Business Corporation Act). A few state laws are silent on the treatment of common transactions, such as treasury stock transactions that result in "losses" or occur at a date on which the corporation has no capital surplus. Problems are compounded because legal authorities often interpret the effects and restrictions of the laws differently. Litigation regarding stock, capital, dividends, and surplus has been frequent and the resulting interpretations by the courts control in many jurisdictions.

The laws are so diverse that exceptions exist to most generalizations of statutory provisions or meanings of terms. Tabulating in this study the provisions and interpretations of the 50 state laws is neither practical nor necessary. A range of the major and frequent provisions of the statutes and of the Model Act, including the 1964 Addendum, that relate to stockholders' equity give sufficient background for accounting recommendations.

Disclosure of legal components. Most of the summary of the corporate form and legal regulations are facts well known to practicing accountants and may seem too elementary to be included in a research study. However, the extent of corporate regulation and its development form the basis for recommending that legal provisions not govern the financial reporting of stockholders' equity but the financial aspects of legal components should be disclosed, at least in notes to the financial statements.

Decisions of Management. Transactions in stockholders' equity and in debt and other securities result from decisions of management pertaining to corporate financing. The advantages, disadvantages, costs, risks, and other factors that necessarily form a part of those decisions are not considered specifically in this study. Those factors are discussed only to the extent that the decisions affect equity transactions and accounting for the results. Thus the many reasons that lead management to decide to issue a debt or an equity security, to redeem or reacquire an equity security, and to distribute a cash or stock dividend are accepted without criticism.

Changes in Equity Not Studied. Opinions of the AICPA's Accounting Principles Board cover accounting for many changes in stockholders' equity, and other accounting research studies include discussions of several changes. The accounting problems in some changes in equity are relatively minor. Those areas not covered in this study are described to clarify its scope.

Results of operations. Accounting for and reporting of results of operations, including adjustments of prior years and other extraordinary items pertaining to retained earnings, are set forth in *APB Opinion 9*. The subject is not reconsidered or discussed in this study, and results of operations are presumed to increase or decrease retained earnings.

Distributions as dividends. Corporate dividends distributed may be in many forms, may require numerous management decisions, and may involve accounting problems. Every distribution to stockholders, many of which recur often, affects stockholders' equity of the corporation. But this study includes only the distributions of equity securities of the same corporation, usually called stock dividends. Accounting for cash dividends and dividends in the form of other assets, so-called dividends in kind, are not specific problems of this study. Presentation of dividend information, such as amounts declared, arrears, and amounts payable, is covered in various pronouncements that are now effective.

Business combinations. Accounting for the changes in stockholders' equity is the only part of the entire problem of business combinations that is considered in this study. The conditions to determine which of two accounting methods apply to a combination and the treatment of the net assets of a combined corporation are not discussed or evaluated.

Minority interests. Accounting Research Bulletins (ARB) and APB Opinions now cover some aspects of accounting for and presenting minority ownership interests in subsidiary corporations included in consolidated financial statements. In addition, an accounting research study in process on intercorporate investments considers that entire topic, and minority interests are omitted from this study.

Specialized and regulated industries. Corporations in several industries may deserve exceptional accounting for stockholders' equity because the organization differs from the usual corporate form or because governmental agencies regulate the operations or presentation of financial statements.

Corporations in specialized fields now often account for and present equity in unique manners. Examples are banks, insurance companies, savings and loan associations, regulated investment companies, and cooperatives. The present practices of those corporations are not described nor appraised in this study. Neither does the study consider whether those corporations should adopt the recommended presentation and accounting procedures. The development of and reasons for existing variations in each field need to be studied to determine if the practices should be continued or be changed to conform with most other corporations.

Numerous governmental agencies prescribe accounting procedures for corporations that are subject to their jurisdictions. The corporations are not necessarily in special industries nor are the sources of stockholders' equity unique. The conclusions of this study are intended to apply to those corporations although existing regulations may not permit them to adopt new accounting procedures for reporting to their supervising agencies. Various agency regulations relating to equity transactions, such as restrictions on the acquisition of treasury stock, are not enumerated or evaluated in this study.

Special features of closely held corporations. Closely held corporations are like publicly held corporations in most respects, and this study does not differentiate between the two in recommending accounting methods. However, some matters of concern to closely held corporations are outside the interests of other corporations. Those special topics—for example, corporations taxed under Subchapter S and personal holding companies—are ignored in this study.

Liquidation and dissolution of corporations. The liquidation and later dissolution of a corporation requires special accounting and reporting. The topic is of less general interest than the presentation and accounting for stockholders' equity of a going concern, and this study is limited to the more frequent problems of continuing corporations.

Similarly, spin-offs and other corporate divestments are mentioned in some contexts in the study but all aspects are not considered.

Organization of Study

The study is concerned primarily with two aspects of stockholders' equity: presentation in financial statements and accounting for transactions that affect stockholders' equity directly. The two aspects are closely related and are closely related in the study. Recommendations for reporting stockholders' equity in financial statements are the basis for recommending principles to be applied in accounting for equity transactions. Further, transactions of a similar type are grouped and evaluated together to show that each type may be treated uniformly. That approach differs from the usual appraisal of an individual type of transaction without regard to others of the same or a similar nature.

For the convenience of readers, the remainder of the study is divided into four parts.

> Part I—Status of Accounting for Stockholders' Equity (Chapters 2, 3, 4, 5, and 6)
> Part II—Solving the Presentation Problem (Chapter 7)
> Part III—Solving the Accounting Problem (Chapters 8, 9, 10, 11, and 12)
> Part IV—Implementation (Chapter 13)

Part I furnishes background for later recommendations by describing the present methods of accounting for and reporting of stockholders' equity. The development of present accounting practices and the major pronouncements related to issuing stock are summarized in Chapter 2. Accounting for decreases in and changes in stockholders' equity are described similarly in Chapters 3 and 4. The varying practices described in the three chapters are compared in Chapter 5 to show the contrasts and conflicts in the factors that determine the accounting procedures and lead to mixed effects on the components of equity. The development of presentation of components of stockholders' equity in financial statements is described in Chapter 6.

Solving the Presentation Problem, Part II, contains Chapter 7. The current presentation of equity and other possible alternatives are evaluated to choose the preferable categories or components of stockholders' equity and the best presentation. The reasons that support the recommendations are explained.

The major part of the study, Part III, is devoted to solving the accounting problem. General principles to be applied in accounting for various kinds of equity transactions are selected and explained in Chapter 8. The accounting procedures flowing from those principles are described in terms of the recommended presentation of sources of equity, but the general principles could also be applied if other components of equity were presented in financial statements. Accounting for increases and decreases in outstanding equity securities according to the recommended principles are explained in Chapters 9, 10, and 11. Other less frequent adjustments of equity, such as recapitalizations and quasi-reorganizations, are discussed in Chapter 12.

The reporting and accounting recommended in Parts II and III would require corporations to restate stockholders' equity and in the future change some accounting procedures. The methods of revising financial statements and changing accounting procedures are considered in Chapter 13, Part IV of the study. The methods recommended are practical.

Part I

Status of Accounting for Stockholders' Equity

Chapter 2 — Issuing Stock

Chapter 3 — Decreases in Stockholders' Equity

Chapter 4 — Adjusting Components of Stockholders' Equity

Chapter 5 — Comparisons of Varying Practices

Chapter 6 — Presentation of Components of Stockholders' Equity

The problems in accounting for and reporting stockholders' equity that are included in this study are described in Part I. The present accounting in the United States, its development, and the features of the results give background for the recommendations that follow in Parts II and III.

2
Issuing Stock

Consideration for Stock Issued

A corporation issues equity securities for consideration received from investors and accounts for the consideration as the first component of stockholders' equity. A basic requirement of the law is that a corporation must receive consideration to issue shares of stock except that consideration is not essential if additional shares are issued to all stockholders and their proportionate interests remain the same.

Accountants often debate the best measure of consideration received and manner of classifying the amount. However, corporate statutes often influence the accounting for the issuance of stock. The range and effects of legal provisions pertaining to capital stock and other components of equity are therefore discussed first. The remainder of the chapter covers the origin and development of accounting practices and the major accounting pronouncements related to issuing stock (1) for consideration in the form of cash, property, or services, (2) in exchange for other securities, and (3) without consideration. Issuing stock that a corporation has reacquired is included in Chapter 3 because a reacquisition initially decreases stockholders' equity.

Legal Regulation

Capital Stock. The Model Business Corporation Act (Model Act) and most state laws provide that shares having a par value may not be issued for consideration that is less than the par value although the shares may be issued at a premium. The laws usually provide that the directors of a corporation may fix the sale price of shares of stock as long as it conforms with limits set by the corporate charter. Frequently laws require that a corporation record the designated par value for each issued share as capital stock and the consideration in excess of that amount as premium on stock. State statutes often specify that a premium on par value stock is paid-in surplus or capital surplus. A few states permit nonassessable stock to be issued originally at less than par value and the agreed consideration represents stated capital.

No par value shares. Most states quickly followed the precedent set by New York in 1912 and enacted laws to permit corporations to issue shares without par value and with a stated value only. The laws covering no par value shares attempted to keep the fundamental separation of capital stock and premium, and lawyers and accountants emphasized capital in excess of stated value of capital stock. Recording the proceeds of sales of no par value stock with a designated stated value for each share is essentially the same as recording proceeds of par value stock. However, many of the current laws permitting stock without par value do not require that a corporation designate an amount as the stated value of each share.

The Model Act states that shares without par value may be issued for consideration fixed by the board of directors. The entire consideration received represents stated capital unless the corporation specifies that only a part is allocated to stated capital.

Corporate Statutes. The Model Act provides that a corporation segregate the interest of stockholders in three categories—stated capital, capital surplus, and earned surplus—and proposes broad meanings for each category.

Stated capital. Stated capital for shares with or without a par value represents the permanent investment of stockholders, but the elements often differ from state to state and the amount in some states is flexible rather than fixed. Generally, stated capital is defined as the total par value of all shares issued or the total consideration received for all shares issued without par value, although a corporation may allocate to capital surplus portions of the consideration received for shares without par value. Some laws restrict the portion that may be excluded from stated capital, some limit allocation to a designated period after the stock is issued, and others prohibit allocation. A few states adopted a concept of stated capital that is an arbitrary amount that a corporation designates for the total outstanding shares of stock.

Earned surplus. Earned surplus as defined in the Model Act represents accumulated and undistributed profits, although transfers of profits to other categories of equity are permissible. The meaning of earned surplus is substantially the same as that favored by the AICPA for retained earnings and similar terms.

Generally, accounting for retained earnings has conformed to legal requirements for designating or recording components of equity. As an example, if the law permits a transfer between capital surplus and earned surplus, an approved transfer is recorded in those accounts and disclosed in the financial statements. The concept of earned surplus as a remainder—that is, retained earnings less transfers to other components of equity—was expressed in *Accounting Terminology Bulletin No. 1* and has been retained in accounting procedures.

> . . . the term *earned surplus* (or *undistributed profits* or *retained income*) means:
>
> The balance of net profits, income, gains and losses of a corporation[1] from the date of incorporation (or from the latest date when a deficit was eliminated in a quasi-reorganization) after deducting distributions therefrom to shareholders and transfers therefrom to capital stock or capital surplus accounts.
>
> [1] Other than gains from transactions in its own shares, and losses therefrom chargeable to capital surplus; see chapter 1(b) of Accounting Research Bulletin No. 43, paragraphs 7 and 8.

Some writers refer to retained earnings as though it were synonymous with the amount of earned surplus as defined in a specific state corporation law. Yet, many state laws permit, or even require, with variations that items other than earnings and dividends be added to and deducted from statutory earned surplus. The resulting amount is not always undistributed earnings of a corporation.

Capital surplus. Capital surplus as defined in the Model Act is determined by deducting stated capital and earned surplus from net assets and represents the remainder of stockholders' equity. Capital surplus in most statutes is more inclusive than paid-in surplus, which usually is limited to a part of the consideration received for shares. Both capital surplus and paid-in surplus is a portion of the investment of stockholders that is less permanent than stated capital and is subject to special rules.

Meanings of terms. Some states have retained the earlier designations of capital and surplus for segments of the stockholders' interest. Capital in those laws often means the par or stated value of issued shares of stock. Accountants and others sometimes add another meaning by referring to total stockholders' equity, including retained earnings, as capital.

The term surplus in some laws now refers to differing sources of equity and caution is needed in using it even with a modifier.

> The concept of surplus under modern corporation statutes and practices must be viewed in the light of developments in the concept of capital and divorced from the simple doctrine of early laws that it was synonymous with profits. In present usage, it is a mixture of profits and amounts that in former years would have been capital.[1]

Corporate Charters. Statutory requirements may dictate some provisions that are included in charters (articles of incorporation) of corporations. Some states allow the provisions of a charter to supersede statutory provisions that are otherwise effective. Provisions of charters may range from granting broad general powers and permissions to setting detailed requirements for securities and stockholders' equity. The total number of authorized shares of each class of stock and the terms of each security issue, such as the class, par value of a share, and the rights and limitations of stockholders, which are usually designated in a corporate charter, often attain the status of legal requirements because the state corporation laws define the permissible terms.

Changes in Legal Capital. The concept of corporate legal capital developed to insure, primarily for the benefit of creditors, a minimum permanent investment in a corporation. But legal capital of a corporation is often no more than a technical limitation having no practical restriction because charter provisions may be changed with little inconvenience. Par value stock may be changed to no par value, a designated high par value may be reduced to a nominal amount, or the par value may be increased. The number of authorized shares may be increased by amending the charter or may be reduced by filing a certificate for retirement of previously outstanding shares. To avoid

---

[1] Ray Garrett, "Capital and Surplus Under the New Corporation Statutes," *Law and Contemporary Problems,* Spring 1958, p. 257.

a formal reduction of legal capital, a few states authorize payment of dividends from stated capital and other states permit distributions in partial liquidation to be deducted from stated capital. Existing legal or stated capital of a corporation is therefore not always maintained intact indefinitely.

Many states permit a corporation to transfer contributed capital or retained earnings to capital stock or other components of legal capital on resolution of the board of directors. The resulting amount of capital stock may exceed the total par value or designated stated value of the issued shares. Total legal capital as defined in some states is not the same as the amount designated as capital stock nor the total of capital stock and paid-in surplus.

The term legal capital in the discussions in this study refers to capital stock, stated capital, or other amounts designated by respective statutes as the required minimum corporate equity.

Accounting Requirements in the Law. The laws generally provide that the legal capital of each class of stock shall be maintained separately according to provisions of the respective corporate charters. Some states require that the par or stated value of issued shares or of issued and outstanding shares be recorded in a separate capital stock account.

Dividing consideration for stock. The presumed requirement to account for consideration received in excess of the par or stated value of the shares issued as capital or paid-in surplus was a major influence and probably in error.

> One may well inquire if the many statutes which sanction the treatment of part of contributed capital as surplus actually *require* such a treatment. Scrutiny of these statutes will disclose that a corporation *may* make such a division but it is not required to do so. Thus use of the prevalent capital-surplus account is largely a matter of following an accounting convention rather than adhering to legal requirements.[2]

But statutory definitions and designations of components of equity

---

[2] Rufus Wixon, "The Nature of Corporate Capital," *The Journal of Accountancy,* September 1946, p. 215.

continue to influence, if not control, the accounting for shares of stock that corporations issue.

Distributions to stockholders. Laws of some states specify that a corporation must keep its books to indicate clearly the division of surplus between the amount that results from earnings and the amount that arises from other sources. Observing the legal measurements of earned surplus is paramount in most states because earned surplus determines the legal amount distributable as other than liquidating dividends. Statutory requirements may also limit other distributions to stockholders. Legal restrictions normally control actions but do not control accounting for and reporting of transactions.

Many of the laws refer to distributions from surplus, dividends payable from surplus, or distributions of surplus. The meanings of those terms are clear to both lawyers and accountants, although critics often point out correctly that the phrases are technically incorrect because assets are distributable; surplus itself is never distributable but serves solely as a measure.

22 Stock Issued for Cash

Recording Proceeds of Sales. The simplest type of issue of stock is sales of shares for cash at amounts equal to or greater than the par or stated value of the shares. With some exceptions, corporations record the par or stated value as capital stock and proceeds in excess of that amount as additional capital.

If stock is sold at a discount, a corporation records the proceeds of sales as capital stock even though the amount is less than the total par value of the shares issued.

Supporting pronouncements. Separating the proceeds of a sale of stock in two components—capital stock and additional capital—has been supported in accounting literature and in pronouncements of the AICPA. *Verification of Financial Statements (Revised)*, published by the Federal Reserve Board in 1929, specified classifications and presentations of equity, and the substance was continued in *Examination of Financial Statements by Independent Public Accountants* which the Institute issued in 1936. Excerpts from the capital stock section of the 1936 bulletin cover basic accounting and presentation.

> The capital stock or stated capital should be shown on the balance sheet in accordance with the statutes of the state under the

laws of which the corporation is organized, the articles of incorporation and the corporation's minutes.

Each class of stock should be stated separately on the balance sheet, with the amount authorized, issued and outstanding and the par value per share. If the stock is of no par value the stated or assigned value per share, if any, should be shown and the redemption price or the amount of preference upon liquidation.

The American Accounting Association also stated in 1936 that a corporation should recognize two major divisions of its capital: paid-in capital and earned surplus. But paid-in capital was further subdivided and included capital stock and paid-in surplus.

Costs of Issuing Stock. A corporation recognizes the consideration received for the stock issued as contributed capital and determines the accounting for the costs of issuing shares of stock by that principle. Therefore, costs of obtaining capital by issuing stock are generally considered a reduction of the related proceeds, and the net amount is recorded as contributed stockholders' equity. Costs directly attributable to realizing the proceeds of stock issued include printing certificates; commissions, fees, and expenses of investment bankers, underwriters, and others; security registration and listing fees; accounting and legal fees; and other similar costs. Usually, issue costs are deducted from contributed components of equity—capital stock or capital in excess of par or stated value. However, legal provisions of some states prohibit deducting stock issue costs from contributed capital but permit deducting the costs from retained earnings. A new corporation usually avoids creating an initial deficit by classifying stock issue costs as deferred promotion and organization costs.

Some industrial corporations in addition to new corporations defer and amortize stock issue costs. The SEC accepts either deferring the costs or deducting them from the proceeds of sale of the securities. *Regulation* S-X lists deferred commissions and expense on capital shares under the heading "Other Assets and Deferred Charges" but states further that the costs may be "shown as deductions from other stockholders' equity."

Stock Issued for Property or Services

Acquired Assets at Cost. To account for stock issued for property or services is more troublesome than to account for cash proceeds of sales of stock because the value of the consideration received is less evident. Prevailing accounting practices are based on the aim of stating assets acquired at cost at the date they are acquired. The long-standing guide in accounting for assets acquired for other than cash was that "cost may be considered as being either the fair value of the consideration given or the fair value of the property or right acquired, whichever is the more clearly evident" (paragraph 4 of Chapter 5, *ARB 43*).

Market price of stock as measure. A publicly held corporation usually considers the current market price of its stock as the best measure of the value of assets acquired for stock unless a quoted market price for the acquired assets is available. A corporation that issues publicly quoted stock for assets, services, or the stock or net assets of another company records the par or stated value of the shares issued as capital stock and records the remainder of the total fair value of the shares issued as additional capital. A business combination accounted for by the pooling of interests method is not viewed as an acquisition of assets for stock, and accounting for stock issued to effect the combination does not conform with the described procedure.

Fair value of consideration as measure. A new or closely held corporation lacks a ready measure of the fair value of stock issued for property or services. Neither the par or stated value of the shares of stock issued nor an arbitrary value fixed by the board of directors is a reliable measure. Until stock of a new corporation is sold, a fair value is not readily ascertainable. The fair value of the property or services acquired may be more clearly evident. Generally, the board of directors determines the value of services received and the value often corresponds with the estimated amount required for a cash payment. The directors may obtain appraisals by independent parties of either tangible or intangible assets acquired, and the assets acquired and the consideration received for the shares issued are usually recorded at a reasonable and realistic estimate of value based on the appraised amounts of the assets.

Stock Rights and Warrants

Characteristics of Securities. A stock subscription right and a stock purchase warrant are similar in that each entitles the holder to exercise the privilege of purchasing shares of stock at a stated price. Although the forms of the instruments are similar, differences between the two privileges conveyed to the holders result from different purposes and cause differences in the substance of related transactions.

The primary differences in the two privileges are that

> one share of stock may be purchased ordinarily with one warrant but with several rights;
>
> rights to purchase stock are usually issued to existing holders of the same stock but warrants may be sold separately or with other securities as a unit, may be issued in exchange for other securities, or may be issued separately without cash consideration;
>
> the purchase price fixed by rights is usually less than the current market price of the stock and the purchase price fixed by warrants is normally greater than the market price of the stock at the date the warrants are issued; and
>
> the privilege to purchase usually extends much longer under warrants than under rights.

The purchase price of stock specified by a warrant may vary before its expiration, usually higher prices at later dates.

Accounting for the issuance of stock on exercise of rights and warrants is the same because of basic similarity in the privileges. The differences in the privileges may result in differences in the date that the consideration for the stock is recorded as additional equity.

Alternative Accounting Practices. Prevailing accounting for the exercise of stock rights and purchase warrants follows the pattern of accounting for cash sales and original issue of shares of stock. A corporation adds the amounts of the proceeds received to capital stock to the extent of the par or stated value of the shares issued and records the remainder as additional capital.

Issued and outstanding stock rights are recorded as a memorandum only. Some stock purchase warrants are sold but not exercised for several years; the proceeds of those sales are recorded as additional capital or as a separate category of equity until the warrants are exercised.

Warrants issued with other securities. Corporations often issue warrants to purchase common stock in combination with preferred stock or bonds. The portion of the proceeds of sales of combined securities allocable to warrants was accounted for in various ways before *APB Opinion 10* was issued in 1966.

Some corporations had adopted the practice of allocating to paid-in capital the portion of the proceeds applicable to the warrants. That practice was endorsed in paragraphs 8 and 9 of *APB Opinion 10*, although the Opinion was suspended temporarily by *APB Opinion 12*. *APB Opinion 14*, issued in March 1969, reinstated the accounting called for in the prior Opinion and stated, in part:

> The Board is of the opinion that the portion of the proceeds of debt securities issued with detachable stock purchase warrants which is allocable to the warrants should be accounted for as paid-in capital. The allocation should be based on the relative fair values of the two securities at time of issuance. . . . However, when stock purchase warrants are not detachable from the debt and the debt security must be surrendered in order to exercise the warrant, the two securities taken together are substantially equivalent to convertible debt. . . .

The recommended procedures now prevail, but before *APB Opinion 10* was issued some corporations had recorded as long-term debt and related discount or premium the entire proceeds of a unit of securities and thus ignored the warrants. Still others adopted a third procedure in which a portion of the proceeds of securities sold was allocated to nondetachable warrants and recorded as a deferred credit. At the time of exercise of the warrants, the deferred credit was reduced by the unamortized discount and the net amount was added to capital in excess of par or stated value of stock. Some of the practices were derived from the various methods of accounting for the conversion feature of bonds.

The proceeds of sales of a unit of preferred stock and attached warrants to purchase common stock are rarely allocated between preferred stock and warrants. The total proceeds become a part of stockholders' equity and allocation is viewed as an unnecessary segregation of components.

Conversions of Securities

The terms of a convertible security, usually a debenture bond or preferred stock, provide that the owner of the security may at his option exchange it for stock of the same corporation under specified conditions. The conversion of debt into preferred or common stock increases total stockholders' equity but, under present accounting practices, the conversion of preferred stock into common stock does not change total stockholders' equity. The conversion of preferred stock shifts equity components.

CHAPTER 2: ISSUING STOCK

Conversion of Debt. Accounting for the conversion of debenture bonds and other debt securities into shares of preferred or common stock is not covered directly in AICPA pronouncements, except that *APB Opinion 10* provided for allocating the proceeds to the conversion feature and reducing the consideration on conversion by the unamortized portion of the allocation. Paragraphs 8 and 9 of that Opinion stated that a portion of the proceeds of convertible bonds should be accounted for as debt discount and that the unamortized debt discount should be accounted for as a reduction of the consideration received for the securities issued on conversion. *APB Opinion 12* temporarily suspended the effectiveness of those paragraphs. The Board studied the problems further and concluded in *APB Opinion 14*, issued in March 1969, that

> . . . no portion of the proceeds from the issuance of the types of convertible debt securities described in paragraph 3 should be accounted for as attributable to the conversion feature.

APB Opinion 14 was effective for fiscal periods beginning after December 31, 1966. "However, if a portion of the proceeds of a convertible debt issue . . . was allocated to the conversion feature for periods beginning before January 1, 1969 that accounting may be continued with respect to such issues."

The basis for the present methods of accounting for conversions of securities is that the consideration received for the stock issued is the amount the corporation received for the security that is converted. Therefore, the conversion of debt securities into stock is viewed as the equivalent of the payment of a liability and the issuance of stock. Bonds outstanding are reduced by the par value of bonds converted and capital stock and additional capital increased by the same amount. Unamortized premium or discount applicable to the bonds converted is similarly transferred to capital stock or additional capital. Conversion results in no gain or loss to the corporation and the transaction is solely a transfer from debt to equity.

Conversion of Preferred Stock. Convertible preferred stock is usually carried at the par or stated value of the issued and outstanding shares and contributions in excess of that amount are included in additional capital. Accounting for conversion of preferred stock into common stock follows procedures similar to those for conversion of debt securities but does not change the total contributed capital. A corporation adds to additional capital an excess of the par or stated value of the preferred stock over the par or stated value of the common stock issued on conversion.

Stock Options

Stock options are rights to purchase shares of a grantor corporation at a stated price either at a specified date or during a specified period and are the same as stock rights and warrants except that typical options are exercisable under limited conditions and are not transferable.

Stock Option and Purchase Plans. This section uses the term stock options to include stock purchase plans because purchases under either arrangement affect stockholders' equity in basically the same way, although the details of option and purchase plans may differ. Usually the differing details are the type of designated optionees, terms of payment, price of stock, and period of exercise privilege. An ordinary fundamental difference is that an employee participating in a stock purchase plan is not permitted to postpone his purchase decision as he may under a stock option plan. The terms of stock purchase plans vary but generally an employee voluntarily agrees to contribute a designated sum periodically (usually payroll deductions) for the purchase of stock to be delivered at the time the installment payments are completed. About half of the stock purchase plans of New York Stock Exchange companies in effect in 1966 allowed an employee to purchase stock at less than the market price, and most of those that were stock purchase-option plans provided that the purchase price was 85% of market price on the date of the offer when the employees authorized the deduction or purchase.[3] Many stock option plans adopted since 1963 set the option price at least equal to the fair market value of the stock on the date the option is granted to meet the tax requirements for qualified stock options. Some corporations have granted to employees the right to purchase restricted stock, and the number and variety of forms of nonqualified stock options have increased in recent years.

The same accounting principles are now applied to all stock option and stock purchase plans regardless of the differences in details.

---

[3] Mitchell Meyer and Harland Fox, *Employee Stock Purchase Plans*, National Industrial Conference Board, Studies in Personnel Policy, No. 206, 1967.

AICPA Pronouncements on Options. Current accounting practices follow the recommendations of *ARB 43*, Chapter 13B, "Compensation Involved in Stock Option and Stock Purchase Plans," originally issued as *ARB 37 (Revised)* in January 1953. *APB Opinion 25*, which was issued in October 1972, modified some parts of Chapter 13B.

A basic problem in accounting for employee stock options is to determine whether or not the agreements contain elements of compensation for services. If stock options involve compensation, its measurement and equitable periodic allocations to income are corollary problems. The amount of compensation, if any, measures a part of the consideration received for the stock, which is an increase in stockholders' equity. The bulletin states in paragraph 1 that "the amount of compensation involved may be substantial and omission of such costs from the corporation's accounting may result in overstatement of net income to a significant degree."

The purpose in granting stock options is considered the primary indication of the absence or existence of compensation. *ARB 43* recognizes the importance of purpose in paragraph 4 of Chapter 13B.

> In general, the terms under which such options are granted, including any conditions as to exercise of the options or disposal of the stock acquired, are the most significant evidence ordinarily available as to the nature and purpose of a particular stock option or stock option plan.

More specific guides are needed to find if options involve a measurable amount of compensation for services because restrictions and conditions on exercise and disposition are found in most options—either compensatory or noncompensatory.

Options without compensation. The AICPA bulletin sets forth criteria to determine if elements of compensation are involved in employee stock option plans. Those not involving compensation may usually be identified by some or all of the following characteristics:

> A means of raising equity capital
>
> An inducement for more widespread ownership of stock of the corporation among its officers and employees
>
> An option price that is not less than a reasonable price for sale of stock to stockholders or public [presumably at date of grant].

Other characteristics have been viewed as indicative but not as decisive standing alone. Noncompensatory stock options may grant the purchase privilege for a short period. Stock option privileges may be available to all employees or a specified large group of employees. If the number of eligible employees is relatively large and the number of shares of stock optioned to each employee is relatively small, the objective of compensation may be incidental. The absence of restrictions on disposition of the stock purchased under options may indicate that proprietary interests of employees are a minor factor but compensation as the major factor does not necessarily follow. A requirement that stock issued for options exercised may be sold only to the corporation at the option price precludes the notion that the option involves compensation for services.

The APB concluded in paragraph 7 of *APB Opinion 25* that at least four characteristics are essential in a noncompensatory plan:

(a) substantially all full-time employees meeting limited employment qualifications may participate (employees owning a specified percent of the outstanding stock and executives may be excluded),

(b) stock is offered to eligible employees equally or based on a uniform percentage of salary or wages (the plan may limit the number of shares of stock that an employee may purchase through the plan),

(c) the time permitted for exercise of an option or purchase right is limited to a reasonable period, and

(d) the discount from the market price of the stock is no greater than would be reasonable in an offer of stock to stockholders or others.

Accounting for the exercise of noncompensatory options conforms with that for other issues of corporate stock for cash. The proceeds of sale represent additional equity and the components are recorded according to the amounts of proceeds and of par or stated value of the stock issued.

Options for compensation. A stock option granted to an employee primarily as an incentive for greater effort involves compensation. Compensatory options usually offer the employee the opportunity to purchase stock at a fixed price for an extended period. The purpose of that type of option is to stimulate more efficient performance of duties or to persuade the employee to remain with the corporation.

Paragraph 1 of Chapter 13B of *ARB 43* states that

> To the extent that such options and rights involve a measurable amount of compensation, this cost of services received should be accounted for as such.

The amount of compensation may be measured by the fair value of the stock option itself. However, the fair value of an option is influenced by the restrictions on transferability that employee stock options usually impose. Many believe that a fair value may not be determined for a stock option restricted in marketability. The committee on accounting procedure stated that an option, even an option to purchase stock at a price above the current market price, may have value but ascertaining that value is not practicable. The conclusion in Chapter 13B of *ARB 43* is that no objective price can be obtained to measure the current value of an option subject to restrictions. Therefore, the only practical method for assigning a value to an employee stock option is to measure the difference, if any, between the fair value and the option price of the stock. *APB Opinion 25* substituted quoted market price for fair value to measure compensation in stock options.

Date To Measure Compensation. The date selected to assign a value to an option and the corresponding compensation may affect materially the recognized costs and resulting stockholders' equity because the market price of stock often fluctuates greatly during the period that an option is outstanding. *ARB 43* states that "there may be at least six dates to be considered for this purpose." The date the

> Plan is adopted
> Option is granted to a specific individual
> Grantee meets all required conditions to permit exercise of the option
> Grantee is first entitled to exercise the option
> Grantee exercises the option
> Grantee disposes of stock acquired through an option.

The committee dismissed two dates as clearly irrelevant in determining the cost to a grantee corporation: the date on which an option plan is adopted and the date on which a grantee disposes of stock acquired through an option. The date on which a grantee has performed the conditions precedent to exercising an option often coincides with the date on which the grantee is first entitled to exercise the option. If they do not coincide, the first exercisable date may be the later date, and in effect the exercisable date controls. The bulletin contains arguments that are pertinent to the remaining three dates—grant, exercisable, and exercised. A summary of arguments for and against each of the three dates and the conclusions in *ARB 43* follow.

Grant date. Although an option is often not exercisable for a designated period after it is issued, perhaps several years, it represents value in the minds of both parties to the transaction, the employer and the employee, at the grant date. A value attaches to an option at the time it is issued and later fluctuations in the market price of a stock should be differentiated from that value. Changes in value after an option is granted affect the optionee but not the compensation costs of the corporation. The employer corporation foregoes at the grant date the alternative of selling stock at the prevailing market price. *ARB 43* concludes that the appropriate date for measuring the value of a stock option to a specific employee is the date that it is granted.

One objection to using grant date in measuring compensation is that the grantee has not performed the contemplated services and the corporation has incurred no accountable obligation at that date. The cost of future services is unknown at the grant date, and only an estimate of compensation cost is possible at that date.

Exercisable date. Advocates of the exercisable date contend that a corporation definitely gives up something of value only at the exercisable date. An option could not be exercised before that date, but at the exercisable date the corporation incurs an obligation to sell stock for a specified price and does not control later transactions. An option is granted as compensation for future services, not those already performed, and values should be measured at the exercisable date when the services are completed and the right to compensation is unconditional.

That rationale was rejected in *ARB 43* for the reasons that

> the value of the option at the exercisable date is not the amount the parties had in mind to fix the compensation, and
>
> the difference between the option price and the market price of the stock at exercisable date has been affected by market fluctuations completely unrelated to the measure of compensation for services of a grantee.

Exercise date. Supporters of the exercise date argue that only at that point is it known that an option will be exercised, the transaction will be completed, and the corporation will incur a cost. Until that date the corporation has no more than a commitment to deliver shares of stock. At the date an option is exercised, the corporation issues stock for less cash than could be realized if the stock was sold in the market; the difference is a cost of the corporation.

Opponents contend that exercise of an option is a personal decision of a grantee, and the timing of the completed transaction should not affect the costs of the granting corporation. The granting of the option right is a valuable consideration for services and should be accounted for at that time. Many other arguments against using exercise date in measuring compensation are the same as those against exercisable date.

Date of property right. The original *ARB 37*, issued in 1948, recognized as one other date to be considered "the date on which the option right becomes the property of the grantee. . . . Upon that date the grantee has met all conditions precedent to receiving the option, and the corporation then has an unqualified obligation under the agreement." The committee concluded that the date of the property right was proper to measure the value of an option. The SEC and many accountants consider that the date of property right of the grantee is the same as the exercisable date. Others believe that the date of property right could coincide with or differ from the date of grant or the date on which the grantee is first entitled to exercise an option. ARB 37 recognized that the property right and grant dates could coincide in stating "the date of the option agreement may coincide with the date at which the option right becomes the property of the grantee." Also, the property "date may not coincide with the date on which the grantee may first exercise his option." The property date could easily be earlier than the exercisable date and requirements for continued employment may in effect place the property date after the exercisable date. The innumerable provisions and terms of stock option plans varied the significance of the property right date for different corporations. The committee eliminated the date of the property right in the revision of ARB 37.[4]

---

[4] American Institute of Accountants, Research Department, "Accounting for Stock Options: Why Accounting Research Bulletin 37 Was Revised," *The Journal of Accountancy*, April 1953, pp. 436-439.

Measurement date for variable plans. Measurement at date of grant remains accepted practice for traditional stock option and purchase plans. *APB Opinion 25*—effective for all stock option, purchase, award, and bonus rights granted by an employer corporation to an individual employee after December 31, 1972—sets a measurement date in paragraph 10b for "variable" plans.

> *The measurement date* for determining compensation cost in stock option, purchase, and award plans is the first date on which are known both (1) the number of shares that an individual employee is entitled to receive and (2) the option or purchase price, if any. That date for many or most plans is the date an option or purchase right is granted or stock is awarded to an individual employee and is therefore unchanged from Chapter 13B of ARB No. 43. However, the measurement date may be later than the date of grant or award in plans with variable terms that depend on events after date of grant or award.

Recognized Compensation. Since *ARB 43* recommends the grant date for measuring compensation, only a few corporations recognize compensation as a part of the consideration for stock issued under qualified options. Qualified stock option plans adopted after 1963 and many earlier ones provided that the option price shall equal the market price of the stock at the date the option is granted. Most stock purchase plans adopted since 1963 provide that the purchase price is no less than 85% of the market price of the stock at date of grant or exercise. Even though a spread between the option price and market price at date of grant was as much as 15% of the market price, measurable compensation often was not considered material and was, therefore, generally ignored.

A few corporations have recognized compensation for stock options if the option price was less than the market price at the date of grant. The corporation recorded the stock issued at the total of cash received and compensation. The compensation costs should be apportioned to the period of service for which the option is given. The period begins with the date of grant and extends to either the exercisable date of an option or the termination date of an employment contract, if any. Therefore, compensation costs measured at the date of grant should be deferred at that date and amortized or portions of the costs should be accrued in the applicable periods. In practice, those treatments are rare. Usually, compensation recognized in employee stock options is not material and is recorded at the date the options are exercised although the cost is determined by the difference in prices at the date of grant. Current practice thereby avoids the unsettled treatment of compensation involved in lapsed options.

Stock Issued for Exercised Options. The choice to issue previously unissued or reacquired shares for exercised stock options is usually a management decision dictated by factors such as dilution of stockholders' interests, number of shares outstanding, cash availability, and listing requirements. A stock option plan may specify that the options are to be granted for treasury stock held, for unissued shares specifically reserved, or for shares that are to be reacquired after the plan is adopted, or that management in its discretion may issue either reacquired or unissued shares for exercised options. The current accounting for treasury shares delivered to an optionee is discussed in the next chapter in the section on dispositions of reacquired stock.

Disclosure of Plans in Financial Statements. The usual absence of compensation for services and the lag between the dates of grant and exercise increase the need to disclose transactions in and status of stock options. The minimum requirements for disclosure of stock option plans are given in Chapter 13B of *ARB 43*. The New York Stock Exchange requires more detailed disclosure of the status of stock options at both beginning and end of a period and the related changes during the period in the number of shares under option. The SEC requires even more comprehensive and detailed disclosure than either the AICPA or the Exchange. Information required for stock optioned to officers and employees is given in Rule 3-16(n) of *Regulation S-X*. The SEC requires disclosure of fair values of optioned stock as of the dates exercisable and exercised. The SEC believes that the information indicates the potential profits to employees and dilution of interests of existing stockholders.

The SEC explained the reasons for adopting the present rule in *Accounting Series Release No. 76*, which was issued in November 1953 after *ARB 37* was revised to measure compensation at the date the option was granted. The Commission had proposed a rule "because of the apparent lack of unanimity of opinion" about determining compensation in stock options. Further,

> The principal point of disagreement was the time at which the determination should be made. Persuasive arguments were advanced for each of three dates, i.e., when the options were (1) granted, (2) exercisable, or (3) exercised.

The Commission considered the comments and suggestions received and concluded that the propriety of using any one of these dates in all cases had not been established, and that determination of, and accounting for, cost to the grantor based upon the excess of fair value of the optioned shares over the option price at any one of the three dates advocated might, in some cases, result in the presentation of misleading profit and loss or income statements.

The SEC also concluded that it should not prescribe a procedure for determining cost to a corporation but rather it should insure that readers of financial statements were furnished sufficient information to appraise the financial effects of stock options.

Business Combinations

Two Methods of Accounting. Accounting for changes in stockholders' equity as a result of a corporation issuing additional stock to effect a business combination is discussed in the context of the two acceptable methods of accounting, the pooling of interests method and the purchase method. The method of accounting for a business combination determines the nature of the increase in stockholders' equity.

Accounting Research Study No. 5, "A Critical Study of Accounting for Business Combinations," by Arthur R. Wyatt and *Accounting Research Study No. 10,* "Accounting for Goodwill," by George R. Catlett and Norman O. Olson describe the origin and development of the purchase and pooling of interests methods of accounting for business combinations. The studies also cite the supporting authoritative pronouncements and their influences on accounting practices. *APB Opinion 16,* issued in 1970, summarizes the development of practices in paragraphs 9 through 14. An earlier accounting practice known as part-purchase, part-pooling is now eliminated because *APB Opinion 16* states that the practice is not acceptable and a single accounting method should be applied to an entire combination.

Pooling of Interests Method. The pooling of interests method of accounting for a business combination presents as a single interest the interests of common stockholders that previously were independent. Paragraph 45 of *APB Opinion 16* states that the "method shows that stockholder groups neither withdraw nor invest assets but in effect exchange voting common stock in a ratio that determines their respective interests in the combined corporation." A business combination may have those features and the Opinion explains the conditions that require a corporation to apply the pooling of interests method. "The combining of existing voting common stock interests by the exchange of stock is the essence of a business combination accounted for by the pooling of interests method."

The method ignores the fair value of stock issued to effect a combination and the fair value of property of the separate corporations. Thus, the existing basis of accounting continues, and the recorded assets and liabilities of the separate corporations generally become the recorded assets and liabilities of the combined corporation. Paragraph 53 of *APB Opinion 16* pertains to accounting for stockholders' equity of the combined corporation.

> The stockholders' equities of the separate companies are also combined as a part of the pooling of interests method of accounting. The combined corporation records as capital the capital stock and capital in excess of par or stated value of outstanding stock of the separate companies. Similarly, retained earnings or deficits of the separate companies are combined and recognized as retained earnings of the combined corporation. . . . The amount of outstanding shares of stock of the combined corporation at par or stated value may exceed the total amount of capital stock of the separate combining companies; the excess should be deducted first from the combined other contributed capital and then from the combined retained earnings. . . .

The principal difficulty in applying the recommended procedures involves the difference in the par or stated values of the common stocks of the separate corporations. Stockholders' equity of the combined corporation equals total equity of the separate corporations, although the resulting components are not always the total of the separate components. The amounts of each component of equity of a corporation issuing stock to effect the combination depend on the provisions of the common stock issued and on the components of equity of the previously separate corporations.

Purchase Method. *APB Opinion 16* provides that all business combinations that do not meet the specified conditions that require accounting by the pooling of interests method should be accounted for as an acquisition of one or more companies. A corporation may issue shares of its own stock to acquire either the outstanding stock or net assets of another corporation. Paragraph 67 of *APB Opinion 16* states the general principle of accounting for the acquisition of an asset by issuing stock:

> An asset acquired by issuing shares of stock of the acquiring corporation is recorded at the fair value of the asset—that is, shares of stock issued are recorded at the fair value of the consideration received for the stock.

The principle is applied in the purchase method of accounting and is discussed in paragraphs 74 and 75 of the same Opinion.

> The fair value of securities traded in the market is normally more clearly evident than the fair value of an acquired company (paragraph 67). Thus, the quoted market price of an equity security issued to effect a business combination may usually be used to approximate the fair value of an acquired company after recognizing possible effects of price fluctuations, quantities traded, issue costs, and the like. . . . The market price for a reasonable period before and after the date the terms of the acquisition are agreed to and announced should be considered in determining the fair value of securities issued.
>
> If the quoted market price is not the fair value of stock, either preferred or common, the consideration received should be estimated even though measuring directly the fair values of assets received is difficult. Both the consideration received, including goodwill, and the extent of the adjustment of the quoted market price of the stock issued should be weighed to determine the amount to be recorded. All aspects of the acquisition, including the negotiations, should be studied, and independent appraisals may be used as an aid in determining the fair value of securities issued. Consideration other than stock distributed to effect an acquisition may provide evidence of the total fair value received.

APB Opinion 16 merely expanded the explanation of the accounting principles that were applicable to acquisitions of businesses since 1957 when *ARB 48* was issued.

An acquiring corporation may distribute previously unissued shares or treasury shares and usually records the fair value of the stock as the consideration received for either type of shares. If previously unissued shares are distributed, a corporation allocates the consideration to capital in excess of par or stated value of stock in the same manner as it allocates the proceeds of sales of stock. A discussion of the procedures to account for treasury stock issued to effect a business combination is deferred to the section on dispositions of reacquired stock in Chapter 3.

Stock Dividends and Stock Splits

Both stock dividends and stock splits require that the corporation issue additional shares of stock pro rata to existing stockholders. Neither a stock dividend nor a stock split changes the assets of a corporation. The proportionate interests of stockholders are not changed by a common stock split or a common stock dividend distributed to holders of common stock, which is the type discussed in this section. Each type of transaction has a diluting effect, although perhaps negligible, on the market price and book amount of one share of stock. Distinctions between the two transactions are purely arbitrary but those distinctions are set in official pronouncements as the basis for determining appropriate accounting.

Distinctions Between Distributions. The two terms, stock dividend and stock split-up, are defined in the first two paragraphs of Chapter 7B of *ARB 43* for the purpose of distinguishing between the distributions.

> The term *stock dividend* as used in this chapter refers to an issuance by a corporation of its own common shares to its common shareholders without consideration and under conditions indicating that such action is prompted mainly by a desire to give the recipient shareholders some ostensibly separate evidence of a part of their respective interests in accumulated corporate earnings without distribution of cash or other property which the board of directors deems necessary or desirable to retain in the business.
>
> The term *stock split-up* as used in this chapter refers to an issuance by a corporation of its own common shares to its common shareholders without consideration and under conditions indicating that such action is prompted mainly by a desire to increase the number of outstanding shares for the purpose of effecting a reduction in their unit market price and, thereby, of obtaining wider distribution and improved marketability of the shares.

Each definition emphasizes that the intent and purpose of the stock distribution is the primary indication of whether it is a stock split or stock dividend. The accounting required for each differs because of the purposes and the beliefs of stockholders that a stock dividend is a distribution of earnings. Briefly, a stock dividend requires capitalization of retained earnings; a stock split does not.

Small and large distributions. Purpose alone is not always conclusive and the resulting effects of a distribution may indicate the type of distribution. If the number of shares issued is so small in comparison with shares previously outstanding that the distribution has no apparent effect on the market price of the stock, the distribution is presumed to be a stock dividend. If the number of shares issued is so great that the distribution materially reduces, or may reasonably be expected to reduce, the market price of the stock, the distribution is treated as a stock split.

Rules of thumb have been set to determine what constitutes a small distribution which is treated as a stock dividend and a large distribution which is treated as a stock split. ARB 43 states that, except for unusual circumstances, a stock distribution of less than about 20% or 25% of the number of shares previously outstanding should be treated as a stock dividend. Distributions greater than those percentages should be treated as stock splits unless they recur frequently.

The New York Stock Exchange in Section A 13 of the *Company Manual* requires that a distribution of less than 25% of the number of shares outstanding before the distribution be treated as a stock dividend. Distributions representing 100% or more of the number of shares outstanding before the distribution should be treated as a stock split. The Exchange requires that distributions of 25% or more but less than 100% be treated as a stock dividend "only when, in the opinion of the Exchange, such distributions assume the character of stock dividends through repetition under circumstances not consistent with the true intent and purpose of stock split-ups." A transaction that is a combined stock split and stock dividend may be treated entirely as a stock split.

The SEC adopted in *Accounting Series Release No. 124*, which was issued in June 1972, the measure of 25% or less for requiring a transfer from retained earnings to other capital accounts.

Terminology. Chapter 7B of *ARB 43* contains a specific recommendation that in describing a stock distribution that is determined to be a split "every effort be made to avoid the use of the word *dividend* in related corporate resolutions, notices, and announcements and that, in those cases where because of legal requirements this cannot be done, the transaction be described, for example, as a *split-up effected in the form of a dividend.*"

The term stock dividend seems firmly fixed in accounting terminology in the United States. However, the word dividend is inaccurate. A dividend implies that corporate assets are transferred to stockholders. A better description is a distribution of stock, but the term stock dividend is used in this study because it is widely accepted.

A distribution of stock of another class to a class of stockholders of a corporation is often called a stock dividend. That type of distribution may change the proportionate interests of existing stockholders and therefore is considered later in this study as a form of recapitalization. Stock dividends discussed in this section and in *ARB 43* are distributions of shares of common stock to the stockholders of the same class of common stock.

Accounting for Stock Dividends. The amount of retained earnings, if any, that should be capitalized for a stock dividend has been controversial, and the required accounting has changed over the years. Current accounting practices arose because of abuses in distributing additional stock in the twenties and criticism of the policy of distributing stock dividends in lieu of cash dividends. At one time the type (or size) of the distribution did not determine the accounting; instead the method of accounting determined whether the distribution was called a dividend or split. Roy B. Kester described that view concisely.

> The essential characteristic of a true stock dividend is the capitalization of a portion of the surplus. Without such capitalization, the issue of stock is merely a stock split-up rather than a stock dividend.[5]

Changes in accounting pronouncements. The usual procedure before *ARB 11* was issued in 1941 was that directors declared a stock dividend as

a percentage of the shares outstanding and the corporation reduced earned surplus the minimum amount for legal requirements, or

a dollar amount to be transferred from earned surplus to capital stock.

The market value of stock first played a part in accounting for stock distributed (other than sales of shares) in the procedures outlined in the 1941 bulletin. The committee stated that after deciding the amount to be transferred from earned surplus to capital stock and capital sur-

---

[5] *Advanced Accounting*, 1946, p. 525. The 1933 edition of the book, before *ARB 11* was issued, contains substantially the same wording. Other authors made the same distinction although Arthur Stone Dewing in the 1934 edition of *A Study of Corporation Securities* stated that the distinction "is not observed in financial parlance" (p. 99).

plus, the directors should decide on the number of shares of stock to be issued by two requirements:

> The number of dividend shares should . . . not exceed the number determined by dividing the amount of earned surplus authorized to be capitalized by the total amount per share in the capital and capital-surplus accounts before the declaration of the stock dividend.

> . . . where such fair market value per share [for the increased number of shares to be outstanding after the stock dividend] is substantially in excess of the amount per share of the combined capital-stock and capital-surplus accounts before the stock dividend, they should fix the number of dividend shares so that the amount charged to earned surplus per share will have a reasonable relationship to such fair market value.

One member of the committee dissented from the bulletin unless the above and other portions of the bulletin "are to be regarded as recommendations in relation to corporate accounting and fiscal policy and not as statements of accounting principles."

The original *ARB 11* was revised in 1952 to provide that a corporation should transfer from earned surplus to capital stock and capital surplus an amount equal to the fair value of the additional shares issued as a stock dividend if the number of shares distributed apparently do not affect the market price of previously outstanding shares. If the number of shares distributed is large enough to materially reduce the market value of one share, the transaction should be described and accounted for as a stock split. The provisions of that bulletin are continued as Chapter 7B of *ARB 43*.

Accounting procedure today. The generally accepted practice is to account for stock dividends in accordance with *ARB 43* "by transferring from earned surplus to the category of permanent capitalization (represented by the capital stock and capital surplus accounts) an amount equal to the fair value of the additional shares issued." The New York Stock Exchange requirement is similar. Section A 13 of the *Company Manual* provides that fair value "should closely approximate the current share market price adjusted to reflect issuance of the additional shares." The fair value is normally based on the closing market price of the stock on the day before the dividend is declared but may be an average of daily prices for a period.

Most state laws require capitalization by a transfer from earned surplus to stated capital of the par value of the additional shares issued or of an amount within the discretion of the board of directors for shares without par value. The legal requirements provide for a minimum capitalization and do not prohibit capitalizing a larger amount.

Closely held corporations. Chapter 7B of *ARB 43* provides that closely held corporations are not required to comply with the accounting recommended for stock dividends. Paragraph 12 reads:

> In cases of closely-held companies, it is to be presumed that the intimate knowledge of the corporations' affairs possessed by their shareholders would preclude any such implications and possible constructions as are referred to in paragraph 10. In such cases, the committee believes that considerations of public policy do not arise and that there is no need to capitalize earned surplus other than to meet legal requirements.

The exception emphasizes that the capitalization requirement for publicly held corporations emerges primarily from public financial policy and not from a general accounting principle. In fact, *ARB 11 (Revised)* first required a reduction of retained earnings for the market value of stock distributed as dividends for reasons of "public interest."

Stock dividends of subsidiaries. Capitalization of retained earnings for a stock dividend is discussed in paragraph 18 of *ARB 51*, "Consolidated Financial Statements," issued in 1959.

> Occasionally, subsidiary companies capitalize earned surplus arising since acquisition, by means of a stock dividend or otherwise. This does not require a transfer to capital surplus on consolidation, inasmuch as the retained earnings in the consolidated financial statements should reflect the accumulated earnings of the consolidated group not distributed to the shareholders of, or capitalized by, the parent company.

Predominant practice for stock dividends. Nearly every publicly held corporation in the United States follows the recommendations of the committee on accounting procedure and New York Stock Exchange. Presentation and disclosure of details varies but the amount transferred from retained earnings to capital stock and additional capital equals the fair value of the additional shares issued. Corporations that distribute treasury shares as stock dividends also account for the fair value of the shares distributed.

The bulletin contains no definition or explanation of a closely held corporation as distinguished from a publicly held one and thus permits some leeway in adopting recommended practices. Corporations in some industries and in some states in addition to closely held corporations do not always follow the recommended practice. Banks are a notable example. Customarily, banks account for stock dividends by transferring from surplus or undivided profits to capital stock an amount equal to the par value of additional shares distributed. Some corporations account for stock dividends at the par or stated value of the stock distributed if the state permits dividends to be distributed from other than retained earnings.

Accounting for Stock Splits. A stock split does not require the capitalization of earnings. If the par or stated value of each share of stock is reduced in the same proportion as the additional shares issued, a stock split does not change the total amount assigned to capital stock.

A corporation need not change the par or stated value of each share of stock, but then the amount of capital stock is increased by the par or stated value of the additional shares issued. Corporations transfer the increase from other capital to the extent available and any remainder from the retained earnings or transfer the entire amount from retained earnings. Either method satisfies legal requirements for the minimum carrying amount of capital stock and is permitted under state laws.

3

Decreases in Stockholders' Equity

Types of Decreases

Total stockholders' equity of a corporation is normally expected to decrease only as a result of losses from operations or dividend distributions that exceed current earnings. The portion of equity contributed by stockholders is commonly envisaged as permanent because statutes restrict distributions of that amount. However, distributions in partial liquidation are permissible. Several forms of partial liquidation are possible—for example, redemption of callable stock is in the nature of a partial liquidation.

Reacquisitions of Stock. Reacquisition of outstanding stock is permissible and usually decreases total stockholders' equity, although the reduction may be only temporary if the corporation later sells or distributes the stock. But a disposition of treasury stock does not always reinstate the total amount of equity. Reacquisitions of stock are described in the first section of this chapter, followed by sections on retirement and other dispositions of reacquired stock.

Recapitalizations. Elimination of a portion of stockholders' equity may accompany the recapitalization of a corporation. However, a recapitalization often changes the components rather than the total of equity. Accounting for recapitalizations is discussed briefly in Chapter 4 on adjusting components of stockholders' equity.

Distributions of Dividends. A recurring decrease in total stockholders' equity is the distribution of dividends, either in cash or in property. A dividend in kind may be a substitute for a cash dividend distributed from earnings. More often a dividend in kind, or property dividend, consists of stock of another corporation and is similar to a liquidating dividend. A corporation may wish or be required to divest its controlling investment in another corporation; the divestiture is often called a spin-off. Accounting for cash and noncash dividends is excluded from this study.

Some corporations offer stockholders the right to exchange shares of stock for securities that the corporation holds as an investment instead of distributing the securities to all stockholders; the transaction fits the category of reacquired stock and not of dividends.

Reacquired Shares of Stock

Reacquired or Treasury Stock. Shares of stock reacquired by the issuing corporation and not canceled and retired are commonly called treasury stock. The term is a misnomer—authorized, unissued shares may also be designated treasury stock. Reacquired stock is a more accurate description. But treasury stock is now accepted, understood, defined in some statutes, and used often in financial statements. Both reacquired stock and treasury stock are used in this study with the same meaning.

Treasury Stock as Asset or Equity. Corporations sometimes recognize stock reacquired for specific purposes as an asset and the transaction has no direct effect on stockholders' equity. Other acquisitions of treasury stock are considered to be equity transactions, and the cost of the stock decreases total stockholders' equity. The accounting practices discussed in this chapter cover reacquisitions that are recorded as equity transactions, although the provisions and restrictions of the laws and corporate charters cover all reacquisitions regardless of the manner of accounting.

Legal Restrictions on Reacquiring Stock. Whether or not a corporation has the right to purchase its own stock and under what conditions are legal questions. Current laws and court decisions have established that corporations in each of the 50 states and District of Columbia are permitted, within limits, to reacquire shares of their own stock. That corporate authority may be granted either by state law or by express powers of a charter if the law is silent or permissive. The laws of the state of incorporation may not only control reacquisitions of stock but also dictate the effects of reacquisitions and of later dispositions on legal components of equity. Reacquisitions of stock are regulated in the categories of redeemable and nonredeemable stock rather than in the distinctions of preferred and common stock.

Redeemable stock. A frequent statutory limitation is that redeemable stock may be reacquired either by redemption or by purchase at no more than the current redemption price. Other limitations are that the corporation remain solvent and that the reacquisitions not reduce net assets below the amount payable to other stockholders with prior or equal rights upon involuntary dissolution. Some states vary the general requirements and modify the restrictions on insolvency or recognition of rights of other stockholders. A corporate charter creating redeemable stock usually specifies the conditions and restrictions of reacquisitions; charter provisions may be more limiting than statutory restrictions.

The Model Act provides that reacquired redeemable shares shall not be reissued and are canceled automatically. Cancellation reduces stated capital of a corporation by the amount of stated capital represented by the canceled shares but only after an official filing with the state of incorporation. Therefore, reacquired redeemable shares never become treasury shares as defined in the Model Act, and canceled and retired shares are restored to the status of authorized but unissued shares.

Nonredeemable stock. Most statutes permit a corporation to purchase its own stock without restriction for a few designated purposes, such as eliminating fractional shares and reacquiring stock from employees under the terms of a plan. Nearly all statutory restrictions on other reacquisitions of nonredeemable stock conform with the view that a corporation does not reduce its legal capital by the purchase of its own nonredeemable stock.

The most common statutory restriction is that the cost of shares purchased may not exceed existing surplus—in many states only unrestricted earned surplus. The Model Act confines "distributions to shareholders to the excess of assets [excluding treasury shares] over the claims of creditors. This achieves the same result sought in the early trust-fund doctrine, without the fictions of a trust or a fund."[1] A typical explanation of the reasons for limiting reacquisitions of stock to the extent of surplus is:

> To allow a corporation to reduce its capital by the purchase of its own shares, is to permit it to return to stockholders funds upon which creditors are presumed to have relied when granting credit to the corporation. Thus, if the corporation is allowed to purchase its own shares without limit, stockholders whose interest in the corporation is residual are enabled to withdraw their capital, partially or wholly, and shift a part of the risk to corporate creditors. . . . Surplus, however, not being a part of the legal capital upon which creditors rely, may be used by a corporation for the purchase of its own shares.[2]

A law specifying that treasury stock may be purchased only from or to the extent of unrestricted earned surplus measures permissible acquisitions, but reducing earned surplus by the cost of the stock is not a necessary accounting consequence.

Generally, nonredeemable stock that is reacquired may be canceled or retained as treasury stock pending later disposition.

Legal status of treasury stock. Several state laws specify that shares held in the treasury are not outstanding. The Model Act specifies that treasury shares are issued shares but not outstanding shares. Most laws provide that reacquired shares may not be voted and no cash dividends may be paid on treasury shares. The prohibition in some laws refers to dividends on treasury shares and thereby outlaws stock dividends as well as cash dividends. Often the laws specifically exclude treasury stock from net assets in determining surplus legally available for distribution as dividends.

Restrictions on earned surplus. The corporate laws of most states provide that distributions to the extent of earned surplus are restricted by the cost of reacquired stock. The restrictions are either temporary or permanent, depending on the statutory provisions.

Some states provide that earned surplus available for dividends is reduced by the cost of treasury stock only as long as the corporation

---

[1] Ray Garrett, "Capital and Surplus Under the New Corporation Statutes," *Law and Contemporary Problems,* Spring 1958, p. 245.

[2] Raymond P. Marple, "The Sources of Capital Surplus," *The Accounting Review,* March 1934, p. 78.

holds the shares. The restriction may be removed and the amount reinstated by sale, distribution, or retirement of the shares. The Model Act does not state specifically whether or not earned surplus is permanently restricted by an excess of the cost of treasury stock over proceeds of sales of the stock.

States with more severe restrictions, such as California and Oklahoma, provide that earned surplus is reduced permanently by the entire cost of treasury stock acquired. A later sale or retirement of the shares in no way changes the original effects of the acquisition and does not reinstate the amount as unrestricted earned surplus. However, some state laws provide that a corporation may distribute dividends to the extent of paid-in surplus as well as retained earnings thus often nullifying a restriction created by the acquisition of treasury stock.

Basic Views of Reacquiring Stock. Corporations have adopted many practices to account for the acquisition and later disposition of treasury stock. The methods of accounting stem from two basic views of the transaction of reacquiring stock. One is often designated "unallocated deduction" or "cost" method and the other "contraction of capital," "par value," or "constructive retirement" method. Total stockholders' equity is the same under either of the two basic methods but, depending on the circumstances, the two methods may produce different components of equity while a corporation holds treasury stock and also after it disposes of the stock.

Unallocated deduction method. The unallocated deduction method views the reacquisition of stock as the initial part of a transaction that will be completed later on the date the stock is sold, distributed, or retired. The cost of treasury stock is a separate unallocated decrease in total equity. As indicated by the term, the cost of treasury shares is retained in a temporary account and is usually presented as a single deduction from all other components of stockholders' equity. Ultimate disposition of the stock determines the effects of the cost on the components of equity.

Contraction of capital method. The contraction of capital method views the reacquisition of stock as a completed transaction—the withdrawal of equity and termination of the rights in the corporation of the related stockholder. All components of stockholders' equity related to the reacquired shares of stock are eliminated as though the stock were retired on the date that it was reacquired.

The contraction of capital method conforms with the view that the reacquisition of stock is a partial liquidation. Since the basic nature of reacquired shares and authorized unissued shares is the same, legal distinctions between the two are disregarded in presenting financial statements. A sale or distribution of treasury stock is viewed as a separate and distinct transaction from its acquisition and is accounted for as though previously unissued shares of stock were sold or distributed.

Authoritative support for accounting. The principal authoritative support for present accounting for treasury stock is pronouncements of the American Institute of Certified Public Accountants. The special committee on cooperation with stock exchanges reported to the New York Stock Exchange on the treatment by a corporation of the purchase and sale of its own stock. A 1938 report of the committee on accounting procedure on the report of the special committee is included in Chapter 1B of *ARB 43*. The pertinent paragraphs relate to disposition as well as reacquisition but they are quoted in entirety because they are often interpreted differently.

> 6. "The opinion of the special committee on cooperation with stock exchanges reads in part as follows:
>
> 7. "'Apparently there is general agreement that the difference between the purchase price and the stated value of a corporation's common stock purchased and retired should be reflected in capital surplus. Your committee believes that while the net asset value of the shares of common stock outstanding in the hands of the public may be increased or decreased by such purchase and retirement, such transactions relate to the capital of the corporation and do not give rise to corporate profits or losses. Your committee can see no essential difference between (a) the purchase and retirement of a corporation's own common stock and the subsequent issue of common shares, and (b) the purchase and resale of its own common stock.'
>
> 8. "This committee is in agreement with the views thus expressed; it is aware that such transactions have been held to give rise to taxable income, but it does not feel that such decisions constitute any bar to the application of correct accounting procedure as above outlined.
>
> 9. "The special committee on cooperation with stock exchanges continued and concluded its report with the following statement:
>
> 10. "'Accordingly, although your committee recognizes that there may be cases where the transactions involved are so inconsequential as to be immaterial, it does not believe that, as a broad

general principle, such transactions should be reflected in earned surplus (either directly or through inclusion in the income account).'

11. "This committee agrees with the special committee on cooperation with stock exchanges, but thinks it desirable to point out that the qualification should not be applied to any transaction which, although in itself inconsiderable in amount, is a part of a series of transactions which in the aggregate are of substantial importance."

Thus the committee on accounting procedure indicated no preference for either the unallocated deduction or the contraction of capital method of initially recording the reacquisition of stock.

Legality of unallocated deduction. Several accountants and lawyers have questioned whether or not the Model Act accomplished an intended purpose of legalizing the presentation of treasury stock as an unallocated deduction from other equity components.[3] The Model Act by its definitions of categories of equity and provisions for restrictions of earned surplus is said to imply that the total cost of treasury stock should be deducted from capital surplus. The analysis leading to that conclusion is: capital surplus by its definition equals total corporate equity less stated capital and earned surplus; the cost of treasury shares does not reduce either stated capital or earned surplus; therefore, the cost of treasury stock is presumed to reduce the residual amount, capital surplus. The effect on earned surplus of reacquiring stock is to restrict distributions to stockholders. A literal interpretation of the words of the Model Act seems to be that capital surplus is reduced by the cost of treasury stock and in addition earned surplus is restricted by the same amount, resulting in a double effect on total surplus. In addition, treasury stock as a separate deduction from other components of equity conflicts with two provisions of the Model Act: (1) that stated capital is not reduced by the reacquisition of stock and (2) that stated capital, capital surplus, and earned surplus are the three components of equity.

---

[3] For example: William P. Hackney, "The Financial Provisions of the Model Business Corporation Act," *Harvard Law Review*, June 1957, pp. 1392-1394; E. George Rudolph, "Accounting for Treasury Shares Under the Model Business Corporation Act," *Harvard Law Review*, December 1959, pp. 324-325; and Robert T. Sprouse, "Accounting for Treasury Stock Transactions: Prevailing Practices and New Statutory Provisions," *Columbia Law Review*, June 1959, pp. 890-893.

Accounting for Preferred Stock Reacquired. Preferred stock is usually reacquired for retirement and often is retired in the same year that it is purchased or redeemed. However, some shares of preferred stock are reacquired with the intention of retiring them in a later year and are disclosed in financial statements as treasury stock. The presentation of treasury stock held at the date of financial statements indicates the treatment at date of acquisition. Reacquired shares are presented in either of two manners:

> Cost of the preferred treasury shares is accounted for as though the stock were retired and preferred capital stock is reduced by the par or stated value of the treasury shares.

> Cost of the preferred treasury shares is shown as a deduction from the total of other components of stockholders' equity.

Neither practice appears to predominate nor are reasons apparent for adopting one or the other method.

Accounting for Common Stock Reacquired. The predominant practice in accounting for common treasury stock is to record the cost of the shares as a separate component of stockholders' equity. However, many corporations allocate the cost of treasury stock to capital stock and additional capital to account for the constructive retirement of the stock. Some corporations follow other practices to account for the constructive retirement of reacquired stock and those are summarized in the section on retirement (page 57). A few corporations deduct the entire cost of treasury stock either from capital stock or from retained earnings.

Retirement of Stock

Stock retired may be previously outstanding shares that a corporation called for redemption, purchased in a securities market, purchased under a tender solicitation, or eliminated in a recapitalization. Some state laws provide that the sole action of the board of directors is sufficient to retire stock. Other states require that the charter be amended to retire shares of stock and the number of authorized shares is reduced correspondingly.

Differing Views of Retirement Accounting. All accountants do not advocate the same accounting for retirements of stock. The controversy centers on the treatment of differences between the purchase price of the stock to be retired and the contributions by stockholders applicable to those shares. Accountants generally agree that if the purchase price is the lesser amount the difference is included in additional capital, but a consensus is lacking for treatment of a greater cost. Assuming that capital stock is reduced by the par or stated value of the shares retired, a summary of the views of accounting for differences follows.

> The difference between the average amount contributed for each outstanding share of stock and the purchase or redemption price of shares retired may affect the components of equity other than capital stock.
>
>> If the cost of the shares is less than the applicable amount of capital stock, the difference is an increase in additional capital.
>>
>> If the cost of the shares is less than applicable contributions but more than the applicable amount of capital stock, the difference remains in additional capital.
>>
>> If the cost of the shares is more than applicable contributions, the difference is:
>>
>>> Preferred stock—a decrease either in additional capital or in retained earnings.
>>>
>>> Common stock—a decrease either in additional capital or in retained earnings, or the difference is allocated to additional capital and retained earnings.

Authoritative support for retirement accounting. Pronouncements of accounting organizations and regulatory bodies support the varied practices adopted to account for retirements of stock. Chapter 1B of *ARB 43* on treasury stock, which is quoted on pages 50 and 51, referred to the retirement of common stock. The committee stated in paragraph 7 that the difference between the purchase price and the stated value of common stock retired should be included in additional capital.

Many accountants believe that capital in excess of par or stated value of stock should not be reduced by more than the pro rata portion applicable to the shares retired. The committee on accounting concepts and standards of the American Accounting Association stated that view in the 1957 revision of "Accounting and Reporting Standards for Corporate Financial Statements."

> Preferably, the outlay by a corporation for its own shares is reflected as a reduction of the aggregate of contributed capital, and any excess of outlay over the pro-rata portion of contributed capital as a distribution of retained earnings.

The AICPA designated pro rata allocation as an additional acceptable practice in paragraph 12 of *APB Opinion 6* dated October 1965. The portion relating to retirement of stock reads:

> When a corporation's stock is retired, or purchased for constructive retirement (with or without an intention to retire the stock formally in accordance with applicable laws):
>
> i. *an excess of purchase price over par or stated value* may be allocated between capital surplus and retained earnings. The portion of the excess allocated to capital surplus should be limited to the sum of (a) all capital surplus arising from previous retirements and net "gains" on sales of treasury stock of the same issue and (b) the prorata portion of capital surplus paid in, voluntary transfers of retained earnings, capitalization of stock dividends, etc., on the same issue. For this purpose, any remaining capital surplus applicable to issues fully retired (formal or constructive) is deemed to be applicable prorata to shares of common stock. Alternatively, the excess may be charged entirely to retained earnings in recognition of the fact that a corporation can always capitalize or allocate retained earnings for such purposes.
>
> ii. *an excess of par or stated value over purchase price* should be credited to capital surplus.

SEC *Accounting Series Release No. 45* issued in 1943 relates to the "treatment of premiums paid upon the redemption of preferred stock." Pertinent excerpts are:

> . . . if the redemption price exceeds the amount paid in on such shares, the excess should ordinarily be charged to earned surplus.
>
> . . . .
>
> "In order to maintain a proper distinction between capital and income . . . it is necessary to consider the entire amount contributed by shareholders as capital regardless of whether reflected in the accounts as capital stock or as capital or paid-in surplus. . . . reflection of a redemption premium paid to one class of shareholders as a diminution or utilization of amounts contributed by another class, or by shares of the same class still outstanding,

would ordinarily be inconsistent with recognition of these principles in that the capital contribution shown for outstanding shares would thenceforth be less than the amount actually paid in on such shares....

. . . .

"If less than an entire issue were redeemed it would not . . . ordinarily be proper . . . to charge against capital surplus contributed by the preferred stock an amount per share in excess of the pro-rata portion of such capital surplus applicable to each share of preferred stock outstanding prior to the redemption in question.

"In some cases a part of capital surplus may have resulted from the prior reacquisition and retirement of preferred or common shares at less than the amounts paid in thereon. Such capital surplus does not therefore represent any amounts paid in on shares still outstanding. . . . ordinarily . . . no objection [exists] to utilizing such capital surplus for the purpose of absorbing the excess of the redemption price over the amounts paid in on the shares being retired."

The quoted highlights from authoritative pronouncements show that support is found for several methods of accounting for retirements of stock. The different views and arguments have contributed to the adoption of varying accounting practices; in addition, some corporations have permitted legal requirements of the state of incorporation to take precedence.

Accounting for Preferred Stock Retired. Accounting for retirement of shares of preferred stock varies with the existing components of stockholders' equity, the purchase price of the reacquired shares, and the discretion of the corporation. The many present practices are classified by combinations of equity contributed for the shares and cost of reacquired shares.

1. Contributed capital equals par or stated value of stock:
    a. cost of reacquired shares less than par or stated value—
        i. difference added to additional capital, or
        ii. difference added to retained earnings.
    b. cost of reacquired shares more than par or stated value—
        difference deducted from retained earnings.

2. Contributed capital exceeds par or stated value of stock (sources of additional capital by class of stock not determinable):
   a. cost of reacquired shares less than par or stated value—
      i. difference added to additional capital, or
      ii. difference added to retained earnings.
   b. cost of reacquired shares more than par or stated value—
      i. difference deducted from additional capital,
      ii. difference deducted from retained earnings, or
      iii. difference allocated and deducted from additional capital and retained earnings.

A few other accounting practices for retirements are found but they are isolated. As examples, an excess of the par value of preferred shares retired over their cost is transferred to common capital stock and a redemption premium on preferred shares retired is deferred to be amortized over the remaining period of the retired issue.

Predominant accounting for retirement. Practices that predominate in accounting for retirement of preferred stock are:

> The excess of par or stated value over the cost of reacquired shares of preferred stock is added to contributed capital.

> The excess of cost over par or stated value of reacquired shares of preferred stock is deducted from either contributed capital or retained earnings; neither practice clearly prevails.

Of course, the contributed equity of a corporation does not always exceed the par or stated value of outstanding stock. If not, the excess cost of retired stock would need to be deducted from retained earnings.

Allocating the excess of cost over the par or stated value of reacquired preferred stock between additional capital and retained earnings is not as frequent as might be expected from recommendations in pronouncements. The annual reports inspected showed that about 5% of the corporations that had additional capital allocated the difference between additional capital and retained earnings; however, the basis for allocating was not disclosed. The sources of additional capital and the amounts applicable to preferred and other classes of stock were not disclosed in published reports. Those factors probably influenced the accounting because capital applicable to common stock was not adjusted for retirements of preferred stock.

Accounting for Common Stock Retired. Reacquiring common stock specifically for retirement is unusual but does occur. Two methods of accounting for common stock retired were followed about equally in the reports inspected. The purchase price of stock reacquired and retired was allocated as follows:

Par or stated value deducted from capital stock, and
1. excess of cost over par or stated value of reacquired shares allocated and deducted from additional capital *and* retained earnings, or
2. excess of cost over par or stated value of reacquired shares deducted entirely from additional capital *or* retained earnings.

Another but exceptional method was to deduct the entire cost of reacquired common stock that was retired from retained earnings. Nearly all of the corporations that followed that method were incorporated in California.

Other Dispositions of Treasury Stock

Legal Restrictions. Several state laws specify that a corporation may dispose of treasury stock only in designated types of transactions, such as selling the shares and distributing stock dividends. Treasury stock may be sold or distributed in most states for any consideration fixed by the board of directors. Since the stock was previously issued and outstanding, the reissue price is not controlled by statute. A corporation may retire treasury stock that is not sold or distributed.

Many state laws do not deal specifically with the results of dispositions of treasury stock, but some statutes indicate through their definitions of terms the intended accounting for dispositions. A few states require that the entire proceeds of sales of treasury stock shall be added to contributed capital. Other states provide that "gains" on sales of treasury stock shall be added to contributed capital.

The Model Act contains no specific requirements for recording the proceeds of dispositions of treasury stock. The definition of earned surplus to include "net profits, income, gains and losses" is often interpreted to mean that earned surplus should include the results of sales or other dispositions of treasury stock. The committee that drafted the Model Act intended the definition of earned surplus "to apply to transactions in capital assets, not to transactions in the corporation's own shares."[4] The AICPA *Accounting Terminology Bulletin No. 1* contains the same definition of earned surplus and a footnote states that gains and losses of a corporation are other than those from transactions in a corporation's own shares.

Accounting for Dispositions of Treasury Stock. Accounting for dispositions other than retirement of treasury stock varies because of differing views of the transactions and differing methods of accounting for acquisitions of the stock. The varied practices in acounting for retirement of stock probably influence accounting for dispositions of treasury stock, whether or not the shares are acquired in expectation of retiring them.

Treatment of unallocated deduction. Accountants who support the unallocated deduction method of recording reacquisitions of stock do not agree on accounting for the later completion of the transaction. Therefore, accounting for the difference between the cost and the proceeds from disposition of stock varies. The different views of appropriate accounting for the proceeds of disposition and the cost of treasury stock carried separately are:

> The difference between the proceeds of sale, or other disposition, and the cost of treasury stock is an adjustment of components of equity applicable to that class of stock. The difference is an increase in additional capital if the cost is less than the proceeds. If the cost is more than the proceeds, the difference is a decrease (1) in additional capital resulting from other treasury stock dispositions, (2) in additional capital that exceeds legal capital, or (3) in retained earnings if all additional capital is legal capital. The difference deducted from

---

[4] Ray Garrett, "Treasury Shares Under the Model Business Corporation Act," *The Business Lawyer,* July 1960, pp. 919-920.

additional capital that exceeds legal capital may be to the extent of

entire amount of available additional capital regardless of origin,

additional capital applicable to same class of stock,

pro rata portion of additional capital applicable to the treasury shares sold (or distributed),

pro rata portion of additional capital applicable to the treasury shares sold (or distributed) and additional capital applicable to stock no longer issued and outstanding, or

pro rata portion of original issue premium applicable to the treasury shares sold (or distributed).

Authoritative support. Chapter 1B of *ARB 43*, which is quoted on pages 50 and 51, contains the general statement that formed the basis for many developments in accounting for treasury stock. The report was prepared for the main purpose of stating a position on "profits" from treasury stock transactions which some corporations included in net income or retained earnings. The generality of the pronouncement led to different interpretations and applications to accomplish the major aims.

American Accounting Association. The committee on accounting concepts and standards of the American Accounting Association recommended in 1957 that all shares reacquired should preferably be accounted for as constructive retirements and that,

> The issuance of reacquired shares should be accounted for in the same way as the issuance of previously unissued shares, that is, the entire proceeds should be credited to contributed capital.

The recommendation also disagreed with the premise of *ARB 43* that a difference between the cost of stock acquired for retirement and its par or stated value "should be reflected in capital surplus" and instead favored pro rata allocation.

Accounting Principles Board. APB Opinion 6, issued in 1965, recognized pro rata allocation as an acceptable practice. That part of the Opinion is quoted on page 54 and the following excerpts from paragraph 12 relate to treasury stock.

When a corporation's stock is acquired for purposes other than retirement (formal or constructive), or when ultimate disposition has not yet been decided, the cost of acquired stock may be shown separately as a deduction from the total of capital stock, capital surplus, and retained earnings, or may be accorded the accounting treatment appropriate for retired stock, or in some circumstances may be shown as an asset in accordance with paragraph 4 of Chapter 1A of ARB 43. "Gains" on sales of treasury stock not previously accounted for as constructively retired should be credited to capital surplus; "losses" may be charged to capital surplus to the extent that previous net "gains" from sales or retirements of the same class of stock are included therein, otherwise to retained earnings.

Business combinations. ARB 48 permitted a corporation to effect a combination by issuing additional shares of presently outstanding stock, shares held in the treasury, or shares of a new issue of stock and to account by the pooling of interests method. *APB Opinion 16* was effective, with certain exceptions, for business combinations initiated after October 31, 1970 and specified as a condition for applying the pooling of interests method that "each of the combining corporations reacquires shares of voting common stock only for purposes other than business combinations."[5] However, a corporation may have reacquired stock previously and held the stock at the date a combination is initiated. Paragraph 54 of *APB Opinion 16* states:

> A corporation which effects a combination accounted for by the pooling of interests method by distributing stock previously acquired as treasury stock . . . should first account for those shares of stock as though retired. The issuance of the shares for the common stock interests of the combining company is then accounted for the same as the issuance of previously unissued shares.

Paragraph 12 of *APB Opinion 6*, issued in 1965, also specified that reacquired stock issued to effect a combination accounted for by the pooling of interests method should be accounted for as retired stock.

Securities and Exchange Commission. Accounting Series Release No. 6, issued in 1938, presented the SEC view that results of transactions in treasury stock represented capital of a corporation.

---

[5] Reacquisitions of stock to effect a business combination accounted for by the pooling of interests method are discussed in the Accounting Interpretation, "Treasury Stock Allowed With Pooling," *The Journal of Accountancy*, September 1971, pp. 80-81.

"... from an accounting standpoint, there appears to be no significant difference in the final effect upon the company between (1) the reacquisition and resale of a company's own common stock and (2) the reacquisition and retirement of such stock together with the subsequent issuance of stock of the same class.

"... when capital stock is reacquired and retired any surplus arising therefrom is capital and should be accounted for as such and ... the full proceeds of any subsequent issue should also be treated as capital. Transactions of this nature do not result in corporate profits or in earned surplus. There would seem to be no logical reason why surplus arising from the reacquisition of the company's capital stock and its subsequent resale should not also be treated as capital."

The SEC has not stated a preference for either the unallocated deduction or contraction of capital method and both are acceptable to the Commission. Rule 3-14 of *Regulation S-X* requires that in financial statements filed with the Commission

Reacquired shares not retired shall be shown separately as a deduction from capital shares, or from the total of capital shares and other stockholders' equity, or from other stockholders' equity at either par or stated value, or cost, as circumstances require.

The Commission accepts in financial statements either allocating the cost of treasury shares as described in paragraph 12 of *APB Opinion 6* or carrying the cost of the shares as an unallocated deduction in equity. The SEC views as unacceptable the practice of deducting from capital surplus the entire excess of the cost of treasury shares over their par or stated value although that practice is approved in *ARB 43*.

Differences in Methods. The recommendations in Chapter 1B of *ARB 43* do not cover accounting for some transactions in treasury stock, such as a corporation without additional capital that reacquires shares or a corporation that sells treasury stock at less than its cost. But the bulletin implies the preferable accounting.

The committee stated that the results of purchase and retirement and subsequent issuance of shares and of purchase and resale should be the same. To attain the same results a corporation would need to follow the recommendations of *ARB 43* to reflect in capital surplus the entire difference between the purchase price and par value of stock retired and include in capital surplus all results of treasury stock transactions, including losses. Identical resulting components of equity also depend on existing components, purchase and resale prices of the stock, and method of accounting for the stock reacquired.

The basic differences in the two methods of accounting for an acquisition and sale of treasury stock in circumstances not covered by *ARB 43* may be illustrated assuming these facts:

1. Existing stockholders' equity of a corporation included:
   (a) contributed equity in excess of par value, and
   (b) no additional contributed equity:

	a	b
Capital stock, $100 par value Issued and outstanding– 1,000 shares	$100,000	$100,000
Contributed equity in excess of par value	10,000	
Retained earnings	50,000	50,000
	$160,000	$150,000

2. The corporation reacquired 100 shares of its stock for $12,000.
3. The corporation sold the 100 shares of reacquired stock for $11,000.

	Unallocated Deduction Method		Contraction of Capital Method	
	a	b	a	b
Stockholders' equity after reacquisition:				
Capital stock	$100,000	$100,000	$ 90,000	$ 90,000
Additional contributed equity	10,000		8,000*	
Retained earnings	50,000	50,000	50,000	48,000
	160,000	150,000	$148,000	$138,000
Capital stock reacquired, 100 shares, at cost	12,000	12,000		
	$148,000	$138,000		
Stockholders' equity after sale:				
Capital stock	$100,000	$100,000	$100,000	$100,000
Additional contributed equity	9,000		9,000	1,000
Retained earnings	50,000	49,000	50,000	48,000
	$159,000	$149,000	$159,000	$149,000

* In accord with paragraph 7 of Chapter 1B of *ARB 43* that "the difference between the purchase price and the stated value . . . should be reflected in capital surplus."

Total equity is the same for circumstances *a* and *b* regardless of the methods of accounting for the acquisition and for the disposition of the reacquired stock.

The two accounting methods produce the same equity components in Column *a* conditions only if the "loss" on the sale of the reacquired stock is deducted from contributed equity. But some accountants oppose reducing equity contributed by stockholders by effects of treasury stock transactions. If the "loss" on the sale were deducted from retained earnings, additional contributed equity would remain $10,000 and retained earnings would be $49,000 under the unallocated deduction method—clearly not the same results as under the contraction of capital method. Column *b* shows that the two accounting methods do not result in the same components of equity if a corporation has no contributed equity in excess of the par value of the stock.

Pro rata allocation to contributed capital. APB Opinion 6 accepts the method preferred by the American Accounting Association which is distinctly different from that of *ARB 43*—reacquired shares are recorded as a contraction of capital and additional capital is reduced by the pro rata portion applicable to the reacquired shares. Components of equity may differ significantly after disposition of treasury stock depending on whether contributed equity is reduced by the entire excess of cost over par value of the stock or by the pro rata portion applicable to stock reacquired.

The results of pro rata allocation when applied to the facts in the previous illustration are:

Contraction of Capital Method

	a	b
Stockholders' equity after reacquisition:		
Capital stock	$ 90,000	$ 90,000
Additional contributed equity	9,000	
Retained earnings	49,000	48,000
	$148,000	$138,000
Stockholders' equity after sale:		
Capital stock	$100,000	$100,000
Additional contributed equity	10,000	1,000
Retained earnings	49,000	48,000
	$159,000	$149,000

Comparing those results with the results of accounting under *ARB 43* shows that the components of equity are the same only if the corporation had no existing additional contributed equity (Column *b*).

Sales of treasury and unissued shares. Both the committee on accounting procedure of the AICPA and the committee of the American Accounting Association stated or implied that the ultimate results should be the same whether a corporation purchases and resells shares or a corporation retires purchased shares and sells previously unissued shares. However, the ultimate components of equity after reacquired stock is sold depend on the components existing at the date stock is reacquired and the method of accounting for the reacquisition. The resulting components of equity under acceptable methods are not necessarily the same as after the sale of previously unissued shares even though total equity is the same. The illustrations show the differences.

Prevalent Accounting Practices. Published reports do not always disclose the accounting for reacquired stock and later dispositions. However, the information available is sufficient to conclude which practices are prevalent and which are probably rare.

Predominant accounting for dispositions. The usual current practices in accounting for dispositions of treasury shares of common stock may be divided according to the two basic methods of recording acquisitions—unallocated deduction and contraction of capital methods. Other variations depend on the nature of the disposition, on the sources and amounts of equity, and on the cost of the reacquired shares. Frequent practices for different combinations of circumstances are shown for each of the two basic methods of recording acquisitions of common treasury stock.

1. Cost of treasury stock carried in a separate account—
    a. Sold in market or under stock option or purchase plan
        i. excess of proceeds over cost of shares added to additional capital
        ii. excess of cost of shares over proceeds deducted from additional capital (sources not determinable), retained earnings, or net income

CHAPTER 3: DECREASES IN EQUITY

b. Distributed under compensation plan or for acquisition of a company

   i. excess of market value over cost of shares added to additional capital

   ii. excess of cost of shares over market value deducted from additional capital (sources not determinable), retained earnings, or net income

c. Issued in a combination accounted for by the pooling of interests method[6]

   i. excess of cost of shares over par or stated value deducted from additional capital or retained earnings

   ii. excess of cost of shares over par or stated value allocated and deducted from additional capital and retained earnings

   iii. excess of cost of shares over par or stated value deducted from additional capital to extent available and remainder from retained earnings.

2. Cost of treasury stock allocated at date acquired—

    par or stated value deducted from capital stock, and

    difference between cost and par or stated value added to or deducted from additional capital (sources not determinable)

   a. Sold in market or under stock option or purchase plan

      excess of proceeds over par or stated value of shares added to additional capital

   b. Distributed under compensation plan or for acquisition of a company

      excess of market value over par or stated value of shares added to additional capital

---

[6] Business combinations accounted for under pronouncements preceding *APB Opinion 16*.

    c. Issued in a combination accounted for by the pooling of interests method

        difference between par or stated value of shares and capital of combining corporations added to or deducted from additional capital.

Other accounting practices. Other accounting adopted for dispositions of common treasury stock is:

    Proceeds of sale of shares added to capital stock.
    Proceeds of sale of shares added to additional capital.
    Excess of cost over proceeds of sale of shares deducted from capital stock.
    Excess of proceeds of sale over cost of shares added to retained earnings.

The accounting for dispositions of treasury stock is often determined by the sources of contributed capital in excess of par or stated value of issued shares, such as capital related to shares that are no longer outstanding or profits on prior dispositions of treasury shares of the same class of stock. Since information on the sources of additional capital is rarely disclosed in annual reports, the extent to which source governs the accounting is not determinable from the financial statements. Some corporations add to retained earnings the excess of proceeds of sales over cost of treasury stock to partially offset greater "losses" that were deducted previously from retained earnings.

A corporation may include the results of disposing of treasury stock in different components of equity in one year and another year. For example, a corporation may adopt a policy to include all "profits and losses" on treasury stock transactions in additional capital. If existing additional capital is sufficient, "losses" are deducted from that amount; if additional capital is nonexistent in other years, the "losses" may be deducted from retained earnings.

4

Adjusting Components of Stockholders' Equity

Issuing shares of stock and decreasing stockholders' equity, which are described in Chapters 2 and 3, obviously change the components of equity. A few transactions, such as a stock dividend and a stock split, shift the amounts of components without affecting total equity and the proportionate interests of individual owners. Other transactions primarily change the components of equity and the accounting is described in this chapter. Some of the changes, for example a recapitalization or reorganization, may modify total stockholders' equity as well as the components.

Changes in Par or Stated Value of Stock

The par or stated value of each share of stock may be changed without changing the number of authorized and issued shares. The board of directors or the stockholders may authorize the change depending on legal requirements and charter provisions. Capital in excess of par or stated value is increased by the amount of an authorized reduction of par or stated value. The total amount required to increase the par or stated value of outstanding shares is usually transferred from additional capital to the extent available and any remainder from retained earnings. However, some corporations deduct the entire increase in capital stock from retained earnings.

Other Transfers Between Components

State corporate laws permit properly authorized transfers between legal components of stockholders' equity in addition to those for stock splits and changes in par or stated value of stock. Transfers may encompass many arbitrary changes in equity components. Customarily, retained earnings is reduced and capital stock or capital in excess of par or stated value is increased the same amount. Sometimes, either of the contributed equity components is reduced and retained earnings increased provided appropriate documents are filed with the state of incorporation.

Recapitalizations and Exchanges

Corporations may be recapitalized, that is, outstanding securities are canceled and are partially or entirely exchanged for other issues. The securities canceled may be long-term debt, preferred stock, or common stock. Frequently, a recapitalization is advisable because a corporation is in default on interest payments or in arrears on cumulative preferred dividends. But sometimes the aim of a recapitalization is to simplify the capital structure or to realign voting rights. In a recapitalization, all stockholders and bondholders and other creditors surrender their claims, equity interests are adjusted, and the existing equity of common stockholders may be eliminated. In effect, a recapitalization is the voluntary formation of a new corporation to carry on operations of the old.

The exchange of outstanding securities in accordance with an offer of a corporation also adjusts the respective interests in the corporation. Recently, the exchange of specific issues of securities in publicly held corporations has been more common than a complete recapitalization that results in an exchange of all outstanding securities.

The terms of exchanges and adjustments of interests in recapitalizations vary greatly and are not reviewed in detail in this chapter. However, the accounting in each recapitalization or exchange follows certain basic procedures. In general, a corporation records as additional equity capital the carrying amount of securities eliminated or exchanged. Capital stock and other contributed capital are adjusted to record newly issued and outstanding capital stock at par or stated value, and all differences in contributed equity are included in capital in excess of par or stated value of capital stock.

Quasi-Reorganizations

Adjustment of Carrying Amounts. The term quasi-reorganization has been adopted to designate the adjustment of components of stockholders' equity as though a corporation had been formally reorganized.

Economic circumstances may warrant the formal reorganization of a particular corporation but equivalent results may be obtained without forming a new corporation or formal court proceedings. The stockholders may instead approve the adjustment of equity of the existing corporation. The procedure permits a corporation to eliminate a deficit in retained earnings, restate the carrying amounts of assets and liabilities, and establish a starting point to accumulate earnings based on restated amounts.

The effect of some quasi-reorganizations is to reduce contributed capital by the amount of an accumulated deficit, however the procedure implies a concurrent adjustment of the carrying amounts of assets and liabilities to current values. Adjustments customarily reduce net assets, and total stockholders' equity is reduced correspondingly. Therefore, a quasi-reorganization often decreases stockholders' equity, although eliminating a deficit is merely a change in components of equity without a change in total stockholders' equity.

Quasi-reorganizations have been infrequent recently but in some earlier periods they occurred often.

Accepted Accounting Procedures. Accounting research bulletins designate accepted accounting for and reporting of corporate readjustments. Chapter 7A of *ARB 43* outlines what may be permitted in a readjustment and what may be permitted after reorganization. The substance of the chapter was first issued in 1939 as *ARB 3*. The first bulletin was issued to amplify and specify application of the following rule adopted by members of the Institute in 1934:

> Capital surplus, however created, should not be used to relieve the income account of the current or future years of charges which would otherwise fall to be made thereagainst. This rule might be subject to the exception that where, upon reorganization, a reorganized company would be relieved of charges which would require to be made against income if the existing corporation were continued, it might be regarded as permissible to accomplish the same result without reorganization provided the facts were as fully revealed to and the action as formally approved by the shareholders as in reorganization.

The procedures for readjustments discussed in *ARB 43* provide that assets should be adjusted to fair but not unduly conservative amounts and potential losses should be recognized at the time of readjustment. Further,

> 6. When the amounts to be written off in a readjustment have been determined, they should be charged first against earned surplus to

the full extent of such surplus; any balance may then be charged against capital surplus. ...

The 1939 bulletin also described the procedures after readjustment. Among those were that

> ... previously earned surplus cannot properly be carried forward under that title. A new earned-surplus account should be established, described as from the effective date of the readjustment.

The bulletin did not refer to the length of time that the dating of a new earned surplus account should continue. Chapter 7A of *ARB 43*, issued in 1953, stated that "this dating should be disclosed in financial statements until such time as the effective date is no longer deemed to possess any special significance" (paragraph 10). The committee on accounting procedure further modified the paragraph by issuing *ARB 46* in 1956.

> The committee believes that the dating of earned surplus following a quasi-reorganization would rarely, if ever, be of significance after a period of ten years. It also believes that there may be exceptional circumstances in which the discontinuance of the dating of earned surplus could be justified at the conclusion of a period less than ten years.

SEC pronouncements. Several accounting series releases of the Securities and Exchange Commission relate to quasi-reorganizations. The present accounting and disclosure practices accepted in AICPA accounting research bulletins are also accepted by the SEC. The Commission stated in 1941 in *Accounting Series Release No. 25*:

> "... a quasi-reorganization may not be considered to have been effected unless at least all of the following conditions exist:
>
> "(1) Earned surplus as of the date selected is exhausted;
>
> "(2) Upon consummation of the quasi-reorganization no deficit exists in any surplus account;
>
> "(3) The entire procedure is made known to all persons entitled to vote on matters of general corporate policy and the appropriate consents to the particular transactions are obtained in advance in accordance with the applicable law and charter provisions;
>
> "(4) The procedure accomplishes with respect to the accounts substantially what might be accomplished in a reorganization by legal proceedings—namely, the restatement of assets in terms of present conditions as well as appropriate modifications of capital and capital surplus, in order to obviate so far as possible the necessity of future reorganizations of like nature."

Regulation S-X that was effective before 1972 provided in Rule 5-02-35(c) that

> Subsequent to the effective date of a quasi-reorganization any description of earned surplus shall indicate the point of time from which the new earned surplus dates and for a period of at least three years shall indicate the total amount of the deficit eliminated.

The rule was amended in 1972; Rule 5-02.39(c) reads

> For a period of at least 10 years subsequent to the effective date of a quasi-reorganization, any description of retained earnings shall indicate the point in time from which the new retained earnings dates and for a period of at least three years shall indicate the total amount of the deficit eliminated.

5

Comparisons of Varying Practices

Features of Present Practices

The prevailing and accepted methods of accounting for customary transactions in stockholders' equity are described and summarized in Chapters 2, 3, and 4. Several facts stand out: procedures to account for equity transactions of a similar type, such as original issues of stock, differ in practice and even in authoritative pronouncements; different corporations account for like transactions differently unless an authoritative pronouncement sets a single practice; the reasons supporting one prevailing practice are sometimes ignored in deciding the accounting for similar transactions; and all accepted procedures are not based on the same factors so that the effects on stockholders' equity are incomparable. Certainly a pattern of accounting is undetectable.

The practices in accounting for transactions in stockholders' equity lack an underlying objective. Perhaps that status can be attributed to the piecemeal development of the procedures over the years. Although the origin of practices may be explained, an explanation alone will not justify continuing the practices.

The many variations may or may not be justifiable and the factors recognized to determine the accounting practices adopted may or may not be reasonable. Conclusions cannot be reached without analysis and appraisal of the different influences that shape present practices.

The attempt in this chapter is to show the contrasts in practices and to find the conflicts in factors that are emphasized. To vindicate or condemn practices is not the purpose of this chapter; rather the purpose is to illustrate the many contradictions today and to show the mixed results.

Contrasts in Prevailing Practices

Current accounting practices are compared in this section to clarify the factors governing the procedures that corporations have adopted. The nature of an individual transaction is often ignored in deciding on procedures. As a result, several other factors, which are discussed in the following paragraphs, determine the accounting and thus the amounts of total stockholders' equity and its components.

Timing of Transactions. Varying views of timing and completing equity transactions are often applied to like transactions with direct but unlike impacts on the accounting results. Some changes in equity are viewed as completed transactions at the date they first occur, others are viewed as completed at the date other related transactions occur, and the effects of still other transactions are measured at more than one date.

The first two views of date of completion are shown by the two acceptable methods of accounting for the acquisition of treasury stock as a change in equity. One is at the date the stock is reacquired and the other is at the date the stock is distributed, sold, or retired. Accounting for stock options exemplifies measuring at two dates—the value of an employee's services obtained is measured at the date an option is granted and an increase in equity, measured by the cash consideration received, is recorded when and if the option is exercised.

The recording of some transactions anticipates that they will be completed at a later date according to specified terms. Total stockholders' equity presented in a balance sheet often includes amounts equal to assets that a corporation has received from nonstockholders. The funds or other property received are not consideration for stock issued; the corporation in return may have issued other securities, but not shares of stock, at the balance sheet date. Therefore, the amounts corresponding to the assets acquired do not yet and may never comprise stockholders' equity. Corporations often view transactions involving the receipt of funds from nonstockholders who may later become stockholders as equity security transactions that are completed in two installments on two different dates.

Funds received for warrants issued illustrate that kind of a transaction. Completing the issue of stock on the exercise of warrants involves two dates, the date the warrants are issued and the date the stock is issued. If viewed as two separate transactions for two distinct securities, total stockholders' equity would exclude the consideration received for warrants issued and outstanding, and equity would increase at the date the warrants are exercised and the shares of stock issued. If viewed as a single transaction for one security, total stockholders' equity would include the consideration for warrants issued as soon as it is received. The assumption of single transaction for one security ignores the differences between a stock purchase warrant and a share of stock.

The alternatives in identifying the dates that transactions occur are accepted indiscriminately. Therefore, the defenses of the related practices often conflict.

Consideration for Stock. The consideration that a corporation receives or distributes is the usual basis of accounting for changes in outstanding equity securities. That procedure is fairly straightforward if the consideration is entirely cash. The funds that a corporation distributes to reacquire shares usually equal the current fair value of the stock; since the distribution almost always differs from the recorded equity applicable to the shares, the corporation must account for the difference. If a corporation receives other than cash or partly cash as consideration for stock issued, accounting for increases in capital stock outstanding relies on recording the fair value of the assets acquired or the fair value of the stock issued, whichever is more clearly evident.

Those outlines of general procedures are altered in some circumstances and are applied to different types of transactions with many variations. Modifications relate to the fair value of stock and the effects of a transaction on equity. Effects are divided in the following discussion as issues of stock and decreases in stockholders' equity.

Fair value of stock. Recording equity transactions at the fair value of stock introduces in the corporate records elements that previously were omitted or recognized only in part. The fair value of stock reflects the recorded resources of the corporation as well as unrealized appreciation and depreciation of its resources and future expectations of the corporation as a going concern. Measuring the consideration for stock issued or reacquired by the fair value of stock means that total stockholders' equity becomes a composite of recorded and unrecorded values at various dates. The resulting book amount of one share of stock after additions and reductions at fair values of stock at different dates is therefore a mixture of values. Accounting for later transactions in an equity security at the fair value of stock is seldom based on the reasons for the value of the stock to differ. Accounting for the components of stockholders' equity ignores the origin of the recorded amounts and later changes in the components.

Date to measure fair value of stock. A corporation may measure the fair value of additional shares of stock issued by the price on a single date or an average of prices during a period. Some current practices recognize one date, others an average, and a few accept either.

To determine the difference between an option price and the fair value of optioned stock, the fair value of the stock is said to be the market price on the date the option is granted. In contrast, the amount recorded for a stock dividend is normally measured by the market price on a single day but may be measured by the average of market prices during a reasonable period. The fair value of stock issued to effect a business combination has been measured by its market price at dates varying from a date during negotiations to the date the shares are issued. Some corporations have selected the date on which the agreement to acquire a business was signed. However, *APB Opinion 16*, which was effective in 1970, stated that the market price for a reasonable period before and after the terms of an acquisition are agreed to was a consideration in determining the fair value of stock issued to acquire a business. In summary, the effective date of a transaction sometimes controls; another date or dates sometimes govern.

Accounting for changes in equity other than newly issued shares may also measure fair value of stock at a single date or an average for a period. The acquisition of treasury stock is recorded at the price paid for the stock. Sales of treasury stock are also accounted for at the amount realized. The prices of both purchases and sales are ordinarily the market price about equal to fair value.

However, the proceeds of other dispositions of treasury stock, such as distribution for a stock option exercised, acquisition of a business, and distribution as a stock dividend, are recorded at the fair value of the stock, but that value is measured in the same manner that the fair value of previously unissued stock is measured for the same type of transaction. Therefore, the fair value may be the market price on the date of the transaction or the average of prices during a period. The fair value of treasury stock distributed for compensation or other operating expenses is not always recognized in accounting for the transaction, and fair values that are recognized are not always measured uniformly.

Issues of stock. The price of additional shares of stock sold to the public is based in general on the current market price of the stock. A corporation records the cash received as the consideration for the stock issued and thereby accounts for the fair value of the stock issued. The fair value of stock issued is accounted for in the issuance of stock for property or services, the acquisition of a business, and the distribution of additional shares of stock as a dividend. However, a corporation recognizes the funds that it receives either on the date the stock is issued or on the date of an earlier transaction as consideration for other equity securities issued. The disparity between funds received and fair value of the stock on either date may often be large. Examples are—

> stock issued for rights exercised is recorded at the proceeds received for the stock,
>
> most stock issued for options exercised is recorded at the option price received, and
>
> stock issued for debentures converted is recorded at the unamortized proceeds of the earlier sale of the debentures.

The nature of a transaction does not determine the accounting adopted to record issuance of equity securities. The type of consideration seems to be a greater influence on the accounting. Generally, the entire consideration for stock is presumed to be the cash received, if any. The total amount received for a single share of stock is rarely cash plus other consideration. However, a corporation does not ignore noncash consideration for stock issued if no cash is received. The financial statements need to show that the directors obtained consideration for securities issued except for those issued proportionately to all existing stockholders.

The obvious exception to those expedients for measuring consideration received is the accounting for a stock dividend. A corporation records consideration for stock issued as a dividend although the corporation receives no cash, other property, or services from the stockholders. In fact, the present accounting for a stock dividend contrasts sharply with one view of the transaction; that is, a stock dividend is an extreme stock subscription right—*no* cash contribution is required for a stockholder to acquire more shares of stock. If accounting endorsed that view and followed current accounting for rights exercised, a corporation would recognize no consideration for the shares of stock distributed as a dividend.

Decreases in stockholders' equity. The consideration distributed to a stockholder for stock redeemed at a specified price is often greater or less than the current market price of the stock; treasury stock may be purchased at its market price; and usually the price of stock acquired under a tender solicitation is above the current market price. A corporation accounts for the changes in equity in all those circumstances at the amounts distributed. The consideration distributed nearly always differs from the portion of contributed equity applicable to the shares acquired and also differs from the proportionate share of total recorded stockholders' equity. Contributed equity applicable to shares reacquired is usually accounted for if it is less than the consideration distributed to retire stock but not always accounted for in other circumstances or for other decreases, such as acquiring and holding treasury stock.

Relative Interests of Stockholders. A basic fact in accounting for stockholders' equity is that each share of stock of the same class or series represents an equal proportionate interest in the applicable component and total amounts of equity. Generally, a well-established, growing corporation has received contributions for stock at various dates and the consideration received for individual shares issued has fluctuated. However, contributed equity and retained earnings are not identified with specific shares of stock and each outstanding share of the same class has equal rights, limitations, and proportionate interests.

Some accepted procedures attempt to account for the proportionate interests of stockholders in various components of equity, but other procedures ignore that transactions may affect the relative interests conveyed by each share of stock.

Dilution of interests. Dilutions of stockholders' relative interests may be distinguished between those that reduce the proportionate interest of one share of stock and those that appear to reduce in addition the value of the overall interest of a stockholder. If the proportionate interest of one share of stock is reduced, the market price of the stock does not necessarily decline correspondingly because an increase in total equity may equal the existing fair value of each share. In reverse, the value of the proportionate interest of one share of stock may be reduced without a reduction in the total interest of a stockholder.

Although other factors may mitigate or counteract the reducing effects, the market price of one share of stock may be reduced by changes in equity such as

> stock split
>
> stock dividend
>
> stock right or warrant exercised at a price lower than market price at date of exercise
>
> stock issued for consideration that is less than the market price of the stock at the date issued
>
> stock issued for conversion of other securities.

Each transaction increases the number of shares of stock outstanding, but all do not always increase assets and earnings by an amount that corresponds to the existing assets and earnings of each outstanding share.

Stock splits and stock dividends do not change the total recorded stockholders' equity but change the number of outstanding shares and therefore often influence the market price of one share. However, those two changes involve existing stockholders only and not the relation of existing and new stockholders.

An increase in total stockholders' equity is recorded for the other changes in equity listed above except a conversion of stock into other stock. But the recorded increase is not always equal to the current market price of the additional shares issued. If the value of the consideration received equals the current market price of the stock issued, the transaction is unlikely to affect the market price of one outstanding share of stock, whether or not the corporation records that value as the consideration received.

Issuing equity securities to new stockholders reduces the relative interests of existing stockholders. The value of a total interest and of one share of stock may also be reduced if the consideration received is less than the fair value of the stock on the date issued or if a part of the consideration is service that becomes an expense of the corporation. For example, an increase in contributed and total equity of a corporation is recorded for shares of stock issued on the exercise of warrants, on the receipt of property or services, and on the conversion of debt securities, but the increase is often less than the total consideration received for the securities issued.

In contrast, two transactions—a stock split and a stock dividend—are accounted for entirely between the existing components of equity; but the accounting for one recognizes fair value and for the other recognizes par or stated value of the stock issued. The par or stated value of additional shares of stock is recognized for a stock split, and the fair value as well as the par or stated value of additional shares is recognized for a stock dividend.

Differences in the prevailing accounting procedures for transactions with a diluting effect may be contrasted easily by comparing stock dividends and stock rights. If the accounting for rights were consistent with that for stock dividends, the difference between the subscription price and the market price of the shares of stock issued would be deducted from retained earnings and added to capital in excess of par or stated value of stock. Conversely, if accounting for stock dividends conformed with that for stock rights, equity components would be unchanged (except to recognize the par or stated value of the additional shares) because a corporation receives no consideration for the additional shares issued.

Accounting for dilution. Two equity transactions—exercise of stock rights and exercise of stock options—increase the number of outstanding shares of stock, reduce the proportionate interest of one share, and increase total and contributed equity. The nature of each transaction and accounting for each may be compared.

The assumption for the comparison is that the market price of one share of stock on the date rights are distributed and options are granted exceeds the exercise prices under both the rights and options. Assuming those prices, the stock rights themselves have a value and customarily trade separately. A stockholder has the option of selling rights issued to him or exercising them. If he sells the rights, his own investment and his total proportionate interest in the corporation is reduced; if he exercises the rights, his own investment is increased and his total proportionate interest is unchanged providing all rights issued are later exercised. In either event, the interest represented by his investment is not affected even though the proportionate interest of one share of stock is reduced because rights are exercised and the number of outstanding shares increased. The exercise of an outstanding stock option has an opposite effect. An existing stockholder's investment remains the same but his total proportionate interest is reduced. In effect, a part of his present interest in equity is transferred to the optionee. Regardless of the different effects on existing stockholders, a corporation now accounts similarly for the exercise of rights and stock options—contributed equity is increased by the additional funds received.

Enhancement of interests. The proportionate interest of one share of stock may be increased by the redemption or the reacquisition of outstanding shares. An increase in proportionate interests is obtained only at a cost; the consideration distributed is customarily greater than the existing book amount of each outstanding share. The accounting procedures that now prevail recognize the consideration distributed as a reduction of total stockholders' equity. However, acceptable practices for each type of transaction vary and the effects of each on the components of equity are not the same. The differing effects on components of equity may change not only presentation of equity but also the amount of equity unrestricted for future distributions to stockholders.

The market price of one share of stock as well as the proportionate interest may increase as a result of a business combination; the market prices of the securities of the combining corporations and terms of the combination determine the effects. Accounting for the combination is now independent of the effects on market prices of stock and proportionate interests of stockholders.

Relative status of stockholders. Equity transactions may modify the relative status of classes of stockholders. Relative status of classes of stockholders refers to the proportionate interests of each class in existing components of equity and interests in future earnings, either as distributions or accumulations. A typical transaction that changes the existing status is the sale and issuance of stock with preferred rights as to redemption, liquidation, conversion, and dividends. Retirement of stock with a prior claim has a reverse effect on the status of the remaining stockholders.

Some procedures in accounting for retirements of preferred stock recognize the change in status of common stockholders; other procedures ignore the effects on components of common stockholders' equity. Accounting for the recapitalization of a corporation ordinarily recognizes the change in status of various classes of stockholders. But the change in relative status resulting from a new issue of convertible preferred stock is disclosed but not accounted for.

Influences on Accounting Practices

Factors That Determine Accounting. The many practices that corporations have adopted to record the changes in and resulting status of stockholders' equity arise from diverse and often overlapping or conflicting factors. The principal factors pertinent to accounting for equity are:

>laws of state of incorporation
>provisions of corporate charter
>class (or series) of stock
>par or stated value of shares of stock
>existing components of stockholders' equity
>purposes of transaction.

The weight given to each of the factors ranges widely in practice and one or another may take precedence. That is clearly evident from the differences in present practices that are not identifiable with one particular factor or combination of factors. Individual corporations often account for similar transactions differently depending on their own concepts of stockholders' equity, earnings, and the nature and purpose of the transaction.

Authoritative Pronouncements. Pronouncements of the AICPA and other authorities that pertain to accounting for transactions in stockholders' equity often recognize several of the influencing factors that are discussed in this chapter. However, conflicting recommendations of different authorities cause confusion, some pronouncements are not comprehensive, and alternative practices are designated as acceptable for some transactions. Some pronouncements are worded in general terms; that leads to diverse interpretations. All of the described conditions are represented in the pronouncements on reacquired stock. Problems in adopting the recommendations in the existing pronouncements are explained and illustrated in Chapter 3.

Regulation of Equity Transactions. Regulation of a corporation and legal status of equity are major influences on accounting for transactions in stockholders' equity which are related directly to other factors, such as the provisions of a corporate charter and the class and par value of stock. Those related factors are included in this section on regulation of transactions.

Influences of legal provisions. The legal restrictions on issuing shares of stock and classifications of components of equity are discussed in Chapter 2. In addition to those regulations, some statutes specify the equity transactions that are permissible and some prescribe the resulting treatment of legal components of equity. Many accountants often presume that the legal effects of transactions conform with the economic effects and thus adopt accounting that follows the regulatory laws. Accounting practices for equity are often defended by asserting that corporate laws require specific accounting or that the accounting must record the legal facts and restrictions. The view that legal requirements are foremost causes many of the differences in accounting between individual corporations and differences for a single corporation in accounting between different dates.

Excerpts from a discussion by Maurice Moonitz and Louis H. Jordan illustrate acceptance of legal control as a premise in accounting for corporate equity.

> . . . all proprietorship accounts are basically and fundamentally homogeneous, identical, and completely interchangeable. Proprietorship is a *quantity* only . . . and therefore can have no natural or normal subdivisions. . . . With the apparent (but not real) exception of the par value of capital stock, proprietorship data are not *independently* determinable.
>
> . . . the classification of proprietorship accounts is imposed upon us from the outside; that is to say, it is the result of a desire or a need to have the proprietorship accounts reflect something *more* than the results of the accounting process.
>
> . . . regulation and control of corporations and of corporate management are needed for the protection of creditors, of stockholders, and of prospective investors. Such needs shape current accounting practices with respect to corporate proprietorship. To understand, then, why a particular practice is followed, we must look not to the accounts themselves or the logic of double-entry bookkeeping, but to these outside forces.[1]

Since many accountants endorsed that view, the basic segregations of stockholders' equity in the traditional components shown in financial statements were derived from legal definitions and requirements.

Laws recognized as primary factor. Several authoritative pronouncements for selected equity transactions recognize that statutory provi-

---

[1] *Accounting: An Analysis of Its Problems,* Volume Two, 1964, p. 141.

sions may be the factor that controls the accounting. Most pronouncements do not specify the circumstances in which they must control but often acknowledge that they may. Excerpts from the indicated pronouncements in the listed areas of equity accounting refer specifically to legal requirements.

American Institute of Certified Public Accountants

APB Opinion 6, Paragraph 13 (1965)—Treasury Stock

> Laws of some states govern the circumstances under which a corporation may acquire its own stock and prescribe the accounting treatment therefor. Where such requirements are at variance with paragraph 12, the accounting should conform to the applicable law.

ARB 43, Chapter 7B, Paragraphs 11 and 12 (1953)—Stock Dividends and Stock Split-Ups

> ... every effort be made to avoid the use of the word *dividend* in related corporate resolutions, notices, and announcements and that, in those cases where because of legal requirements this cannot be done, the transaction be described, for example, as a *split-up effected in the form of a dividend.*
>
> In cases of closely-held companies .... there is no need to capitalize earned surplus other than to meet legal requirements.

American Accounting Association

Accounting and Reporting Standards for Corporate Financial Statements, 1957 Revision—Equities, Treasury Stock

> ... statutory requirements are particularly restrictive in this area of corporate activity and, to an important degree, are controlling in the reporting of such transactions.

Some prominent accountants have expressed similar views for other equity transactions.

Legal aspects in practice. All accounting practices for equity transactions are not based on the contention that legal aspects are uppermost, but some are. Legal requirements control in accounting for a stock split but are secondary in accounting for a stock dividend for which legal permissions take precedence. As another example, accounting for the cost of treasury stock as an unallocated equity deduction and for later dispositions of the stock makes no attempt to recognize legal provisions. Since many state laws permit various practices or are silent on the treatment of some transactions, each corporation cannot adhere to specified legal provisions to cover all transactions.

Class and par or stated value of stock. Each class of stock is separated in accounts and financial statements, and accounting for transactions recognizes the individual classes with one exception. All shares of treasury stock recorded at cost in a separate account and shown as an unallocated equity deduction in financial statements does not distinguish the classes of stock held but sometimes a note discloses the components of the total cost.

Accounting for treasury stock acquisitions under the unallocated deduction method does not recognize the par or stated value of the shares and existing components of equity are unchanged. However, procedures for recording the acquisition of treasury stock under the contraction of capital method and for recording some other equity transactions account for the par or stated value of stock.

84 **Existing Equity Components as Decisive Factor.** Unless legal requirements or practices set in authoritative pronouncements dictate other accounting, the composition of existing components of stockholders' equity is likely to be the primary factor in determining the accounting for equity transactions that decrease total equity or change components. The derivations of various amounts is the determining factor even though a corporation may characterize the components alternatively according to designations in the state laws, sources of equity, or availability for dividends and other transactions. Similar accounting for like transactions depends on the sources and amounts of capital stock, capital in excess of par or stated value of stock, and retained earnings or deficit. If the approved procedure for a given transaction reduces capital in excess of the par or stated value of capital stock, obviously, the accounting of a corporation without additional capital is not always the same as that of a corporation with additional capital. Capital in excess of par or stated value of stock is often viewed as directly related to a specific class of stock but not to all outstanding stock, either pro rata by class or all classes. Also, equity resulting from a given type of transaction is often viewed as pertaining to the same but not another type of transaction; for example, "losses" resulting

from the disposition of treasury stock may be deducted from equity derived from earlier dispositions.

Classification of components. The accounting for many equity transactions aims to maintain the original sources of the components. As an illustration, net proceeds of sales of stock are included in capital stock or allocated to contributed equity components to differentiate from retained earnings. Transactions other than sales of original issues for cash may also distinguish sources of equity, such as sales of treasury stock that was carried at cost. However, some prevalent procedures for retirement of stock do not attempt to account for the applicable contributed equity, and the consideration distributed for the shares retired may be deducted from various components.

Shifts between components of equity alter the designation of sources and obscure the origins of equity. That result is produced not only by discretionary transfers between components but also by accepted accounting procedures for some transactions. For instance, accounting for stock dividends designates retained earnings as contributed equity. The opposite is the result of accounting for retirement of stock as a deduction from retained earnings—it leaves original contributed equity intact.

Purpose of Transaction. The purpose of a transaction in stockholders' equity has been emphasized as a basic determinant of some accounting practices. The purpose is said to indicate the economic effects of a transaction and the economic and financial facts are interrelated. On that assumption, purpose is the starting point for the distinctions between stock splits and stock dividends, between compensatory and noncompensatory stock options, and between reacquisitions of stock for retirement and for later distribution. Many transactions are accounted for without regard to purpose, such as issue and exercise of stock rights, change in par value of stock, and retirement of stock. Purpose is seldom the sole determinant of practice and usually is only one influencing factor.

Some corporations recognize purpose in accounting for treasury stock purchased for later distribution. The accounting and presentation depend on the purpose for which the stock is held, exemplified by treasury stock carried as an asset. Other corporations account in the same manner for all stock reacquired regardless of a single or several purposes for which it is held.

Results of Varying Practices

Practices in accounting for transactions in stockholders' equity have evolved from many influences. Often the solution proposed for a specific problem was related to existing procedures for similar transactions. Other solutions were entirely independent without an attempt to coordinate the answer with other existing practices. As a result, some procedures may be suited to isolated situations. Each factor pertinent to accounting methods is undeniably significant, but individual choice often dictates which one takes precedence if the factors conflict. Similar transactions of different corporations are treated differently with different results but without distinct reasons. The tremendous range of practices in accounting for reacquisition of stock and retirement and disposition of treasury stock illustrates the differences.

Considering the effects of transactions on the interests of remaining stockholders seems to be pushed to the background. If present practices result in the same total stockholders' equity and the differences are in components only, the selection of an accounting treatment may be of no consequence. However, the significance of components of equity and interests of stockholders are relevant to accounting for transactions. Some equity transactions may affect results of operations even though other changes would offset the effect on total stockholders' equity. Accounting often slights the economic effects and other factors; that neglect needs to be examined to find if it is justified. The appropriate determinants of accounting for transactions in equity are selected in Chapter 8.

6

Presentation of Components of Stockholders' Equity

Traditional Presentation

Components in Financial Statements. The traditional components of stockholders' equity in financial statements are capital stock, capital in excess of par or stated value of capital stock, and retained earnings. Regardless of variations in the titles or the number of divisions, nearly all components fall into the three major classifications.

Customarily, the components of stockholders' equity shown in financial statements are: the total par or stated value of each separate class or series of stock, either issued or outstanding shares; contributions by stockholders in excess of capital stock amounts as premium or paid-in capital; and retained earnings (earned surplus). All contributed capital in excess of par or stated value of capital stock is usually presented as a single amount and the amounts from each principal source are separated in supporting records only. A number of corporations without preferred stock outstanding show contributed capital in the balance sheet as a single amount and disclose in a note the amounts of capital stock and additional capital that comprise the combined amount.

Treasury stock. Treasury stock should not be identified as a separate category of equity. The presentation of the cost of treasury stock as a separate deduction from components of stockholders' equity shows that a corporation postponed accounting for the effects of transactions on the components of equity.

Appraisal of assets. A few corporations classify as a separate component the additional equity resulting from an appraisal of assets. Recognizing appraised values as equity is rare today unless recorded as part of a quasi-reorganization. But some corporations appraised assets and recorded an increase in value as a component of equity in earlier years and the increase remains as part of equity today.

Influences on Presentation. The current presentation of components of stockholders' equity is largely determined by tradition. The reporting practices have in turn been influenced by legal provisions and accounting pronouncements. Authoritative accounting pronouncements specify as approved or permitted some practices in reporting stockholders' equity. However, the provisions of controlling corporate statutes are often the greater influence.

Legal requirements. Most statutes require or imply that transactions related to stockholders' equity shall be recognized in the financial accounts. However, the Model Act does not prescribe either specific accounts that must be maintained in the corporate records or the presentation of equity in financial statements. Many of the prescribed legal aspects of transactions and definitions, which are summarized in Chapter 2, have been carried over to financial presentation.

Provisions of state laws rarely specify the information that must be disclosed in annual reports, but a few state laws do require that certain amounts must be shown in annual reports to stockholders.[1] Disclosure in notes to financial statements presumably satisfies the statutory requirements.

Accounting pronouncements. Authoritative pronouncements that concern presentation of stockholders' equity pertain to classification of surplus. *Examination of Financial Statements by Independent Public Accountants,* which the AICPA issued in 1936, contained

> Where practicable the nature of the surplus should be shown on the balance sheet divided under principal classifications such as:
> (a) Earned surplus (or deficit).
> (b) Capital or paid-in surplus.
> (c) Surplus arising from revaluation.

Later pronouncements of the AICPA contain substantially the same requirements for presentation.

---

[1] An example is contained in Section 21.20, Capital and Surplus, of the Michigan General Corporation Act.
> A corporation shall at all times keep its books in such manner as to indicate clearly the division of the surplus accounts between surplus arising from earnings and surplus arising from other sources and it shall likewise indicate clearly such items in its annual reports to the state and its annual reports to its shareholders.

Regulation S-X of the SEC requires the following disclosure for other stockholders' equity:

> ... Separate captions shall be shown for (1) paid-in additional capital, (2) other additional capital and (3) retained earnings (i) appropriated and (ii) unappropriated.

Equity contributions by nonstockholders. A few corporations have considered that the receipts of certain assets from nonstockholders as well as stockholders represent contributions to equity even though stock is not issued in exchange. The types of transactions vary but an example of one is land for a plant site received from a governmental unit. Usually the addition to equity has been included in capital in excess of par or stated value of stock. That treatment is supported by *Accounting Terminology Bulletin No. 1* which states that capital surplus represents, in addition to contributed capital in excess of par or stated value and results of transactions in a corporation's own stock, "capital contributed other than for shares."

Terminology in Financial Statements. Retained earnings in earlier years was titled surplus or preferably earned surplus to distinguish the amount from paid-in surplus. Corporations have modified through the years the designations for categories of surplus, particularly since the AICPA committee on terminology recommended that the terms capital surplus and earned surplus be avoided. However, some corporations have not adopted the recommendations of the committee to revise the titles of equity components. Statistics published in *Accounting Trends & Techniques* show the trends and current terminology in the annual reports of 600 selected companies. Typical designations as alternatives for capital surplus or paid-in surplus are:

> Additional (paid-in) capital
> Other capital
> Capital in excess of par (stated) values.

Some descriptions indicate the source and others are general to cover several sources. Typical alternatives for earned surplus are:

> Retained earnings
> Earnings retained (employed or reinvested) in the business
> Accumulated earnings.

Accumulated losses from operations are usually captioned "deficit" in financial statements.

Reductions of retained earnings. The AICPA committee on terminology stated in *Bulletin No. 1* that if "the amount of retained income has been reduced as a result of a stock dividend or a transfer by resolution of the board of directors from unrestricted to restricted capital, the presentation should, until the fact loses significance, indicate that the amount shown as retained income is the remainder after such transfers." However, relatively few corporations disclose earlier reductions of retained earnings by transfers to capital stock and additional capital. Still fewer disclose the total cumulative amount transferred from retained earnings for stock distributed as dividends. Corporations have followed the practice of "dating" retained earnings for a reasonable time after a quasi-reorganization. "Dating" indicates that components of equity have been transferred, but the amounts of earlier changes are not always disclosed.

Presentation of Treasury Stock. The presentation of treasury stock depends primarily on the method of accounting for the cost of reacquired shares. Most corporations report the cost of common stock reacquired as a separate item pending disposition of the shares; others allocate the cost to equity components as a constructive retirement of outstanding shares. Reacquiring stock is interpreted as the first step of an incomplete, undetermined transaction. The total cost of treasury stock is shown as a separate, negative component of stockholders' equity. The description of the deduction varies from a brief "Treasury Stock, at cost" to "Common Stock purchased and held for specific purposes, xxx shares at cost of $xxx."

Other less typical presentations of treasury stock held are:

cost of treasury shares deducted from the total of capital stock and additional capital applicable to the same class of stock

cost of treasury shares adjusted to the market price of the stock at the date options to purchase stock are granted

cost of treasury shares distributable under a compensation plan deducted from the liability for deferred compensation—with or without disclosure.

Corporations that account for reacquired shares as though retired and allocate the cost directly to capital stock and other components of equity usually disclose the number of shares held as treasury stock in the description of that class of stock or in a note. The cost neither appears as a separate component of equity nor is disclosed after the period in which the stock is reacquired.

The presentation of preferred treasury stock does not always agree with a corporation's accounting for or presentation of common treasury stock. That is, some corporations account for preferred treasury stock as a contraction of capital and account for common treasury stock as an unallocated deduction.

Treasury stock as an asset. AICPA pronouncements permit "in some circumstances" including as an asset the cost of treasury shares held. The provision is generally interpreted to apply to shares held for a specific purpose, such as a compensation plan. The cost of treasury stock classified as an asset is significant in a number of publicly held corporations and at least a general explanation of the purpose often accompanies the classification. Some corporations show part of the treasury shares held as an asset and the remainder of the shares as an unallocated reduction of stockholders' equity.

Disclosure of Rights and Restrictions. Most financial statements disclose not only the par or stated value of each share but also the numbers of authorized, issued, and outstanding shares of stock. A corporation may be committed to issue additional shares under outstanding options or warrants, other outstanding securities with conversion privileges, or agreements to acquire another business. The number of authorized shares that are reserved to cover commitments is usually disclosed in a note.

Rights of classes of stock. If more than one class of stock is outstanding, redemption prices, conversion rights, preferences as to dividends and distributions in liquidation, and differences in other rights, such as participation in dividends or unusual voting rights, are at least indicated in the general description of the security and are sometimes described in a note.

Some corporations present preferred stock at the total redemption or involuntary liquidation prices rather than par or legal stated values.

The recommendation in paragraph 10 of *APB Opinion 10*, "Omnibus Opinion—1966," is to disclose in the equity section of a balance sheet an aggregate involuntary liquidation preference that is considerably in excess of the par or stated value of preferred shares. The current *Regulation S-X* of the SEC states for preferred shares that "aggregate preferences on involuntary liquidation, if other than the par or stated value, shall be shown parenthetically in the equity section of the balance sheet."

Paragraph 11 of *APB Opinion 10* states

> In addition, the financial statements should disclose, either on the face of the balance sheet or in notes pertaining thereto:
> a. the aggregate or per share amounts at which preferred shares may be called or are subject to redemption through sinking fund operations or otherwise;
> b. as called for by paragraph 35 of APB Opinion No. 9, the aggregate and per share amounts of arrearages in cumulative preferred dividends.

The current listing agreement of the New York Stock Exchange provides that annual financial statements shall disclose any default in cumulative dividend requirements and sinking or redemption fund requirements.

Restrictions on distributions. A corporation has usually invested the funds derived from retained earnings in operating assets, and the amount of retained earnings is not a measure of funds available for distributions as dividends. Some readers, however, presume that the amount of retained earnings indicates the amount of dividends that a corporation is allowed to distribute if funds were available. Therefore, restrictions on payments of dividends imposed by statutes and contractual requirements are disclosed in financial statements to indicate limitations that the directors must observe. Although the remainder of retained earnings is not necessarily available for distribution, some corporations disclose the amount not restricted.

Appropriated earnings. A corporation that has appropriated retained earnings for a specific purpose segregates the total accumulated earnings between unappropriated and appropriated and discloses both amounts in the financial statements with a description of the purposes of the appropriations. Appropriated earnings are sometimes labeled "reserves." Chapter 6 of *ARB 43* prescribes that reserves for general undetermined contingencies or indefinite possible future losses should be created by appropriating retained earnings and "should preferably be classified in the balance sheet as a part of shareholders' equity." An appropriation of retained earnings by directors is a discretionary restriction on dividend distributions.

Status of Current Presentation

Customary Equity Components. The purpose of presenting the customary equity components is often said to be to show the legal status of corporate capital. But even that aim is rarely achieved. The stockholders' equity sections of most balance sheets have become a hodgepodge of mixed and meaningless figures.

Capital stock shown at the par value of issued or outstanding shares may or may not be total legal capital. Capital stock shown at stated value may be either more or less than legal capital. The amount designated as capital stock is not significant unless it coincides with legal capital.

Some corporations describe accurately the sources of capital in excess of par or stated value of shares of stock and others caption the amount uninformatively as "other capital," "paid-in capital," or "capital surplus." Thus the total of capital stock and additional capital may or may not convey information.

Transfers from retained earnings to capital stock or additional capital obviously lose their original designation. Thus a general classification of capital surplus may include a conglomeration of items applicable to several classes of stock, either presently or previously outstanding. A few corporations describe additional capital as "capital contributed and earnings capitalized in excess of stated value of common stock." That caption, of course, tells something—differing components of equity are combined in one amount—but its only value is to serve as a flag.

Resulting retained earnings is invariably a residual amount that does not purport to represent total earnings retained by a corporation. In addition, transfers of contributed capital to earned surplus, which are permitted by some states, commingle two distinct sources of stockholders' equity.

Distributions of earnings. Many accountants claim that one component of stockholders' equity that has meaning is retained earnings reduced by the amount of restrictions on distributions. The resulting amount is intended to indicate the maximum distributable as dividends. Relatively few stockholders find the upper limits of dividends payable useful data; dividends declared are based on many financial considerations, not the legal availability of earned surplus alone. Unless a corporation is in financial difficulty, distributable retained earnings is a minor factor in deciding the amount of dividends to declare. The financial policy of nearly every large publicly owned corporation limits current dividends to a portion, often no more than 50%, of earnings for the year and dividends distributed rarely exceed current earnings. A preferred stockholder's interest in retained earnings is negligible unless dividends are in arrears or he has participating or conversion rights.

Alternatives Possible. One evidence of the lack of interest in the customary equity components reported in financial statements is that stockholders show indifference to and readily approve changes in legal capital. Security analysts, creditors, accountants, and lawyers may examine the details of changes in equity to determine the effects of transactions not otherwise disclosed. However, most readers of current financial statements find that the elements of stockholders' equity now presented are uninformative. They therefore look for changes in total equity and ignore changes in the components.

Conventional presentation of components may be futile and other alternatives may be more informative and useful. Alternatives are considered in Chapter 7 to recommend either retaining current presentation of components of stockholders' equity or adopting a better presentation.

Part II

Solving the Presentation Problem

Chapter 7 — Recommended Components of Equity

Current presentation of stockholders' equity as well as possible alternative presentations are analyzed in Part II for the purpose of recommending the best presentation.

7

Recommended Components of Equity

Purposes of Equity Accounting

Useful Reporting. The overall aims in accounting for stockholders' equity need to be decided before considering the details of accounting for specific transactions. The advantages of the results of feasible alternatives may then be appraised objectively.

This chapter evaluates the merits of presenting selected information without regard to existing pronouncements and practices. Present practices and recommendations are, of course, among the feasible alternatives but need not set limits in agreeing on necessary, pertinent, and desirable information. The ultimate purposes of accounting for stockholders' equity should determine the methods and manner of presenting and disclosing desired information in financial statements.

Appraisal of Influencing Factors. An analysis of the many factors that may influence accounting practices and presentations will help to decide whether all of the factors or, if not all, which ones should be recognized. The importance or immateriality of each of the present major influencing factors—such as laws, economic effects of transactions, and existing components of equity—need to be part of the evaluation. Probably no single factor can control to the exclusion of all others in all circumstances. Some factors conflict or produce different results for different corporations and perhaps they should be abandoned unless they can be reconciled with defensible reasons.

The effects of state laws illustrate the range of influence. Meeting statutory requirements is considered in this study because some legal requirements influence accounting and some legal aspects may need to be recognized either in accounting or presentation of statements. But that status does not imply that legal requirements must be the sole controlling factor. State laws are diverse and cannot furnish a uniform basis of accounting for equity transactions of all corporations. Pleas for improvement and uniformity between primary provisions of the different state laws have been unheeded for over 40 years. The applicable state laws should not control the accounting unless it is possible to show that the components of stockholders' equity vary according to the state of incorporation not only for legal purposes but also for financial purposes.

Selection of Presentation. The preferable basic presentation of stockholders' equity is the subject of this chapter. The discussion assumes that a corporation has been operating as contrasted with a new corporation.

Accounting principles that should apply to specific kinds of equity transactions are recommended next in Chapter 8. Analyses of the nature of various types of transactions in later chapters demonstrate that the recommended principles suit the presentation recommended in this chapter to disclose desired information.

Impact of Corporate Equity

Distinctive Features of a Corporation. The corporation as a legal entity separate from the individuals who pooled resources to form the enterprise is unlike the proprietorship or partnership enterprise in significant ways. The capital of a proprietor or a partner in an enterprise, regardless of its source, is subject to his withdrawal unless restricted by agreement, and claims may be asserted against his personal assets to satisfy obligations of the enterprise. A proprietorship or partnership enterprise is in effect a segregated segment of the assets owned by an individual or by a group.

Accounting separately for the invested capital and accumulated earnings of a proprietorship or partnership is unnecessary, and periodic earnings of the enterprise are usually added to the invested capital of the owners. Enterprises may recognize transactions with partners or proprietors as changes in their invested capital and ignore the sources of accumulated capital. Although withdrawals may be earmarked as withdrawals of investments or of earnings, a separation is meaningless because the two components of capital are interchangeable. But withdrawal of the entire interest of a proprietor or partner dissolves the existing enterprise, although a new enterprise may continue the operations.

The limited liability of stockholders, the corporation as a continuing legal entity, and corporate ownership divided into transferable shares produce distinctive characteristics of corporate equity. In general, stockholders are liable for no more than their respective investments in a corporation, and claims to satisfy corporate obligations cannot be asserted against other assets that they hold. A compensating feature is that, with some exceptions, the original contributions of stockholders are legally permanent investments in a corporation. A stockholder may not withdraw at his option either his share of original contributions or his share of corporate earnings; distributions of corporate assets to stockholders require and depend on authorization of the board of directors, often at its sole discretion. A stockholder, however, may transfer at his discretion all or part of his interest without the knowledge or permission of the corporation; that becomes his only optional means of withdrawing his investment. The transfer of a stockholder's interest does not change the financial status of a corporation, and the corporation need not record the transfer except in the registration records supporting the outstanding shares.

Accounting for Corporate Proprietorship. The established idea of accounting for the total interests of proprietors, either of individual partners or of a sole proprietor, is inadequate for a corporation. A corporation attempts to identify the total proprietorship of each class of stockholders and the elements of proprietorship instead of the interests of individual owners of the enterprise. Corporate proprietorship represents the interests of a constantly changing group of stockholders, and a corporation does not record their individual investments. The proportionate interests of individual owners of a corporation are determinable directly from the corporate financial statements but their individual investments are not. Since the details of individual transactions are not freely available to stockholders as they are to partners and proprietors, the classification of equity transactions and the summary of corporate equity in financial statements become significant in furnishing needed information on the changes in and status of the proportionate interests of stockholders.

Interests of stockholders. The total stockholders' interest represents the reported net resources of a corporation, and an individual stockholder is concerned with his proportionate interest in those resources. If the proportionate interest of a stockholder changes, the financial statements should show the reasons for the change, the amounts of the related transactions, and the resulting effects on the components of stockholders' equity. Transactions may or may not change total equity, but a corporation should report a change in the proportionate interest of a share of stock.

Alternative Presentations of Equity

The standard, time-honored presentation of three equity components is not mandatory and other presentations of financial information are possible. Stockholders' equity may be presented in many ways, such as classifying by type of consideration received or segregating by dates received or earned. Numerous components could be established depending on the types of transactions of an individual corporation. Since all facts related to stockholders' equity cannot be shown in a single selected format, the foremost need is to decide what information about equity is desirable and how to present it concisely in the financial statements.

Several accountants have proposed answers but most suggestions have been ignored or given scant attention. Suggested alternative presentations fit generally into three broad groups: classifying equity by its sources, segregating invested capital and retained earnings, and presenting a single amount for total stockholders' equity. Representative reasons for advocating each of the three proposed types of alternative presentations are described in this section and cover the major arguments for various methods.

Sources of Equity. Financing—assets contributed—and operations are the primary sources of equity in a corporation. Many accountants recommend dividing total equity into the two component sources and believe that readers of financial statements are entitled to that information. Some advocates emphasize the importance of both sources of equity and others stress one source or the other. Those who propose presenting the sources of equity usually observe that financial presentations need not follow legal definitions.

Raymond P. Marple commented on the significance of stockholders' equity in discussing the presentation of a balance sheet.

> To properly assess the relative importance which should be accorded the balance sheet, it is necessary to consider the function it serves and the relative importance of that function. To describe it as a statement of financial position tells little about the balance sheet. It would be much more appropriate to refer to it as "a

statement of the sources and composition of company capital." If this were done, and the form of the statement revised to better display the sources from which the capital was obtained and the forms in which it is held, the function of the balance sheet would be much clearer.[1]

Mr. Marple had written many years before that an essential in financial statements was a segregation of funds invested in a corporation by its owners from capital earned by the corporation. He acknowledged that the separation did not conform with legal distinctions.

> ... the state legislatures and courts of this country have not seen fit to recognize completely this distinction between invested and earned capital, but have adopted a concept that is here called legal or stated capital. ... the practice has been to set up arbitrary limits instead of following the fundamental distinction between invested capital and earned capital.[2]

Other advocates of subdividing equity by origins cite the economic significance of the components. For example, James L. Dohr wrote:

> The fact of outstanding importance in connection with the net economic capital is that of its origins, i.e., whether contributed by way of an investment of capital in the enterprise or whether "earned" or "accumulated" or resulting from the profitable conduct of business. This conclusion is inescapable whether the matter be approached by an economist, a lawyer or an accountant. ... the financial statement must show correctly the extent to which the present economic capital of the enterprise has been built up through the profitable conduct of business.[3]

In discussing distinctions of various kinds of surplus, Samuel J. Broad wrote in 1938:

> The basis of accountancy is the fundamental economic concept of the distinction between capital and income. Looking at a corporation from the viewpoint of its relation to its owners or stockholders, capital may be briefly described as the money or assets they have invested in the corporation, and income as the increment resulting from the use of the capital, including services which the capital has made available. Unfortunately, in attempting to rec-

---

[1] "The Balance Sheet—Capital Sources and Composition," *The Journal of Accountancy*, November 1962, pp. 57-58.
[2] *Capital Surplus and Corporate Net Worth*, 1936, p. 8.
[3] "Capital and Surplus in the Corporate Balance Sheet," *The Accounting Review*, March 1939, pp. 39-40.

oncile with this fundamental idea the numerous and varying statutory and legal doctrines (some of them fictitious, such as those which permit a corporation to consider only part of a stockholder's contributions as capital and the balance as surplus), we have wandered into a maze of intricacies which obscure the underlying facts....

I would like to make a plea for a return to first principles. I would like to see the amounts contributed by stockholders considered as capital regardless of the form of the contribution.[4]

William D. Cranstoun recommended that equity "appear in two parts, capital and surplus." Surplus would be "limited to the net accretions occurring through other causes than capital contributions."[5] William A. Paton interpreted the proposal to restrict reported surplus to the cumulative amount of undistributed profits to result in the following presentation of surplus:

Surplus (undistributed profits):
    Designated as legal capital xxx
    Legally available for dividends xxx   xxx[6]

F. W. Thornton stated concisely and emphatically that disclosing retained earnings was necessary.

There is no item in a balance-sheet so illuminating as "earned surplus." Anything that misrepresents the amount that a corporation has saved out of profits is deplorable and wrong.[7]

William J. Vatter recently discussed investment contributions and retained earnings:

There are various account titles and captions used to describe different aspects of corporate stock equities. . . . when the state granted limited liability as a feature of corporate organization, it also established the requirement of legal capital. . . . Any amount of corporate stock equity over and above the legal capital is "surplus" from the legal viewpoint. Thus, when par value shares are

---

[4] "Is It Desirable to Distinguish between Various Kinds of Surplus?" *The Journal of Accountancy*, April 1938, pp. 281-282.
[5] "Some General Observations on Surplus," *The Journal of Accountancy*, January 1938, p. 69.
[6] "Is It Desirable to Distinguish between Various Kinds of Surplus?" *The Journal of Accountancy*, April 1938, p. 287.
[7] "Stated Capital and Treasury Stock," *The Journal of Accountancy*, August 1934, p. 152.

issued for consideration greater than the par amounts, the premium is an excess over legally required par value and is "surplus."

From a business viewpoint, however, the legal requirement of a stated capital is of less consequence than is the necessity for setting a starting point from which gains and losses can be measured. . . .

There is a difference between amounts *put* into the business by investment, and amounts *left* in the business by the actions of management. . . .

. . . the distinction between amounts put in the business and those left in the business is at least a workable primary classification of corporate stock equities. Indeed, there are many accountants who would insist that this is the only classification needed for practical reporting purposes.[8]

After analyzing the nature of ownership equities and several theories of corporate equity, Eldon S. Hendriksen recommended that stockholders' equity be classified by sources.

Classification of stockholders' equity by its source is generally considered to be the major classification objective in balance sheet presentation. This emphasis is not misplaced because a description of the sources of capital provides useful information regarding the historical development and the current position of the corporation. Corporate growth provided through internal sources of funds is relevant information when compared with a firm that has grown entirely through the sale of preferred and common stocks or through the sale of debentures.[9]

Invested Capital. Many accountants suggest that stockholders' equity should be segregated to show separately invested capital and retained earnings. The term invested capital is used with different meanings but often it refers to capital contributed for stock outstanding and for stock issued previously and to retained earnings transferred to capital.

Robert T. Sprouse and Maurice Moonitz recommended that invested capital should include legal transfers from retained earnings. They first explained that the economic and financial status of equity was essential information but then qualified their appraisal to make that status secondary to conflicting legal factors.

---

[8] "Corporate Stock Equities—Part 1," Morton Backer, Editor, *Modern Accounting Theory*, © 1966 (Englewood Cliffs, N.J.: Prentice-Hall), pp. 257-258.

[9] *Accounting Theory*, 1965, p. 405.

Historically, accounting for stockholders' equities, perhaps more than any other aspect of accounting, has been strongly influenced by legal concepts and statutory provisions. Financial statements, however, are primarily economic rather than legal documents and, accordingly, an accounting which reflects the basic economic distinctions is paramount.

In accounting for stockholders' equities, therefore, a fundamental distinction is maintained between *invested capital* and *retained earnings*. *Invested capital* refers to the portion of stockholders' equity which arose from the commitment of assets to the enterprise, including transfers from retained earnings, and which will not be withdrawn or reduced except as permitted by law. *Retained earnings* or *earned surplus* designates the portion of stockholders' equity which arose from operations. The amount of retained earnings is uncommitted in the sense that the board of directors has the power to decide (a) to distribute assets to stockholders as a share of the earnings of the enterprise and thereby reduce the amount of earnings retained, or (b) to designate some part or all of the amount of retained earnings as invested capital.

. . . .

The significance of the amount of capital stock is purely legal in nature.

. . . .

... capital in excess of par or stated value of capital stock .... is not necessary but when properly arranged it does permit information of an essentially legal nature to be disclosed.[10]

Their explanation is endorsed by those who contend that statutory requirements govern the presentation of equity in financial statements. Henry Rand Hatfield expressed a traditional view.

There are many accountants who speak somewhat slightingly of what they call the "legal definition" of capital, or stated capital. But it cannot be too strongly insisted that it is in its legal character that the capital of a corporation is significant. It is a mildly interesting piece of information to learn how much the stockholders actually put into the business.[11]

Total Equity. Another alternative to the traditional presentation of equity is to show total stockholders' equity as a single amount. Several accountants state that the standardized form of reporting components of stockholders' equity has lost significance and is not

---

[10] *Accounting Research Study No. 3*, "A Tentative Set of Broad Accounting Principles for Business Enterprises," 1962, pp. 41-43.
[11] *Surplus and Dividends*, 1943, p. 5.

useful. They say also that it does not furnish information necessary for investors and in some ways the reporting may mislead. A single amount of total common stockholders' equity is proposed as more useful.

Excerpts from two of the proposals illustrate the arguments.

> What is the usefulness of these subdivisions of stockholders' equity in the balance sheet? The most frequent answer is that the amount of retained earnings indicates the limits to which dividends can be paid. It is also sometimes suggested that it is useful to distinguish between a corporation's dedicated capital and the retained earnings that have not been earmarked for any purpose.
>
> . . . .
>
> To the extent that the large, publicly owned corporations . . . have financed their own growth internally . . . by retaining rather than distributing earnings, the significance of "retained earnings" as limiting the amount available for dividends has lost force. . . .
>
> Even if distinctions among types of common-stockholder equity may have largely lost significance from the standpoint of being the practical factor limiting dividends, it may still be suggested that, when the currency has been relatively stable, there is usefulness in segregating and identifying retained earnings as an index of cumulative growth from within, or of showing stockholders both invested capital and earned but undistributed increment. The point with regard to the individual stockholders carries little weight, however; most of them bought into the corporation much more recently than the time when its original capital was paid in, and many since the last new capital flotation. . . .
>
> Historical statistics on the cumulative amount of income earned but not distributed may well be useful to financial analysts and economists as indices of past growth, conservatism in paying dividends, and accordingly, financing from within. For many companies, however, such statistics are no longer pure: portions of retained earnings have been capitalized in connection with stock distributions to stockholders, acquisitions and mergers for stock, and the like. The significance of amounts of reported retained earnings has been impaired accordingly.
>
> In summing up consideration of the corporation's obedience to the admonition that it maintain a distinction between capital and income, these conclusions seem warranted: (1) corporations often impound and identify as permanent capital more than the minimum legal capital; (2) what accountants call capital (the sum of amounts for capital stock and capital surplus) still falls short—usually, far short—of the corporation's capital indefinitely invested in the business; and (3) if the reported amount of accumulated retained income is inaccurate, it is on the side of understatement because

additional amounts often have been reclassified as capital which actually have been earned and retained by the corporation.

What does this mean to the stockholder? It adds up to, in essence, the practical concept that the entire common-stockholders' equity is the corporation's "capital." Distinctions among "capital stock," "capital surplus," and "retained earnings" are not, for most large corporations, useful to anybody.[12]

It appears that little data of any significance to the investor is conveyed by the current practice of subdividing the common shareholder's section of the balance sheet. For the investor's purposes, the common shareholders' equity on the balance sheet is only a residual figure needed to balance the accounting equation for it appears to have no apparent usefulness to the investor in making his investment decision. So long as this is the case, any attempt to subdivide the common shareholders' equity is unnecessary. . . . An alternative method of presenting the equity should be found. One alternative would be to show the sum of the original contributions plus the profits retained as a single figure.[10]

[10] This particular approach has sometimes been referred to as the "stewpot" approach. Professor Sidney Davidson of the University of Chicago was the first person whom the author heard refer to it in such a fashion.

The stewpot approach to the presentation of the common shareholders' equity has two advantages over the current practice.

1. It would prevent the reader of the statement from being misled by the data presented.
2. It would allow more time for the analysis of the useful data which should be present in the annual report.[13]

Raymond J. Chambers also recommended that stockholders' equity be shown as one sum but modified his recommendation by "the amount paid in . . . would be shown parenthetically."[14]

Nearly 30 years ago A. C. Littleton discussed the importance of stated capital and legal requirements as protection for creditors of a corporation.

---

[12] Herman W. Bevis, *Corporate Financial Reporting in a Competitive Economy*, 1965, pp. 59-61.

[13] Jacob G. Birnberg, "An Information Oriented Approach to the Presentation of Common Shareholders' Equity," *The Accounting Review*, October 1964, p. 968.

[14] *Accounting, Evaluation and Economic Behavior*, 1966, pp. 286-287.

The thought persists that some substitute may be found for stated capital as the measure of protection offered the creditors of limited liability corporations, and that corporation law needs no complicated array of stock and surplus accounts to accomplish its purpose, however useful they may be to management and accountants.

Perhaps a single net worth account to represent the whole residual equity would suffice without necessarily distinguishing the sums which represented capital and those representing profits. Does the protection of creditors necessarily depend upon limiting withdrawals to profits? If an adequate relationship is maintained between total assets and total debt, is that relationship not a protection? Is the protection any better for being made up of invested capital rather than accumulated profits? As far as creditors are concerned, does it matter whether capital is lost or withdrawn, provided they are still protected by an ample margin?[15]

Equity for each type of security. One recent recommendation is to classify equity on the basis of the equity of preferred stock and the equity of common stock.

Whenever there is more than one class of stock, the owners' equity can be classified on the basis of the equity of each class of stock. The major problem is on what basis to allocate the owners' equity to each class. There are several alternatives that can be used. In all the alternatives, a specific amount is assigned to the equity of preferred stock, and any residual owners' equity is assigned to the common stock. The alternative methods of valuing preferred stock are by par value, liquidation value, call price, and the capital paid in by preferred stockholders.[16]

The equity assigned to each class of preferred stock should be based upon the capital contributed by each group of preferred stockholders. The residual equity would belong to the common stockholders and would be equal to their contributed capital plus the undistributed earnings.[17]

Since the proposed classification combines the amount contributed by

---

[15] "A Substitute for Stated Capital," *Harvard Business Review*, Autumn 1938, p. 83.

[16] Kermit Charles Natho, Jr., "A Study of the Principles Used in the Classification of the Owners' Equity Section of the Balance Sheet," Ph.D. dissertation, Louisiana State University and Agricultural and Mechanical College, 1970, p. 196.

[17] *Ibid.*, p. 199.

common stockholders and retained earnings, the proposal is a variation of presenting total equity as a single amount.

Selection of Most Informative Presentation

Stockholders' equity as customarily presented in financial statements is described in Chapter 6, and three suggested alternative methods with typical reasons proposed by the advocates of each method are described in this chapter. A uniform presentation in financial statements of United States corporations is recommended in this section. The purposes of the recommended method are to furnish the maximum useful information and to exclude unnecessary details. The traditional presentation is rejected as the preferred method.

Present Practice Relies on Legal Concepts. Presentation of three traditional components of stockholders' equity derived from the early practice of attempting to recognize the legal status of components of equity. William J. Vatter identified the derivation of popular practice.

> It is remarkable how often our accounting procedures and even accounting thought are conditioned by historical patterns. Once a certain notion is accepted and used, it is extremely difficult to drop procedural and mental patterns associated with that notion. The legalistic concept of capital has had a definite impact upon accounting for corporate stock equities, and the patterns of accounting in this area are still greatly influenced by legal notions.[18]

The circular effect of recognizing legal status was explained thus:

> Perhaps the real mystery, however, is the need in the law, and even more especially in the accountants' balance sheet, for any division of the proceeds from stock issues, par or no par, into stated capital and capital surplus. It will surely be conceded that from an economic viewpoint any subdivision of the original stockholders' investment contribution between par and excess of par or between stated value and excess of stated value is utterly spurious. This statement has been made by so many accountants so many times that it has now become trite. It must be concluded that the accounting profession has continued to observe this distinction only in order to disclose legal information to some extent. Now it appears quite possible that the legal profession has perpetuated the

---

[18] "Corporate Stock Equities—Part I," Morton Backer, Editor, *Handbook of Modern Accounting Theory*, 1955, p. 373.

distinction in an effort to align modern statutory law and modern accounting practice.[19]

A discussion of purposes of stated capital and the related functions of accounting concluded with the observation that "other and better methods may be available" but "it is more difficult to shelve history than logic."[20]

Legal concepts not controlling. The 1947 report of the committee on revision of the statement of principles of the American Accounting Association explained that

> . . . the Committee feels it cannot necessarily follow the statutes and the courts for the law has its purposes and often is not an appropriate guide to good accounting ideas and sound concepts.[21]

> This [Committee view] is especially true in so far as equities are concerned. Many interpretations and expedients have been adopted as accounting principles and rationalized as such because they are provided for in various corporation laws. Accounting principles must be developed without regard to legal expedients which may be available at any given time if it is hoped to obtain acceptable provisions in corporation laws.[22]

The highly technical legal capital and surplus are undeniably important for many decisions but are secondary for presentation of financial statements and are more in the nature of supplementary information. If legal aspects of equity are presented in financial statements, the diversity of corporate laws would introduce diverse presentations. F. W. Thornton explained that the best accounting practice is not affected by territorial boundaries.

> These statutes [of states and territories] prescribe what a corporation legally may do; they do not prescribe the manner in which it shall state what it already has done. Accountants' balance-sheets

---

[19] Robert T. Sprouse, "Accounting Principles and Corporation Statutes," *The Accounting Review*, April 1960, p. 251.

[20] Henry G. Manne, "Accounting For Share Issues Under Modern Corporation Laws," *Northwestern University Law Review*, July-August 1959, p. 289.

[21] Hale L. Newcomer, "Introductory Statement," *The Accounting Review*, January 1948, p. 10.

[22] James R. McCoy, "Equities," *The Accounting Review*, January 1948, p. 23.

are intended to show what transactions have taken place and the present financial position; they are financial, not legal, exhibits.

If corporation statutes should govern the form of balance-sheet these statements would vary according to the state of incorporation; what is legally right in one state may be a criminal offense in another. But accounting ethics are not defined by geographical limits; what is fair presentation in New York is fair presentation in Laputa.[23]

The influence of time is similar. Corporate laws in some states have been amended frequently and some statutes have been amended drastically. The financial status of corporate equity is not changed overnight by new legal provisions even though the legal status may be changed.

Accounting was criticized more recently for its dependence on legal concepts.

> ... legal requirements, whether embodied in statutes or court decisions, can only follow and attempt to consolidate business practices. . . . In fact it is customary, and perhaps wise, for the legal requirements to follow at some distance behind the generally accepted principles developed by business men and accountants in the course of their work, while in financial presentation we must always be developing and breaking new ground.
>
> . . . .
>
> Statutory pronouncements and court decisions can therefore be expected to consolidate advances made in accounting—not to be the starting point for them.
>
> There is danger in too great an emphasis on the legal elements in accounting.[24]

An article analyzing the principles and measurement of business income included a statement that applies to stockholders' equity as well.

> Even if the law moves slowly and holds accounting to an unsatisfactory set of conventions, it is all the more important that accountants should themselves take the initiative to experiment and to reflect.[25]

Some critics of existing laws have stated that, since accounting and

---

[23] Letter to editor, *The Journal of Accountancy,* August 1933, p. 152.

[24] Howard Ross, *The Elusive Art of Accounting,* © 1966 (New York: Ronald Press Company), pp. 98-99.

[25] Iain W. Symon, "Business Income: Some Reflections on its Principles and Measurement," *The Accountant's Magazine* (Scotland), August 1968, p. 426.

law are complementary, adopting preferred accounting for equity transactions would cure many statutory deficiencies.[26]

Legal capital not always disclosed. The traditional three components of stockholders' equity do not always disclose legal capital. Since legal capital is defined in some statutes to be the amounts received for stock issued, the par or stated value of issued capital stock may not be the legal capital. Legal capital covers all classes of stock and apportioning stated capital between different classes of stock has no effect on legal capital. Capital in excess of par or stated value combined for all classes of stock may or may not represent a part of legal capital of a corporation.

One evidence of the artificiality of legal capital is that without an official change a corporation does not always maintain it as an inviolate amount. Legal capital is defined as an amount that cannot be reduced, withdrawn, or paid out without statutory authority. Can it be contended that the amount is not reduced if a deficit exceeds "other capital"? Some state laws recognize this possibility and provide that actual capital may be reduced by a deficit from operations resulting in capital impairment, legally distinguished from capital reduction. However, losses do not technically reduce legal capital in most states and the amount of loss must be restored before dividends may be paid. Also, a corporation that reacquires its own stock reduces stockholders' equity but it postpones accounting for the effects on equity components, including legal capital, if it shows treasury stock as an unallocated deduction from other components of equity.

Possible uses of legal capital. Legal capital as the fixed amount of par or stated value of issued shares or stated capital is a margin that a corporation is expected to maintain with certain exceptions, supposedly to serve creditors and stockholders. The total amounts and details are expected to be useful information in appraising financial status and future financial management, but legal capital of a well-established United States corporation is often today a minor part of total equity. The original purposes of showing legal capital separately now appear outmoded by the legal provisions that permit voluntary changes.

Creditors rarely rely on the legal capital of a corporation for assurance of collection or even for a safeguard. A creditor under a short-

---

[26] For example, Michael A. Lerner and Kenneth I. Solomon, "Accounting and the Law Intertwined: A Case Study of the Need for Uniform Accounting Principles," *The Georgetown Law Journal*, April 1968, pp. 670-687.

term loan is primarily interested in the availability of cash to pay the obligation. Most long-term creditors consider that factors such as current and future earnings, available funds or other resources, and other obligations indicate the probability of collection and extend credit on those bases. Many creditors limit their risks by insisting on covenants that restrict dividends and other distributions in addition to the statutory restrictions. Legal capital is unlikely to be of consequence to a creditor unless continuing operations of a corporation are uncertain or bankruptcy is imminent.

Legal capital and par or stated value of capital stock mean little to owners of equity securities. A holder of preferred stock may be interested in the par value of his shares if it determines his dividends, redemption price, or rights in liquidation. A holder of common stock probably ignores the par or stated value of his shares; the amount and nature of his relative interest in existing equity of the corporation is the focus of his attention.

Directors and management of a corporation are necessarily concerned with legal capital, legal status of distributions, and legality of reacquiring stock. The information is required to fulfill their responsibilities and avoid possible liabilities in authorizing transactions. But the legal information now disclosed in published financial statements may not be adequate for that purpose. Information on capital and retained earnings disclosed in financial statements must be supplemented by additional statistics and advice from counsel.

Invested Capital Derived From Legal Status. Advocates of presenting invested capital start with the basic presumption that sources of equity are of primary importance but vary that presumption to recognize the effects of legal transfers between components. Although presenting invested capital displays some portion of the corporate legal status, it is a mixture, showing neither sources of equity nor legal capital. Since the distinction between invested capital and contributed capital is not apparent to readers of financial statements, they may misinterpret both invested capital and retained earnings. The proposed divisions of invested capital and retained earnings therefore have little or no advantage over the customary presentation.

The recent trend for corporations without preferred stock outstanding to combine capital stock and capital in excess of par or stated value of stock and present that one amount as stockholders' capital is a step in the direction of showing invested capital. The combined amount includes earnings capitalized and transferred to capital stock or additional capital by charter amendment, action of the board of directors, or distribution of stock dividends. The original sources are no longer identified. One fact deserves emphasis: the *source* of equity is not always the same as a *label* of capital stock or retained earnings. Earnings retained do not cease to be earnings because a portion is transferred to other equity components.

Invested permanently. Some accountants argue that a transfer from retained earnings to legal capital shows that the amount is permanently invested in the corporation. However, retained earnings are invariably invested even though the amount is not designated legal capital or invested capital. Permanency does not depend on classification.

Total Equity Restricts Information. Nearly all arguments for presenting a single amount for stockholders' equity do not defend it as best practice but rather object to presenting the customary three components of stockholders' equity. No justifying reasons have been found for showing one amount without disclosing informative components. Important, available, and useful information would be combined into one amount—a useful amount, of course—but more information could be revealed easily.

Total equity as a single amount seems to be based on the view that the amount is a "balance"—merely a difference between assets and liabilities. Seemingly, the idea that stockholders' equity is determined by specific factors is rejected. Stockholders' equity is increased by investments of owners and by earnings; stockholders' equity is decreased by withdrawals or distributions to owners and by losses.

Inadequate disclosure. An objection to a single amount for equity is that the combining of other items and contributions by stockholders may deliberately hide the disposition of contributions. The presentation would not reveal the extent to which contributions had covered accumulated losses or had been distributed to stockholders as dividends. Disclosure of either circumstance is necessary and thus a combined amount would need to be further explained in some manner.

Early practice. Some corporations did in fact follow the practice of showing equity as one amount in the 1920s but the presentation was criticized as leaving the stockholder in the dark. The corporate balance sheet should show instead the "composition of capital as derived from contributions, from surplus earnings, and from revaluation of assets."[27]

Views of AICPA. An early committee of the AICPA on the definition of earned surplus considered the proposal that equity be shown as one amount and rejected the suggestion because it lacked support. The views of the committee are shown in excerpts from an article that summarized the reasons underlying the adopted definition of earned surplus.

> It has been urged that where the capital stock of a corporation has no par value, the distinctions between capital stock and the various sorts of surplus have become lost and that net worth should be displayed, for balance sheet purposes at any rate, as a single figure. The argument gains plausibility in those instances in which additional shares of no-par stock are sold after surplus has accumulated, and after an enhancement in the share valuation has occurred because of such accumulation. Should not all surplus be transferred to capital stock account upon the sale of a substantial block of no-par-common shares? The answer is not difficult. The selling price of the new shares depends not so much on the size of surplus as on the proven ability of the company to pay dividends.
>
> . . . .
>
> . . . the great majority of accountants favor the separation of contributions of stockholders from surplus and the separation of capital surplus from surplus arising from earnings. No argument was presented which would justify any other procedure. . . .[28]

Presenting total equity obviously avoids some accounting problems because distinguishing the components of equity that are involved in a single transaction is unnecessary. Combining different kinds of items in other areas by reducing the accounting classifications would also simplify the accounting process. An early Institute statement, Special Bulletin No. 18 of March 1923, answered a question about transferring surplus to capital stock and included comments on equity as one amount.

> The proprietary equity represented by capital stock without par value is the excess of assets over liabilities. But this equity needs some classification. It would be about as logical to issue an income statement showing one item for expenses without classifica-

---

[27] John R. Wildman and Weldon Powell, *Capital Stock Without Par Value,* 1928, p. 8.
[28] E. L. Kohler, "The Concept of Earned Surplus," *The Accounting Review,* September 1931, p. 207.

tion as to set up a balance-sheet with the proprietary equity shown as a lump sum.

That part of the bulletin has not been replaced and is still authoritative.

Total divided for classes of securities. A division of total equity by classes of securities earmarks a part as the interest of preferred stockholders and the remainder as the interest of common stockholders. Retained earnings are assigned automatically to the interest of common stockholders, which may be contrary to the facts. As an example, a corporation may distribute retained earnings to preferred stockholders as dividends or to redeem outstanding preferred stock. Also, holders of convertible preferred stock may assert their potential claim on retained earnings by exercising the privilege to convert. Holders of securities that carry the potential acquisition of equity securities may also have a claim on retained earnings and a part of the amount may be diverted from the interest of common stockholders. Classifying the entire amount of retained earnings as equity of common stockholders fails to highlight the interests of holders of all securities.

Sources of Equity Recommended. Financial statements are prepared primarily to present the economic and financial aspects of a corporate entity. The aim of accounting is to provide necessary and relevant data to understand those aspects of the entity. Corporation laws should not automatically control accounting in the area of equity any more than they do in other areas.

Attempting to disclose only the legal status of equity or presenting total stockholders' equity restricts unnecessarily the usefulness of information supplied in financial statements. The legal concept of corporate capital, ordinarily limited to the par or stated value of either issued or outstanding stock, emphasizes restrictions on withdrawals of total equity and is incompatible with the going concern concept. An amount designated for issued or outstanding shares of stock does not equal either contributed or total equity.

Financial aspects foremost. In contrast, presenting sources of equity would furnish information pertinent to several financial areas and useful in evaluations and decisions. Sources of equity are contributions by stockholders and retained earnings, two distinct parts of equity of a profitable corporation. The consequence of legal aspects of stockholders' equity is not denied by recording transactions to display their economic results.

Some accountants state that current financial statements accomplish a major objective of showing the sources of equity. In fact, the caption of the stockholders' equity section of some corporate balance sheets is "Sources from which capital was obtained" or something similar. But the components shown are the traditional ones of capital stock, additional capital in excess of par or stated value of stock, and retained earnings. Obviously, sources are not evident or determinable from those customary components unless none of the typical equity transactions have occurred.

To present the sources of equity in financial statements, the traditional terminology and components need to be abandoned and contributions by each class of stockholders need to be segregated from earnings retained in the corporation. Those users of financial statements who are interested in total stockholders' equity and believe that components are of no consequence would have available the amounts they view as vital. Other users would find sources highlighted and available immediately from the amounts shown in the financial statements.

Recommended Presentation

Components of Equity. Stockholders' equity in the following form would present needed information concisely and also disclose some legal aspects. The effects of shares of treasury stock are disregarded at this point in the discussion.

Stockholders' Equity:
  Contributed by:
    Preferred stockholders
      Outstanding—xxx shares
        (Note x) $xxx,xxx
    Common stockholders
      Outstanding—xxx shares
        (Note y)   xxx,xxx $xxx,xxx

  Earnings retained in the business:
    Appropriated for common stock
      legal capital (Note y)   xxx,xxx
    Unappropriated (Note z)   xxx,xxx   xxx,xxx
                                                                 $xxx,xxx

Note x—Par value, terms of redemption, priority in dividends and liquidation, conversion privileges, participations, and accumulated dividends in arrears, if any.

Note y—Par value and explanation of par or stated value of outstanding shares in excess of capital contributed by common stockholders, such as the par value of additional shares issued as stock splits or stock dividends, and other appropriations of retained earnings for legal capital.

Note z—Restrictions on distributions of dividends.

A corporation that has more than one class of preferred or common stock issued and outstanding should show separately the contributions by each class of stockholders. The interests of holders of different classes are not the same and some transactions change the interests of one class but not another. The distinctions between the various classes of stock should be described in the notes.

Distinctive features. Both recommended and traditional presentations result in the same total stockholders' equity. Distinguishing characteristics of the proposed presentation are:

Total equity contributed by each class of stockholders is shown as one amount; portions of contributions (proceeds of sales of stock) designated for legal purposes as capital stock and as a premium or contributed excess are combined, avoiding capital or paid-in surplus.

All retained earnings are so designated, whether or not a portion has been appropriated for legal capital. The sources of stockholders' equity are not changed by authorized transfers in legal components and stock splits, stock dividends, and other changes in securities that do not revise the interests of stockholders.

A restriction on retained earnings imposed by a transfer to legal capital is shown as an appropriation of retained earnings without changing the amount of equity derived from contributions by stockholders. Other restrictions resulting from preferred dividends in arrears and contractual agreements are disclosed in notes.

Terminology. The recommended presentation retains the term stockholders' equity as a caption because it is now used in many reports and apparently is understood.

The subcommittee on surplus of the AICPA committee on accounting procedure reported in 1942

> ... that the Institute should recommend and encourage as preferable:
>
> (1) the description as "net corporate investment" of what is now sometimes called "net worth," "proprietorship," or "stockholders' equity."[29]

The recommended terminology was not adopted in practice, although a few corporations use a caption of stockholders' investment. Perhaps investment would be confused with assets classified as investments.

James L. Dohr, research director of the Institute, commented on the committee report and various designations for the excess of assets over liabilities. He concluded that:

> The meritorious designations would seem to be those which indicate, so far as possible, the nature of the excess as consisting of proprietary investment as increased or decreased in the course of business.... In this category are such items as "proprietary investment," "contributed capital and accumulated earnings," "net corporate investment," and "contributed capital and accumulated income." By the use of the words "investment" or "contributed" the historical origin of the excess is indicated although perhaps neither, taken by itself, suggests the increase due to reinvested or retained profits, or the decrease due to losses.[30]

He recognized that the term "equities" has some support in accounting theory but

> Its use may be objected to, however, on the grounds (a) that it also fails to indicate the basis of valuation except erroneously in so far as it implies present values, (b) that it is in conflict with its well established use in the law where it means an asset, (c) that as conventionally used it covers liabilities as well as the excess and therefore fails to indicate the basic distinction between borrowed capital and venture capital, (d) that it would be more appropriate

---

[29] *The Journal of Accountancy,* May 1942, p. 452.
[30] "Names Wanted—A Problem in Terminology," *The Journal of Accountancy,* August 1942, p. 136.

if applied to the interest of the stockholder stated on the basis upon which he acquired his shares, whether from the corporation or from another stockholder.[31]

Several other suggestions for substitute captions have merit and may be preferable:

>Equity Interests
>Ownership
>Owners' (Stockholders') Interests
>Funds Contributed (Supplied or Invested).

The caption residual equity is one suggestion that is suitable for issued and outstanding common stock and other residual securities. But the equity of senior securities without residual characteristics would need to be excluded from a residual section, and the resulting differences in presentation of senior securities and residual equity in various corporate balance sheets would likely perplex stockholders.

None of the suggested terms are clearly superior to stockholders' equity, which has the advantage of wide acceptance today. Presenting the component sources of equity should overcome objections to the term equity.

The suggested presentation changes conventional terms to avoid confusion with those that now emphasize legal aspects. Total contributed equity could be called capital stock but the new meaning of the term would not be distinguishable from the many meanings now. The term capital can be used conveniently in its legal sense of par value or stated value of stock or stated capital. The recommended presentation is therefore adaptable to statutes in different states.

Other sources and appropriations. Revaluation of assets may be a source of equity in a few corporations. A revaluation of individual assets and liabilities often relates to retained earnings but a revaluation of all assets for changes in the price level should be separated from the primary categories of contributions by stockholders and retained earnings.

Appropriations of retained earnings for specific purposes in addition to legal capital should be presented as separate appropriations.

---

[31] *Ibid.,* pp. 135-136.

Maintaining sources of equity. Sources of stockholders' equity need to be maintained in accounting for equity transactions if financial statements are to be interpreted uniformly. The consideration received for newly issued equity securities obviously increases the contributions by stockholders. Problems in those transactions involve measuring the amount of consideration other than cash. If transactions in equity securities reduce stockholders' equity, the effects of those transactions on the two primary component sources of equity need to be accounted for. Later chapters on equity transactions describe the problems in detail and demonstrate solutions.

Customary Disclosures. The presentation recommended in this chapter discloses selected information in supporting notes. Some present disclosure practices are retained and others are eliminated for the reasons explained in this section.

Disclosure of legal capital. Legal facts about equity of a corporation may be necessary information for management, creditors, and some governmental authorities. However, legal capital may be shown without being the primary classification in a balance sheet. That view was expressed over 25 years ago.

> It must be recognized that the corporation is a business enterprise as well as a legal entity. This duality requires of accounting the difficult task of presenting economic data as well as reflecting the purely legal aspect. The difficulty is perhaps most marked in connection with the reporting of capital, for here business and legal concepts are quite different. In law there is a tendency to view capital as a designated quantity which sets a limit upon the withdrawal of funds invested by the stockholders. . . . Business needs are not adequately served if the terminology and organization of the statements are too strongly influenced by legal concepts and considerations.
>
> It is submitted that the managerial and financial uses of corporate statements are more frequent than the strictly legal uses, and that customary usage should control the form of presentation rather than incidental usage. This position is the more reasonable in that its acceptance need not impair the usefulness of statements from the legal standpoint. Thus legal capital can be shown as a detail under total paid-in capital.[32]

---

[32] W. A. Paton and A. C. Littleton, *An Introduction to Corporate Accounting Standards*, 1940, p. 106.

Facts relating to stockholders' equity that are required by law to be disclosed may be included in explanatory notes—that is distinctly different from presenting the amounts as components of equity in the balance sheet. Disclosure in a note is satisfactory from a legal view and does not ignore legal requirements. Information on legal status may be readily available from subsidiary accounts maintained in conformity with statutory provisions and definitions. Subsidiary accounts serve the purpose that "when the law specifically establishes obligations or places limitations on certain rights or determines the effect of certain transactions, accountants must reflect the facts as the law fixes them."[33] Notes to financial statements may contain the amounts of legal capital, stated capital, paid-in capital, capital surplus, earned surplus, or other items defined and required in the respective state laws.

The amounts of capital stock and retained earnings disclosed in presenting stockholders' equity and in notes would not necessarily coincide with the amounts of legal components (such as stated capital, capital surplus, and earned surplus) that are required for decisions of management. Information in addition to that in financial statements would need to be prepared with the advice of counsel and furnished to the directors and management of corporations from time to time as requested.

Liquidation preference. The recommended presentation discloses in a note the amount to which preferred stockholders are entitled in liquidation. An alternative presentation that is recommended in paragraph 10 of *APB Opinion 12* is to show the total liquidation preference in the balance sheet rather than in a note. Disclosure in either manner is satisfactory and should depend on the quantity and types of other information to be disclosed.

Preferred stock should not be carried at the amount of liquidation preference unless that amount coincides with the contributions received for the stock. Presenting shares of stock at the amount of prior claims in liquidation anticipates an event—that a corporation is to be liquidated. The liquidation preference is not an obligation of a corporation that is a going concern. Contributions of preferred stockholders can be increased to a greater liquidation preference only by reducing retained earnings and thus both sources of equity would be misstated.

---

[33] Carman G. Blough, "Balance Sheet Presentation of Treasury Shares," *The Journal of Accountancy,* April 1963, p. 75.

Restrictions on reacquiring stock. Bond indentures and other agreements with creditors frequently commit a corporation to observe restrictions on equity transactions in addition to restrictions imposed by law. Most of the restrictions relate to distributing dividends, acquiring treasury stock, and retiring stock.

A frequent limitation in contracts and agreements covering loans is that the corporation may reacquire no shares of its own stock as long as the debt or a specified portion of the original debt is unpaid. Other limitations may be that treasury stock may be acquired only if specified working capital ratios are maintained or retained earnings after the acquisition exceed a specified amount. Some loan agreements provide that a corporation may reacquire its own stock only with the express permission of the creditor.

Creditors insist on those and similar provisions in agreements to assure that the corporation will not divert funds needed to satisfy its loan obligations. Ordinarily the acquisition of treasury stock is outside usual operations, and restrictions on equity transactions do not require disclosure unless they are likely to affect future operations. However, restrictions imposed on distributions of dividends should be disclosed.

Other disclosures. The illustrated format does not disclose in the equity section or a note the number of authorized shares of each class of stock. The value of that information in financial statements is doubtful because a corporation may readily change the number of authorized shares. Directors and management are responsible for limiting commitments to issue additional shares to the authorized number; compliance does not need to be singled out for disclosure.

Sometimes stockholders have approved and authorized the directors to issue shares of stock of a class other than the outstanding stock. The authorized but unissued stock should be described in a note because the rights of the potential stockholders usually differ from those of the existing stockholders and issuing the stock may change the existing proportionate interests.

Commitments to issue additional stock should be disclosed as part of the explanations of contingent equity securities, pending acquisitions, and terms of other obligations to show the maximum additional shares of stock that are issuable under existing arrangements.

The par value of each class of stock may be increased, decreased, or eliminated easily and is not significant financial information. Disclosing the par value of stock in a descriptive note meets legal requirements. The difference between contributed equity and the total par value of outstanding stock is explained by an appropriation of retained earnings. Descriptive notes should also disclose other characteristics of each class of stock.

The portions of retained earnings that pertain to different classes of stock are essential but subsidiary information. If holders of preferred stock have a prior claim on retained earnings because dividends are in arrears or the stock is entitled to participate with the common stock, those facts may be disclosed, preferably in a note.

Contingent Equity Financing. Stockholders' equity in the recommended presentation represents the ownership interests of issued and outstanding shares of stock. Variations in securities issued by a corporation and other financing arrangements may result in contingent interests in the equity of a corporation. Convertible debt, stock purchase warrants, and stock options encompass rights entitling the holders of those securities to become stockholders at their options during specified periods and illustrate contingent stockholder equity interests. Until the privileges are exercised, the consideration received for those securities is not and may never be equity of the corporation and the holders are not and may never be stockholders. A corporation may also have agreed to issue additional stock later for additional compensation for services or for other liabilities; satisfying those liabilities may depend on the occurrence of specified events instead of the choice of a claimant. The status of corporate financing is shown more clearly if all securities and liabilities representing contingent equity interests are presented in a separate classification in a balance sheet.

Consideration for nonequity securities. A corporation may issue contingent equity securities with the expectation that the consideration received will later increase equity, but as long as a holder of the security retains his prerogative not to acquire an equity interest, the financing received requires a distinct classification. None of the contingent equity interests share currently in the distribution of earnings although the consideration received from security holders is a source of nonequity financing and the corporation may incur additional expenses for the use of the funds. Debating the most predominant of the mixed characteristics of a given security as a basis for determining its classification in traditional categories becomes useless. Placing the securities in a separate category emphasizes the present status and potential additions to equity.

The present practice of adding a part or all of the proceeds of sale of contingent equity securities to stockholders' equity at the date of sale conveys the impression that the transaction directly increases corporate equity applicable to outstanding shares of stock. The facts are the opposite—equity securities issued later for contingent equity financing usually decrease the interest of an outstanding share of stock.

The proceeds assigned to warrants at the date they are issued are now added to stockholders' equity. Thus the proceeds are accounted for as permanent capital of a corporation. A typical contention is that the accounting "may be justified by the fact that the issuer receives a portion of the assets in return for warrants and that the amount never has to be repaid."[34] True, a corporation is not obliged to repay the amount assigned to warrants; however, the corporation is obliged to later settle in some manner for outstanding warrants unless they lapse. The terms of the obligation are ignored if the initial classification is stockholders' equity.

The amount of contingent equity financing does not necessarily equal future additions to stockholders' equity. A corporation often receives additional consideration at the time contingent equity claims are exchanged for equity securities. Or, contingent financing may not be added to equity because securities of a contingent equity nature are reduced by the distribution of corporate funds and the privileges to become stockholders are no longer available. For example, a convertible debt obligation may be paid in full at maturity date or redeemed at par or a premium at a call date, or stock warrants may be purchased and canceled. A separate classification highlights the possible changes in resources, liabilities, and equity.

Liabilities shown separately. Contingent equity financing represents liabilities of the corporation but they are unique. They are claims that are not necessarily satisfied by distributing resources of the corporation. The settlement dates are undeterminable because the stated redemption or due date of a security is not necessarily the date it will be settled.

---

[34] Pierre Royer, "Long-Term Warrants as Financing Instruments," Ph.D. dissertation, University of Michigan, 1970, p. 102.

The amount of settlement is also undeterminable in advance; that is, the value of an equity security that may be issued to replace convertible debt, options, or warrants is not known until the settlement date.

Classifying contingent equity financing in a separate category immediately preceding stockholders' equity earmarks the nature of the securities or agreements as contractual claims that may be replaced later by equity interests. Presenting each type of security or agreement separately discloses the consideration received, and a description of the terms discloses the possibility of later equity transactions. The number of shares of stock that may be issued for each of the various outstanding securities and agreements should also be disclosed.

Securities representing contingent equity financing often involve contingent expenses and a separate balance sheet classification calls attention to that characteristic. The consideration received in the exchange of contingent equity securities for the interest of a stockholder may include assets or services that can be measured only at the date of the exchange. The contingencies for expenses of the corporation and the potential decrease of the proportionate interests of stockholders are disclosed clearly by adequate descriptions of the nonequity securities.

Debt classified as equity. Some authors have argued that convertible debt loses its debt characteristics and acquires equity characteristics at the point that its conversion value is greater than its redemption value. Thus the change in nature justifies a change in classification. A conclusion of typical arguments is:

> . . . those convertible bonds whose conversion value exceeds the call price and all convertible preferred stocks should be classified as owner's equity on the statement of financial position since a preponderance of the decision factors indicate equity. Once that value has been attained the characteristics of convertible bonds undergo a major transition. The maturity date and maturity value no longer have significance as a debt characteristic because the corporation can either call the bonds and force conversion or the investors can voluntarily convert, which they would certainly do rather than have their bonds redeemed at the lower price. The prior claim on assets upon liquidation is unimportant when the company is performing well enough for its stock price to be increasing.
>
> In addition to the above factors which lose their significance when the conversion value exceeds the call price of the bond there are certain positive changes. First while the periodic claim on income is fixed by the interest rate, the bondholders have an interest

in the retained earnings which they can acquire whenever they desire and the value of their investment reflects that interest by keeping pace with the market value of the common stock. Second, the conversion privilege becomes operational and the potential dilution of earnings becomes a real possibility because the corporation can call the bonds anytime it chooses knowing that conversion will occur when the call notice is issued.

. . . .

In the practical application of the above general conclusion it may be desirable to add a cushion to the critical point of equality between conversion value and call price. Otherwise fluctuations in the market price of the common stock could result in the bond being frequently alternated between debt and equity classification on the statement of financial position. The size of the cushion could be based upon the probability of market fluctuations for the individual company. This practical adjustment in no way negates the general conclusion, rather it serves only to minimize the frequency of changes in the statement of financial position classification of convertible bonds.[35]

The primary objection to the presentation that is advanced in that argument is that it anticipates a change that has not occurred. Outstanding debt securities retain their designated rights and claims until they are converted. The fact that they may be modified by a later election is not the same as a conversion. Their classification as contingent equity financing shows both the present status of the securities and the potential changes.

Terminology. Several authors of recent articles on specific types of securities have argued for excluding from stockholders' equity the consideration received for those securities. They recognize that a separate classification of nonequity securities would improve the presentation of financial statements. Some suggestions for captions and the reasons are described briefly.

> ... warrants ... should not be lumped in with other equity interests. ... The sale of warrants by a corporation on its unissued stock is ... an open transaction. ... The book value of the outstanding common stock should not benefit while the transaction is still unresolved. ... consideration received for warrants [should be treated] as a deferred credit capital account titled "Common Stock Warrants Outstanding." This account should be segregated from other equity

---

[35] Levis Duval McCullers, "Convertible Securities—Debt or Equity?" Ph.D. dissertation, University of Florida, 1969, pp. 176-178.

> interests until such time as the warrants are either exercised or written off as expired.[36]
>
> ... controversy over earnings per share is symptomatic of less than ideal reporting of income and ... how that income is distributed among the various interests having an equity in it. ... potential stockholders (holders of convertibles, rights, warrants, etc.) have a valid equity in earnings retained....[37]
>
> ... the joint debt and equity elements of convertible debentures are inseparable and yet also mutually exclusive ... hence, both elements should be reported simultaneously. ... using an intermediate balance sheet section [between liabilities and stockholders' equity] ... would ... call attention to their indeterminate nature and thus emphasize their hybrid characteristics.[38]
>
> ... Opinion No. 15 .... has removed the cloud of illusions surrounding deferred equity [—convertible securities, warrants and options].[39]

Deferred, potential, and contingent each convey the idea of future equity interests. But contingent is recommended in this study because the term is broader and covers various securities or agreements.

Advantages of Sources of Equity. The two sources of invested funds are essential to understand the means of financing a corporation and to evaluate the existing capital structure. Many readers of financial statements may use sources of equity only indirectly in their evaluations of past and future performance, but the information should not be denied them. Presenting total equity only may be superior to the customary components but it fails to furnish the maximum useful information.

Useful information supplied. A reader of financial statements that show the sources of stockholders' equity may obtain useful facts quickly

---

[36] William Schwartz, "Warrants: A Form of Equity Capital," *Financial Analysts Journal*, September-October 1970, pp. 99-101.

[37] Peter H. Knutson, "Income Distributions: the Key to Earnings per Share," *The Accounting Review*, January 1970, pp. 55, 58.

[38] Dudley W. Curry, "The Financial Reporting of Convertible Debentures," Ph.D. dissertation, Stanford University, 1969, pp. 198, 200.

[39] James T. Powers, "APB Opinion No. 15 and Its Implications," *Financial Analysts Journal*, May-June 1970, p. 70.

without searching and compiling details. Illustrative significant facts are:

> Proportions of equity derived from contributions by stockholders and results of operations
>
> Changes, both total and details of expansion and contraction, during a period in each source of equity
>
> Results of using all assets furnished by creditors and stockholders are shown in the separate amount of retained earnings
>
> Overall corporate policy for retention and distribution of earnings
>
> Effects of dividend policies on existing equity components and on obtaining future financing
>
> Relation of contributions by stockholders to funds obtained from creditors
>
> Flexibility of capital structure as indicated in descriptions and amounts of sources of total financing
>
> Potential effects of reacquiring outstanding shares of stock
>
> Potential equity interests shown as contingent equity financing segregated from interests of existing stockholders
>
> Revenue and expenses related to income producing operations and to financing shown by additions and reductions to equity segregated by sources.

An accumulated deficit resulting from operations and prior distributions of earnings would be disclosed regardless of the legal status of and transfers between capital and surplus.

This study shows in later sections that accounting for sources of equity results in accounting for all activities of a corporation—financing transactions as well as income producing operations.

Aid in analysis of securities. Ratios of stockholders' contributions to total equity and to debt, flexibility of capital structure, changes during a period, and contingent equity interests indicate potential and beneficial changes in temporary financing and in equity financing. The information helps to appraise existing and obtainable leverage of stockholders.

Many financial ratios calculated for corporations today are not based on contributions by stockholders and retained earnings partly because the two components of equity are not available. Total equity is necessarily substituted because the traditional components are not significant.

The past earning power of a corporation is one factor required in analyzing the potential of a security. To determine that factor and estimate future results, the changes in both contributed equity and debt securities must be ascertained. Unless the primary sources of stockholders' equity are separated, increases and withdrawals of contributed equity become intertwined with retained earnings and conclusions derived from the analysis of changes may be incorrect.

Another factor used in appraising the potential of a security, especially a common stock, is the rate of return on equity. Some analysts view a rate of return based on book equity as a limited tool and compute a return on restated equity. Earnings during a period are required for each method of computing a return. The return applicable to residual equity securities may be computed easily if securities with a fixed or prior claim to earnings are shown separately. But an average rate of return on residual securities computed on the basis of total equity for those securities lumps together the effects of many factors. An overall rate supplies little information for analysis and the recommended presentation of sources of equity facilitates a more meaningful appraisal. Fluctuations in the rate of return should be attributed to the changes in retained earnings; this implies that a basic rate of return should be assumed for total contributions to equity. By separating contributions and earnings, the benefits of a corporation having retained a portion of earnings can be evaluated and potential benefits and future trends can be estimated.

Potential changes in the proportionate interests of stockholders resulting from an increase or decrease in outstanding stock can be determined more precisely if equity is separated by sources. Computations of that kind are necessary if a corporation is to acquire another enterprise by issuing additional shares of stock; the premium over existing book equity of one share affects the future rate of return on outstanding shares. Otherwise, an increase in earnings appears to result from an addition to retained earnings. That could lead to an incorrect appraisal of the benefits of acquisitions effected by issuing additional stock.

Simplification and understanding. Presenting sources of equity would simplify financial statements and correspondingly increase the understanding of readers. Even though Eric L. Kohler predicted that presentation more than 20 years ago, it is still a minority practice.

> At some day not far distant it seems quite likely that paid-in surplus will be merged with other contributions from stockholders, and a single figure for capital will be displayed on published balance sheets for each class of stock.[40]

Further, he encouraged accountants to develop theories free from legal bias and

> ... seek to have the concepts of capital surplus and paid-in surplus removed from the statute books, and to have all contributions of stockholders classified as paid-in capital. This simplification would add measurably to the understanding between corporations and stockholders; and it would automatically eliminate most of the variations now found in net-worth practices.[41]

---

[40] "Surplus," Thomas W. Leland, Editor, *Contemporary Accounting*, 1945, Chapter 4, p. 1.
[41] *Ibid.*

Part III

Solving the Accounting Problem

Chapter 8 — Recommended Accounting for Equity Transactions

Chapter 9 — Increases in Equity Securities — Individual Interests Reduced

Chapter 10 — Increases in Equity Securities — Individual Interests Unchanged

Chapter 11 — Decreases in Equity Securities

Chapter 12 — Adjustments of Equity

General principles to be applied to account for various transactions in equity securities are recommended in Chapter 8. The principles are consistent with the presentation of components of equity recommended in Part II. Applications of the principles to typical transactions in equity securities are explained and illustrated in the last four chapters of Part III.

8

Recommended Accounting for Equity Transactions

The recommendation in Chapter 7 is to present the sources of stockholders' equity—contributions by stockholders and retained earnings—in financial statements. That presentation of components has many advantages and would furnish useful information. The next step is to select principles to account for equity transactions in a manner that will supply the source components of stockholders' equity.

Equity transactions covered exclude accounting for dividends distributed to stockholders except the distribution of stock of the corporation. Results of operations for a period change the retained earnings component of equity and that change is a transaction in equity. However, the only aspect of accounting for results of operations that is within the scope of this study is the reporting of services and costs of financing that are received as consideration for stock.

Selecting Principles for Transactions

Influencing Factors. The major factors influencing the present accounting for equity transactions are discussed in Chapter 5. Comparisons of existing practices in that chapter show differences in the factors that are recognized and in the effects and nature of transactions that are emphasized. The purpose of this chapter is to select the factors that should determine accounting for stockholders' equity and to establish general principles that a corporation should apply to account for various transactions in its equity securities.

Need for Uniform Treatment. General guiding principles selected for all transactions in equity securities should achieve the purposes of accounting for changes in components of equity and furnishing desired financial information. Individual types of equity transactions should not be analyzed in isolation, and accounting procedures should not be selected piecemeal. Debate of accounting for stockholders' equity is usually in terms of one type of transaction without regard to other similar transactions, and a precedent set by existing practices has often been ignored for a new type of transaction. As a result, some present procedures are contradictory and all treatments are not now consistent.

Many types of equity transactions are related, and the nature, effects, and purposes of various transactions may be compared to group those with similar characteristics. Types of transactions are grouped in that manner in Chapters 2, 3, and 4 as issuing stock, decreases in equity securities, and changes in components of equity. The possible effects on net income and equity components of each group of transactions may be appraised and coordinated with the presentation of information that is recommended in Chapter 7 to select improved accounting practices.

The principles recommended in this chapter are applied to the groups and individual types of transactions in later chapters. The results are then analyzed to decide if they are justifiable. Analysis requires considering other views of preferable practices and views that now decide accounting procedures for equity transactions. The conclusions cannot be proved in the sense that obtainable evidence will show that the results of the recommended principles are the best; however, the results of the selected principles can be supported by logical reasoning.

The aim in this study is to propose solutions in terms of general principles and thus furnish a pattern for later transactions in circumstances that are not now foreseen.

Features of Sources of Equity. The presentation of sources of equity recommended in Chapter 7 designates the sources as contributions by stockholders and retained earnings. The discussion further explains that contributions by stockholders represent the consideration received for outstanding stock and that the contributions for different classes of stock should be shown separately. Identifying and presenting sources of stockholders' equity leads to several maxims that need to be heeded in selecting accounting principles for equity transactions.

Stockholders' equity is limited to (1) consideration received for the shares of stock outstanding (contributions by stockholders) and (2) retained earnings; therefore, stockholders' equity excludes consideration received for securities other than stock.
(Revaluations of assets to recognize appraisals or price increases are exceptions and should be presented as a separate component of equity.)[1]

Contributions by stockholders are divided into the total consideration applicable to each class of stock.

Consideration received for shares of stock issued is reduced by the direct costs of obtaining the consideration.

Contributions by stockholders comprise the cumulative amounts of consideration received at different dates, reduced by withdrawals of contributions.

A proportionate part of the total contributed equity applicable to each class of stock is applicable to each outstanding share of that class of stock.

Contributed equity is reduced by the proportion applicable to a reduction in the number of outstanding shares of stock.
(The accounting for the total consideration distributed to effect a reduction in stock and for the reduction of contributed equity depend on the equity transaction.)

Retained earnings is increased by periodic net income, the residual amount of the results of operations that is applicable to the interests of stockholders.

Retained earnings is reduced by the entire corporate cost incurred for equity financing, whether or not paid in cash and whether or not distributed as dividends. That is, consideration to stockholders for furnishing contributed equity is accounted for and deducted from retained earnings.

---

[1] Revaluations are those recognized in accounting on the historical-cost basis and exclude restatements for changes in general price levels described in *APB Statement 3*.

Those maxims form the basis for developing the principles recommended to account for transactions in stockholders' equity of corporations.

Factors To Determine Accounting. Factors that influence present accounting practices are discussed in Chapter 5 and many are found to be irrelevant, for example, the laws of the state of incorporation. Other factors are now recognized sporadically but not consistently. Those factors that should determine the accounting for issuing stock, decreases in equity securities, and changes in components of equity are:

> Effects of a transaction on the proportionate interest in equity represented by one share of stock.
>
> Purpose and nature of a transaction—a security transaction that is related entirely to equity is distinguished from one that involves operations or creditor financing.
>
> Date a transaction occurs—recognition of financial effects is neither delayed nor anticipated.

The amounts of an equity transaction as well as the existing components of equity of course influence the financial results, but amounts should not be the crucial factor in setting accounting procedures.

Arguments in Chapter 7 supporting the recommended presentation of sources of equity conclude that legal requirements and definitions are not controlling for financial reports and that disclosure of legal capital in financial statements is sufficient. Changes in legal components of stockholders' equity that do not change contributions by stockholders or retained earnings should not be recognized in accounting for the components of equity. Similarly, statutory provisions need not control the financial accounting for equity transactions.

Recommended Principles

The features of sources of stockholders' equity and the factors that should influence accounting for transactions in equity securities, which are enumerated in the preceding section, can be combined in establishing general principles that should be adopted to account for all types of equity transactions.

Transactions in Equity Securities. The principles applicable to accounting for transactions in equity securities of a corporation are few and relatively simple. Briefly,

> A transaction in an equity security occurs and is completed on the date that an increase or decrease in outstanding shares of stock is effective.
>
> A transaction in an equity security is recorded at the amount of the consideration a corporation receives or distributes for the security.
>
> The consideration equals the cash or fair value of other assets that a corporation receives or distributes unless the transaction does not involve cash and does not change the existing proportionate interests of stockholders.
>
> The fair value of other assets that a corporation receives or distributes for an equity security is measured by the fair value of the security unless an estimated value of the asset is more reasonably determinable.
>
> The fair value of an equity security as a measure of consideration is based on market prices of the stock.
>
> The result of a transaction in an equity security is recognized as changes in contributions by stockholders and in retained earnings based on the nature of the transaction.
>
> Costs of equity financing are deducted directly from retained earnings.

The recommended principles are derived from the features of sources of equity and the selected factors to influence accounting although they are expressed in a different format.

The fair value of a share of stock is determined by many factors, only some of which are now recognized in financial statements. Since transactions in equity securities, both increases and decreases, occur at various times at different fair values of the securities, the cumulative amounts of components of equity are now and will continue to comprise a mixture of values. As a result, accounting for equity transactions can account for the proportionate interests of stockholders but cannot attempt to account for the value of outstanding shares of stock.

Purpose and nature of transactions. The selected factors and accounting principles refer to the purpose and nature of equity transactions. Purpose and nature are general terms but they imply that a transaction must be analyzed to determine why it occurs, what it accomplishes, and its effects on net income and component sources of stockholders' equity. The various kinds of transactions need to be scrutinized in this study to learn the essence of their natures and the financial results.

Many equity transactions entail financing costs and benefits that should be recognized as changes in retained earnings, either directly or as a part of net income. Later chapters of this study, which show that the selected principles are appropriate, necessarily discuss in detail the nature of various equity transactions, their relations to sources of equity, and corporate costs of financing.

Date of transaction. The selected principles state that a transaction in an equity security occurs and is completed on the effective date of an increase or decrease in outstanding shares of stock. That means that a transaction occurs and is completed simultaneously. Thus, an earlier or later transaction related to an increase or decrease in outstanding stock is independent. Each transaction is accounted for separately.

Effective date refers to that date on which the parties involved agree irrevocably to a transaction. A corporation may at a later date, sometimes after a long delay, issue or reacquire the certificates evidencing the ownership of shares of stock that the parties agreed to on an effective date. The physical delivery of certificates and the effective date of a transfer of stock rarely coincide. Delivery is later evidence of a transaction that occurred earlier.

Proportionate interests unchanged. The recommended principles bar recording noncash consideration for transactions in equity securities that do not change the proportionate interests of stockholders. The basis for the exclusion is that some transactions in equity securities are without economic substance and merely change the number of shares of stock representing an equity interest. Total stockholders' equity and equity components are neither increased nor decreased and the proportionate interests of stockholders are unchanged. A stock split or a reverse split are clear examples of a transaction of that type. Recording an amount as consideration received or distributed would misstate equity components because the change in outstanding securities has no financial effect on stockholders' equity.

Sources of equity. Applying the recommended principles of accounting for transactions is described in terms of the two component sources of equity recommended in this study, that is, contributions by stockholders and retained earnings. However, the same principles should be applied even though contributions by stockholders are presented in financial statements as capital stock and capital in excess of par or stated value of stock. Additional capital, of course, would need to comprise remaining contributions only. That amount would differ significantly from the additional capital of many corporations today because a part of retained earnings is now often designated as capital.

Consideration Other Than Cash. Unless the consideration is cash or property whose value can be measured objectively, such as a security with a recognized market value, a measure of the consideration that a corporation receives or distributes for an interest in its equity is the least clear-cut and least undisputable of the proposed principles. The fair value of an equity security issued is designated in the list of principles as the best measure because both parties to the transaction recognize that amount in their arrangements and it represents the additional contribution to equity at the effective date of the transaction. Other measures fail to show the effects of a transaction on the components of equity and on the proportionate interests of existing stockholders.

Adequate consideration. The parties in a typical agreement to transfer stock for assets are a potential stockholder and a corporation. The stockholder transfers an asset to the corporation and accepts in exchange a number of shares of a security which have a determinable fair value. The corporation reduces the proportionate interests of existing stockholders by issuing additional shares in exchange for a resource. Since the issue of stock increases the total outstanding shares of stock and each outstanding share carries a pro rata interest in total equity, a portion of the proportionate interests of existing stockholders is transferred to other stockholders. Each party views the consideration as adequate and equitable. The transaction is comparable to issuing stock for cash except that the consideration received lacks a ready monetary measure. The directors are obliged to issue new stock only for fair and adequate consideration in relation to the fair value of outstanding stock, whether the consideration received is cash or other assets.

The reasonableness of recording the fair value of stock issued as the measure of the consideration received may be illustrated by showing the effects of assigning no carrying amount to resources that a corporation receives. If a corporation assigns no amount, presumably the assets received are of no value and issuing additional stock dilutes the interests of existing stockholders. The results are shown by assuming that recorded stockholders' equity of $300,000 is represented by 10,000 shares of stock with a fair value of $50 a share (based on recent market prices of $47 to $52 a share). The corporation issues 10,000 additional shares of stock to a new stockholder. If the corporation receives no consideration for the new stock, the dilution of the value of the interests of existing stockholders is a maximum of $250,000—one half of $500,000, the total fair value of the outstanding stock. The existing proportionate interests in recorded equity are also reduced one half. However, a corporation cannot issue additional shares of stock unless the fair value of the consideration received for the security is adequate to maintain the fair value of outstanding shares of stock. The fair value of the consideration received for the additional stock is therefore necessarily about $500,000. Assigning to the consideration an arbitrary amount ranging from zero up to the fair value understates the consideration received and implies that the transaction dilutes the value of the interests of existing stockholders.

Fair value of assets received. Some accountants frown on the fair value of stock issued as a measure of the consideration received for stock and insist that accounting principles require an independent valuation of the asset received. Otherwise, the original cost (carrying amount) of the asset may be inflated if the current price of a security is inflated. The contention does not fit with the historical-cost basis of accounting. The cost of an asset acquired for cash may be inflated or deflated over the fair value estimated by independent appraisal. Since the asset is acquired by exchanging one resource (cash) for another resource, no one suggests that the cost should be adjusted immediately to another value. The disbursement of cash is said to be the key to the difference between assets purchased and assets received as consideration for stock. The entire exercise ignores that the resources representing the existing interests of stockholders are to be accounted for—they may be exchanged for resources of another form or they may be reduced by a transfer to new stockholders. If reduced, the addition of new resources by the new stockholders should offset that reduction. An independent appraisal of the fair value of an asset received as consideration for stock is no more representative of the appropriate carrying amount than it would be for an asset purchased for cash.

The permission for corporations to issue stock for property or services to the "extent of the value thereof" means that directors are obliged to determine the value of the consideration received, using reasonable judgment to appraise the value. The value referred to is "value *to the corporation* or value for the corporate purposes rather than value in an outside market."[2] An independent appraisal may assist in judging value for corporate purposes but does not set the amount of consideration received.

Fair value of stock opposed. An objection voiced to using the fair value of stock issued based on market prices of the stock as a measure of consideration received is that the current market price of the stock may be inflated or deflated and therefore does not correspond to the underlying value of one share. However, negotiations of the parties are based on market prices of the stock and assets transferred are measured in relation to those market prices. Since an equity security transaction is arranged between two parties, each accepts the terms of the transaction in the belief that he is to receive fair and adequate consideration.

If the price of $50 a share in the illustration on page 140 is excessive, a potential stockholder would likely be reluctant or unwilling to accept 10,000 shares of stock for his consideration that has a fair value of $500,000. The directors would be limited to issuing no more than about 10,000 shares of stock because they are obliged to issue stock at approximately its fair value. Assuming that the transaction is completed, the new stockholder accepts 10,000 shares of stock and at that date he can realize $50 a share in the marketplace.[3] Similarly, a present stockholder

---

[2] David L. Dodd, *Stock Watering* (The Judicial Valuation of Property for Stock-Issue Purposes), 1930, p. 104.

[3] A stockholder is unlikely to realize a price of $50 a share on a single date for one half of the outstanding shares of stock. The assumed amounts illustrate easily the factors involved in a customary type of transaction.

can realize $50 by selling a share of stock even though that price may be high. Unless the value of the assets received is about $50 a share, the market price of the stock is ordinarily expected to decline reflecting dilution of the value of the interest represented by one share of stock.

A variation of the argument is related to a corporation's issuing stock for another business and the agreement provides that the number of shares of stock issued depends on the market prices of the securities of both corporations. If the market price of the stock of the acquired corporation is excessive, the fair value of the new shares issued may be greater than the fair value of the assets contributed. Some accountants contend that a transaction with those conditions dilutes the interests of existing stockholders but that the dilution will be reported through later results of operations. Others argue that the stock issued should be recorded at less than fair value. Those arguments ignore the duty of directors not to dilute or impair the values underlying outstanding shares of stock. Reporting the financial results of transactions as they occur is imperative. Certainly, a dilution of the interests of stockholders because a corporation receives inadequate consideration for stock should be reported immediately. Recording less than the fair value of stock issued does not change the facts but may postpone recognition.

Price fluctuations. A recurring objection to measuring consideration received by the fair value of the stock issued for property is that market prices of securities fluctuate, especially that the market price may later decline. The fall of stock prices in 1970 is often used to illustrate that assets contributed for stock issued in 1969 would be recorded at excessive amounts a year later. However, the assets contributed and recorded in 1969 and the value of the assets and the stock in 1970 are independent matters. The transaction considered in this study is the 1969 contribution of assets for stock.

The fallacy of the objection is illustrated by comparing the transaction with the acquisition of another asset whose market price fluctuates as much or more than many stocks did in 1970—a membership on a stock exchange. A corporation records a membership on a stock exchange at its cost or fair value at the date acquired with the knowledge that a change in its market price is inevitable. The pattern of change is usually tied to stock market activity. Neither the completed transaction nor the consideration distributed depend on future market prices of the exchange membership.

Costs of financing as part of consideration. The fair value of stock issued as a measure of consideration received may seem unreasonable because a corporation may not retain the entire consideration as recorded assets. A part of the consideration may be costs that expire and become expenses and thus reduce retained earnings as costs of equity financing. That fact underscores the need to account for the entire consideration received. Unless financing costs are recognized, the interests represented by outstanding shares of stock may be reduced without the financial statements containing evidence of the reason for the reduction.

Accounting has long recognized that consideration for stock may be services as well as property and that those services may take several forms, among them providing corporate financing. Thus, recognizing consideration received as a current expense or costs of financing does not alter the principle that the fair value of stock issued is a reasonable measure of consideration received.

Fair Value of Security. The market price of an equity security on a single day may not indicate the fair value of the security because the price may be affected by isolated events or the trend of trading.[4] The effects of material circumstances that either increase or decrease market prices should be eliminated in determining the fair value of a security. If the market prices of a stock have been stable or followed a continuous trend over a long period, a fair measure of value of the stock may be the market price before an extraordinary event that affects all marketable securities. If the market prices of a stock have fluctuated erratically during a recent period, a fair measure of value of the stock may be an average of market prices for a period. The length of period needed depends on the nature of events and the magnitude of price fluctuations but usually would be several weeks and rarely would exceed a few months.

Adjustments of market price. The calculated market price of a security may need to be reduced for two factors to set a fair value—issue costs and quantities. A corporation incurs costs to issue additional

---

[4] Some authorities defend market price as the estimate of fair value. For example, Eugene F. Fama wrote that "If the random walk theory is valid and if security exchanges are 'efficient' markets, then stock prices at any point in time will represent good estimates of intrinsic or fundamental values." ("Random Walks in Stock Market Prices," *Financial Analysts Journal*, September-October 1965, p. 59.)

shares of stock for cash and accounts for the proceeds less the costs as an addition to equity. The determination of the fair value of securities issued for noncash assets should recognize that a corporation would ordinarily deduct from the proceeds of sales of stock the costs of obtaining cash consideration. Therefore, a reasonable market price may be reduced by estimated issue costs.

The second factor, quantity, requires comparing the number of shares of stock issued for noncash assets with the number of shares traded in the market. If the quantity issued for noncash consideration is significantly greater, the calculated market price may need to be reduced to obtain a fair value for the larger number of shares. A reduction recognizes that a seller of a large quantity of securities often allows a price concession for the benefits of an immediate single transaction.

However, sometimes a calculated market price should not be reduced to obtain the fair value of a security. For example, a number of shares of stock which is large enough to carry control of a corporation may command a premium over the current market price. But that premium is an advantage held by the seller that he transfers to the purchaser. That benefit is unrelated to the consideration received by a corporation. A corporation issuing a large number of shares of stock to a single stockholder should neither recognize a premium nor reduce the reasonable market price to determine the fair value of the stock.

A calculated fair market price of stock traded publicly may also need to be reduced to measure the fair value of unregistered shares of stock, often called letter stock or restricted stock. A corporation would be required to incur the costs of registration before the value of restricted stock is comparable with the price of freely traded shares. Sales of restricted stock at a discount and their effects on components of equity are discussed in Chapter 9.

Costs of Financing. The following explanation of financial transactions will help in later analyses of the effects of equity transactions.

> Financial transactions may be defined loosely as those transactions aimed at making resources available for the income-directed activities of the enterprise. The acquisition of resources through the investments of owners, by borrowing, and—if the term is interpreted broadly—by reinvestment of earnings, are all financial transactions as is also the return of resources to the interests who supplied them.[5]

---

[5] R. K. Mautz, "A Proposed Accounting Technique for Reporting Financial Transactions," *The Journal of Accountancy*, July 1952, p. 82.

Transactions related to financing and those related to revenue producing activities are distinguishable. But those distinctions may not help in deciding if the costs of financing should reduce retained earnings directly or net income. Customarily, costs incurred to obtain creditor and debt financing are reported as operating expenses, and similar costs related to preferred and common stock financing are reductions of retained earnings. Some accountants have challenged the presentation of costs of equity financing and others have recently questioned the reporting of costs of debt financing, particularly convertible debt securities.

Net income vs. retained earnings. Various possibilities of presenting net income range from excluding all financing costs, of both equity and debt financing, to recognizing all financing costs, including dividends distributed to stockholders. Combining all financing costs is said to show the total cost of compensating those who furnish corporate financing regardless of shifts in debt and outstanding equity securities.

Admittedly the capital structure of a corporation is discretionary with management. But the results of changes should be apparent in financial statements. The present concept of net income as the residual amount applicable to interests of stockholders is the most informative presentation. Dividends and other distributions to stockholders are not the only benefits that accrue to the holders of equity interests; undistributed earnings also pertain to those interests. Therefore, net income as now reported represents operating profits reduced by costs of non-equity financing for the period and applicable taxes. The reported net income shows the results of the leverage involved in the capital structure of a corporation as well as earnings for the benefit of all equity interests. Net income determined on that basis increases retained earnings, and disposition in the current or future years of net income depends on actions of the directors. Thus corporate costs of equity financing should be deducted directly from retained earnings.

Therefore, financing costs involved in equity transactions are analyzed in this study in terms of the present concepts: those related to debt securities are deductions in arriving at net income and those related to equity securities are direct reductions of retained earnings. That is, the present distinctions between debt securities and preferred stocks are retained even though the two types of securities are similar in many respects. All costs of financing with debt securities are deducted from net income even though the debt obligation may be satisfied in part by issuing equity securities. The terms of some securities reflect characteristics of both debt and equity securities. If so, the transactions are complex, and distinctions in the type of financing costs are clouded. The nature and purpose of the transaction often indicate the type of costs incurred.

Entire costs of financing. The attempt in this study is to identify all costs and expenses in equity transactions and to recommend accounting for them. Some costs of financing are not now recognized by accepted accounting practices although similar costs in other transactions are now accounted for. The failure to report financing costs means that readers of financial statements are able to interpret the effects of transactions only with additional analyses. The information furnished in financial statements is often insufficient for correct estimates or supplementary computations.

The contradictions in recognizing financing costs in present accounting procedures are demonstrated by the differences in accounting for the conversion of preferred stock and accounting for the redemption of preferred stock. A conversion of preferred stock into common stock is now accounted for by a transfer of the par or stated value of the preferred stock to capital stock and additional capital. The accounting recognizes no difference between the security surrendered and the security distributed in exchange. In contrast, the consideration distributed to redeem a preferred stock ordinarily differs from the par or stated value of the stock. Accounting recognizes the difference as a change in the other components of equity—additional capital and retained earnings.

Maintaining Sources of Equity. Presenting stockholders' equity as contributions by stockholders and retained earnings requires maintaining the distinctions in recording equity transactions. Most procedures in accounting for equity transactions today commingle the two primary sources of equity, and the original classifications are therefore lost. Equity transactions increase as well as decrease total equity and an analysis of the effects of the various types of transactions determines the changes in individual sources.

A frequent objection to showing sources of equity is that attempts to maintain the division will fail and, therefore, it should not be started. Most objections are couched in terms of the traditional accounting for equity transactions—in terms of capital stock, additional capital, and surplus. The detailed analyses in later chapters show that a division by sources is feasible, but a brief summary of typical arguments and the rebuttal is included at this point.

William J. Vatter summarized and discussed the customary claim of accountants that attempts to classify stockholders' equity in the two categories of contributions by stockholders and retained earnings will run into difficulties.[6] Special circumstances are said to call for additional classifications and computations that make presentation of equity more complicated than investment contributions and retained earnings. One basic issue is that corporations are required to maintain minimum legal capital, which is not necessarily the same as the amount stockholders invest, and special accounts are needed to report technical legal capital and contributions in excess of legal requirements. The conclusions in earlier parts of this study are that elements of legal capital are not required classifications in financial statements and that disclosing legal capital meets statutory requirements. The discussion of three other common issues is summarized in the following table, accompanied by suggested rebuttals.

Discussion of Issues	*Suggested Rebuttal*
Classes of Stock	
Stock equities must be subclassified to report the amounts of each class of shares. Problems arise from specific features of special classes, such as preferences in dividend distributions or in liquidation, participations, cumulative dividend rights, and conversion privileges. When accumulated dividends of nonparticipating preferred stock have been paid, the equity in retained earnings is properly assumed to be entirely that of the common shares; but the priority of preferred rights for dividends not met and participations should be recognized in reporting retained earnings in a balance sheet.	Prior or participating rights of preferred stockholders should be disclosed but the classification of components of stockholders' equity as contributions and earnings should not be changed because the rights exist. The destination of retained earnings on a liquidation basis is not primary disclosure data for a going concern.

---

[6] "Corporate Stock Equities—Part 1," Morton Backer, Editor, *Modern Accounting Theory*, 1966, pp. 258-259 and Part 2, pp. 267-300.

| *Discussion of Issues* | *Suggested Rebuttal* |

Reclassifications and Dilutions

Transfers between retained earnings and investment contributions may change legal capital and shift the relative status of stockholders. Transactions in this category are donations, conversions, stock dividends, stock splits, warrants, and options. Recognizing the transactions raises problems in adhering to the two basic classifications and complicates equity presentation.	Reclassifications of components now cause confusion in reporting and interpreting equity. Many changes affect legal capital but do not alter the sources of equity. The important facts of sources of equity may be retained in presentation and legal capital may be disclosed in addition.

Appropriations and Reserves

Subclassifying retained earnings for legal restrictions, contractual relations, or financial considerations may be justifiable and advisable. A stockholder is entitled to a report of income in terms of its disposition. To show the purposes for which earnings are retained, all retained earnings would be stated in terms of appropriations or reserves. Invested capital is not classified based on purposes, but a different classification for retained earnings is reasonable because of the nature of earnings.	The sources of equity show how a corporation obtained resources not how it used those resources. Total retained earnings are appropriated for business purposes; identifying specific amounts for one purpose benefits no one. Funds are commingled and, after investment, an initial designation is no longer significant. Restrictions on the payment of dividends to the extent of retained earnings should be adequately disclosed. Restricted is not the converse of available; this fact is disclosed more clearly if retained earnings are not subclassified.

Pooling of Interests Method. Accounting for equity in a business combination accounted for by the pooling of interests method is unique. Unless a new corporation is formed and issues securities to effect the combination, one corporation increases its outstanding equity securities but measures the consideration received by neither the fair value of the assets received nor the fair value of the stock issued. The concept underlying pooling of interests accounting is a combining of two separate entities to continue operations as one combined entity. The concept puts the transaction in a distinct category, not an increase in outstanding equity securities of a corporation.

The securities issued to effect a combination accounted for by the pooling of interests method are viewed as securities of the combined entity and not those of an existing corporation. The combined entity is new in one respect but continuing in another—that is, the combined corporation substitutes for the combining corporations, which cease to exist, but retained earnings of the combining corporations are carried forward as retained earnings of the corporation resulting from the combination.

The principles recommended in this study to account for equity transactions therefore cannot apply to accounting for a business combination by the pooling of interests method. The corporation that issues stock to effect the combination does not record the fair value of the consideration received. Instead the contributed equity and retained earnings of each combining corporation should be carried forward to obtain the two component sources of stockholders' equity of the combined corporation. That procedure pursues the idea that previously separate entities continue as one entity—thus the pooling of interests method of accounting.

Combining the component sources of equity conforms with the recommendations of this study to present contributions and retained earnings separately. Legal capital of the resulting combined corporation may be more or less than contributed equity, as in either of the separate combining corporations, but maintaining the original classification of equity by sources should prevail in accounting for stockholders' equity of the combined entity.

Application of Principles

The comparisons of varying accounting procedures in Chapter 5 show that present practices do not conform with the principles recommended in this chapter. One benefit of applying the same principles to all transactions is that transactions of a similar nature have the same effects on components of equity and results of operations of all corporations. Another benefit is that the two primary sources of equity would continue to be informative and useful regardless of the variety or frequency of transactions.

The general principles recommended in this chapter may be applied to various types of transactions in equity securities. First, the substance of the transaction must be analyzed, and that leads to discerning the effects on components of equity. The purpose of a transaction is often one indicator of its substance.

The next three chapters on accounting for increases and decreases in outstanding equity securities are devoted to methods of applying the general principles. The factors related to the accounting are outlined, and the reasons that justify the effects on equity components accompany the explanations. Other changes in stockholders' equity that do not always change the number of outstanding equity securities, such as quasi-reorganizations and transactions with nonstockholders, are discussed in the last chapter of Part III.

9

Increases in Equity Securities—Individual Interests Reduced

General principles to record transactions in equity securities are recommended in Chapter 8. Namely, a corporation records the issuance of a security at the amount of consideration received which equals the cash or the fair value of other assets received in the transaction; the fair value of other assets is measured by the fair value of the equity security issued unless the estimated fair value of the asset is determinable. Applications of the recommended principles to increases in equity securities are demonstrated in this chapter and in Chapter 10.

Types of Transactions

Corporate transactions with many different labels increase the number of outstanding equity securities. Yet the types of transactions are few. The discussion of increases in outstanding equity securities is divided in this study by types of transactions rather than labels alone to show more readily the consistency of the accounting recommended.

One basic division is between transactions that reduce the proportionate interests of existing stockholders and those that change the number of securities but do not change the stockholders' proportionate interests in corporate equity.

Another distinction in the types of transactions is that a corporation may receive consideration for securities issued or may issue additional securities without consideration. A corporation receives some kind of consideration for issuing additional securities that reduce the proportionate interests of existing stockholders, although the form of consideration is often other than cash or only partly cash. The comparison of practices in Chapter 5 shows that present practices often limit the consideration recognized to the cash received and ignore the portion of the consideration representing services.

Several types of transactions may dilute the value of an outstanding share of stock. A decline occurs if a corporation increases the number of shares of stock without increases in assets and earnings that correspond to those amounts related to each outstanding share.

Types of increases in outstanding equity securities are divided in this study into those that reduce the proportionate interests and those that do not change the proportionate interests. Whether proportionate interests are changed is essential information that should be reported in financial statements. Transactions that reduce the proportionate interests of existing stockholders are the most frequent and are discussed in this chapter. Those that do not change the proportionate interests are discussed in the next chapter.

Sales and Original Issues

To prevent diluting the value of the interests of existing stockholders, the directors of a corporation are obliged to issue common stock to new stockholders for consideration that is about equal to the fair value of an outstanding share. A proportionate interest in total equity needs to be distinguished from the value of that interest because a change in proportionate interests may have no direct financial effects on the interests of stockholders.

Many increases in outstanding equity securities under various terms and arrangements can be characterized as sales. All distributions for consideration of previously unissued shares as contrasted with reacquired shares fit the designation of "Sales and Original Issues"; but the transactions discussed under this designation are limited to sales for cash, property, or services that are not set by special arrangements that defer the acquisitions of equity interests—for example, warrants and stock options—which are discussed separately.

Consideration of Cash or Property. Sales of additional shares of stock for cash are authorized at a price that is approximately equal to the market price of outstanding shares. Then the total number of outstanding shares increases, the total value of corporate resources also increases, and the proportionate interest in the corporation represented by one share of stock is reduced, but the fair value of one share of stock remains about the same. The present procedure of recognizing the net proceeds of sales as the consideration received for new shares issued conforms with recording the contributions by stockholders as additional corporate equity. To conform with the recommendations in this study that equity transactions be recognized as changes in the contributed and retained earnings components of equity, a corporation should add the entire consideration received to the contributed component of equity instead of allocating the proceeds between capital stock and capital in excess of par or stated value of stock.

The procedures for recording the proceeds of sales of stock for cash also apply to consideration that is an asset for which a fair value may be determined objectively, such as a security with a quoted market price.

Sales or distributions of treasury stock increase outstanding equity securities and also reduce the proportionate interests of individual stockholders. Thus the effects are the same as sales of previously unissued shares. However, accounting for treasury stock depends on the accounting for the cost of the shares reacquired. Reacquiring shares of stock decreases outstanding equity securities, which is the topic of Chapter 11. Therefore, sales and distributions of treasury stock are considered in that chapter with accounting for the acquisition of treasury stock.

Services as Consideration. A corporation may issue additional equity securities for a variety of consideration, for example, services of officers and employees, services of outside firms and individuals, and nonequity funds furnished to finance corporate operations. The directors of a corporation approve the number of shares of stock to be issued for services under the same requirements that they authorize a cash sales price of additional equity securities—the corporation must receive adequate consideration in relation to the current fair value of the stock issued.

The present basis for determining the value of services received in exchange for shares of stock conforms with recognizing the fair value of assets received. That fair value is measured by the value of the asset (services) received, often the same amount that would have been required for a cash payment, or the fair value of the stock issued in exchange whichever is more reasonably determinable.

Distributions To Satisfy Liabilities. Distributing previously unissued shares of stock to satisfy corporate obligations is no longer a rare transaction. The obligations satisfied are often liabilities for compensation to employees for services but sometimes are other liabilities, such as pension costs. The more customary transaction is to distribute previously unissued shares to employees to satisfy compensation arrangements. Reacquired shares rather than original issues are usually distributed to satisfy other liabilities and the accounting is discussed in Chapter 11.

A corporate liability for compensation to be satisfied by issuing and distributing stock of the corporation may be fixed in terms of a dollar amount or of a number of shares of stock. If the compensation liability is a dollar amount, the number of shares of stock distributed is ordinarily determined by the market price of the stock at the date distributed. Therefore, the consideration received by the corporation and the amount of the liability both equal the current fair value of the shares issued. If the liability is designated as a number of shares of stock, the dollar amount of the corporate liability fluctuates with changes in the market price of the specified number of shares. The arrangement obligates the corporation to deliver shares of stock and the amount of the liability can be measured only by the fair value of that number of securities. The fair value of shares of stock at the date distributed represents the consideration received for the shares of stock issued to satisfy a liability to deliver securities. That fair value also corresponds to the amount of the liability of the corporation at the date the securities are distributed. Therefore the recorded consideration received for stock issued and the reduction of the compensation liability are equal.

Although arrangements and terms may vary, all distributions of previously unissued stock to satisfy liabilities increase contributed equity by the fair value of the additional shares of stock at the date the stock is issued. The effects on stockholders' equity are the same as sales for cash or services except that distributing stock may affect the corporate liabilities for taxes.

Common Stock Issued at a Discount. Some corporations issue stock with specified restrictions on the sale and transfer of the shares, and the shares are often called restricted or letter stock. The consideration received for each share is usually less than the fair value of an outstanding share. The absence of the features of freely transferable and registered stock justifies a nominal discount in the selling price. A price concession recognizes that new stockholders have agreed to postpone the usual rights to dispose freely of the stock. Since the corporation avoids some issuing costs, the consideration received is about the same as the net proceeds of sales of registered shares of stock would have been.

Nature of large discount. However, some corporations have issued restricted common stock with discounts that far exceed the customary costs of registering the securities and underwriting fees. Unregistered stock at a large discount is usually issued as a private financing arrangement with one or a few stockholders who agree that the stock represents an investment to be held for a designated period. Some corporations offer to sell to employees restricted stock at a large discount from fair value. The offers are usually a part of a compensation plan and the accounting discussed in the section on stock options applies to those issues of stock.

Recording the cash proceeds of the sales as the entire consideration received may be inadequate reporting of the financial effects of the transaction. An analysis of the substance of a typical transaction follows to reveal the nature of a large discount.

A corporation issues shares of common stock at a large discount from the current fair value of outstanding shares, sometimes as little as 50% of the current market price, because needed financing is unobtainable on lower and satisfactory terms. A corporation would ordinarily prefer creditor financing, even with high interest rates, if funds were available from that source on acceptable terms. Generally, a corporation resorts to issuing restricted stock at a large discount because financing with alternative securities is impracticable—either the prospects and financial condition of the corporation are poor or the supply of capital is scarce. Deciding practicality and satisfactory terms are influenced by accounting because present accounting does not require that all costs of equity financing be recognized.

Restrictions on transfers of stock sold at a large discount are incidental to the primary purpose of obtaining corporate financing. The restriction is a concession by the purchasers and avoids an increase in the number of shares of stock available for trading in the marketplace during the agreed period.

Return to investors. Common stock is issued at a large discount because investors will furnish corporate financing only on the condition that the expected return exceeds the normal return of other stockholders. Restricted stock ranks equally with all other outstanding shares of stock of the same class for dividend purposes during and after the restriction period. But restricted and other outstanding shares of stock are not equal in other respects until after the restriction period ends. The sources of the return to purchasers of discounted stock for their investments of funds are future equality of the new and old shares of stock and dividend distributions. Therefore, the consideration received for the ownership interests represented originally by shares of discounted stock includes costs of equity financing.

Equity financing costs. Issuing restricted common stock at a significant discount entails financing costs for the new capital at a higher rate than the cost of funds invested by existing common stockholders. The return on each dollar invested for discounted stock is greater than the return on each dollar of the fair value of investments of existing stockholders. The purchasers of discounted stock are compensated by a lump sum reduction in the purchase price of the stock in place of larger periodic returns in the form of preferential dividends. The effects of the transaction are comparable to those from issuing a class of stock with prior claims that is convertible into ordinary common stock at the end of a restriction period.

Since all outstanding shares of common stock have identical claims on current and retained earnings of a corporation, a part of the interests of existing common stockholders is transferred to new restricted stockholders through the issuance of additional shares at a large discount. Existing stockholders accept the preferential terms of the newly issued stock because the transaction satisfies financing requirements for operation of the corporation.

The difference between the fair value of the stock issued and the cash consideration received represents corporate cost of equity financing incurred at the date the stock is issued. The entire cost of equity financing should be recognized in the financial accounts. Compensation to new stockholders for the financing furnished is a part of the consideration for the stock; therefore a corporation should record the entire consideration received for the stock issued, not the cash only. Since the new stock issued is similar to other outstanding shares except for transferability, the consideration for restricted shares sold at a significant discount should be the fair value of other outstanding shares reduced by estimated costs of registering the stock. The remainder of the difference is a financing cost which the corporation should defer and amortize over the period of restriction. The financing cost relates to equity financing; therefore the periodic amortization should be deducted from retained earnings. The consideration received is contributed equity which remains after the restriction ends, but amortization of the financing cost may be allocated reasonably to the restriction period because it represents the minimum period of direct benefit.

Stock Purchase Warrants

Nature of Warrant Transactions. Consideration received for stock purchase warrants issued is in the nature of a deposit on later possible sales of stock, and a corporation assumes a commitment to issue equity securities under the terms of the warrants. Since warrants themselves do not represent an ownership interest, a corporation should exclude from stockholders' equity the consideration received for outstanding warrants. The consideration should be classified as contingent equity financing, described in Chapter 7, as long as the warrants remain outstanding.

Increases in outstanding equity securities from issuing stock on the exercise of stock purchase warrants differ from other sales of stock for cash in two respects only—the cash consideration is specified in the warrant, which is often issued far in advance of the stock, and that amount is not necessarily the entire consideration that the corporation receives.

Issuance and Elimination of Warrants. The primary aim of a corporation in accounting for transactions in its stock purchase warrants should be to record as a part of stockholders' equity the entire consideration received for stock issued. If the total consideration exceeds the cash received, the difference represents some kind of "services" received. The corporate objective in issuing stock warrants should identify the nature of the services received and thereby the accounting for those services. The complexities of some warrant transactions and of some related securities often obscure the actual corporate purposes.

Corporations issue warrants under conditions so varied that the nature and effects of issuing and exercising those sold separately, those issued for other than cash, those sold in combination with other securities, and those distributed in business combinations are best considered individually in this section.

Variations in transactions. Stock purchase warrants may include unusual provisions or may be involved in special transactions. The more familiar exceptional circumstances and their treatment in this section are described in the following paragraphs.

Although most stock purchase warrants designate an exercise price that is more than the market price of the stock that a warrant holder is privileged to buy (privilege stock) at the date the warrants are issued, sometimes an exercise price is less than the current market price of the stock. The characteristics of warrants that offer an immediate benefit through an advantageous exercise price are considered in this section to determine if accounting for the transactions at issuance and exercise of those warrants should differ from that for the more usual warrants.

Holders may exercise warrants or allow them to lapse, and some corporations have paid the holders for the right to cancel outstanding warrants. A few stock purchase warrants are redeemable at a specified price at the option of the issuing corporation. Each possibility is discussed in this section.

Some warrants do not stipulate an exercise period and are therefore called unlimited or perpetual warrants. That feature does not change the nature of the transactions but merely extends the term and is not considered as a separate problem.

A few corporations issue warrants in exchange for shares of outstanding common stock and retire the stock. That type of transaction is a form of reorganization and is discussed in Chapter 12.

Some securities called stock purchase warrants have the characteristics of stock rights or stock subscriptions and should be accounted for according to their natures regardless of their titles.

Exercise of Warrants Sold Separately. A separate cash sale of warrants to purchase stock at a designated price above the current market price of the stock is the least complex of the many types of warrant transactions. An analysis of the transaction will demonstrate its nature and the factors involved in the issuance and exercise of warrants without adding other complications of coupling with another security, redemptions, and variable features.

Outstanding warrants. A corporation sells warrants and receives funds, which it may use to finance operations, but assumes no obligation to pay interest and repay principal, as it would for borrowed funds, and grants no dividend and other rights, as it would for equity funds from stockholders. The obligation of the corporation is to deliver an equity security when the holder of a warrant elects to pay the additional designated price. The amount of the ultimate corporate obligation is uncertain at the time a warrant is sold, but the corporation is willing to assume an unfixed liability to gain the advantage of obtaining funds from other than credit or equity sources.

The corporation has in effect accomplished two things: (1) obtained funds without incurring current expenses for their use and (2) insured that the cash consideration for an equity security issued later will exceed its current market price. One may fairly assume that in the absence of those benefits a corporation would not sell warrants with the accompanying uncertain liabilities but instead would obtain loans or sell equity securities at the market price.

The purchaser of a stock warrant advances funds to a corporation and accepts an uncertain return that depends entirely on the later market price of the stock that he is privileged to purchase. He foregoes a current return in the form of dividends or interest on his investment. If the price of the stock rises, his warrant may be valuable and his return spectacular. Conversely, the stock purchase privilege may later convey no advantage, and the warrant may have no value.

Consideration for stock issued. The consideration received for the stock issued on the exercise of warrants is composed of three parts: cash received on exercise of the warrants, cash proceeds of sale of the warrants, and consideration for the earlier financing supplied to the corporation. The financing expense that the corporation incurs for the use of funds other than equity funds is a part of the total consideration received for the stock issued. Another part of the financing expense results from the benefit the corporation derives from arranging for the future sale of an equity security at a price higher than its market price at the date the purchase privilege is granted. A corporation may improve its later financial position over that derived from selling stock at a lower current market price. However, separating the components of the financing expense is impossible, and a corporation should account for the expense in total.

The fair value of shares of stock issued on the exercise of warrants is the most reasonably determinable measure of the total consideration that a corporation receives for the stock. That measure conforms with the arrangements agreed to by both parties to the warrant transaction—the corporation is obliged to deliver securities of unknown value at an indefinite date for a fixed sum. The difference between the total consideration for the stock issued and the cash received represents a cost of corporate financing. A corporation should record the total consideration received as contributed equity at the date the stock is issued and eliminate from contingent equity financing the proceeds of the sale of outstanding warrants.

The accounting then recognizes the contingent consideration to be distributed for financing that is involved in the sale and exercise of warrants. The amount of contingent financing costs depends on the success of the corporation and is one form of incentive financing, similar to contingent interest.

Fair value of stock issued. The market price of privilege stock that the holder of a stock purchase warrant may obtain on exercise ordinarily reflects, at least in part, the potential dilution of the proportionate interest of one outstanding share from the exercise of outstanding warrants.[1] Therefore, the consideration received for stock issued may be measured by the market price of the stock at date of exercise without an adjustment for the greater number of shares of stock that will be outstanding after the warrants are exercised. Other factors that a corporation may need to recognize in setting a fair value of stock based on its market price are discussed in Chapter 8.

Illustration of sale and exercise. The financial effects of exercising a stock purchase warrant that is sold separately for cash may be illustrated with simple but representative facts assumed:

> A corporation sells for $3 in year X a warrant to purchase one share of stock at $25 during the period from X+1 to X+11. The market price of the stock is $20 a share at the date the warrant is sold.

---

[1] A study of the ratio of the price of stock to the earnings per share and the effects of potential dilution assuming conversion of outstanding debt and preferred stock are described by Eugene M. Lerner and Rolf Auster in "Does the Market Discount Potential Dilution," *Financial Analysts Journal,* July-August 1969, pp. 118-121. Peter W. Bacon and Edward L. Winn, Jr. discussed recognition in the market of the impact of conversion in "The Impact of Forced Conversion on Stock Prices," *The Journal of Finance,* December 1969, pp. 871-874.

The market price of the stock is—
- $25 a share in year X+2
- $28 a share in year X+3
- $29 a share in years X+4 and X+5.

The warrant holder exercises his privilege and purchases one share of stock for $25 in year X+6 at the date the market price of the stock is $30 a share.

A warrant holder obtains no direct benefit from the warrant if he exercises his privilege to purchase stock while the market price of the stock is less than or equal to the exercise price plus the purchase cost of the warrant. Thus, he is unlikely to exercise the warrant in years X, X+1, X+2, and X+3. Some exceptions are possible; for instance, a holder may exercise a warrant at a time that the market price of the stock is above the exercise price but below the exercise price plus cost of warrant because he expects dividend distributions to compensate for the excess total cost of the stock. A warrant holder is most likely to delay exercising his purchase privilege until the market price of the stock is greater than his total cash consideration, such as in year X+6.

The fair value of the stock issued is $30, and the corporation receives $28 cash. Thus the total consideration received of $30 includes $2 corporate consideration for financing. The financing consideration represents the cost of the use of $3 for the period from year X to year X+6 and for the assurance in year X that stock may be sold later for cash of more than $20.

Recognizing financing expenses. A corporation should recognize either as operating expenses or as costs of equity financing the financing consideration it distributes on the exercise of warrants. The decision is important because operating expenses would reduce net income and equity financing would reduce retained earnings directly. The purpose of selling stock purchase warrants should be the factor that determines the designation. The ultimate objective of the corporation is to obtain equity financing, and the funds received for contingent financing are related to the resulting equity interests rather than directly to the interim liability that is equal to the proceeds of sales of the warrants.

As described earlier, a corporation is not obliged to pay interest or declare dividends on the funds it receives for warrants issued but is obliged to compensate warrant holders if it later receives consideration for stock. The financing consideration distributed should be deducted from retained earnings to maintain the distinction of including debt financing expenses in net income and costs of equity financing in retained earnings.

The recommended procedure is similar to but not the same as accounting for dividends distributed to stockholders. Dividends, representing a return to stockholders for their investments, are deducted from retained earnings; financing consideration, representing a return to purchasers of warrants for their contingent equity investments, should also be deducted from retained earnings. If a warrant holder elects to assert his purchase privilege, he also asserts his privilege to claim a portion of retained earnings and to participate in future earnings. The fair value of the stock that he receives reflects a portion of the retained earnings as well as unrealized appreciation.

The return to a warrant holder may be at a lower rate than that to a stockholder because dividends are distributed to stockholders between the dates the warrant is sold and exercised. But the warrant holder accepts that disadvantage since he may limit his risks by postponing his decision to invest in corporate equity and the possibility of a higher rate of return later is attractive.

Corporate costs of equity financing with warrants could be estimated at the time warrants are sold and allocated to each fiscal period in which the warrants are outstanding. That procedure could be defended in principle but is impracticable, and the recorded allocation would require adjustment, perhaps significant, to the fair value of stock at the date the warrants are exercised. The benefits of recording costs of financing before warrants are exercised would be limited because the costs would reduce retained earnings and increase the amount of the warrants classified as contingent equity financing until the date of exercise. Another influence to account for the costs of financing with warrants at the date they are exercised is that the warrants may never be exercised due to the relation of market and exercise prices. Accounting for the lapse of warrants is discussed separately in this section.

Another method of recognizing the costs could be to record the excess of the market price of stock over the maximum cash consideration on the basis that fluctuations in the price of the stock determine the periodic costs of financing. For example, using the facts in the illustration on pages 160 to 161, costs of financing would be recorded as follows:

Years X to X+3	-0-
Year X+4	$1
Year X+5	-0-
Year X+6	$1

Obviously, recording annual increases in market price could fail to spread the financing costs equally to each period that the warrants are outstanding. The market price of the stock may fluctuate significantly and not follow a continuing upward trend; if so, to accrue financing costs according to changes in the market price of the stock is more objectionable.

The various circumstances mean that the most practicable procedure is for a corporation to recognize the total financing costs as a reduction of retained earnings in the period that warrants are exercised. The description of outstanding warrants may disclose adequately the potential reduction of retained earnings without periodic transfers of uncertain future costs between retained earnings and contingent equity.

Exercise of Warrants Issued for Other Than Cash. Warrants may be issued without a cash consideration. Those issued for noncash consideration are usually for services, such as those of underwriters and promoters. The value of the consideration received in the form of services should be measured and recorded as a corporate liability for outstanding warrants the same as for warrants sold for cash. The nature of the transactions is the same; the only difference is the nature of the consideration received.

The value of the services that a corporation receives can be estimated even though the additional costs of financing with warrants are uncertain and the corporation does not recognize an estimate of the costs at the date the warrants are issued. An argument may be that estimates of services are impracticable at the date the warrants are issued and unnecessary because the amount would be adjusted at the date the warrants are exercised later. But an estimate recognizes the consideration received for the warrants issued, and those services received are distinct from later costs of financing. Intervening financial statements should show clearly the contingent equity financing until the outstanding warrants are exercised.

Exercise of Marketable Warrants Sold in a Unit. Many stock purchase warrants are sold in combination with senior securities as a unit. Warrants are most often sold with debt securities, but some corporations have sold units of common stock and stock purchase warrants. Although sold as a unit, detachable warrants that are traded separately and the other securities have distinctive characteristics. Dispositions of the two securities are also distinctive. Dispositions (redemption, maturity, and exercise) of the two securities that concern the issuing corporation ordinarily are independent and occur at different dates. A corporation should therefore account separately for the issuance and later transactions in each of the securities.

Allocation of proceeds. A corporation should record the proceeds of sale of each primary security and warrant that is traded separately but is issued as part of a unit. The proceeds of sale of a unit of debt security or preferred stock and detachable warrants may be allocated between the primary security and the warrants based on the market prices of each at the date both are traded separately. By allocating the proceeds, a corporation recognizes that the selling price of either the debt security or the preferred stock alone would have been less than the combined unit and segregates the proceeds applicable to those securities and to the warrants. The sales price of a unit is not necessarily equal to the market price of the component securities because the features of a unit differ from those of the individual securities. Allocation based on market prices of the individual securities at the same date recognizes the relative weights that the marketplace gives to the features of those securities.

A corporation now accounts for interest and dividends paid to the holders of senior securities sold in a unit and for disposition of those securities the same as for other debt securities and preferred stock. Allocating the proceeds of sale of a unit of debt and warrants increases the related debt discount or reduces the related debt premium; amortizing the larger discount or smaller premium in turn reduces periodic net income.

The consideration that a corporation receives for a share of common stock sold as a unit with stock purchase warrants may be less than the fair value of an outstanding share of stock if the consideration is determined by allocating the proceeds of sale of the unit based on the market prices of each security. Analysis of the transaction should show (1) if a difference between fair value and allocated proceeds results from financing costs incurred or (2) if the proceeds should be allocated between the stock and warrants to record the stock at its fair value. If the transaction involves costs of equity financing similar to those of issuing stock at a large discount, the costs should be recognized as part of the consideration received. Thus, the stock issued would be recorded at current fair value.

Warrants outstanding and financing costs. The nature of a separate sale of stock purchase warrants and of a sale as part of a unit are alike although the evidence of corporate purpose is not always obvious in a unit sale. Thus, the accounting for allocated proceeds should be the same as for separate proceeds of sale. Proceeds allocated to warrants should be shown as warrants outstanding and classified as contingent equity financing. The final costs of financing with warrants, measured by the fair value of the stock issued, should reduce retained earnings at the date the warrants are exercised.

Debentures surrendered for exercise. Some stock purchase warrants provide that the purchase price of the privilege stock may be paid in cash or by surrendering debentures of a face amount equal to the purchase price. The form of payment does not change the nature of the transaction of issuing stock on the exercise of warrants. The corporate liability for outstanding debt is settled to the extent that debentures are surrendered, and that amount is part of the consideration received for stock issued.

Exercise of Nonmarketable Warrants. Some lenders accept a unit of securities, such as long-term notes and warrants exercisable separately, in lieu of a higher interest rate or an earlier maturity date, for granting postponed installment payments, or for some other concession. Neither the debt nor the warrants are traded publicly, and the market price of neither can be estimated objectively. Creditors are willing to forego defined advantages, for example a higher fixed return or earlier payment, for the possibility of a larger return through the future value of the stock purchase warrants. The corporate purpose of issuing the warrants is to obtain current benefits in credit financing—to obtain equity financing is incidental. In fact, postponing the payment of costs of credit financing may be the sole objective.

Sometimes a corporation is unable to borrow required funds because the current money market and the possibilities of inflation make lending with a fixed return and repayment unattractive. Some creditors will advance funds if a corporation adds the potential benefits of stock purchase warrants. Usually, the private lenders agree not to sell the warrants to others but may detach the warrants from the debt and exercise the warrants.

Credit financing expenses. A corporation agrees to the provisions of stock purchase warrants and a combined loan after it projects future corporate earnings and ranges of market prices of its stock and estimates the financial effects of exercising the warrants. An evaluation of those factors is necessary to decide if the corporate consideration to be distributed on exercise of the warrants approximates the benefits to be derived from the provisions of the loan. The corporation may use those projections as a basis to accrue each period the estimated costs of financing with warrants although the total costs are not determinable until the warrants are exercised. Periodic warrant financing expense plus interest on the loan should reduce net income as credit financing expenses because the stock purchase warrants comprise part of the debt financing arrangements.

A corporation should not assign a part of proceeds of the debt or loan to the warrants at the date of issuance. Instead, the financing expenses accrued each period should be recorded as the carrying amount of the warrants, classified as contingent equity financing. The adjustment of estimated to actual financing expenses, measured by the fair value of the stock at the date the warrants are exercised, should be included in net income on the same basis as other nonrecurring debt expense, such as that for redemptions, that is, extraordinary if material.

Nondetachable warrants. Warrants that are not detachable from another security of a unit are similar to the conversion privilege incorporated in the provisions of convertible securities, which are discussed in a separate section of this chapter.

Differences in accounting. The accounting procedures recommended in this section provide that the financing expenses related to warrants traded separately and those for which no market exists are recognized in different periods. Also, the financing expenses related to warrants traded separately reduce retained earnings directly and those related to nonmarketable warrants reduce net income.

The nature of the securities and the purpose of the related borrowing transactions justify the differences in accounting. All costs of issuing and exercising warrants reduce retained earnings; but costs of those issued to obtain equity financing are a direct reduction, and costs of those issued as a part of credit financing are a reduction of net income. The recommended accounting does not change total financing costs even though the expenses related to credit financing are recognized, at least in part, each period.

Exercise Price Below Market at Date Issued. The exercise price specified in a few warrants is below the market price of the privilege stock at the date the warrants are issued. Warrants with those provisions are usually issued in combination with preferred stock, debenture bonds, or loans, and the warrants are not traded publicly. The warrant is related directly to the financing obtained from the combined security.

The exercise privilege obviously has a realizable value to the holder at the date the warrants are issued although he may postpone purchase of the stock and the value of the privilege may later increase. The warrants carry an immediate value that is independent of potential enhancement in the market price of the stock. The intent of management is to distribute compensation for services—for example, advisory services or underwriting—or to grant a discount on the sales price of the security. The amount of compensation distributed or discount granted may be measured by the difference between the exercise price and the fair value of the stock at the date the warrants are issued. Issuing warrants that convey an immediate benefit and the later exercise or lapse of the warrants are distinct transactions.

Recording warrants issued. Since directors are obliged to receive adequate consideration for all securities issued, the proceeds of warrants as well as the other combined securities should be measured at the date issued. The compensation recorded for services or price concession should also be recorded as the consideration for the warrants at the date the units of securities are issued. The proceeds assigned to warrants represent a discount on the proceeds of the other securities issued in combination with the warrants. If the purchase privilege is granted with debt securities or loans, the discount to be amortized is increased by the carrying amount assigned to the warrants. For example, a corporation obtains a loan of $100,000, issues to the lender 10,000 warrants to purchase common stock at a price $2 less than the current price of the stock, and records the warrants and the discount on the loan at $20,000.

Financing costs on exercise. Financing costs directly related to the warrants are uncertain and not determinable until the warrants are exercised. Cost is then measured by the difference between the exercise price plus the carrying amount of a warrant and fair value of the stock issued. That cost relates to equity financing obtained through exercise of warrants and should be accounted for the same as for warrants sold separately, that is, deducted from retained earnings at the date of exercise.

Distributions in Business Combinations. Some corporations issue a unit of convertible debt and stock purchase warrants in exchange for the outstanding equity securities of another corporation. The transaction is similar to the sale of a unit of debt and warrants except that the consideration received lacks the objective measure of cash proceeds. Instead the fair value of the securities issued may be more reasonably determinable, the same as in determining the consideration received for newly issued shares of common stock in exchange for stock of another corporation. If separate market prices of the debt security and the warrant are available, a corporation should record the consideration for each security on the basis of market prices. The consideration received for securities for which market prices are unavailable should be based on appraised values of the securities. The consideration assigned to warrants issued should be accounted for as contingent equity financing the same as for warrants sold separately.

Lapse of Warrants. Holders of warrants to purchase stock may find that the price of the stock does not reach or exceed the designated purchase price during the privilege period. Under those conditions a warrant holder will not exercise his warrant unless he wishes to acquire the stock for reasons other than financial return, such as to obtain control. The proceeds of sale or other consideration received for warrants should not be shown as contingent equity financing after the end of the privilege period. The consideration and the transaction determine the disposition of the carrying amounts of the warrants.

The purchaser of a warrant pays for the privilege of later purchasing the stock at less than its market price at the later date. The corporation assumes an uncertain obligation for costs as a part of the financing arrangements. If the earnings and future prospects of a corporation or general market conditions do not produce a market price for its stock that is high enough to attract exercise of the warrants, the corporation incurs no additional expenses but benefits to the extent of the consideration received for the warrants. The warrant provisions are a part of the overall equity financing and all results, expenses as well as benefits, should be recognized as a part of financing costs. A corporation receives consideration for potential equity financing—equity never materializes.

Therefore the carrying amount of warrants that expire unexercised should be transferred to and increase retained earnings. By adopting that procedure, a corporation recognizes the results, both benefits and costs, of equity financing arrangements as changes in retained earnings. Contingent equity financing was not converted to stockholder interests, and the carrying amounts of the warrants accrue to the benefit of the existing stockholders.

Unexercised warrants issued originally as a part of credit financing arrangements are an exception to the accounting recommended in the last paragraph. The carrying amount of warrants unexercised at the end of the privilege period should reduce the expenses of credit financing included in net income.

Cancellation of Warrants. A corporation may want to eliminate the possibility of increasing the number of outstanding equity securities through the exercise of warrants and arrange to compensate the holders for canceling their purchase privileges. That arrangement can be negotiated if an individual or another corporation holds all or most of the warrants. A corporation is permitted to buy its widely held warrants in an open market but rarely does it.

The corporation pays a financing cost equal to the difference between the payment and the carrying amount of the warrants. The cost should reduce retained earnings in the period paid. The effects of the cancellation on retained earnings are the same as those of the exercise of warrants. The claim of warrant holders on undistributed earnings and future earnings is satisfied by paying cash instead of distributing shares of stock.

Warrants redeemed. Redemption of warrants is of the same nature as a cancellation. The only difference is that the redemption price, equivalent to a cancellation price, is not negotiated but is set by the original provisions of the warrant.

Stock Options

A corporation issues additional shares of stock at the time optionees exercise outstanding stock options. The new shares of stock convey rights of stockholders equal to the rights of each other outstanding share of stock of the same class. On the date of exercise of an option, a corporation issues additional shares, the number of outstanding equity securities increases, the corporation recognizes the consideration received as an increase in contributions by stockholders, and the proportionate interests of existing stockholders change.

A corporation may distribute treasury stock on the exercise of employee stock options, and the special features of those transactions are discussed in the section on reacquired stock in Chapter 11. This section covers the distribution of previously unissued shares which increases the number of outstanding equity securities.

Similarities of Options and Warrants. The basic characteristics of stock options are similar to those of stock purchase warrants, and the obligations of an issuing corporation are the same for each security. The primary differences are that most warrants are transferable privileges and involve outsiders and their financing of the corporation, but most stock options are nontransferable privileges and involve employees and their services to the corporation with corporate financing a minor factor. The similarities mean that the same accounting principles apply to the exercise of each type of privilege because the impacts on corporate equity are similar. The differences mean that analyzing and recording stock option transactions may be more complex and that services of employees ordinarily affect net income.

Stock options may be granted to other than employees of a corporation. Sometimes a corporation issues options to underwriters or others as compensation for their past services. The nature of the issuance and exercise of options issued to outsiders is the same as that for nontransferable stock purchase warrants. Therefore, the accounting for the stock options should correspond to that for warrants issued for the same purpose.

The discussion in this section is in terms of a customary stock option that specifies an option price that is equal to or not less than 85% of the fair value of the stock at the date the option is granted. The discussion also pertains to a plan that grants the privilege to purchase stock at a large discount from fair value of the stock.

Consideration for Stock Issued Under Options. Although a corporation receives cash equal to the option price for the stock issued on exercise of an option, that amount is not an objective measure of the entire consideration received because employee option stock is issued for cash plus services of the optionee. Compensating employees—usually officers and executives—for services is recognized as the primary purpose of typical stock option plans. Option rights are not always granted as a part of a formal employment contract but the terms of an option usually require, with some exceptions for death, that an optionee is permitted to exercise his options only if he is an employee. In fact, stock options plus salary are often attractive as a compensation package.

A corporation should recognize as additional equity an amount assigned to services received as consideration for securities issued. Services received may be the entire consideration or only a part of the consideration as in the exercise of stock options. Services received are expected to enhance the business even though the amount assigned to those services is usually treated as an expense of operations and not as a continuing asset of the corporation.

The problems of measuring and accounting for services received under stock option plans have long created controversy. However, measuring the amount to be assigned to services received and accounting for the corresponding cost of services as compensation expense are separate problems.

The discussion in Chapter 2 on present prevailing practices shows that exercising some stock options granted to employees does not depend on their performing services for the corporation. But those option plans are relatively scarce. The conditions and nature of the related equity transactions are similar to those of other sales of stock for cash, and accounting for the stock issued and the consideration received should be the same.

Accounting now ignores some consideration. Present accounting practices rarely recognize the services received as consideration for option stock. Apparently the failure to account for the entire consideration evolved and was accepted because few were satisfied with the various proposed alternative solutions. Total stockholders' equity is the same whether a corporation records as the consideration received for option stock issued (1) the cash received from an optionee or (2) the cash proceeds plus an amount for services received and includes the amount assigned to services in net income as compensation expense. However, the amounts of the two component sources of stockholders' equity depend on the accounting, and the differing effects on results of operations may be significant. Accounting should recognize and report the separate financial effects of transactions even though counter effects are equal. By including in contributed equity all consideration received for stock issued and in net income all compensation for services performed by employees, a corporation avoids understating contributions of stockholders and overstating net income and retained earnings by equal amounts.

The fact that a part of the consideration received for option stock is omitted from the financial statements is not now clearly disclosed in explanatory notes. Even though notes could be improved, disclosing the effects of stock option transactions is an inadequate substitute for accounting for those effects. The proportionate interests of existing stockholders are reduced because additional shares of stock are issued for the options exercised. Unless the option price equals the fair value of an outstanding share of stock at the date the option stock is issued, which is unusual, a portion of a stockholder's interest in corporate resources is transferred to the optionee. That transfer is expected to be justified by the value of services performed for the corporation.

The treatment of employee stock options can justifiably follow the principles of accounting recommended in this study for increases in outstanding equity securities. Methods of recognizing the substance of issuing and exercising stock options are discussed in the following paragraphs.

Value of Services. The value of services performed by an optionee could measure a part of the consideration received for the stock issued under options if the services could be valued independently. However, the benefits that a corporation derives from services of an employee determine the value of those services to the individual enterprise. The relation of the services of each optionee to his respective employer corporation is unique, and a combination of distinctive factors determines the value of an optionee's services. Those characteristics of value of services pertain regardless of the form of consideration—cash, stock of the employer corporation, stock options, insured annuity, or other assets. The value of specific services received for each type of compensation is presumed to be reasonably equal to the value of the consideration given to an employee because a corporation is obliged to receive adequate value for distributions to employees.

Although making a reliable independent estimate of the value of services received is impracticable at the time a stock option is granted, while it is outstanding, or after it is exercised, a corporation may usually determine readily the value of the consideration distributed for services under option plans. Equality of the two amounts is implied by the requirement to receive adequate consideration for stock issued. That procedure for measuring consideration received conforms with that adopted for other assets received for corporate securities issued.

Estimates of services recommended. Several other methods of estimating the value of services of optionees have been recommended.

They include equivalent cash payments, amounts determined and agreed to by the parties to the agreement, and income tax deductions foregone. Each suggested method assumes that the consideration that a corporation is to distribute later in the form of stock is fixed at the date of an option agreement and can be measured at the date of agreement. Those assumptions are fictitious, and none of the suggested methods reflects the terms of stock option arrangements and the transactions as they occur.

The provisions of a stock option plan determine the amount of the consideration that a corporation becomes contingently obligated to distribute to an optionee. The amount may well depend on later events.

Some arguments support the recommendation to measure the equivalent current cash salary that would be required for the services of an employee. The method assumes that two distinct types of compensation can be equated and measured interchangeably. A cash salary does not correspond to a stock option in nature, results, or benefits. The accounting should measure the effects of an option arrangement on operations and equity not those of an alternative arrangement that the corporation did not adopt.

Contingent Consideration for Services. Corporations are permitted to and do arrange for future services, including services of employees, although the ultimate consideration is unknown at the time of the agreement. If an arrangement for services involves unknown costs, it is unrealistic to try to force accounting for the costs of a plan into some other pattern.

A stock option does not provide for fixed consideration for services determined at the date the option is granted to an employee; rather the option commits the corporation to later deliver securities of presently unknown value—a contingent amount which may fluctuate. Accounting and presentation should highlight the contingency while stock options are outstanding.

Fair value of stock as a measure. Both the corporation and the optionee expect the market price of the corporation's stock to increase during the option period. If the option price equals the market price of the stock at the date the option is granted, the purchase privilege has no value and the option plan has failed to accomplish its purpose unless the market price rises. A corporation determines the number of shares of stock to be covered by options granted to an individual employee by an estimate of the value of the stock at the date he may purchase the stock and management judges that estimate in relation to the estimated value of an employee's services, his cash salary, and other employee benefits. Since consideration for services is accounted for as compensation, management of a corporation obviously intends—in fact is obliged—to obtain value for stock issued but the value of services of an optionee is not determinable in advance. The estimated value of future services of employees may change after options are granted and the earnings of the corporation reflect the change in value of those services based on performance, ability, and efforts of employees. In turn, the market price of stock reflects earnings and expectations of earnings. Incentive compensation in the form of stock options ties the consideration for employee services to changes in corporate earnings reflected in the fair value of option stock.

Plans carry risks. The terms of a stock option assure an employee that he has the right to receive additional compensation for his services to the extent that the benefits of his services are reflected in the later value of the stock. His rewards are not always commensurate with his efforts because the compensation he receives and an independent value of his services are equal only to the extent that the later fair value of the stock reflects that value of his services. The value and productiveness of all employees' services are only two of many factors that affect the market prices of stock and other factors may offset well-intentioned services. Similarly, other events unrelated to services may enhance the value of a corporation and the related market price of its stock. At the time of an option agreement, a corporation is assured that it has the right to receive employee services but the value of those services is unknown at that date. Both the consideration that a corporation is to distribute to an employee for his services and the incentive compensation that the employee is to receive are determined later. Each party assumes risks.

Daniel L. Sweeney explained explicitly the risks in stock options.

> In any option plan there is a risk of loss to both contracting parties. The optionee might realize no benefit for services performed under the option. The corporation might be required to forego a much larger cash sum during the option period than they wished to pay in cash compensation at the date the option was granted. Yet, the expectation of market increase must be such that it outweighs the expectation of loss and thus provides a desirable speculation acceptable to both parties. It is desirable to the corporation as a

means of obtaining valuable services for a minimum current cash outlay, and it is desirable to the optionee as a means of obtaining a larger amount of income than could otherwise be obtained on a straight cash payment basis.[2]

Absence of consideration for services. Stock option plans are predicated on an increase in the market price of the stock. But during the period that a stock option is exercisable, the fair value of the stock may remain the same or decline from its market price at the date the option is granted. The absence of an increase in price does not imply that the services themselves were of no value, but the benefits of the services may be offset by unfavorable events. The benefits of the services are not measurable objectively, and the corporate obligation for compensation for services is in terms of the stock to be issued. If an employee exercises his privilege when the option price is not less than the fair value of the stock, the corporation incurs no additional expense for his services because it distributes no consideration to the employee.

Contingent Plans Acceptable. Accounting for stock option plans may and should recognize the contingent compensation for services which is a part of the arrangements. Plans that commit a corporation to later distribute contingent amounts of compensation are now acceptable practices. Bonus plans and phantom stock plans illustrate common arrangements of that type, and the contingent aspects of each type of plan are described in this section.

Bonus plans. A plan for bonuses based on a percentage of earnings involves contingent compensation for services. The amounts of compensation are uncertain until the corporation determines earnings without that reduction, and the resulting bonuses are recognized as an expense of current operations. Despite litigation regarding methods of computing a bonus base and allegations of excessive compensation (the same as for cash payments of fixed salaries) bonus and other plans for sharing profits have been upheld as a corporate business practice. In general, the restrictions on plans are that the bonuses awarded must be reasonable in relation to services performed.

The nature of the contingent incentive compensation portion of a stock option plan and a bonus plan are the same; the purchase of stock

---

[2] *Accounting for Stock Options,* 1960, p. 23.

for cash by employees does not change the essential characteristics of contingent consideration for services. The final amount of one depends on the price of option stock and the final amount of the other depends on earnings. That is, the award is not fixed but is specified in terms of later events.

The similarities of bonus and stock option plans are underlined by the terms of some option plans that make the exercise of options contingent on the prosperity of the corporation. Exercise of an option may be permitted only if annual earnings reach a designated amount or increase a designated percent over base period earnings.

Contingent stock plans. Some variations of deferred compensation plans involve awards of contingent stock, for example, "phantom" stock, "shadow" stock, and share or basic units. Those plans have one common characteristic—a corporation grants an award to an employee in terms of shares of the employer's stock; the shares of stock are not distributable but are used to measure compensation that is to be distributed later. The amount distributed is usually determined by a later market price of the stock or by dividends paid on equivalent shares of stock after the date of award. In fact, stockholders have challenged phantom stock plans of some corporations because the final amount of compensation was not fixed and determinable at the date of award.

The distribution to an employee under a phantom stock plan may be in the form of cash or securities, but the significant point is that the amount of compensation is contingent on events unknown at the date of award. Phantom stock plans are similar to stock option plans in that respect because the final amount distributable for stock options exercised is also contingent on later events. But present accounting for the two types of plans is completely unlike. Amounts distributed under phantom stock plans are recorded as compensation expense for services received. Apparently, receiving the option price as cash consideration for stock issued on the exercise of stock options means that ignoring the rest of the consideration is permissible.

Reasonable Compensation. The granting of a stock option commits a corporation to potential compensation for future services of employees. In effect, an employee agrees to perform services for an undesignated amount of compensation and the corporation agrees to deliver securities of undesignated value for a specified amount of cash. Even though the value of services of an employee estimated independently at various dates is not necessarily equal to the fair value of the securities issued less the option prices, which is the consideration distributed to the employee, the relationship of the two must be reasonable.

Arthur H. Dean commented on the legal aspects of consideration for stock options.

> When the directors enter into a contract which in substance will result in a gift of corporate assets because of the lack of a fair relationship between the value of the consideration to be given by the other party and the value of the consideration being given by the corporation, the contract may be held unenforceable by the courts, or if enforceable, the directors may be held liable for waste of corporate assets in making it. Where the contract has to do with employment and is executory in character, it will generally be held unenforceable.[3]

He also discussed the principles of several court cases on consideration for stock options and stated

> . . . the board of directors must be in a position to sustain the burden of proof that in granting a stock option to a particular employee, such option when added to the recipient's cash salary, pension rights, and rights under deferred profit-sharing plans, if any, does not result in the payment to such employee of an amount in excess of the true value of his services over a particular period.[4]

The reasonableness of compensation under stock option plans has been questioned in many stockholders' suits but

> . . . even though an option may represent large potential profits, the courts have shown no inclination to regard the highest potential profit as equivalent to fixed monetary compensation and have not been disposed to strike down this form of compensation for "unreasonableness" merely because profits are greater than the fixed salary which might otherwise have been paid.[23]
>
> [23] "If the option was perfectly valid when given it would be difficult for this court to fix a precise market value which the stock might attain within the definite term as an ultimate limit and constitute the exact boundary line between a valid and an invalid exercise of such option. The advance in value of the shares was clearly the hope and expectation of all the parties. . . ." Wyles v. Campbell, 77 F. Supp. 343, 350 (D. Del. 1948). . . .[5]

---

[3] "Employee Stock Options," *Harvard Law Review*, June 1953, p. 1422, Copyright 1953 by The Harvard Law Review Association.

[4] *Ibid.*, p. 1423.

[5] George Thomas Washington and V. Henry Rothschild, 2nd., *Compensating the Corporate Executive*, Volume II, © 1962 (New York: Ronald Press Company), p. 574.

Some states have enacted legislation

> ... providing that except for fraud, the judgment of the board of directors of a company which has granted an option shall be deemed conclusive as to the consideration for the option and its sufficiency. [See Note]
>
> This form of statute does not wholly eliminate the requirement of consideration. If consideration exists, the statute seeks to apply to the option the same law relating to the sufficiency of the consideration as has long applied to shares of stock issued in return for services. When there is consideration in one form or another at the time the option is granted, the statute is intended to preclude the court from substituting its judgment for that of the board of directors as to whether the services were at least equal in value to the value of the option. An option to an executive can provide incentive only if it may involve substantial profit; and if such profit is subject to review at a subsequent time, perhaps years later and with hindsight applied to the situation as it existed at the time the option was granted, the option may lose much of its function.[6]

All of the legal requirements for reasonable compensation and the incentive nature of stock options lead to the conclusion that for accounting purposes the consideration received (services plus cash) may be presumed to equal the consideration given—the fair value of the stock issued.

Fair Value of Stock Issued. A fair value of stock issued is determinable, and the preceding analysis shows that the difference between the fair value and the option price of the stock should measure the services received as part of the consideration for the stock issued. That same amount is the corporate cost of compensation for services. The fair value of stock issued for stock options should be determined at the date an optionee exercises his privilege of purchase. That is the date on which the equity transaction occurs—the corporation distributes consideration to an optionee and increases stockholders' equity. The fair value of stock at other dates is related to the transaction, but the

---

[6] George Thomas Washington and V. Henry Rothschild, 2nd., *Compensating the Corporate Executive*, Volume II, pp. 578–579.

Note: In Gallin v. National City Bank of N.Y., 152 Misc. 679, 704, 273 N.Y. Supp. 87, 115 (Sup. Ct. 1934) "Judge Dore added: 'The rule is established that directors of a corporation acting as a body in good faith have a right to fix compensation of executive officers for services rendered to the corporation, and that ordinarily their decision as to the amount of compensation is final except where the circumstances show oppression, fraud, abuse, bad faith or other breach of trust. . . .'" (*Ibid.*, p. 892.)

amount of the consideration that the corporation distributes is uncertain until the option is exercised.

Alternative values. Neither the date an option is granted nor the date an option is first exercisable fixes the terms or occurrence of the transaction of issuing shares of stock. A corporation assumes a commitment at the date it grants an option and the corporation can no longer alter the commitment at its discretion. An optionee obtains at the exercisable date the right to decide later if and when it may be to his advantage to purchase shares of stock to obtain additional compensation. Until exercised, a stock option is comparable in some respects with other sales commitments or agreements of sale. Thus the sale of stock occurs at the date a stock option is exercised and services of employees contributed before that date are similar to deposits on contracts of sale. However, a cash deposit is a fixed amount; in contrast, the amount to be assigned to services received can be estimated as the services are performed but is not final until later. The nature of the transaction is not changed because the commitment of the corporation may ultimately entail issuing equity securities.

The weakness of using the price of stock at grant date to measure the consideration received for stock issued under an option is clear if the option price equals the market price at that date, a common provision. Then the value of services received and the cost of compensation would be zero. The only possible argument is that the corporation incurs no cost because it disburses no funds. That argument would trap a corporation into an attempt to defend issuing its stock at less than fair value and an assertion that services of employees were something other than consideration for stock issued.

Measuring the consideration for stock issued under options on the entitlement date was supported in the original *ARB 37* by the following comparison of issuing stock under options to that under a profitsharing bonus:

> Customarily, compensation is due upon performance of a service agreed upon. If compensation is paid in cash, the work is usually first performed for a stipulated period. The charge accrues during the period and payment falls due at the end of the period. In the case of compensation paid in stock as a bonus at the end of a period, the amount of the compensation is not definitely determined until the end of the period. In such cases, the amount of the compensation would be the fair value of the bonus shares at the end of the period, although there might be a recording of estimated accrual during the period. (Par. 4)

Daniel L. Sweeney stated in his criticism of the concept advocated in the bulletin:

> The most obvious flaw in the above argument is in relating the issuance of bonus stock—which *must* be valued at the date of issue—to the issuance of stock under a stock option. The action is the same in both instances; but in the case of the bonus stock, the compensation bargain is for bonus stock as the medium for effecting payment, so the value of the stock must be equal to the value of the services; while in the case of the stock option, the option itself is the medium for effecting compensation and is the unit which reflects the service cost involved.[7]

His contention that the bonus and option are not alike and the value of the stock issued should not be measured the same overlooks that the option is not transferable—the employee realizes nothing until he exercises his privilege to purchase stock and the corporation satisfies its liability by issuing shares of stock.

Consideration received by employees. The procedure recommended in this study for a corporation to recognize as services received the fair value of the consideration distributed less the option price of the stock issued is not based on the argument that the corporate expense should equal the consideration received by an employee. A corporation anticipates that an optionee will realize as a minimum the difference between the market price of the stock on the first disposable date and the option price, less any tax effects. The price of the stock is expected to rise. If the price rises, the difference is greater on the first disposable date than on the date the option is exercised. Thus the consideration that the corporation distributes is less than the amount the employee receives. Price increases or price decreases after the first disposable date are unrelated to the employers' consideration for services, and the amount an employee realizes depends on the personal investment decisions of each optionee.

Market value of stock. The fair value of stock issued at the date an option is exercised should represent a reasonable computation based on market prices of similar quantities of the stock which is discussed in Chapter 8. A fair value may be the average of market prices over a reasonable period to eliminate freakish fluctuations or may be the current market price adjusted to eliminate the effects of isolated events

---

[7] *Accounting for Stock Options*, 1960, pp. 114-115.

or a temporary trend of trading. The number of shares issued for stock options is rarely large in relation to shares traded by the public and the current market price of stock need not be adjusted for blockage.

Dilution of Stockholders' Interests. The exercise of stock options is often acknowledged to dilute the interests of stockholders. For example,

> Perhaps the most serious complaint against stock option plans is that their cost is nearly invisible to shareholders. Books can be balanced without showing any expense on the financial statements, since corporate assets are not diminished. Yet there is no magical way of putting money into one pocket without taking it from another. Stock options are actually taken out of the shareholders' pockets by diluting their participation in control and equity.[8]

A part of the interests of existing stockholders in corporate resources and future earnings is transferred to optionees; the amount transferred is a reduction of retained earnings and is measured by the difference between the total consideration and cash received.

In theory, the market price of one outstanding share of stock declines because the cash consideration from an optionee for an additional share of stock does not equal the current market price; the remainder of the consideration for the stock is services of the optionee which is compensation expense. The reduction in the price of stock is not attributable to a cash consideration which is less than the fair value of the stock but is attributable to compensation expense which reduces net income. In practice, a price reduction is often not evident because (1) the compensation expense for services of optionees (and also the benefits derived) have an impact on earnings of several periods, (2) the number of shares ordinarily issued for options is small in relation to the number of shares of stock outstanding, and (3) other factors also influence the market price of the stock.

A frequent statement is that the dilution of stockholders' equity resulting from issuing additional shares on the exercise of stock options should be recognized as compensation costs. That statement is probably a shortcut of the facts involved in the transaction: the fair value of stock issued measures the consideration distributed and it also measures the consideration received; the difference between the total

---

[8] Alfred F. Conard, "Financial Problems of the Business Enterprise—Getting the Money Out," *University of Illinois Law Forum*, Fall 1954, p. 456.

and cash consideration received represents compensation for services which reduces the retained earnings component of stockholders' equity as an expense of operations.

The dilution of stockholders' equity is sometimes discussed in terms of an opportunity cost to the corporation—the difference between the price at which the stock could have been sold and the option price of the stock.[9] Discussions in those terms introduce irrelevant conditions; the accounting is not a matter of what would have happened if events were different. Rather, the accounting should recognize what did happen; the determination of total consideration received for stock issued under options cannot ignore that a part of it is services of optionees.

Recognizing Compensation for Services. A frequent objection to recognizing as compensation the difference between the option price and the fair value of stock issued is that the amounts may be large, thus reducing net income significantly. Regardless of the amounts involved, the financial statements should show the consideration for services as compensation to present the results of operations adequately. The directors of a corporation are responsible for obtaining services of a value approximately equal to the consideration distributed for those services.

An employee receives the opportunity to limit his risks—until he exercises an option he may invest only his services. A corporation relinquishes its right to control or limit its risks except by the terms of the option agreement and the number of shares subject to option. Those arrangements are intended to serve as a greater incentive to optionees. Most employee stock option plans provide that an employee may not within a designated period dispose of stock acquired under options without a penalty. Therefore, an employee cannot limit his risks after he exercises a stock option except that his services indirectly affect the prices of the stock during the holding period. Measuring the corporation's consideration for services (compensation) at the date an

---

[9] As examples, E. R. Dillavou suggested that as the first of six reasons to measure the value of an option by the value of the stock at the date the option is exercised (*The Accounting Review*, July 1945, pp. 320-326), and Dwight R. Ladd stated that "the cost of options must be imputed in terms of the opportunities the corporation loses by entering into and completing the option arrangement" (*Contemporary Corporate Accounting and the Public*, 1963, p. 134).

option is exercised prorates to both parties the risks from the date an option is granted.

Compensation period. An employee agrees that in return for a stock option he will perform services for a corporation from the date the stock option is granted to at least the date he may exercise the option. The service period usually varies from that minimum and may be set by an employment contract; employee services are often related to the limitations on disposing of the option stock acquired. Corporations often prohibit dispositions during the holding period that is required for favorable tax treatment, and many option plans now adopted provide that an optionee must hold for at least three years the stock acquired by exercising an option. A few corporations extend the holding period and provide that an employee may not sell stock purchased under options until he terminates his employment by the corporation. Restrictions on disposition mean that an optionee defers the realization in cash of his compensation for services.

A corporation usually grants an option with the intention of obtaining services from date of grant to the first permissible disposition date, and the optionee and corporation in effect agree to a minimum period of services by the terms of the option. The period from date of grant of the option to the earliest disposal date after the first permissible exercise date represents the shortest period the employee must perform services to obtain benefits. That basis is appropriate for allocating corporate expenses because the corporation contemplates that the optionee will perform services during that period in exchange for the rights conferred by the option.

The first date of permissible disposition of stock acquired under options varies because the required holding period invariably runs from date of exercise. Since an employee is often permitted to exercise his option over an extended period, perhaps as much as five years after date of grant of a qualified option and longer of a nonqualified option, the first permissible disposition date is known only after the option is exercised. Revising the allocation period each time an option is exercised would be impracticable in accounting for compensation for services. The accrual periods in a single corporation might then range from three years to eight years or more for services under different options. Since an optionee, not the corporation, controls extending the period beyond the minimum, adjusting the compensation period for delayed exercise is unnecessary.

The compensation related to a stock option granted as a part of a formal employment contract should be allocated over the initial term of the contract. Extending the allocation to the first permissible disposition date may be advisable if the contract provides for renewal to that date.

The recommended allocation period does not necessarily match the expenses with benefits because the benefits of the services of optionees may extend beyond the allocation period. Actually, the allocation period fits with the performance period the same as cash salary payments. Corporate benefits may not be restricted to the periods in which the services are performed for any type of consideration. A summary on the assumptions of benefits of services was:

> The traditional accounting for employee services follows the assumptions that the benefits from such services are consumed in the period when the services are rendered. This assumption may be valid in some cases and not in others. The services represented by the stock option are no different from services paid for with cash. The author is not prepared to offer an alternative to accounting for employee services generally. Therefore, by default, he concludes that benefits derived from employee services represented by stock option plans may be regarded as consumed in the same period in which the services were invested.[10]

Estimated compensation. The nature of stock options makes the cost of services of optionees indefinite at the time the options are granted. Unestimable and indefinite are not parallel. Both the corporation and the optionee estimate potential compensation before reaching an understanding, even though the estimate may be informal. Those estimates, the same as other estimates, may later be found incorrect. That does not refute that the corporation estimates its consideration for services, and corporate management would be irresponsible without that procedure. Therefore, at the time a corporation grants stock options it should estimate the fair value of the stock at the date the options are exercisable and account for the difference between that estimate and the option price as the estimated compensation for services of optionees.

Accounting for estimated compensation produces more informative financial statements even though the estimates are clearly subject to

---

[10] R. E. Blaine, "Accounting for Employee Stock Option Contracts," *The Canadian Chartered Accountant,* January 1967, p. 71.

later adjustment. Also, stockholders voting on proposed option plans should be furnished estimates of the total compensation involved instead of merely the number of shares of stock to be optioned. One company official expressed the need this way:

> Monetary values represent the universal language of business. In determining the profitability of an enterprise, the magnitude of an expansion program, or the reasonableness of the president's salary, the first question asked generally concerns the amount of money involved.
>
> When it comes to stock options, however, neither industry nor the accounting profession has accepted the responsibility of reporting to stockholders any economic value. How, therefore, can a stockholder begin to judge whether or not a proposed option plan is reasonable?
>
> . . . .
>
> Furthermore, he is never given any accounting for the value of these options at the time they are issued, when they become exercisable, or after they are exercised.[11]

He argued further that the values of options should be established at the date they are granted and recognized as compensation for services. One of his comments on the results applies to estimating consideration as recommended in this study.

> Critics may argue that this leaves too much room for the exercise of judgment, but I would much prefer to be in the position of defending my judgment on a particular issue than to be guilty of not applying judgment at all.[12]

The estimated consideration is unlikely to equal the difference between the option price and fair value of the stock at the date an option is exercised. Minor variations, either more or less, may be ignored because the fair value of the stock is itself an estimate. A corporation should recognize other than minor variations from the estimate in accounting for the consideration received for the stock issued. Ordinarily, the revised compensation may be recognized in the remaining period of service, and compensation expense of prior periods need not be revised.

---

[11] Edwin D. Campbell, "Stock Options Should Be Valued," *Harvard Business Review*, July-August 1961, p. 52.

[12] *Ibid.*, p. 57.

Since the recognized consideration for services represents compensation for a period of years, theoretically, compensation for each period should be the present value of a portion of the total expense. But the customary service period now involved in most option plans is three to five years, with a maximum of eight years for qualified plans. In addition, the consideration for services is distributed to the optionee before the entire service period has expired. In fact, some stock options are exercised shortly after they are granted but the service period extends for three more years. The combinations of advance and postponed distributions of consideration for services should affect a computation of present value. Those offsetting effects on the results of operations for each period do not warrant the additional computations of present values, and allocating the consideration on a time basis should be satisfactory.[13]

Services before exercise of option. The services performed by an optionee are not a contribution to stockholders' equity before he exercises his stock option. An optionee is entitled to become a stockholder under certain conditions. But until shares of stock are issued to him his contribution of services is not part of stockholders' equity and his services convey none of the rights and obligations of a stockholder. The granting corporation is the only party that assumes a future obligation. The corporation should record periodically an estimated liability for services of an optionee or, alternatively, record the entire estimated compensation as a liability with a corresponding deferred charge at the date options are granted. The corporation has agreed to settle the liability for services by later issuing stock at the option price.

---

[13] Deferred compensation plans involve a similar problem of recognizing an obligation to be settled at a later date. Henry R. Jaenicke stated that in measuring the amount of compensation in deferred stock plans "Theoretically, it should be possible to value the award on the basis of the present value of the share-units awarded in any particular year, discounted from date of issue to date of grant. Assumptions as to the value of the shares at date of issue, the appropriate interest rate to be used, and expected increases in the deferred awards resulting from crediting the employee's account for dividends declared on the phantom shares, would probably prevent any solution along these lines from obtaining any widespread acceptance. Hence, at a possible sacrifice of relevance for objectivity, the measurement of the compensation based on the full fair market value of the stock is probably justified." "Accounting for Restricted Stock Plans and Deferred Stock Plans," *The Accounting Review,* January 1970, p. 125.

The liability for services of employees to be satisfied by issuing option stock should be classified as contingent equity financing. The corporation has assumed an obligation, but the outcome depends on actions of the optionee. The election to invest funds and increase equity of the corporation is discretionary with the optionee.

A part of the consideration for services measured and recognized as an addition to stockholders' equity at the date of exercise of an option satisfies the option liability recorded before that date. The remainder of the consideration for services is a deferred charge to operations during the previously determined allocation period.

Adjusting compensation expenses. The amount of compensation and its allocation period may require adjustment for reasons other than a difference between the estimated consideration for services and the excess of the fair value over option price of the stock at date of exercise. For example, employment of an optionee may be terminated before the end of the selected allocation period. If so, unamortized deferred compensation should be written off as an expense of the period of termination. Since the corporation will not receive services in the remainder of the projected employment period, the remaining deferred compensation should be viewed and classified as an expense of termination of employment.

Disqualifying dispositions of option stock may also affect unamortized deferred compensation. If an employee disposes of stock acquired under an option before holding it the time required for beneficial tax treatment, the corporation is allowed a tax deduction equal to the difference between the option price and the fair value of the stock at date of exercise. The deduction is allowed in the year of the disqualifying disposition, but the tax effects should be allocated to corporate net income in the same periods as the compensation costs.

Terminated options. If an optionee never exercises his privilege to purchase stock and his option lapses, a corporation should apply the recorded liability for services of the optionee to reduce current compensation expenses. In effect, the corporation obtained services of an employee without distributing consideration to him. Identifying those events that influence the employee's decision not to exercise an option and forego compensation is usually impossible. An allocation to prior periods would be impracticable even though the reduction of the liability may relate in part to compensation of prior periods. The canceled liability is a change in accounting estimate, and a corporation may therefore write off the liability in the period that the option terminates.

Convertible Securities

Individual issues of convertible securities are all alike in some characteristics but vary significantly in other attributes. Each convertible security provides that it may be exchanged for another security that conveys different rights, privileges, restrictions, and limitations. Nearly all convertible securities carry senior, prior rights—either those of debt obligations or preferred stock—plus a privilege to convert into common stock of the same corporation.[14] Although other terms of conversion exist, such as debt convertible into other debt securities or preferred stock, the accounting illustrated in this section is discussed in terms of the predominating conversion of senior securities into common stock of the same corporation.

Many of the variations between individual issues are in the detailed provisions of the convertible securities, such as senior rights, conversion period, and changes in the conversion privileges at specified intervals. The basic characteristics of convertible securities remain the same despite the variations except that some are debt and others are senior equity securities.

Comparison of Convertible Debt and Equity Securities. Convertible debt securities and convertible senior equity securities have many likenesses. The securities carry the right to obtain equity interests of common stockholders in exchange for relinquishing the prior rights conveyed by a senior security. Holders who exchange their securities indicate their willingness to contribute to the common stockholders' interests, their acceptance of greater risk, and their desire to obtain a larger return on their investments to replace their claims or senior equity interests.

The conversion privilege is an integral provision of the security itself and the right may not be transferred or assigned separately. Converting may not be an economic advantage to a holder at the date the senior securities are issued. The future value of the right is at best an estimate.

---

[14] Securities of some corporations are convertible into common stock of the parent of the corporation.

However, the right to convert is one of the many factors that enter into determining both the selling price of an issue of convertible securities and the specified rate of return on the security.

Uncertainties. The provisions of conversion privileges mean that an issuing corporation as well as the holders of its convertible securities face uncertain results. Although conversions may be permitted only during designated periods on varying terms, the holder of a convertible security generally controls whether or not it is exchanged for common stock. An issuing corporation is able to retain no more than limited control over conversions through redemption provisions and financial policies that influence the market price of its common stock.

Most convertible securities specify that the issuing corporation may call the security for redemption under designated conditions and terms. Therefore, a corporation may call a security before the conversion privilege is advantageous to eliminate the exchange right or may call the security when the conversion privilege is valuable to force an exchange. Corporations sometimes issue convertible securities with an ultimate goal of increasing the common stock equity and plan to achieve that goal through exchanging the securities and eliminating the senior rights without redeeming the securities. The plan may be for the exchange to occur before a certain date, but the timing is always uncertain because earnings expectations are often off schedule. Since the time of the exchange, if any, is unknown and the number of common shares issued often depends on the date that the exchange occurs, a corporation's commitment to deliver common stock in exchange for outstanding senior securities is not fixed.

Even if a corporation wishes to force conversion, the conditions that make that step advisable are not predictable far ahead with certainty. Various corporate financial policies that determine sources of financing, financing expenses, and dividend distributions influence the market price of the common stock that in turn influences the conversion of senior securities.

The original purchaser of a convertible security accepts an uncertain return because the conversion privilege he obtains may or may not be a future benefit. The conversion price is usually higher than the market price of the common stock at the date a convertible security is issued. A holder of a convertible security is assured that his senior rights will continue, but the potential additional return is unknown at the time the corporation issues the security. Purchasers after the original issue also accept an uncertain return although the uncertainties diminish as the conversion period becomes shorter.

Reduction of stockholders' interests. A consequence of issuing convertible senior securities is that later the proportionate interests of existing common stockholders may be reduced. Conversion increases the outstanding shares of common stock and transfers a part of the interests of existing common stockholders to new common stockholders. Funds invested originally in a convertible security are less than the fair value of the common stock acquired in exchange because holders do not exercise their conversion privileges unless the expected return on the common stock that may be acquired is greater than the return on the senior security. Therefore the exchange of a convertible security reduces the value of an outstanding share of common stock. A corporation accepts the potential dilution of the value of the interests of common stockholders as a part of the financing arrangement for convertible debt or senior equity securities. The purchaser of a convertible security obtains a claim to an uncertain additional return on his investment. The amount of the return and actual dilution of the interests of other stockholders depend on conditions prevailing at the time of conversion.

Convertible debt and equity securities differ. All convertible securities are alike in the respects described but they also differ. They differ not because of the conversion privilege but because of differences between debt and equity securities.

Accounting problems of both convertible debt and convertible equity securities involve the consideration received for common stock issued on conversion and a difference between that consideration and the carrying amount of the securities converted. The consideration received for the common stock issued is measured most reasonably by the fair value of the common stock at the date it is issued, the same as for other transactions that furnish corporate financing and later increase outstanding equity securities. Since debt securities and preferred stock convey different senior rights and limitations, the effects of converting each type of security are considered separately.

Outstanding Convertible Debt. The provisions of convertible debt securities obligate the corporation to repay the principal amount but also allow the exchange of outstanding securities for equity interests of a common stockholder in lieu of repayment. Therefore, a convertible debt security is a source of contingent equity financing. Chapter 7 stated that a corporation should classify the consideration received for convertible debt in that category along with warrants, stock options, and similar obligations, but each type of security should be shown separately. Convertible debt securities are similar to other debt in provisions for interest payments, repayment, and redemption, and the premium or discount determined by the proceeds received should be accounted for the same as for other debt; that is, the securities should be shown at face amount, less discount or plus premium.

Distinctive classification. A classification as contingent equity financing distinguishes convertible debt from other long-term debt that must be satisfied by the payment of cash and groups together all contingent equity financing. Until converted, a convertible debt security is a debt obligation, and no part of the proceeds of sale is a contribution to equity of the corporation. The contingent equity classification shows clearly its status as potential equity as well as an existing obligation; the description should disclose the number of additional shares of stock that may be issued in exchange. Attempts to classify convertible debt entirely as a debt or as an equity security fail because the security is unique and never wholly fits either category.

Allocation for conversion privilege. Conversion privileges of debt securities are often compared with warrants sold with debentures as a unit, and the conclusions are that both are calls on equity securities with the same final effects on stockholders' equity. Thus the accounting should be the same. If that conclusion is discussed in terms of present accounting for detachable stock purchase warrants—that is, the proceeds of sale of warrants are allocated to additional capital—the contention is that a part of the proceeds of sale of convertible debt should similarly be allocated to additional capital. However, accounting for warrants was discussed earlier in this chapter, and the analysis led to the recommendation to recognize the contingent equity characteristics of warrants until exercised and to recognize the related financing costs as a part of the consideration received for stock issued on exercise of warrants. Classifying the face amount of convertible debt as contingent equity financing puts the accounting for proceeds of sale of convertible debt and debt issued with stock purchase warrants on the same basis.

Obviously, a debtor corporation could allocate some portion of the proceeds of sales of convertible debentures to the conversion privilege and show that amount as a separate item of contingent equity financing.

But that presentation would be confusing and perhaps also misleading because the corporate liability for outstanding debt would be understated. The corporate obligation cannot be split to settle separately a part relating to debt and a part relating to the conversion privilege. Both are settled simultaneously by redemption, conversion, or repayment. The carrying amount of a debt obligation settled by conversion to common stock becomes a part of the contributions to equity.

Interest expense. Interest accrued on outstanding convertible debt according to the terms of the security should be a financing expense included in net income. The interest rate may be affected by the conversion privilege the same as other factors affect the stated rate. However, the accounting should recognize the specified terms of the debt not other assumed terms, such as interest on nonconvertible debt. For example, loans placed privately normally provide for a higher rate of interest than those sold publicly, but accountants do not propose to assume that private loans were obtained publicly and therefore record the interest expense as it would have been under different conditions.

Redemption of convertible debt. Accounting for convertible debt securities redeemed or paid at maturity should be the same as for other debt securities and involves no changes in outstanding equity securities. Accounting for conversion of a debt security into common stock affects stockholders' equity directly.

Conversion of Debt Securities. Accounting for the conversion of debt securities depends on the nature of the related financing and equity transactions. A corporation that issues convertible debt securities receives funds and assumes an obligation not only to repay the principal amount and to pay interest periodically but also to deliver equity securities of a then unknown value instead of repayment if the holder elects. A corporation satisfies its outstanding debt obligation by distributing shares of common stock to a holder of a debt security who exercises his privilege to convert. The consideration distributed to a debt holder to satisfy his claim should be measured by the fair value of the common stock delivered at the date of conversion; that amount similarly reflects the consideration received by the corporation for the additional stock issued. If the measure of the consideration received for the stock were the fair value of the convertible security, the result would be the same. Since a convertible debt security carries rights to obtain an interest in existing common stockholders' equity, the price of the convertible issue fluctuates with the market price of the common stock if conversion is feasible.

A debt security is converted to common stock only if the fair value of the stock is greater than the face amount of the debt.[15] The difference between the consideration distributed measured by the fair value of the stock issued and the face amount of the debt securities converted (adjusted for unamortized premium or discount) measures the financing expenses that a corporation incurs. The corporation assumed at issue date an uncertain obligation for financing expenses in addition to the stated interest under the provisions of a convertible debt security. Conversion reduces the book amount of the existing interests of common stockholders because the transaction involves a financing expense included in net income, but that amount plus the carrying amount of the debt is a contribution to equity for the additional common stock issued.

The recommended recognition of financing expenses involved in convertible debt is similar to accounting for additional interest payable on debt securities if corporate earnings reach a specified level. Each security involves contingent additional consideration for the use of creditors' funds.

The committee on accounting concepts and standards of the American Accounting Association recommended in its 1957 Statement that the expense involved in the conversion of debt be recognized in the period of conversion.

> Any difference between the amortized amount of a liability as reflected in the accounts and the amount of assets released or equities created should be recognized as a gain or loss in the period of liquidation. When a liability is discharged by conversion to a stock equity, the market value of the liability is ideally the measure of the new equity created. However, if a reliable market price for the liability is not available, the market value of the stock issued may be used.

Obviously a difference between the market price of a convertible debt security and the market price of the shares issued in exchange would be negligible because a disparity would be momentary. Therefore, the results of the recommendation to measure the market value of the lia-

---

[15] An exception may be that privately held debt is converted to common stock to permit a corporation to borrow additional funds.

bility are equivalent to recognizing the fair value of the stock issued as recommended in this study.

Conversion privilege and inflation risks. One objection which will surely be aimed at the recommended procedure is that the financing expenses may be large and the expenses recognized on conversion will increase as the price of a common stock rises. The nature and purpose of the conversion privilege no doubt explain that result. Built into a coupon rate on a debt security is compensation not only for the use of funds and the credit risks assumed but also for the risks of inflation. Since changes in the return on money are less predictable during periods of inflation, compensation through the fixed yield on a security is unattractive to investors. A conversion privilege is more satisfactory to offset the effects of unstable prices and entitles the security holder to a direct return for his risks of inflation. Thus the financing expenses for convertible debt securities rise or fall with the fair value of the common stock.

Conversions and redemptions. The procedures recommended in this study to account for expenses on conversion of debt may be compared with accounting for the redemption of a debenture. The potential expense involved in conversion is one factor determining other variables of a debt security at the time of issuance—the selling price and coupon interest rate. Similarly, the potential expense of a redemption provision is a factor in setting the selling price of a debt security. The final amount and period of the related expense for either the redemption or conversion features may be anticipated but is uncertain. If a debenture is called for redemption at a premium, a corporation now recognizes the redemption premium as a financing expense of that period—perhaps as an extraordinary item depending on the amount of the premium paid. The potential redemption premium is not accounted for periodically in advance of call.

In theory, a premium paid is not an expense of the period of redemption; rather, the amount should be allocated to the entire period that the bonds are outstanding. That procedure is impracticable, however, because any method of allocation selected in advance is so arbitrary that the results may be meaningless. Neither should a corporation anticipate the conversion of a debt security and attempt to recognize additional financing expenses periodically. Both redemptions and conversions result in financing expenses that are uncertain until the transactions occur.

Warrants Attached to Debentures. Some corporations issue debentures as a unit with nondetachable stock purchase warrants. A provision that the warrants may be exercised only by surrendering debentures equal to the purchase price of the privilege stock makes the financial terms of the unit equivalent to those of a convertible debenture. The debt obligation may be satisfied by issuing stock on the exercise of the warrants the same as on the exercise of a conversion privilege. The stock purchase warrants and the conversion privilege are both integral parts of the debt financing arrangements. The consideration for the additional stock issued under both arrangements should be measured by the fair value of the stock, and the debt financing costs should be measured by the difference between the fair value of the stock distributed and the consideration received at the time of the sale of the debenture or the unit.

A difference between convertible debentures and debentures with stock purchase warrants attached is that one arrangement involves a single security and the other two securities, but the accounting should be essentially the same. Both outstanding stock purchase warrants and the debentures to which they are attached should be classified as contingent equity financing. Outstanding warrants may be shown separately at no carrying amount or may be shown as part of the description of the debentures. Either method discloses the existing obligation and the contingent equity interest.

Results of Recommendations. The accounting recommended for debt converted to common stock and separable debt and nonmarketable warrants (warrant section, pages 157 to 169) results in similar expenses included in net income but the timing of the expenses differs. The expenses related to convertible debt are included in operations for the period of conversion, and those related to units of debt and nonmarketable warrants are included in operations for the periods the warrants are outstanding. The warrants are a separate outstanding security; they may be exercised and the related debt securities may remain outstanding. In contrast, the liability for convertible debt is extinguished at the date it is converted.

Total stockholders' equity is the same under the recommended procedures and the current practice of recording the carrying amount of debt as an addition to equity at the date the securities are converted. But current practice is undesirable because it overstates net income and retained earnings by omitting financing expenses and understates contributions by stockholders by omitting part of the consideration received for stock issued. Unless the results of financing with convertible securities are recorded and displayed adequately, the periodic results of operations are uninformative and designated sources of stockholders' equity lose meaning.

Conversion of Preferred Stock. A convertible preferred stock is distinguished from a convertible debenture because it is an equity security forming a senior part of stockholders' equity. The proceeds of sales of convertible preferred stock should be classified as equity contributed for that class of security. A conversion of preferred stock into common stock reduces the shares of one class of equity securities and increases another, both of which are components of stockholders' equity.

The conversion privilege of preferred stock is one of the factors determining the dividend rate and the proceeds of its sale. The privilege to convert is stipulated by the terms of a preferred stock issue and the issuing corporation may not modify that right. Convertible preferred stock conveys both senior and residual rights of stockholders. The senior claim for dividends and preference in liquidation is augmented by a residual claim on retained earnings. The senior claim is satisfied by the periodic distribution of dividends on the preferred stock, and the residual claim is asserted by exercising the conversion privilege. The holder of convertible preferred stock controls the satisfaction of his residual claim by his election to convert or to retain his senior security.

Consideration for common stock. A preferred stockholder may elect to convert his interest into an interest of a common stockholder, and a corporation should recognize the fair value of the common stock issued as the consideration received for the stock. The amount represents the consideration that the corporation distributes to satisfy the senior interest and the residual claim. The fair value of the common stock issued in exchange for preferred stock is invariably greater than the contributions for the converted shares of preferred stock. The difference between those amounts should be a reduction of retained earnings.

A feature of convertible preferred stock is that the holders are offered an equity in earnings above the designated dividend rate. A conversion of the preferred stock transfers to the new common stockholders the benefits accumulated to that date as well as a potential equity in future earnings. Since the customary return in the form of dividends is not a reduction of net income, the reduction for the consideration involved in conversions of preferred stock should not be included in periodic results of operations.

Granted, total stockholders' equity is the same if the contributed preferred equity is transferred to contributed common equity which is the present practice. But present practice does not reduce retained earnings by the consideration distributed to the former preferred stockholders. Holders of outstanding preferred stock have elected to contribute to the corporation their earlier equity contributions and their claims on retained earnings in return for the interest of a common stockholder.

The accounting recommended in this study for the conversion of preferred stock to common stock fits with the frequent corporate objectives of either facilitating the sale of an issue (a "sweetener") or raising common equity capital indirectly.[16] A corporation accomplishes those objectives by offering an additional return to the holders of convertible preferred stock and should recognize the distribution of that amount as equity financing costs.

Comparison with redemption. The conversion of debt securities was compared earlier with the redemption of debt securities; the conversion of preferred stock may also be compared with the redemption of preferred stock. Anticipating the redemption of preferred stock and allocating a redemption premium to various periods is impracticable. The premium paid to redeem preferred stock is now often deducted from retained earnings, and that practice is defended in Chapter 11. Since the nature of the costs of redemption and conversion are the same, the same arguments apply to recognizing the consideration distributed on conversion as a reduction of retained earnings.

Acquisition of a Business

Accounting by the Purchase Method. Corporations often issue additional equity securities to acquire another business. The discussion in this section is limited to business combinations that are effected by issuing shares of stock, at least in part, and accounted for by the purchase method. It excludes those combinations effected entirely by distributing assets and by assuming liabilities and those accounted for by the pooling of interests method.

---

[16] Hussein H. Elsaid discussed the reasons for using convertible preferred stock in "The Function of Preferred Stock in the Corporate Financial Plan," *Financial Analysts Journal*, July-August 1969, pp. 112-117.

The general principles recommended in Chapter 8 should be applied in accounting for shares of stock issued to acquire another business. Thus the consideration received for the stock issued should be measured by the fair value of the stock unless the fair value of the assets received is more reasonably determinable. Since the acquired assets comprise a going concern, the fair value of the business acquired is ordinarily not determinable with the same objectivity as the fair value of the stock issued.

Measuring consideration received. A corporation estimates the fair value of a business that it plans to acquire. Then that value and the fair value of one share of stock determine the number of shares to be issued to acquire the assets of the business or its capital stock. The obligation of directors to obtain adequate consideration for stock issued means that a corporation may appropriately measure the consideration received for stock issued in a business combination by the fair value of the shares issued. The market price of stock at the date it is issued is the starting point for determining its fair value, but that price may be adjusted for various factors which are discussed in Chapter 8.

Present practices of measuring the total consideration received for stock issued to acquire a business conform to the recommendations in this study.

Accounting for consideration received. An acquiring corporation should recognize the acquisition of a business as an increase in stockholders' equity as of the date shares of stock are effectively issued and the assets received as consideration are transferred to the corporation. The consideration received should increase the equity contributed by stockholders. Recording the consideration as contributed equity applies to either preferred stock or common stock issued for a business. A corporation sometimes issues both preferred and common stock to acquire another business and the consideration received for each type of security should be measured by the fair value of that security. The recommended practice fits with recognizing the sources of equity for each class of stock and therefore differs from the present practice of designating a part of the total fair value of the stock issued as preferred and common stock and the remainder as additional capital.

The terms of some acquisitions require that a part of the total consideration to the transferor of the assets is to be distributed at later dates. An acquiring corporation should record as of the date of acquisition an obligation to distribute cash or debt securities later. The total consideration for the acquisition is resolved but part of the payments are postponed.

Accounting for the assets and liabilities making up the total consideration received for stock issued in a business combination is beyond the scope of this study. A major section of *APB Opinion 16*, "Business Combinations," concerns the problems of recording the acquisition of a business by the purchase method and *APB Opinion 17*, "Intangible Assets," provides accounting for goodwill and other intangible assets acquired in business combinations.

Delayed Determination. Some arrangements provide that a corporation acquiring another business may be obliged in specified circumstances to issue additional shares of stock after the date the combination is effected. The consideration received for stock issued may not be finally determined until several years after assets are transferred to the acquiring corporation. The types of arrangements and specified conditions are numerous but all are usually grouped as acquisitions involving contingent consideration.

The remainder of this section contains a discussion of accounting for stockholders' equity in the most common arrangements for contingent consideration. However, the number of arrangements for contingent consideration is limited because assuming a commitment to issue additional stock in the future to settle an earlier acquisition is impracticable unless the acquired business is closely held.

Contingent consideration. An acquiring corporation and a business to be acquired negotiate the number of shares of stock to be issued based on the estimated fair value of the assets to be transferred and the fair value of the stock to be issued. The parties may not agree that one or the other of the two measures is satisfactory because the fair values of the assets of the parties to the combination are uncertain. The uncertainties preclude a mutually satisfactory settlement at the date of acquisition, and the parties may delay final settlement pending later events.

If so, the acquired business or its owners transfer assets to the acquiring corporation as a contribution to equity; the acquiring corporation issues shares of stock evidencing the new interest in stockholders' equity. However, the acquisition is not completed at the date the assets are transferred. The carrying amount of the assets, the number of shares of stock issued for the contributed assets, or both are not final until the acquisition is resolved at the end of a designated contingency period. The consideration received does not represent contingent equity financing because the corporation receives a contribution to stockholders' equity and grants rights to new stockholders by issuing shares of stock. However, measures of the consideration received are contingent.

Arrangements for contingent consideration result from unresolved measures—either the fair value of the consideration received or the fair value of the stock issued for that consideration. Each measure and typical purposes for the arrangements are analyzed separately in this discussion.

Fair value of consideration unsettled. The fair value of the consideration received may not be determinable to the satisfaction of both parties negotiating a business combination. A transferor may contend that the fair value of his assets is greater than the market value of the shares of stock that a corporation is willing to issue. A contingent arrangement that relates the final number of shares of stock to be issued to later performance of the acquired assets may be an acceptable solution.

Corporate directors are obliged to issue stock whose fair value is about equal to the demonstrated fair value of the consideration received. However, they may agree to issue more shares of stock for the consideration and the number of shares is specified in terms of the future level of earnings of the acquired assets, usually with a proviso that

> earnings equal or exceed a specified amount for individual specified periods,
>
> cumulative earnings equal or exceed a specified amount for a specified period, or
>
> earnings increase at least equal to a specified rate during a specified period.[17]

Some arrangements are in terms of the earnings level of a specified segment of the acquired assets rather than entire operations. However, resolving the contingency is not tied to the earnings of the combined corporation because the fair value of the consideration received is the doubtful item. The parties agree that the later results may substantiate

---

[17] W. Robert Reum and Thomas A. Steele, III explained and illustrated types of contingent arrangements in "Contingent Payouts Cut Acquisition Risks," *Harvard Business Review*, March-April 1970, pp. 83-91.

a larger amount to be assigned as fair value of the assets that the transferor contributed earlier to corporate equity. The arrangement therefore specifies a maximum number of shares of stock to be distributed under certain conditions. The minimum number of shares of stock is determinable, and the acquiring corporation issues that number at the date the assets are transferred.

Recording additional consideration. Assets are contributed to the acquiring corporation, and the minimum amount to be recorded as consideration received is determinable and recorded at the date of acquisition. The acquiring corporation should record the stock issued at its current fair value. The final amount of the consideration received is resolved by later events, and the minimum may increase.

The maximum number of shares to be distributed contingently is set by the terms of the agreement, but the amount of consideration for the stock is open because the fair value of the common stock of the acquiring corporation at later dates is uncertain. If the terms of the contingent arrangement are satisfied and the acquiring corporation is required to issue additional shares of stock, the stock issued should be recorded at its fair value at the date issued.

In negotiating contingent arrangements, the parties usually consider that the fair value of the stock to be issued is expected to fluctuate and that the fair value at the date of settlement is uncertain. Thus the consideration is uncertain. The terms of arrangements also recognize that settlement of an acquisition is delayed for the length of the contingency period and that the transferor foregoes dividend distributions and other rights of stockholders to the extent that stock is issued after the assets are transferred. Part of a final settlement is therefore in effect a return for postponing that settlement.

An amount equal to the current fair value of stock that is recorded as contributed equity at the date of settlement should be allocated between the assets acquired as consideration and costs of financing. The amount recorded originally for the assets acquired should be increased by the fair value of the additional stock issued, discounted at an appropriate rate for the contingency period. The remainder of the fair value of the stock should be deducted from retained earnings as a cost of equity financing.

The recommendations in this study differ from the practices endorsed in *APB Opinion 16*. This section recommends that a part of the consideration for the additional stock issued be recognized as costs of equity financing rather than entirely as the value of assets acquired. The recommendations apply to arrangements contingent on the earnings of the acquired assets and exclude those contingent on earnings of the combined corporation.

Measure of consideration unsettled. Parties to a combination may not agree that the current market price of the stock of the acquiring corporation represents its fair value at the date the assets are transferred. The parties may agree on the approximate fair value of the assets acquired, but the acquiring corporation may contend that the current market price of its stock is below its fair value because the market price does not recognize the fair value of its assets. Thus the acquiring corporation is unwilling to issue stock with a total market value equal to the agreed fair value of the assets. The party transferring assets may contend that the fair value of the stock is no greater or may be less than its current market price. Therefore, the number of shares of stock issued on the basis of the current market price or a higher value would be inadequate, and the transferor is unwilling to accept the stock as a final settlement.

An alternative that may be satisfactory to both parties is to arrange that later results of operations will determine the final number of shares of stock issued for the acquired business. Later operations of the combined corporation may be evaluated in terms of net income in future periods or of the market price of the stock of the acquiring corporation. The values of the assets of the acquiring corporation affect significantly those combined results. The parties may be willing to assume that future results which equal or exceed expectations demonstrate that the earlier fair value of the stock of the acquiring corporation was equal to or greater than its market price and vice versa.

An arrangement for contingent consideration because the fair value of the measure of the consideration is uncertain usually specifies that the acquiring corporation is obliged to issue additional shares of stock in various circumstances. Although arrangements may be in several forms, issuing more shares of stock is commonly in terms of failing to meet a specified condition, often

> Dependent on level of earnings—
>> earnings of the combined corporation for specified periods equal or exceed a specified amount.
>
> Dependent on market price of stock of the acquiring corporation—
>> market price at a specified date equals or exceeds the market price of the stock at date of acquisition, or

market price at a specified date equals or exceeds a specified amount.

Sometimes an agreement specifies averaging market prices of the stock of the acquiring corporation for a period instead of specifying a price at a single date.

The arrangement in effect guarantees that the transferors of the acquired business receive a specified minimum consideration that conforms with the fair value of the acquired assets. The total number of shares of stock is tentative although some arrangements specify a maximum number of additional shares. The final settlement may vary with earnings or market price of the stock of the combined corporation. Otherwise, the number of shares issued originally satisfies the terms of the arrangement.

Arrangement illustrated. A typical arrangement for contingent consideration because the measure of the consideration is doubtful illustrates the factors involved. The assumed facts are:

Corporation A negotiates to acquire in May 19x1 the assets of Corporation B in exchange for shares of common stock of Corporation A.

The fair value of the net assets of Corporation B is about $6,000.

The market price of common stock of Corporation A in May 19x1 is $50 a share.

Corporation A argues that the fair value of its common stock in May 19x1 is $60 a share and that the later market price of the stock will demonstrate that value. Corporation B agrees to accept contingently in May 19x1 100 shares of common stock of Corporation A.

Corporation A agrees to issue additional shares of common stock to the stockholders of Corporation B in May 19x5 unless the market price of its stock is $70 or more at that date. The market value of $7,000 for 100 shares in May 19x5 discounted at the earnings rate of Corporation A, reduced by dividends distributed, is about equal to $6,000, the fair value of the acquired assets in May 19x1. If the market price of common stock of Corporation A is less than $70 a share in May 19x5, Corporation A will issue additional shares of stock so that the market value of the total shares issued to Corporation B will equal $7,000 in May 19x5.

Illustrations of a range of results in May 19x5 are:

Market Price of Corp. A Common Stock	Market Value of 100 Shares of Corp. A Common Stock	Additional Shares of Corp. A Common Stock Issued	Reason for Result
			Measure of $60 in 19x1 was:
$40	$4,000	75 ($3,000)	High
50	5,000	40 (2,000)	High
60	6,000	17 (1,000)	High
70	7,000	None	Fair
80	8,000	None	Low

As long as the market value of 100 shares of common stock of Corporation A equals $7,000 or more in May 19x5 the parties are satisfied that the fair value of the measure was at least $60 in May 19x1. Corporation A issues additional shares of stock to Corporation B to the extent that performance after the combination fails to support the measure of $60.

Recording stock issued. The fair value of the consideration received for stock is not in doubt in the illustrated contingent arrangement. Therefore, the assets acquired and consideration received for the stock issued at date of acquisition should be recorded at the agreed fair value of the assets—$6,000 in the example. The consideration received exceeds the current market value of the stock issued, which is permissible. But a corporation should record equity securities issued to acquire a business at not less than the current fair value of the stock issued to effect the combination.

The carrying amount of the assets remains the same whether or not the corporation issues additional stock at the end of the contingency period. If later results require the corporation to issue more shares of stock for the acquired assets, the shares are issued without recording consideration because the original measure of consideration for each share (assigned value of a share of stock) was excessive.

The fair value of the acquired assets is unchanged but the proportionate interests of the stockholders in the combined corporation do not represent the ratio between that value and the value of the acquiring corporation if the tentative measure at date of acquisition was incorrect. The stockholder interests are adjusted at the settlement date by issuing more shares of stock to recognize a fair measure of the consideration. The additional contribution to equity was recorded based on the best but a tentative measure at the date of acquisition.

An arrangement for contingent consideration specified in terms of the market price of the stock not declining is intended to substantiate the fair value of the stock at date of acquisition. That arrangement differs from the above illustration of an argument that fair value exceeds the market price of the stock. Thus, the consideration recorded originally should be the fair value of the stock issued at the date the assets are acquired. Additional shares issued because the market price of the stock declines should be recorded without consideration.

The recommendations in this section and the practices recognized in *APB Opinion 16* result in the same amounts recorded as stockholders' equity except that the Opinion does not approve the method to account for contingencies based on combined earnings.

Securities issued to escrow agent. Some corporations provide that a maximum number of shares of stock are issued for an acquired business and all or part of the securities are placed in escrow. The terms of the arrangements are usually the reverse of those that require the acquiring corporation to issue additional shares of stock. Therefore, the purposes of the arrangements and the tentative measure indicate the accounting for a later return of stock to the acquiring corporation.

Status during contingency period. At interim dates, a corporation can determine the number of shares of stock that would be issuable under contingent arrangements on the basis of the price of the stock and the other conditions existing on those dates. That status is preferably disclosed in a note explaining the outstanding shares of stock and contributions by stockholders. Although the arrangements involve contingencies, they are not contingent equity financing in the sense that equity is potential—the corporation has received consideration and has issued shares of stock. Only the final amount of consideration is contingent. The status of escrow agreements should also be disclosed in notes to financial statements.

Illustration of Recommended Accounting

A reduction of the proportionate interests of stockholders that occurs because outstanding equity securities are increased is shown more readily by the principles recommended in this study than by present procedures. Corporations now fail to recognize the entire compensation for services, all financing costs, and the effects on existing equity components of many transactions.

An illustration contrasts the results of recommended and present accounting for some customary transactions in typical circumstances—perhaps doubling the number of outstanding shares in ten years is more than normal. The facts and the transactions assumed are:

In the first year, a corporation sold 1,000,000 shares of $1 par value common stock for $5 a share.

In the fifth year, the corporation sold at par $6,000,000 face amount of 4½% debentures due in 20 years and convertible into common stock at $10 a share. The market price of the common stock was $9 a share on the date the debentures were sold.

In the seventh year, the corporation sold at par $5,000,000 face amount of 5% debentures due in 12 years with 300,000 detachable warrants to purchase common stock at $13 a share during the next five years. The common stock was then selling at $11 a share. The proceeds were allocated $303,000 to the warrants and $4,697,000 to the debentures based on the market prices of the two individual securities.

At the end of the seventh year, the corporation granted to employees options to purchase 100,000 shares of common stock during a five-year period beginning one year after date of grant. The option price was $11 a share, the market price of the stock at date of grant. Management estimated that the price of the stock would be $12 at the date the options were exercised. Total compensation of $100,000 (100,000 shares at $1 a share—$12 less $11) was to be accrued over four years beginning in the eighth year at the rate of $25,000 a year because optionees were required to hold the stock acquired for three years.

The corporation retained earnings of $2,720,000 from results of operations for 10 years; $500,000 of that amount was retained from net income of $900,000 in the tenth year.

At the beginning of the eleventh year, the market price of the common stock was $14 a share, and at that time the debentures were converted, the stock options were exercised, and the stock purchase warrants were exercised.

Recommended Accounting

Balance Sheet at end of tenth year:—

Long-Term Debt—5% Debentures due 19xx:		
Principal amount	$ 5,000,000	
Less unamortized discount	202,000	$ 4,798,000
Contingent Equity Financing:		
4½% Debentures due 19xx, convertible into 600,000 shares of common stock	6,000,000	
Warrants to purchase 300,000 shares of common stock at $13 a share	303,000	
Employee options to purchase 100,000 shares of common stock at $11 a share	75,000	6,378,000
Stockholders' Equity:		
Contributed by common stockholders, 1,000,000 shares outstanding	5,000,000	
Retained earnings	2,720,000	7,720,000

* * * * * * * * * *

Results of Transactions at beginning of eleventh year:—

Reduction of retained earnings:		
Expenses included in net income—		
Conversion of debentures—		
Fair value of 600,000 shares of stock	$ 8,400,000	
Face amount of debentures	6,000,000	$ 2,400,000
Exercise of stock options—		
Fair value of 100,000 shares of stock	1,400,000	
Proceeds of sale of stock	(1,100,000)	
Total compensation expense for four years	300,000	
Accrued compensation ($25,000 for three years)	(75,000)	225,000*
Adjustment for equity financing costs—		
Exercise of warrants—		
Fair value of 300,000 shares of stock	4,200,000	
Proceeds of sale of stock	(3,900,000)	
Proceeds of sale of warrants	(303,000)	(3,000)
Total reduction of retained earnings		2,622,000
Additions to equity contributed by common stockholders,		
1,000,000 shares at $14 a share		14,000,000
Stockholders' Equity:		
Contributed by common stockholders, 2,000,000 shares outstanding	19,000,000	
Retained earnings	98,000	19,098,000

* $75,000 is compensation expense of eleventh year and $150,000 is an extraordinary item to adjust compensation for the three preceding years.

Present Accounting

Balance Sheet at end of tenth year:—

Long-Term Debt:			
5% Debentures due 19xx			
Principal amount		$ 5,000,000	
Less unamortized discount		202,000	$ 4,798,000
4½% Convertible debentures due 19xx			6,000,000
Stockholders' Equity:			
Capital stock, 1,000,000 shares of $1 par value		1,000,000	
Capital in excess of par value		4,303,000	
Retained earnings		2,795,000*	8,098,000

* * * * * * * * * *

Results of Transactions at beginning of eleventh year:—

Additions to equity:		
Capital stock, 1,000,000 shares at $1 a share		$ 1,000,000
Capital in excess of par value—		
Conversion of $6,000,000 debentures less par value of 600,000 shares of stock	$ 5,400,000	
Proceeds of sale of $1,100,000 for stock under options less par value of 100,000 shares of stock	1,000,000	
Proceeds of sale of $3,900,000 for stock under warrants less par value of 300,000 shares of stock	3,600,000	10,000,000
		11,000,000
Stockholders' Equity:		
Capital stock, 2,000,000 shares of $1 par value	2,000,000	
Capital in excess of par value	14,303,000	
Retained earnings	2,795,000	19,098,000

* $2,720,000 plus $75,000 to eliminate compensation expense of $25,000 a year accrued in each of three years.

The amount of total stockholders' equity after the increases in outstanding common stock is the same under both accounting treatments, but the present accounting procedures recognize the effects as changes in capital stock and additional capital only.

The illustrated transactions result in reducing by one-half the proportionate interest of one share of stock. Present accounting makes it appear that the sole change in equity was a contribution by new stockholders. By limiting the contribution to the cash received, present accounting does not disclose the equity interest transferred by existing stockholders to new stockholders. Recorded stockholders' equity expressed in share amounts for both accounting methods shows the differences.

	End of Tenth Year	After Transactions at Beginning of Eleventh Year
Recommended Accounting		
Contributed by common stockholders	$5.00	$9.50
Retained earnings	2.72	.05
	$7.72	$9.55
Present Accounting		
Capital stock	$1.00	$1.00
Capital in excess of par value	4.30	7.15
Retained earnings	2.80	1.40
	$8.10	$9.55

Since each outstanding share of stock has an equal interest in equity and earnings, the new shares issued in the eleventh year are not distinguishable from the shares outstanding at the end of the tenth year. Under present accounting, one-half of the retained earnings seems to apply to the newly issued shares. On the contrary, retained earnings applicable to the original 1,000,000 shares has been reduced more than one-half because the corporation received a part of the consideration for the new shares in the form of services rather than cash.

10

Increases in Equity Securities—Individual Interests Unchanged

The proportionate interest of an individual stockholder in the equity of a corporation remains the same after some increases in outstanding equity securities. Those kinds of increases in equity securities are the subject of this chapter. They differ from most increases in outstanding equity securities that reduce the proportionate interests of existing stockholders, which are discussed in Chapter 9.

Distributions of stock rights, stock splits, and stock dividends do not change the proportionate interest of an individual stockholder although they usually reduce the proportionate interest represented by a single share of stock. Increases in outstanding securities resulting from the three kinds of distributions are not all alike because a corporation issues additional shares of stock for consideration in one type and issues shares without consideration in the other two.

The discussion of unchanged proportionate interests of stockholders is divided between increases in outstanding stock for consideration received on exercise of stock subscription rights and increases in outstanding stock without consideration—stock splits and stock dividends.

Stock Issued for Consideration

Stock Subscription Rights. Present practices in accounting for the distribution of stock subscription rights and for the subscription to shares of stock are described in Chapter 2. Briefly, a corporation recognizes the cash received as the consideration for stock issued on exercise of stock rights. Current accounting for the exercise of stock purchase warrants is the same despite some differences between the two securities, which are also explained in Chapter 2.

Stock purchase warrants are ordinarily distributed to other than existing stockholders and their exercise reduces the proportionate interests of existing stockholders. But some securities that carry privileges to purchase additional shares of stock are distributed ratably to holders of outstanding stock and are called warrants because the designated exercise price and exercise period are those customarily contained in stock purchase warrants. The financial effects of exercising warrants of that type and of stock subscription rights are the same and the recommendations in this chapter apply to both securities.

Proportionate interests retained. One feature of stock subscription rights sets them apart from all other transactions that increase outstanding equity securities and contributions to stockholders' equity. A corporation distributes rights to existing stockholders in the same proportions as their existing interests. Each outstanding share of stock of the same class is treated exactly the same. Existing stockholders receive the subscription rights, and nonstockholders do not share in the distribution of the rights. In fact, issuing stock rights rather than selling new shares to new stockholders permits present stockholders to avoid a dilution of their proportionate interests.

If a subscription right entitles the holder to purchase stock at a price below the current fair value of the stock, that difference is reflected in the fair value of each right distributed to and owned by an existing stockholder. A stockholder may retain his proportionate interest in the corporation by investing additional funds or he may realize a part of his existing investment by selling his subscription rights. Either way, the proportionate interest in a corporation available to an individual stockholder remains intact and its disposition or retention is within his discretion.

The proportionate interest of an individual stockholder will be less after stock rights are distributed and exercised if he elects to sell his rights. Selling rights is comparable with selling a part of an existing interest and has no effect on equity of the corporation.

Proportionate interests of stockholders change, of course, if all stock rights are not exercised. But a rational assumption is that a stockholder will either exercise rights that have a value or sell them and someone else will exercise them.

Distribution and exercise of stock subscription rights have the same effects on the total amount and components of stockholders' equity as ratable additional contributions of funds without the corporation issuing additional shares of stock. The two transactions differ because stock rights are traded separately, and the later exercise of those sold to nonstockholders and other stockholders modifies the existing proportionate interests of stockholders. The results of a stockholder's selling his stock subscription rights are distinct from the effects of the corporation's distributing the stock rights.

The effects of distributing subscription rights are described in Chapter 5 and contrasted with the effects of granting and accounting for stock options.

Proceeds added to contributed equity. Since a distribution of stock subscription rights does not change the existing proportionate interests of stockholders, exercise of the rights and issuance of additional shares of stock involve no consideration other than the cash received and no financing compensation. The present method of recording the cash consideration received as additional equity conforms with the accounting principles recommended in Chapter 8 of this study.

However, present procedures divide the consideration received between capital stock for the par or stated value of the new shares issued and additional capital for the remainder of the proceeds. The entire cash consideration received for subscribed stock should be added to contributed equity under the recommended policy of segregating the two sources of stockholders' equity.

Issuing additional shares of stock usually changes legal capital of a corporation, and the transaction may affect an appropriation of retained earnings for legal capital. An addition to contributed equity resulting from the exercise of stock rights is usually greater than the par value of the stock issued and may be large enough to eliminate the need for all or part of an appropriation of retained earnings for legal capital. If so, the directors may authorize a transfer of all or a part of earnings appropriated for legal capital to unappropriated retained earnings.

Warrants Distributed Pro Rata. Some rights to purchase stock that are issued to existing stockholders are called warrants because they are exercisable over an extended period and the exercise price is higher than the market price of the stock at the date the rights are distributed. Each stockholder holds the same claims, rights, and interests as he did before the distribution; after the distribution two securities—warrants and stock—represent his original interest. The total equity of the issuing corporation is unchanged until the stock purchase warrants are exercised.

The effects of a stockholder selling warrants received in a ratable distribution are the same as those of his selling stock subscription rights received. A corporation should not account for a stockholder's sale of his warrants any more than it would account for the sale of a part of the shares held by a stockholder.

Effects on market value. The market price of a share of stock plus the market price of a related warrant may be greater than the market price of the stock before a corporation distributed the warrants. Some accountants cite that fact as evidence that a corporation distributed something of value to its stockholders and should therefore account for the value of that distribution, the warrants. A more plausible explanation of the increased market value is that the sum of the parts is greater than the whole. Distributing a warrant separates an existing equity interest into two portions, one with greater risk and one with lesser risk. Although the value of the package is the same, the market value of the package increases because some investors find the greater leverage of a warrant attractive.

Outstanding warrants. Warrants distributed to all stockholders differ from stock subscription rights because the extended exercise period means that the warrants may be outstanding at the end of several fiscal periods. Each stockholder is treated equally at the date warrants are distributed, but the stock and warrants are separate securities either of which may be held or sold. Stockholders who acquire their equity interests after warrants are distributed need to be informed of the overhanging possibility of additional shares of stock being issued at the option of the holders of stock purchase warrants. Therefore, a corporation should show at no carrying amount in the contingent equity financing section of its balance sheet the outstanding warrants that were distributed originally to all stockholders and should describe the terms and other characteristics of the warrants in a note to the financial statements.

Stock Issued Without Consideration

Stock Splits and Stock Dividends. Stock splits and stock dividends are considered together in this section because they are of the same nature and are alike in their effects on corporate equity and the investments of stockholders. The present distinction between the two distributions of stock is relative size, that is, the number of shares of stock in relation to the shares outstanding. The dividing point is wholly arbitrary. Both transactions are aptly described as the pro rata distribution of additional shares of stock to stockholders of the corporation without consideration.

The customary stock dividend discussed in this section is a distribution of common stock to existing common stockholders. The laws of some states and some corporate charters prohibit distributions of other than common stock dividends on common stock. However, the term stock dividend also encompasses preferred stock distributed to common stockholders and common or preferred stock distributed to holders of preferred stock. Distributions of stock as dividends that realign existing rights and obligations of holders of equity securities are discussed in Chapter 12 on adjustments of equity.

Ratable distributions. A corporation that splits its stock or distributes a stock dividend distributes additional shares proportionately to all stockholders of the same class but neither distributes funds or other assets nor receives cash or other assets. The committee on accounting procedure recognized those facts in paragraph 6 of *ARB 43*, Chapter 7B. Stock splits and stock dividends do not change total stockholders' equity, the proportionate interests of the existing stockholders, or the two component sources of stockholders' equity.

The only change resulting from either a stock split or a stock dividend is in the proportionate interest of one share of stock. A statement repeated again and again is true but ignored today in United States accounting—the interests of individual stockholders in a corporation are the same after a distribution but are represented by more stock certificates, more pieces of paper.

Effects on equity. Existing practices of publicly held corporations in the United States account for the par or stated value of stock distributed as stock splits and for the fair value of stock distributed as stock dividends. Total stockholders' equity is unchanged by the accounting for either distribution; only the components of equity are changed. The changes are now recognized in the traditional components of capital stock, capital in excess of par or stated value of stock, and retained earnings.

The present accounting requirements for stock dividends may have acquired some early proponents because corporations often issued stock at its par value. Corporate equity therefore consisted of capital stock at par value and retained earnings, and the statutes required that a corporation transfer from retained earnings to capital stock an amount equal to the par value of additional shares of stock issued as a dividend. Those circumstances are little related to equity today because the par or stated value of capital stock is often a nominal portion of the proceeds of sales and fair value.

Present accounting practices have a curious effect on retained earnings: distributing a small number of shares of stock, that is less than 25%, reduces retained earnings more than distributing a large number of shares (retained earnings may not even be changed for a stock split).

Distinctions between distributions. Some accountants argue that large and small stock distributions should be accounted for differently because a stockholder receives something of value in a small distribution, and the value of his entire interest increases. A greater market value of a stockholder's interest is used as evidence to bolster the argument. Some studies show that an apparent increase in the total value is temporary, and the marketplace ultimately adjusts the prices of stock to eliminate an increase after a distribution of additional shares.[1] Furthermore, an increase in the total market value usually shows no correlation with the market value of the additional shares distributed. Many of those who have analyzed changes in the market value of an interest after a stock dividend have concluded that the effects of the many influences cannot be isolated.[2] Therefore, evidence is probably lacking to support the statement in *ARB 43* that in numerous instances stock dividends have no "apparent effect upon the share market price."

The argument to account for an increase in market value also loses its force because the total market value of an equivalent number of shares is often greater after a stock split. In fact, the corporate purpose of a stock split is to make a security more attractive and thereby enhance the market price.

Determining whether a distribution of stock is a stock split or a stock dividend has been the subject of some court cases. The accounting has

---

[1] C. Austin Barker studied the effects of stock dividends and stock splits on the market prices of stocks. Summaries were published in articles in *Harvard Business Review* of January-February 1956, May-June 1957, and July-August 1958.

[2] M. Richard Sussman, *The Stock Dividend,* 1962, studied the influence of stock dividends on the market prices of stocks. His conclusions on pages 68 and 69 began, "The average results produced by this study were in direct contrast to those of the Barker study. . . ."

often been a crucial factor in the decisions as opposed to the ratio of distributed shares to the number of previously outstanding shares.[3] Henry G. Manne's observation on the relevance of size is pertinent.

> The reasoning, as we have seen, is that if the distribution is large enough to affect the market price, the shareholder will thereby be informed that he is not receiving an additional value but rather is having his former value divided into a greater number of smaller pieces. Conversely, if there is no effect on the market price he may conclude that he has received something of value. What is evidently meant here is that if the distribution is too small to have a *measurable* effect on the market price, it will be considered a dividend. But it would be very difficult to establish that any distribution of shares by the corporation could ever be small enough to have no effect whatever on the value of existing shares.[4]

The arbitrary basis for distinguishing between stock dividends and stock splits is illustrated not only by the percentages of the number of outstanding shares chosen—20%, 25%, 100%, etc.—but also by the fiduciary accounting treatment prescribed in some state laws for stock dividends received. Some states require that the periods in which a corporation accumulated earnings determine the income or principal nature of a stock distribution, and other states apply an arbitrary percentage of the number of outstanding shares for the distinction. For example, Article 2-A of the New York Personal Property Law (Uniform Principal and Income Act) provides that distributions of shares amounting to 6% or less of the outstanding shares shall be considered income and those amounting to over 6% shall be entirely principal.

Value of stock distributions. A sampling of pro and con opinions in the debate on stock dividends ranges from

> "The stock dividends give tangible recognition of the shareholder's increased investment in the business." to

> "It doesn't give the stockholder a thing he hasn't got already."[5]

---

[3] Henry G. Manne, "Accounting For Share Issues Under Modern Corporation Laws," *Northwestern University Law Review*, July-August 1959, pp. 319-320.
[4] *Ibid.*, p. 320.
[5] Robert Sheehan, "The Big Payout," *Fortune*, November 1956, p. 240.

The idea of a change in the total of a stockholder's investment resulting from a stock dividend contrasts sharply with the effects of a cash dividend. A stockholder also receives something he already *has* if a corporation distributes a cash dividend. In effect, the value of his stock investment is reduced by the dividend he receives. The corporation has divested assets—cash—and the value of a stockholder's investment is reduced correspondingly. But the stockholder may dispose of the cash received at his discretion. The net assets of a corporation remain the same after a stock dividend is distributed and the interest of each stockholder in those assets likewise remains the same.

Nearly all reasons to support recognizing the distribution of stock dividends as a reduction of retained earnings are variations of the dissenting argument of Justice Brandeis in the famous case in 1920 on taxation of stock dividends—*Eisner* v. *Macomber* (252 U.S. 189). He argued that a stock dividend is equivalent to distributing a cash dividend which the recipient stockholders apply to purchase additional shares of stock of the corporation; a stock dividend is comparable to distributing cash dividends and subscription rights and applying the cash dividends to exercise the rights. The distribution of a stock dividend is said to merely bypass two transfers of cash.[6]

If actuality is ignored, a case can be built to show that the results of two cash transactions and distributing a stock dividend would be the same. Retained earnings are a part of the stockholders' interests in a corporation but are available to the stockholders only if the directors declare a dividend distribution. All earnings that a corporation retains increase the stockholders' interests in the corporation without the concurrence or discretion of the stockholders. If the parallel were followed to its conclusion, all retained earnings would be transferred to contributed equity with or without a corporation's distributing additional stock certificates.

If a distribution of stock is viewed as a single transaction rather than as replacing two transactions, the market value of the shares of stock

---

[6] Some courts have accepted the notion that stock dividends in effect telescope two separate transactions. Henry G. Manne cited cases in "Accounting For Share Issues Under Modern Corporation Laws," *Northwestern University Law Review,* July-August 1959, pp. 322, 323, and notes.

distributed is not pertinent to the accounting. A concise criticism of the present incongruous accounting is:

> Actually the market-price formula has no logical basis. Underlying the capitalization process is the concept of a stockholders' equity consisting of two main sections, (1) capital and (2) accumulated earnings. And the act of capitalization consists of making a transfer from the second section to the first. Accordingly there is no rhyme or reason in using a market price per share, representing the current value of the total equity per share, including *both* capital and invested earnings, in effecting a transfer from one section to the other. Moreover, it should be borne in mind that the total book value per share will seldom even approximate the appraisal of the market.[7]

Defects of Present Accounting. The primary defense of accounting for stock dividends at fair value of the shares distributed is that investors may believe that a corporation has distributed assets as a dividend and the accounting should follow that belief. The result of that accounting is not to clarify but rather to enhance the erroneous belief because retained earnings are reduced by the fair value of stock distributed to the stockholders.

Furthermore, the accounting requirement to transfer from retained earnings to permanent capital an amount equal to the fair value of a stock dividend loses its impact in those states that permit a corporation to distribute a cash dividend to the extent of paid-in or capital surplus. The route may be circuitous; but, if a cash dividend reduces capital surplus that has been increased because of a stock dividend, the results may be the same as if no amount was transferred from retained earnings for the stock dividend.

Limitation on stock dividends. A recommendation in *ARB 11* was that the amount of earned surplus capitalized for a regularly recurring stock dividend should not exceed the amount of current income because stockholders are likely to interpret the dividend as a notice that the corporation has current income. Requirements that the fair value of stock dividends plus cash dividends may not exceed earnings in the year of distribution have been suggested to prevent a corporation from hiding poor current earnings. Instead, the linking of a stock distribution

---

[7] William A. Paton and Robert L. Dixon, *Essentials of Accounting*, 1958, p. 665.

and current earnings reinforces the idea that a corporation is distributing earnings to its stockholders.

Distributions of treasury stock. The odd results of existing accounting for stock dividends is illustrated by the accepted accounting for treasury stock distributed as a stock dividend. If a corporation distributes treasury stock that is carried at cost as an unallocated deduction from equity, retained earnings are reduced by the fair value of the stock and the difference between the cost of the stock and its fair value is transferred to additional capital. Thus, assets were distributed to reacquire the stock, and contributions by stockholders were reduced; but the accounting displays neither of those effects. Rather, retained earnings are reduced by the entire cost of the treasury stock and further adjusted at a later date for the fair value of the treasury shares. A corporation has therefore not capitalized retained earnings. An appraisal of the transaction is:

> Such a so-called stock dividend is simply stock watering which does not represent net worth or surplus, but only a prior disbursement of the purchase price to a former shareholder. The withdrawal of assets in favor of a former shareholder is no basis for a free distribution of additional shares to the remaining shareholders; to call it a "dividend," either in stock or in property, is entirely misleading.[8]

Substitute for regulation. Present accounting procedures plus labeling the distribution a dividend hides the significance of a pro rata stock distribution to an investor and the effects on stockholders' equity. The purpose of accounting is not to police financial and management practices that the public or regulatory agencies believe are undesirable or that companies may have abused. Misrepresentation of corporate distributions may be controlled by other means than accounting. Regulatory agencies may exercise control by providing for their approval of proposed announcements and notices to stockholders.

Recommended Accounting. Neither contributions of stockholders nor retained earnings are changed by the pro rata distribution of stock as a split or as a dividend. A distribution of additional shares of stock reduces the proportionate interest of one share of stock but does not change the components of stockholders' equity. Therefore, a corporation should record the additional number of outstanding shares of

---

[8] Henry W. Ballantine, *Ballantine on Corporations*, 1946, p. 484.

stock and retain the same dollar amounts of components of stockholders' equity.

Typically, letters to stockholders say:

> The stock split increased your stock holdings in the Corporation but it did not change your proportionate equity in the Corporation.

> This stock dividend does not change your equity in the Company; however, sale of any portion of this stock dividend will reduce your equity accordingly.

Those sentences tell the whole story. Why try to make the accounting change it?

The method of accounting for stock distributions recommended in this study would permit a corporation to report both components of equity according to their sources.

Legal capital requirements. A corporation may need to appropriate retained earnings to meet legal capital requirements for the increased shares of stock if stockholders' equity is presented as recommended in this study. However, no appropriation of earnings will be required if existing contributed equity equals or exceeds the legal capital for the new number of outstanding shares of stock as defined by the laws of the state of incorporation.

Financial decisions of corporate management. This study is limited to accounting for distributions of stock. The advisability or desirability of distributing shares of stock to existing stockholders is beyond the scope. The pertinent factors in those decisions depend on corporate financial management and are not accounting matters. The advantages, disadvantages, costs, and tax and legal aspects of distributing stock dividends as well as stock splits are analyzed and available in many articles.[9]

---

[9] As examples, Benjamin Graham, "Stock Dividends," *Barron's*, August 3, 1953, p. 3 ("They Can Save the Investor Many a Tax Dollar") and August 10, 1953, pp. 5-6 ("An Analysis of Some of the Major Obstacles"); Stephen H. Sosnick, "Stock Dividends are Lemons, Not Melons," *California Management Review*, Winter 1961, pp. 61-82; A. C. Whitaker, "The Stock Dividend Question," *The American Economic Review*, March 1929, pp. 20-42; Thomas York, "Stock Dividends from the Viewpoint of the Declaring Corporation," *The Accounting Review*, March 1941, pp. 15-33.

11

Decreases in Equity Securities

Presenting contributions of stockholders and retained earnings separately is impossible unless accounting for decreases as well as increases in outstanding equity securities recognizes the changes in components of equity resulting from the transactions. Equity transactions must be analyzed and accounted for as they relate to contributions by stockholders and retained earnings, not to total stockholders' equity alone. Since each outstanding share of stock of the same class is represented by an equal portion of the total of the components of equity applicable to that class, a share is no longer identified or identifiable with a specific contribution to equity or with a specific portion of retained earnings. Both equity components are associated with the outstanding shares of stock, and the consequences of reducing those shares must be accounted for and allocated to both components of equity.

Reacquiring a part of the outstanding shares of stock is the principal manner of decreasing equity securities and total stockholders' equity, either permanently or temporarily. Reacquisition may be the first step to retire stock although corporations reacquire stock for various other purposes. This chapter covers various aspects of accounting for reacquisitions of stock.

Factors To Determine Accounting

Appropriate procedures to account for reacquired shares of stock, including shares for retirement, should be determined in relation to individual factors, which are outlined briefly in this section and discussed more fully in the applications of the procedures in numerous situations.

Characteristics of Equity Securities. The characteristics of stockholders' equity and outstanding equity securities are fundamental factors in determining the accounting for reacquired stock. The nature of the equity interests of preferred and common stockholders cannot be presumed to be the same. Thus the equity interest of each class of stock requires separate study. The results of financing with a senior security as opposed to a residual equity security may be significant in accounting for reacquisitions of stock. In turn, hybrid securities that embody characteristics of both senior and residual equity may require distinctive treatment. Retirements and other dispositions of reacquired shares of preferred and common stock need to be examined separately because the accounting results of the transactions may or may not need to be the same.

Purpose and Nature of Transactions. Reacquisitions of stock are separable primarily by two factors: (1) the purpose for which a corporation reacquires its own stock and (2) whether the reacquisition is required or optional. The purpose of reacquiring stock usually indicates the nature of the transaction; however, sometimes that purpose is not evident, or at least certain, until the corporation disposes of the reacquired shares.

Similarly, dispositions of reacquired stock are separable by their purposes and whether distributions of treasury shares are required or discretionary. Although the purposes of a retirement and a distribution of reacquired stock are diverse, that cannot be the sole division of dispositions because the purposes of distributions of stock may be so numerous that all distributions should not be grouped together.

The following discussion of purposes of reacquisitions of stock and later dispositions is divided between retirements, other dispositions, and required acquisitions for specified dispositions.

Retirement of stock. Corporations usually intend to retire the preferred stock that they reacquire, although some acquire preferred treasury stock for other purposes. Corporations occasionally intend to retire common stock that they reacquire but ordinarily intend to hold the shares temporarily and to sell or distribute them later.

Preferred stock is retired primarily for one of two reasons:

> Terms of the issue require either redemption by call at specified times or periodic redemption through a sinking fund.

Advantages accrue to common stockholders from retiring outstanding preferred shares. Funds required for retirement may be supplied by retained earnings or replacement financing which may be a new issue of preferred stock or other securities.

Both reasons may pertain to either partial or entire retirements of preferred issues. The reasons are analyzed in the retirement section of this chapter to find their effects on the interests of other preferred stockholders and common stockholders and on the sources and costs of financing a corporation.

Retiring common stock is discretionary with a corporation except that sometimes a closely held corporation provides for retirement at the discretion of a stockholder or his estate. Retiring stock is normally expected to produce a benefit for the remaining common stockholders; earnings for each remaining share are expected to increase because either net income is not reduced in the same proportion as the number of shares or a stockholder is willing to sell his securities to the corporation at a bargain price. Benefits to remaining stockholders are not always pecuniary, or perhaps the financial benefit is indirect because the corporation may reacquire and retire stock to eliminate a troublesome or dissatisfied stockholder.

Reacquisitions not for retirement. The purposes of acquiring treasury stock, either preferred or common, can be divided basically as either financing or operating. Even reacquisitions of stock that are required by the terms of the issue, such as stock that a corporation must purchase from terminating employees, fit either a financing type of purpose or an operating purpose if part of a compensation plan. Dispositions of treasury stock also fulfill either financing or operating purposes.

Various transactions in treasury stock are of a financial nature. They are separate and apart from the ordinary business operations of a corporation, and their financial effects should not be commingled in net income. In contrast, some treasury stock is acquired or shares held are set aside for specific operating purposes. Stock transactions may apply to arrangements that are a part of normal operations, and the entire costs related to the arrangements should ordinarily reduce net income.

Each type of purpose—financing and operating—for acquiring treasury stock needs to be analyzed for its effects on stockholders' equity and on expenses of operations or costs of equity financing. The purposes differ and the accounting for types of transactions may need to distinguish each purpose. The timing of the designation of purpose, that is, whether it is before or after the stock is reacquired, is relevant because the timing usually indicates the intent of management. An influence on the accounting may be that the purpose of reacquiring stock is not always designated or stock reacquired for one purpose may be switched later to another purpose. Accounting procedures recommended in later sections of this chapter are divided between stock reacquired for financing purposes and stock reacquired for operating purposes. Undesignated reacquisitions and changes of purpose are recognized in the discussion.

Required acquisitions for specified dispositions. The board of directors of a corporation sometimes authorizes and directs management to acquire treasury stock for a specific purpose. Some corporations or some plans and agreements require that management distribute treasury stock for compensation arrangements and for acquisitions of other businesses. Others provide that at the option of management either treasury shares or previously unissued shares may be distributed for a named arrangement. Still others require that management distribute previously unissued shares. Some plans provide that deferred distributions of compensation may be stock or cash at the option of either the corporation or the employee. If an arrangement provides that either treasury shares or previously unissued shares may be distributed at the discretion of management, the directors may instruct management to adopt a plan for uniform procedures to be followed in satisfying the terms of the arrangement.

Weight given to purpose. No evidence exists that determining appropriate accounting can be based solely on either the purpose of the acquisition or whether the acquisition and disposition of treasury stock is required or optional. Both factors merit appraisal. Other factors that must be considered are (1) the proceeds of sale or amount of liability satisfied by the distribution of treasury stock and (2) various combinations of the purchase price of reacquired stock and the amounts of components of stockholders' equity. Often treasury stock transactions are substitutes for other transactions, and that fact may be related to the accounting.

Legal Requirements To Be Recognized. The effects of legal regulations on reacquiring and retiring stock is another factor related to accounting for transactions in reacquired stock. State laws governing the acquisition of treasury stock aim in one way or another to restrict purchases of treasury stock to protect creditors and stockholders. Since creditors have the right to rely on a corporation's maintaining legal capital, purchases of treasury stock are often forbidden except to the extent of accumulated retained earnings (or earned surplus) as defined in the statutes. A corporation that reacquires outstanding common stock may shift part of the risks of common stockholders to holders of senior securities. Some reacquisitions of shares, depending on the purchase price of the stock and existing components of equity, are said to discriminate among stockholders. For those reasons the states have enacted rules to limit acquisitions of treasury stock, but the many statutes are now complicated and unlike.

Listing agreements with stock exchanges may also restrict a corporation in purchasing and redeeming its own stock. Typical provisions require a corporation to report transactions or contemplated transactions and permit redemptions only by lot or on a pro rata basis.[1] The SEC limits reacquisitions of a corporation's stock to prevent manipulation of prices of the stock. Decisions in specific cases furnish precedents that guide other corporations in determining permissible reacquisitions of stock.

Effective legal provisions may not control the accounting but may set a limit on transactions. Recognition of legal aspects as discussed in this chapter is based on the recommendation earlier in the study that a corporation disclose legal capital in financial statements but the laws not govern the classification of components of stockholders' equity.

Preferred Stock Retired

Status of Preferred Stock. All preferred stock issues cannot be placed in a single general category because the different terms produce securities with varied characteristics. An issue of stock may be titled preferred but in substance be similar to common stock and represent a continuing investment in the corporation. For example, if a preferred stock is noncallable, noncumulative, and participates with the common stock in distributions and voting control, its security characteristics are more those of a common stock than those of a senior security.

The unique characteristics of convertible preferred stock do not set it apart for purposes of discussing retirement of preferred shares. The conversion feature is an additional privilege for the holders of those shares but if the stock is retired rather than converted the additional

---

[1] For example, New York Stock Exchange Listing Agreement, Section I, pars. 7-10.

rights are ineffective—the retired preferred stock retained its status as a senior security to the end. Conversion of preferred stock, which is covered in Chapter 9, reduces the outstanding shares of that class of stock but it also increases the outstanding shares of common stock.

Many preferred stocks are similar in nature to long-term debt securities. Except for the tax effects of paying interest as contrasted with dividends, both types of securities have the same effect on the share of earnings and the equity interests of common stockholders. However, a contractual obligation to pay interest involves greater risk for common stockholders when conditions are adverse than does an obligation to distribute preferred dividends. Some preferred issues are more flexible than bonds because the stock may be redeemed at any time at the option of the corporation. The typical preferred stock discussed in this section on accounting for retirement is a redeemable, cumulative, and nonparticipating issue with preference in liquidation which should be viewed as an alternative to a method of financing with a long-term debt security. A corporation is often able through purchases in a securities market or a tender offer to reacquire and retire preferred stock that is titled as nonredeemable, and the discussion also covers those transactions.

Equity contributed by preferred stockholders. A preferred stock may be issued at a premium over its par value and the reasons for the premium are vital in accounting for the disposition of contributed equity at the time the stock is reacquired or retired. An issue price of preferred stock at its par value or above is based on a combination of factors, including the dividend rate and terms of redemption. The price is selected to provide an estimated return on the funds invested by a stockholder for the period the stock is outstanding, assuming that the designated dividend will be paid each period. If the dividend rate specified for a preferred stock issue would result in a higher return on the par value than the current rate for comparable securities, the issue price includes a premium to compensate for the higher future dividends. That situation is comparable to selling bonds at a premium to equalize the coupon rate and current lending rates.

Terms of a preferred stock issue that require redemptions at specified dates or at specified prices are determined at the time the dividend rate and issue price are set and all are interrelated. The cost of redemptions is a part of costs of equity financing and a corporation is aware at the time the sale of stock is arranged that it is obliged to incur the cost later.

Dividends, premiums, and redemptions of preferred shares have the same effects on the equity of common stockholders as do interest, premiums or discounts, and redemptions of bonds, although the periods selected to recognize the costs are not always the same. A significant difference, however, is that dividends distributed to preferred stockholders reduce retained earnings directly and do not reduce net income as do interest expenses.

Discretionary redemptions. A corporation that is not required but has the option to redeem and retire outstanding preferred stock normally exercises its option only if management expects a benefit to accrue to the common stockholders. Contributions by common stockholders and retained earnings may be sufficient to finance the operations of a corporation, and management expects that eliminating a prior dividend right of preferred stockholders will increase the return on the interests of common stockholders. But earnings that may be retained may not always be adequate for required financing, and funds to redeem outstanding preferred stock may need to be obtained from selling a new debt security or another preferred stock issue. If the costs of financing with replacement securities—that is, interest, dividends, redemption premium, etc.—are less than similar costs for the redeemed preferred stock, the resulting benefit accrues to the common stockholders.

Accounting for Costs of Preferred Stock Retired. The purchase or redemption price of preferred shares reacquired may occasionally equal the average amount originally contributed for each outstanding share of preferred, whether the contribution equals or exceeds the par value. However, prices are nearly always greater or less than the contributed equity and those prevailing conditions are discussed first.

Contributed equity of preferred stock exceeds cost. Shares of preferred stock originally issued at par or stated value or at a premium may be reacquired for retirement at less than the average amount contributed for a share of the stock. The differing reasons for varying circumstances are analyzed separately.

Cost equals or exceeds par value. Some issues of preferred stock are redeemable at par or stated value or at a premium that is less than the contributed premium. Also, the price of shares purchased in a securities market may approximate those specified redemption prices. The interdependence of issue price, premium, and specified dividend rate leads to the conclusion that an excess of contributed equity applicable to the retired shares over the cost of those shares should be added to retained earnings. A corporation then recognizes all equity financing costs, including dividends, as a reduction of retained earnings.

The interests of preferred stockholders are liquidated at less than their contributions and transferring to retained earnings a premium on preferred stock or the difference between an original premium and cost of reacquired stock reduces the effects of preferred dividends paid previously. The resulting retained earnings are the same as if the stock had been issued at a lower premium or at par value with a lower dividend rate. Issuing the preferred stock was a method for the corporation to obtain equity financing, and the entire net costs (dividends less the difference between funds collected and repaid) should be included in retained earnings.

Even though a premium, or difference, is an adjustment of dividends paid during the years the stock is outstanding, it need not be amortized periodically. The premium on preferred stock differs from the premium on bonds because every stockholder, preferred or common, assumes equity risks and is not guaranteed a specified dividend and redemption price. Amortization would anticipate the occurrence of uncertain events, such as the declaration of a dividend and a call for redemption. Further, amortization of premiums on stock would periodically switch the equity components of contributions and retained earnings without an effect on net income because dividends distributed and other costs of equity financing should be deducted directly from retained earnings.

After preferred stock is redeemed and retired, a premium contributed originally by the preferred stockholders no longer applies to outstanding shares of stock. The premium applicable to retired preferred stock could be classified as contributed equity only if it were a *donation*. None of the facts support that designation. Preferred stockholders purchase equity securities that convey specified senior rights and limitations but they do not donate funds to a corporation. If all outstanding preferred stock is retired, the stockholders' equity section of a balance sheet should then show as contributed equity only the contributions by the common stockholders.

Cost below par value. Preferred stock originally sold at par or stated value or at premium may occasionally be reacquired for retirement not only at less than the proceeds of the issue but also at less than its par or stated value. A price that low comes about because: (1) the specified dividend rate is low compared with the current return on comparable securities or (2) the market appraises that the prospects of the corporation do not assure continued dividend payments. Either of the circumstances result from conditions that already have or ultimately will decrease the retained earnings component of equity.

A corporation often lacks an incentive to reacquire its outstanding preferred stock voluntarily if the dividend rate is low in comparison with other securities and the corporation needs equivalent financing. Since replacement financing could be obtained only at a higher rate, dividend distributions would remain the same because the lower amount of new financing would be offset by the increased dividend rate on funds equivalent to the cost of the shares reacquired.

However, the terms of a preferred issue may require a corporation to retire a specified number of shares periodically or the corporation may foresee benefits in eliminating some features in the preferred stock. If so, the corporation would purchase stock in the market at a price below the redemption price. The difference between the purchase price and equity contributed for those preferred shares represents a benefit of having obtained financing earlier on advantageous terms. That benefit should be included in retained earnings at the time the shares are retired because it is a part of overall costs of equity financing.

A simplified illustration using assumed facts will show the effects of required retirements of equity financing with favorable terms. A corporation sells a share of 4% preferred stock at its par value of $100. Several years later the market rate for similar financing is 8% and the market price of the stock drops to $50. To finance a required retirement of stock the corporation needs to sell a similar security, but preferred stock can be of $50 par value with a dividend rate of 8%. Dividends in future years are the same dollar amount as before, but the interest of a holder of one share of preferred stock is now $50. The benefits of the earlier financing at the rate of 4% apply to the interests of the common stockholders and therefore $50, the difference between $100 par value and purchase price of $50, should be added to retained earnings at the date the corporation reacquires the 4% preferred stock.

If the effects of reacquisitions on financing costs are disregarded, one benefit of eliminating a low priced preferred stock could be the possibility of improved market prices for other outstanding securities of a corporation. Also, a corporation may no longer require the financing supplied by an outstanding low dividend preferred stock and reacquiring the stock to eliminate a right to prior dividends may be desirable. A market price that is less than the contributed equity applicable to the preferred shares offers an additional benefit for the common stockholders. Paying preferred dividends in prior years on excessive financing reduced the equity interests of the common stockholders. The difference between the purchase price of the preferred shares retired and the applicable contributed equity should therefore be added to retained earnings to partially compensate for the earlier deductions of preferred dividends from retained earnings.

Different factors are involved if depressed operations indicate uncertainty that the corporation can maintain earnings and continue dividend distributions. The market may expect the equity of the common stockholders to decline more. The proportion of earnings distributed as dividends to preferred stockholders in at least some earlier periods was probably excessive in relation to amounts available for common stockholders and those earlier preferred dividends reduced the retained earnings applicable to the common stockholders' equity. The effect of prior dividend payments may be counteracted by adding to retained earnings the difference between the cost of the preferred shares retired and the applicable contributed equity.

Cost of preferred stock exceeds contributed equity. Circumstances are reversed if the cost of preferred shares reacquired exceeds the applicable contributed equity. The terms of a preferred stock issue may require redemption at a designated price, and at the time of issuance a corporation assumes the future costs of redemption as a part of the financing costs. The issue price and specified dividend rate reflect the effects of required future redemptions. The excess of the cost of reacquired shares over applicable contributed equity should be deducted from retained earnings. The deduction represents additional costs of equity financing incurred at the time of redemption rather than during each year the stock was outstanding. The additional costs of redemption as well as the preferred dividends are deductions from retained earnings because they pertain to equity financing.

The decision to reacquire preferred stock voluntarily at a cost greater than applicable contributed equity is based on two possibilities: (1) replacement financing is obtainable at a lower rate or (2) required corporate funds are obtainable from earnings. Retiring preferred stock in either event benefits the common stockholders by increasing future earnings applicable to their shares. Therefore, the difference between the cost of the preferred shares retired and applicable contributions is properly deducted from retained earnings at the time of retirement as an additional cost of equity financing. The transaction is unrelated to contributions of the common stockholders and affects only accumulated and future earnings. A portion of retained earnings is relinquished currently for future benefits.

Cost of preferred stock equals contributed equity. Some issues of preferred stock are redeemable at par or stated value or occasionally the stock may be purchased in a securities market at par value. If the original amount contributed for a share equals its par or stated value, the cost of shares reacquired and their retirement should be accounted for as a reduction of equity contributed by the preferred stockholders.

If the cost of reacquired shares equals the par or stated value plus a contributed premium on the shares, retiring the shares simply reduces the contributed equity applicable to the preferred shares retired.

Summary of recommended accounting methods. The recommended accounting for retirement of preferred stock in all combinations of costs of the reacquired stock and contributed equity results in eliminating the equity contributed for the retired shares and in transferring the difference between cost of the retired stock and applicable contributed equity to retained earnings. That procedure was justified by analysis of the reasons for retirements and the conditions that determined the proceeds of issues of preferred stock. More than one reason may underlie the results of some transactions, but the effects should be accounted for the same.

In analyzing present practices, some accountants have pointed out the inconsistency between the customary accounting for a cost of reacquired preferred stock that is more than contributions and a cost that is less. George O. May stated in a discussion of alternatives:

> ... if a premium [cost of stock reacquired in excess of contribution] represents final adjustment of the share of profits going to the preferred stockholder the same should be equally true of a discount. Upon this view, the discount would be a credit to earned surplus—not as a gain but as an adjustment of a previous debit for dividends. Most accountants would reject this view as to discounts, and many of them may, therefore, be unwilling to accept it as to premiums.[2]

Rejecting "this view" without supporting reasons or arguments is unacceptable.

The main objection usually given to adding redemption discount to retained earnings is that a payment in excess of contributions cannot

---

[2] "Premiums on Redemptions of Preferred Stock," *The Journal of Accountancy*, August 1941, p. 129.

be regarded as a dividend because the rights to dividends are established by contract and redemptions do not enlarge those rights. Yet the rights of redemptions are also established by contract. The analyses of various circumstances in this chapter show that the effects of retiring preferred stock at more or less than applicable contributed equity should be recognized in retained earnings as part of costs of equity financing. Dividends, redemption prices, and issue prices are so closely interrelated that their financial effects should be recognized similarly. Counterproposals are essentially assertions that amounts assigned originally to contributed equity are always and forever contributed equity unless distributed in cash to the contributors or their successors.

Common Stock Retired

Status of Common Stock. Common stock discussed in this section may be of more than one class. Distinctions between different issues are usually variations in voting rights, dividend participations, and claims in liquidation, but all issues are residual equity securities. An issue of stock may be named preferred but have the characteristics of a separate class of common stock rather than senior, prior rights of preferred stock, and a corporation should account for its retirement as it does for common stock. Conversely, some securities titled common stock have the characteristics of preferred stock, and accounting for their retirements should follow the recommendations for preferred stock.

Equity of common stockholders. Contributions by common stockholders and earnings retained by a corporation represent the residual ownership of an entity. Unless a corporation is relatively new, outstanding shares of stock have usually been issued for differing consideration and, except for recent purchasers of stock under option or purchase plans, the present stockholders of large, publicly owned corporations have rarely furnished the recorded contributions. Outstanding shares cannot be said to be identifiable with specific contributions, even though on occasion a corporation could trace the amounts contributed, but each share needs to be identified with a pro rata portion of total contributions applicable to the class of stock and of retained earnings. The presentation of stockholders' equity proposed in this study shows retained earnings in two parts, if necessary: the portion appropriated for legal capital and the unappropriated remainder. Each share of outstanding common stock is therefore identified with a pro rata portion of each of the two categories of retained earnings.

Each outstanding share of stock of the same class is identical; the rights and limitations conveyed by each are the same and the legal status of each is uniform. As a result, each buyer of common stock acquires a proportionate interest in the equity of a corporation.

The retirement of shares of common stock is the withdrawal of a proportionate interest in the equity of the corporation. All types of retirements of common stock represent a reduction in total stockholders' equity and affect each component of common equity. If the cost of reacquired stock were equal to the pro rata portion of contributed equity and retained earnings, each component of equity would be reduced by the precise pro rata share. Costs equal to proportionate equity probably never occur except for reacquired stock of an open-end mutual investment fund. The cost of stock reacquired by other corporations is almost always more or less than the pro rata portion of the common stockholders' equity. Retiring a part of the common shares is therefore equivalent to withdrawing an aliquot portion of total contributed common equity and distributing a portion of retained earnings.

Accounting for Costs of Common Stock Retired. The interpretations of equity of common stockholders and effects of retirements may be projected to various combinations of costs of reacquired stock and components of equity. The purpose is to determine in this study the accounting for retirements of common stock that will be most informative and objective for all stockholders and investors.

Purchase price exceeds equity interest. A corporation reacquires common stock for retirement at a price that exceeds the proportionate share of equity because it anticipates that the remaining stockholders will benefit in the future. Management believes that distributing the amount is warranted because opportunities to invest the funds are not sufficiently profitable or other financing can be obtained at a lower cost. Contributed equity should be reduced by the pro rata portion applicable to the retired shares to record the withdrawal and distribution of funds to stockholders. The remaining contributed equity represents the portion applicable to the number of common shares that remain outstanding.

A corporation should deduct from retained earnings the excess of the purchase price of retired shares over applicable contributed equity. That excess represents not only the allocable share of retained earnings but also the excess of cost over the proportionate part of total recorded equity. Deducting the excess cost from retained earnings is justifiable because the retirement is expected to produce increased future earnings. The reasons for anticipating greater earnings after retiring a part of the common stock often vary with prevailing conditions. Examples are: financing costs may decline if funds are replaced from alternative sources; unless a corporation uses all available funds to advantage, eliminating the required cost for idle funds may increase the return to the remaining stockholders; a portion of the purchase price over proportionate equity in the corporation may represent unrealized appreciation of the corporation's assets not yet recognized in the financial statements—in effect, a corporation distributes to a withdrawing stockholder his proportionate part of the appreciation that the corporation expects to recognize later.

Analyses of typical reasons that the purchase price of retired shares exceeds the applicable portion of total equity show that deferring the excess cost to future periods may be appropriate. However, allocating that excess to future periods is impracticable. An excess results from many diverse factors, and the portion allocable to a single period would be an unreliable estimate of the influences of each of the several factors. Deducting the excess cost from retained earnings at the time stock is retired has the same total financial effects as deferring and allocating the amount although admittedly the timing is arbitrary. Some factors may influence net income of future periods, but assessing the amount of the factors related to operating income and the amount related to distributions of earnings is impossible.

Equity interest exceeds purchase price. The purchase price of common stock reacquired may be less than the proportionate part of total equity or even of contributed equity. Factors depressing the market prices of the securities may create the possibility that reacquiring and retiring shares of common stock will benefit the remaining stockholders. Future prospects of a corporation may be poor—perhaps losses have already been incurred or a disastrous event has occurred. A stockholder may believe that the assets cannot produce an adequate return on his investment or that the carrying amount of specific assets is too high. Therefore, he concludes that his interest in the corporation is not equal to the book amount of his equity and he is willing to sell his securities at a price below his recorded equity. A price of the stock below the equity applicable to one share recognizes an unrecorded decline in resources of the corporation.

A corporation should record as withdrawn the portion of contributed equity applicable to common stock retired regardless of the purchase price of the reacquired stock. The remaining contributed equity represents the pro rata amounts applicable to outstanding shares. If the purchase cost is less than contributed equity applicable to the retired shares, the difference should be added to retained earnings. Viewed in relation to past events and expected future events, that accounting is appropriate. Reacquiring stock at a reduced amount represents a pro rata reimbursement by the retiring stockholders to the remaining stockholders for unrecorded depreciation. The effects of transactions or events to the date of retirement are thereby allocated to the retired shares. The resulting effects of losses, write-downs, or other reductions in equity recognized in the future will be included later in retained earnings through periodic net income.

Summary of recommended accounting methods. The accounting for retirement of common stock recommended in this study culminates in eliminating the equity contributed for the retired shares and transferring the difference between purchase price and applicable contributed equity to retained earnings in all circumstances. That treatment is justifiable in theory except for its timing. Most differences represent at least an estimate of the proportionate part of unrealized appreciation or depreciation of assets including unrecorded goodwill. The differences could be recorded separately and later allocated as adjustments of profits and losses realized. But the practical difficulties of identifying and matching the unrealized and the realized appreciation and depreciation make it expedient for a corporation to record the adjustment in retained earnings at the time stock is retired.

Analysis of the factors that cause differences between the purchase price and the related portion of equity is now applied in some accounting procedures. The treatment of daily retirements of stock of mutual investment companies is an illustration. The companies recognize in their financial statements unrealized appreciation and depreciation and relate a portion of the cost of shares reacquired to the valuation amounts.

The proposed procedures do not recognize a profit or a loss on retirement of common stock. On the contrary, the accounting procedures recognize that retiring common stock requires the distribution of corporate assets and a corresponding reduction in corporate equity. They allocate the reduction to the component sources of equity according to the nature of the transaction.

Changes in categories of retained earnings. A retirement of common stock may require reclassifying the categories of retained earnings that are designated as appropriated for legal capital and unappropriated, as recommended in this study. For example, if retained earnings had been appropriated for legal capital to effect a stock split, a retirement of shares should reduce both the appropriation for legal capital and contributed equity by the proportions applicable to the retired shares. Unappropriated retained earnings should be reduced by the remainder of the purchase price of the reacquired stock.

A simple illustration of those reductions assumes these facts:

A corporation issued 10,000 shares of $5 par value stock for $8 a share. Legal capital in the state of incorporation is the par value of issued shares of stock and excludes paid-in premium.

The corporation retained earnings of $125,000.

The corporation distributed in 19xx one share of $5 par value stock for each share held. The directors authorized that contributed equity in excess of legal capital be designated additional legal capital and that retained earnings be appropriated for the remainder of the required legal capital.

The corporation reacquired 2,000 of the 20,000 outstanding shares of stock for $25,000 and retired the 2,000 shares.

	Before Reacquisition and Retirement of Stock	After Retirement of Stock
Stockholders' Equity:		
Contributed by common stockholders		
Outstanding—		
20,000 shares (Note)	$ 80,000	
18,000 shares (Note)		$ 72,000
Earnings retained in the business:		
Appropriated for legal capital (Note)	20,000	18,000
Unappropriated	105,000	90,000
	125,000	108,000
	$205,000	$180,000

Note—(Before Retirement) The par value of the 20,000 outstanding shares of stock is $5 a share or $100,000; retained earnings of $20,000 is appropriated for legal capital representing the excess over contributed equity of the par value of 10,000 shares of stock distributed to effect a two for one split in 19xx.

Note—(After Retirement) The par value of the 18,000 outstanding shares of stock is $5 a share or $90,000; retained earnings of $18,000 is appropriated for legal capital representing the excess over contributed equity of the par value of 9,000 shares of stock distributed to effect a two for one split in 19xx.

Since the original paid-in premium is not required to be legal capital in the state of incorporation, the corporation is permitted to designate that amount as legal capital to effect the two for one split. The remainder of the par value of the additional shares of stock issued is shown as an appropriation of retained earnings. Alternatively, the directors may appropriate from retained earnings the entire par value of the additional shares ($50,000 in the illustration). That appropriation, however, would restrict the distribution of retained earnings more than is required and perhaps confuse the presentation of reacquired stock. The legal capital of a corporation as well as contributed equity are reduced proportionately for shares retired.

Stock Reacquired for Financing Purposes

The sections on stock reacquired for other than retirement are divided between stock reacquired for financing purposes and for operating purposes. The discussions apply to either preferred or common stock.

Financing Purposes of Transactions. A corporation reacquires its own stock for financing purposes in transactions that underlie using available funds, revising sources of financing, anticipating conversions of securities and exercise of stock purchase warrants, distributing stock dividends, and effecting business combinations. Each type is discussed in the following paragraphs.

Using available funds. A corporation may use uncommitted funds to advantage by reacquiring its own stock and holding the shares temporarily. Whether or not that is a proper or the best use of corporate funds is outside the scope of this study. A depressed current market price may offer a potential benefit to the corporation or its stockholders from acquiring and later selling treasury stock. The reduction in dividend payments while the shares are held as treasury stock and later sales of the shares at higher prices both increase the stockholders' equity. Of course, a potential selling benefit will not materialize unless the price of the stock rises, and a corporation may retire the treasury shares rather than sell them at the purchase price or less.

Revising sources of financing. A corporation's existing sources of financing may not be the most advantageous combination of debt and equity securities nor of senior and common equity securities, and the easiest and least costly means of modifying the outstanding securities may be to reacquire outstanding stock. Also, reducing the outstanding stock with or without increasing other securities may be desirable. A corporation may wish to reduce equity temporarily but not retire stock. It may be able to obtain the desired reduction by purchasing and holding stock in the treasury. A corporation may later increase the equity of that class of stock by selling the treasury stock and avoid incurring underwriting and other costs required to issue new shares.

Anticipating conversions of securities and exercise of warrants. Outstanding securities of a corporation may carry the privilege for the holders to convert them into other securities, or outstanding warrants may entitle the holders to purchase equity securities. Many corporations may wish to issue previously unissued securities when and if securities are converted or warrants are exercised. Other corporations may wish to forestall an increase in outstanding equity securities, usually common stock, by reacquiring outstanding stock and reserving it for later distribution to the holders who elect to convert securities or exercise warrants.

The possible advantages of that action must be weighed against the disadvantages of depleting funds, at least for a short period, by the purchase price of treasury stock. Using corporate funds to acquire treasury stock could wipe out the advantages of issuing convertible securities or warrants. The restrictions of SEC Rule 10b-6 on reacquiring stock of a class that is covered by a registration under a continuous offering may effectively eliminate using treasury stock for conversions and exercise of warrants.

Distributing stock dividends. The logic of acquiring treasury stock for the purpose of distributing a stock dividend in lieu of a cash dividend is elusive. However, a corporation is alleged to benefit because it can distribute funds without transferring retained earnings to capital stock or increasing the number of outstanding shares. An increase in outstanding stock may affect the market price of the stock and the amount of cash needed for future dividends.

If treasury stock carried as an unallocated deduction from equity is distributed to stockholders, no part of retained earnings is required to be transferred to capital stock. The reasoning that makes that a benefit to either the corporation or stockholders is roundabout and largely illusory. Funds are not distributed to the continuing stockholders; instead, funds are distributed to the stockholders who sell their interests. The distribution of funds to reacquire stock reduces the interests of continuing stockholders. The distribution of more certificates for the same interests reduces the proportionate interest of one share. All in all the results are opposite to the supposed benefits to stockholders.

Often a corporation distributes stock as a dividend because available funds are inadequate for a cash dividend. But a purchase of treasury shares requires corporate funds. Corporations acquire and then distribute treasury shares instead of previously unissued shares as stock dividends for only one reason—to avoid increasing the number of outstanding shares with possible effects on market prices of the securities, pertinent ratios, and future dividends. That feature is lost, however, unless the treasury stock is acquired and distributed in the same fiscal period. Reacquiring and distributing stock in the same period reduces available funds the same as does distributing a cash dividend. That result is contrary to the reason for the distribution of stock.

An actual benefit of distributing treasury shares as a stock dividend is that a corporation may conserve cash in later years. If a corporation distributed previously unissued stock as a dividend, the total cash to be distributed as dividends could remain the same only if the dividend rate were reduced. Apparently, that possible benefit does not loom large in the financial planning of corporations.

Effecting business combinations. A business combination may be completed by distributing treasury shares of a corporation. Some managements are wary of distributing previously unissued shares for a combination because an increase in the number of shares outstanding may affect the market price of the stock. A combination has a direct effect on the earnings per share of stock, rate of return on investment, and other ratios and thus probably an indirect effect on security prices. The possibility of an adverse effect may be minimized if the total shares outstanding are not increased. A corporation may be able to purchase another business for cash but may choose to use stock. Several factors often lead a corporation to use available funds to reacquire its own stock to exchange later when acquiring another corporation, although previously unissued shares are available to effect the combination.

Financing purposes pertain to equity components. All of the types of transactions described are financing in nature. They are not directly related to the operations of a corporation but to the ownership interests of equity stockholders and may change the components of stockholders' equity. One could contend that procuring adequate financing is a necessary corporate activity and the related costs are current operating expenses. Some treasury stock transactions outlined in this section, such as a business combination or sale of stock for more than its purchase price, do provide a corporation with additional resources. But the related costs or benefits are not current financing expenses or income. Rather, they are more comparable with costs of issuing additional shares of stock and a premium included in the issue price of shares of stock. Other treasury stock transactions reduce funds available and the problem is to recognize the related costs.

A corporation may not have earmarked treasury stock as acquired for specific purposes. Undesignated reacquisitions of stock should nearly always be assigned to the area of financing purpose—using available funds to acquire stock at a favorable price is invariably the reason.

Results of Transactions. The results of reacquiring equity securities for financing purposes are appropriately reflected in the accounts and financial statements as direct changes in stockholders' equity and excluded from current operations. Both total equity and components of equity are affected by reacquisitions of stock. The proportionate interests of the remaining stockholders are changed, that is, the decrease in outstanding shares increases the proportionate interest of each continuing share of stock.

This section analyzes the changes to be recognized in contributed equity and retained earnings, the principal categories recommended for presentation of stockholders' equity, but disregards the bookkeeping required in subsidiary accounts.

Reacquisition is in effect retirement. Purchasing treasury stock for financing purposes is equivalent to distributing portions of contributed equity and retained earnings to withdrawing stockholders. The effects on components of equity should be recorded on that basis at the time the treasury shares are purchased to show the status and components of equity applicable to the remaining stockholders. Remaining stockholders view the acquisition of treasury shares for no specific purpose other than to reduce the number of outstanding shares as a distribution of available funds to other stockholders and a reduction of contributed equity and of retained earnings. The funds represent a portion of the total investment of stockholders in the corporation, and the entire distribution reduces total stockholders' equity.

The reacquisition of stock constitutes in essence the retirement of stock and the transaction should be accounted for as a retirement. Formal retirement of the shares is not a prerequisite for that accounting. Stockholders who retain an interest in the corporation are entitled to be informed of the portions of remaining equity represented by contributions and by undistributed earnings.

Opposition to constructive retirement. Many accountants oppose the constructive retirement of treasury stock and advocate the unallocated deduction method. Most arguments against constructive retirement are based on legal factors or legal restrictions. For example, accounting as a constructive retirement was said to violate the trust fund theory:

> Under the latter theory, stated capital is a trust fund for the protection of creditors, and almost without exception the state laws provide that corporations may not declare dividends, nor reacquire their own shares, other than out of the excess of assets over the amount of aggregate liabilities and stated capital—in other words out of surplus .... deducting reacquired shares from capital ... offends the law which prohibits the reduction of the trust fund by other than formal action.
>
> . . . .
>
> It is inconceivable that the aforementioned excess [redemption price over the par or stated value] can be considered a distribution

to the retiring stockholders, for such a concept offends the law concerning preferential distribution of earnings to any stockholders within a class or group without making distribution in like proportion to every stockholder of that class.³

The following statement exemplifies opposition to retirement accounting.

> The concept wrongly injects into corporate accounting fundamental theories of partnership accounting; it seems to imply that every share of stock of each class has a vested interest in every dollar which was contributed in respect of that share, just as every dollar which a partner contributes to the capital of the firm becomes a credit to his capital account to which he is entitled upon withdrawal. The "corporate fiction," well established in law and accountancy, looks upon the corporation as an entity separate and apart from those who have contributed capital; each stockholder having only an undivided equity in the net worth of such corporation.... Assets are pooled, liabilities are pooled, and stated capital is pooled.⁴

That statement overlooks the fact that each share of stock is identified with a pro rata portion of the related total component sources of equity. That is not the same as saying that each dollar of contributed equity is identified with a particular share of stock. The discussion in Chapter 7 shows that the bases of accounting for partnership capital and stockholders' equity diverge because the owners' interests represented by shares of stock are transferable without knowledge or permission of the corporation.

Unallocated deduction. The quotations show that legal restrictions on acquiring treasury stock set the stage for ready acceptance of the unallocated deduction method of accounting. Acquiring treasury stock does not reduce legal capital of a corporation in most states because a reduction requires formal action. Recording the cost of reacquired stock in a separate equity account is an expedient to comply technically with the laws. A concise reply to the contention that acquiring treasury stock does not reduce capital is

> To subscribe to such a conclusion, however, is to hold that temporarily a corporation may exist as an entity with no other stock-

---

[3] Victor H. Stempf, "Accounting Standards," *The Journal of Accountancy,* January 1942, pp. 72-73.
[4] *Ibid.,* p. 73.

holders than itself, that capital which has been withdrawn from a business is still in the business, and that capital which is non-existent, or nominal only, is as effective in earning profits as that which actually plays a part in the corporation's operations. Obviously, this is adding fiction to fiction.[5]

Some accountants argue that the unallocated deduction method of recording reacquired stock is "the most simple and direct presentation, which displays the true suspense character of treasury stock."[6] However, the arguments supply no defense that the transaction is incomplete; suspense is assumed.

One author suggested that accountants adopted the unallocated deduction method because they were unable to satisfy themselves as to the classification of components of stockholders' equity. Deducting the cost of treasury stock from all components made unnecessary analysis of the elements of equity.[7]

Effects recognized as transactions occur. The legal restrictions on reacquiring stock emphasize that the transactions are withdrawals of funds by stockholders. Regardless of the bookkeeping for reacquisitions of stock, total stockholders' equity is reduced by the cost of treasury stock even though legal capital is unchanged. The total cost of stock reacquired is significant, but holding a single amount in abeyance obscures the effects of the reacquisition. A reacquisition is a completed transaction, but a single amount shown in suspense camouflages its effects on financial statements and remaining stockholders' equity.

Delaying to account for the effects of stock reacquisitions on the components of equity does not aid in understanding the current financial position of a corporation. Funds are disbursed, the stock is reacquired, and both the total equity of the corporation and its components are reduced. Future equity transactions—for example, distribution of the shares to acquire another company—are unrelated to the event that has already occurred—the reacquisition of outstanding shares and re-

---

[5] George R. Husband, "The Corporate-Entity Fiction and Accounting Theory," *The Accounting Review*, September 1938, p. 250.

[6] Victor H. Stempf, "Accounting Standards," *The Journal of Accountancy*, January 1942, p. 73.

[7] H. G. Bowles, "Treasury Shares on the Balance-sheet," *The Journal of Accountancy*, August 1934, p. 104.

duction of stockholders' equity. Components of equity as well as total equity change at the date stock is reacquired, not months or years later.

Recording reacquired stock. The effects on components of stockholders' equity of acquiring treasury stock and later selling or distributing the shares should be the same as purchasing and retiring shares and later issuing additional shares. Management may exercise the option to retire treasury shares and sell or distribute previously unissued shares or to sell or distribute treasury stock. The financial results should be the same for either decision.

One difference in accounting for the retirement of stock and the acquisition of treasury stock is in recording the effect on the portion of retained earnings appropriated for legal capital. Retirement of common shares ordinarily reduces contributed equity, retained earnings appropriated for legal capital, and unappropriated retained earnings. In contrast, acquiring and retaining treasury shares does not change the existing legal capital in many states because treasury shares are unretired shares and remain a part of the total issued and outstanding shares under legal definitions. Therefore, retained earnings appropriated for legal capital may need to be increased and unappropriated retained earnings reduced by an amount equal to the legal capital of the treasury stock acquired. An illustration of the presentation of appropriations follows. To facilitate comparison, the assumed facts are the same as the illustration of retirement (pages 236 and 237) except that reacquired shares are held in the treasury and later sold.

> A corporation issued 10,000 shares of $5 par value stock for $8 a share. Legal capital in the state of incorporation is the par value of the issued shares of stock and excludes the paid-in premium.
>
> The corporation retained earnings of $125,000.
>
> The corporation distributed in 19xx one share of $5 par value stock for each share held. The directors authorized that contributed equity in excess of legal capital be designated additional legal capital and that retained earnings be appropriated for the remainder of the required legal capital.
>
> The corporation reacquired 2,000 of the 20,000 outstanding shares of stock for $25,000. Legal capital is not reduced when stock is reacquired.
>
> The 2,000 shares of treasury stock were sold for $30,000.

CHAPTER 11: DECREASES IN EQUITY SECURITIES

The directors authorized that retained earnings previously appropriated to meet legal capital requirements be designated unappropriated retained earnings.

	Before Acquisition of Treasury Stock	After Acquisition of Treasury Stock	After Sale of Treasury Stock
Stockholders' Equity:			
Contributed by common stockholders			
Outstanding—			
20,000 shares (Note)	$ 80,000		$102,000
18,000 shares (Note)		$ 72,000	
Earnings retained in the business:			
Appropriated for legal capital (Note)	20,000	28,000	
Unappropriated	105,000	80,000	108,000
	125,000	108,000	
	$205,000	$180,000	$210,000

Note—(Before Acquisition) The par value of the 20,000 outstanding shares of stock is $5 a share or $100,000; retained earnings of $20,000 are appropriated for legal capital representing the excess over contributed equity of the par value of 10,000 shares of stock distributed to effect a two for one split in 19xx.

Note—(After Acquisition) The par value of the 18,000 outstanding shares of stock is $5 a share or $90,000; retained earnings of $28,000 are appropriated for legal capital representing the excess over contributed equity of the par value of 9,000 shares of stock distributed to effect a two for one split in 19xx and the par value of 2,000 shares of treasury stock.

Note—(After Sale) The par value of the 20,000 outstanding shares of stock is $5 a share or $100,000.

Retained earnings equal to the par value of treasury shares sold, distributed, or retired may be transferred to the unappropriated classification. Total retained earnings after the sale of treasury stock is the same as if the stock were retired, as illustrated on pages 236 and 237, but the appropriation for legal capital is no longer required because total contributions by stockholders exceed legal capital.

Treasury stock held. The clash between the legal and financial status of treasury stock often creates confusion in the financial reporting of the number of shares of stock. One claimed advantage of the unallocated deduction method is that a legal status of treasury stock as issued shares is shown more easily than under the contraction of capital method. However, reacquired shares are no longer either issued or outstanding from a financial viewpoint.

The number of shares held by stockholders is now often unclear in financial statements because the total number of issued shares, which includes treasury shares, is shown without an explanation. The most useful presentation is to show as issued and outstanding the number of shares held by stockholders and to disclose the number of treasury shares excluded. The number of shares issued and outstanding under the applicable statutes may also be shown in that presentation.

Since the recommendation of this study is to treat treasury stock acquired for financing purposes as constructively retired at the time the stock is acquired, disclosing the total purchase cost of treasury stock held is unnecessary. The cost of treasury stock and the number of shares reacquired may be significant information in some historical summaries. The information may be necessary to interpret correctly various statistics, such as earnings per share. If the distribution of retained earnings is restricted to the extent of the cost of treasury stock held or previously acquired, the restriction in excess of appropriated earnings should be disclosed in the financial statements.

Dispositions of Treasury Stock for Financing Purposes. Briefly, issuing additional shares of stock increases contributed equity and total stockholders' equity of a corporation. The financial aspects of issuing previously outstanding shares or authorized and unissued shares are not significantly different. Acquiring treasury shares terminates some stockholder rights, and issuing or reissuing shares creates stockholder rights.

Recording all sales alike. Assuming that treasury stock acquired for financing purposes is recorded as though the shares were retired, later issuance of the shares should be recorded the same as newly issued shares. That method conforms with the facts and circumstances. Typical dispositions of treasury stock do not involve retained earnings. A corporation has neither distributed earnings nor earned anything by reissuing treasury shares; the proceeds of sales or distributions of stock increase contributed equity. That aspect is underlined by the fact that the corporation could have chosen to complete the transactions with previously unissued shares. The financial effects on stockholders' equity should not differ because of an arbitrary choice of shares.

The effects of a sale of treasury shares and of a sale of newly issued shares are comparable. A purchaser of either treasury shares or previously unissued shares in the customary profitable corporation pays an amount greater than the contributed equity applicable to each share of outstanding stock. Obviously, that excess represents retained earnings and unrealized appreciation, including future prospects, applicable to the shares sold. An individual buyer indicates that he is willing to contribute funds as his equity investment in the corporation. A purchaser of stock in a securities market is unaware that a corporation is the seller of treasury stock but that fact would be of no consequence in his decision to buy or in setting the price.

New stockholders contribute additional capital to a corporation. They can never *contribute* earnings. The additional contribution modifies the components of each stockholder's proportionate part of total equity. Existing stockholders' proportionate interests in contributed equity and retained earnings are modified and their total interests are modified because the additional shares of stock are not sold at the existing book amount.

Argument to maintain contributed equity intact. Accountants sometimes object to the same accounting procedures for the issuance of treasury shares and of previously unissued shares because the treasury shares are still issued shares and equity funds were contributed at the time the shares were issued originally. The contributed equity applicable to those shares is said to never change regardless of perhaps repeated reacquisitions and dispositions. The reissue price of shares may be more or may be less than the pro rata portion of contributed equity or of total equity, but some accountants believe that the reissue price is not pertinent.

The argument goes:

> Certainly one who purchases treasury stock is not contributing capital. The capital represented by the stock he buys was contributed by the original subscriber, it is still in the corporation, and it was not paid out of the corporation when the latter acquired the shares of treasury stock.[8]

The argument is based on the contention that the corporation is a holder of its own stock and the purchaser replaces the corporation by buying one of the assets of the corporation. That analysis leads to the conclusion that acquisitions and dispositions of treasury stock are not equity transactions at all. The reacquired shares are assets of the corporation, and the differences between the cost of shares and reissue price are clearly part of net income.

That is the conclusion except for corporations chartered in states whose laws provide that the reacquisition of shares reduces stated capital and the issuance of treasury stock increases stated capital.[9] Therefore the components of equity and assets could be changed materially if a corporation transferred its charter from a state requiring reduction of legal capital to a state requiring retention of legal capital.

Other distributions of treasury stock. The recommendation to account for sales of treasury stock as though previously unissued shares were sold fits with the circumstances of other dispositions of treasury stock for financing purposes. Applications of the recommendation are discussed in the following paragraphs.

Distributed for business combinations. Stock issued to acquire either the assets or stock of another corporation should be recorded at the fair value of the assets or the fair value of the stock issued whichever is more reasonably determinable. The changes in equity are the same whether treasury or previously unissued shares are distributed to complete the acquisition. The increase in stockholders' equity is similar to that resulting from the sale of additional stock.

Treasury stock transactions for the acquisition of another corporation relate strictly to the equity of the continuing corporation. Although the

---

[8] Robert H. Montgomery, "Dealings in Treasury Stock," *The Journal of Accountancy,* June 1938, p. 473.

[9] *Ibid.,* p. 474.

directors may require that management reacquire shares to be distributed for that purpose, the acquisition of a business is itself not a part of the benefits or expenses of operations. By recording the reacquisition of stock as a retirement and the distribution of shares as a new issuance, a corporation keeps intact its distinction between contributed equity and retained earnings.

One argument may be that if a corporation uses treasury stock to acquire another company, the corporation may realize more than the cost of the stock on its disposition because the consideration received exceeds the cost, and that excess should be recognized as a profit. The argument is often defended by equating the distribution of treasury stock with the distribution of other assets, such as marketable securities of a third corporation. A corporation distributing other assets does recognize the difference between cost of the assets and their current value as a profit. Distributing treasury stock cannot be validly compared with distributing other securities because a corporation acquires an investment security and treasury stock for basically different purposes. Securities of other corporations are acquired for one of several operating purposes—return on investment as revenue or appreciation, control, or economy in operations. Another business is acquired primarily to expand overall operations and only indirectly for the described operating purposes. Neither the acquisition of the treasury stock nor the acquisition of another business is a part of operations.

Conversions of securities and exercise of warrants. Increases in equity securities through the conversion of other securities and the exercise of stock purchase warrants should recognize the total consideration received for the issued stock as described in Chapter 9. Using treasury stock has no effect on the financial aspects of the transactions—the increase in contributed equity. Increases in contributed equity may involve costs of financing, and a corporation may have acquired treasury stock to limit those costs, but the costs relate to equity financing and reduce retained earnings. Unless treasury stock is recorded as retired at the time acquired, a part of the financing costs may never be reported and accounted for.

Distributed for stock dividends. Distributing additional shares of stock as a dividend does not change the proportionate interests of stockholders. The accounting should not differ because the shares distributed are identified as treasury shares or as previously unissued shares. Neither component of stockholders' equity—contributed equity and retained earnings—is changed by the distribution of additional shares. The par or stated value of the additional shares needs to be recorded in subsidiary records to meet legal requirements but the sources of equity are unchanged.

Adjustment of appropriated retained earnings. The components of retained earnings may need to be adjusted for the effects on legal capital of the issuance of treasury stock. The entire appropriation of retained earnings for legal capital may no longer be required, and the directors may authorize that the amount be returned to the unappropriated category. The adjustment and sale of treasury shares is illustrated in the section on recording the reacquisition of stock on pages 244 and 245.

Stock Reacquired for Operating Purposes

Operating Purposes of Transactions. A corporation may acquire treasury shares or may reserve shares held to comply with specific arrangements related directly to operations. The purpose of many arrangements—stock option or purchase plans, profitsharing or bonus plans, or deferred compensation contracts—is to compensate employees for services that they furnish to the corporation. Stock option and purchase plans and profitsharing plans that involve distributions of stock often substitute for larger current cash payments. Occasionally treasury shares are used to cover a few other operating expenses, such as accrued costs of a pension plan, commissions of salesmen, and donations to charities. Those distributions of stock are classed with operating purposes because they relate to expenses incurred for normal business operations.

The described transactions should be viewed as a part of operations because of their natures and purposes; distributing stock to satisfy liabilities does not change the underlying nature and purpose of incurring costs. The operations aspects of the transactions do not take on a unique character because treasury stock is involved, however, the accounting may be more complex than for the distribution of previously unissued shares. Accounting for treasury stock transactions for operating purposes usually varies because the shares distributed must be either treasury stock or previously unissued shares or optionally may be treasury stock or unissued shares.

Results of Transactions. Corporate aims and intended results of treasury stock transactions for operating purposes are of first importance. Treasury stock specifically acquired for a designated operating purpose is necessarily presumed to pertain to results of operations and is related only indirectly to sources of financing and components of equity. A requirement that a corporation acquire and distribute treasury stock is the decisive factor for allocating to net income the benefits or costs of completing the distributions of the stock. The total costs of arrangements that contemplate that the corporation may incur costs to acquire stock become a part of the related operations. For example, a board of directors may authorize and direct management to reacquire stock to comply with an operating objective, and the decision is made with the full knowledge that reacquiring the stock is virtually certain to entail costs. Sometimes the anticipated costs may be reduced because the fair value of the stock rises after it is reacquired. But a benefit from the arrangement is possible only under certain combinations of circumstances, as shown later in this section.

Treasury stock is an alternative. Most treasury stock transactions for operating purposes are substitutes for other forms of consideration for costs incurred. Deferred compensation payable in shares of stock of the employer corporation serves as a good illustration. Alternatives to that arrangement could be larger current salary payments, deferred cash payments, purchase of insurance or annuity contracts, deferred or current distributions of marketable securities or other assets, and possibly others. If one of the alternatives were selected, the corporation would without question recognize the distributions as cost of compensation. The analysis in this section aims to find if choosing the alternative of distributing treasury stock should affect the costs of compensation which are then allocated to operations.

Distributing treasury stock does not alter the nature or purposes of the basic transaction. The costs incurred relate to providing compensation for services of employees, an operating expense. Many accountants are reluctant to recognize all the costs as part of net income if the compensation arrangement involves treasury stock. Those beliefs no doubt stem from the 1938 AICPA view that no "profit or losses" on treasury stock transactions could be included in net income. However, that statement was written in the context of a corporation trading its own shares, not in the context of acquiring and distributing treasury stock for operating expenses. Today corporations often reacquire stock specifically to meet obligations set by a prearranged plan to distribute stock to employees and others.

Variety in distributions of stock. Treasury stock distributed to cover operating expenses may be divided between two distinctly different situations: (1) treasury shares are acquired because they are required for distributions and (2) treasury shares held are required to be distributed or the distribution of either treasury or unissued shares is discretionary.

Unless treasury stock is acquired specifically for required distributions, the results of transactions are not identifiable with a specific operating purpose and its related costs. The financial effects of distributing undesignated treasury shares should be the same as if previously unissued shares were distributed. The requirement to acquire treasury stock governs whether the results of treasury stock transactions should be recognized in net income.

Variations of arrangements and circumstances for distributing reacquired stock for operating purposes are endless. The more usual circumstances and arrangements for compensation involving distributions of stock illustrate numerous existing variations.

1. Management is required to distribute previously unissued shares of stock and

    reserves authorized and previously unissued shares at the date either the commitment is assumed or the obligation is incurred or

    reserves no stock.

2. Management is required to distribute shares of treasury stock held at the time the plan is adopted.

3. Management in its discretion may distribute either previously unissued shares or treasury shares of stock and

    reserves authorized and previously unissued shares at the date either the commitment is assumed or the obligation is incurred,

    reserves shares of treasury stock held at the time the plan is adopted at the date either the commitment is assumed or the obligation is incurred,

    acquires treasury stock after the plan is adopted and

reserves reacquired shares at the date either the stock is purchased or the obligation is incurred, or

reserves no stock.

4. Management is required to acquire treasury stock after the plan is adopted and to distribute reacquired shares.

5. Management in its discretion may distribute either previously unissued shares or treasury shares of stock but is directed by the board of directors to adopt and carry out a plan of distribution and designates the shares to be distributed as

authorized and previously unissued shares,

treasury stock held at the time the plan is adopted, or

treasury stock to be acquired later.

The four described circumstances that require or may involve the distribution of treasury stock (2 through 5) are distinct.

If management is required to satisfy an obligation by distributing reacquired shares already held as treasury stock (2 above), the transaction is no different from distributing previously unissued shares. Designating treasury shares for a compensation arrangement simply earmarks the specific shares to be distributed. Accounting for their issuance should correspond to that for newly issued shares or the sale of treasury shares. The acquisition of the treasury stock for financing purposes, which includes shares for undesignated purposes, should have been accounted for as though the shares were retired. The issuance of the treasury shares for compensation or other liabilities should be recorded as additional contributed equity as described in the financing purpose section of this chapter.

If management has the choice to distribute previously unissued shares or treasury shares to satisfy an obligation (3 above), benefits or costs of using treasury stock cannot be considered part of the compensation arrangement. The arbitrary choice of treasury stock is a physical identification of the shares but is unrelated to the costs of compensation. Otherwise, additional costs or benefits would be eliminated merely by deciding to distribute previously unissued shares. Two similar transactions of one corporation could result in different expenses of operations because management selected one or the other shares of stock. The only significance of acquiring and reserving the treasury stock after a plan is adopted is that the corporation is assured that sufficient shares will be available at the time stock is needed for distribution under a plan.

If management is required or adopts a plan to purchase stock to be reserved as treasury shares for a purpose (4 and 5 above), benefits or costs after the shares are reacquired are directly related to the operating purpose of the transaction and includable in results of operations. The reacquisition of stock is not discretionary but is required to complete the arrangements adopted. The corporation disburses cash to acquire the shares and holds the shares to issue later to satisfy its obligation. Unless treasury stock is distributed to satisfy the obligation, cash or its equivalent would be the substitute. The costs should be the same whether the corporation distributes cash to employees or disburses cash to purchase treasury stock for distribution. The reason for the reacquisition of stock determines the accounting for the costs of the stock transactions.

Required and discretionary distributions. One clear distinction between treasury stock transactions required for operating purposes and those in which treasury stock is optional is that management does not control the proceeds of required dispositions. The consideration received for either distribution or sale under a plan are set by the terms of the plan. Compliance is not discretionary, and the consideration is designated by provisions of the plan. Management may not advance or postpone distributions of stock to alter the proceeds of dispositions.

Treasury stock acquired for and required by operating arrangements is set apart from that for financing purposes because the stock is not directly related to equity financing and existing equity interests. Operating transactions affect retained earnings through periodic net income but have no effect on existing contributions of stockholders.

Recording reacquired stock. Cost is the appropriate carrying amount of treasury shares acquired for distributions under an operating arrangement. Shares of treasury stock acquired and held to comply with terms of operating plans are to be distributed ultimately to satisfy either an accrued liability or a commitment for a potential liability.

It follows that treasury stock required for operating purposes should be shown as an asset of a corporation. The corporation has used available funds to reacquire the stock and in turn holds the stock as an asset to be distributed later to satisfy liabilities. The securities are earmarked for distribution to cover designated costs. The fact that the securities are stock of the corporation does not change the nature of the entire transaction. The acquisition of the stock does not reduce the equity of the corporation temporarily; a substitute asset is acquired to satisfy liabilities. Retained earnings are reduced by the expenses accrued as liabilities and to reduce them further by all or a part of the purchase price of the treasury stock would be meaningless and perhaps even misleading.

Changes in market value of the stock need not be recognized currently. Later market prices of the stock and provisions for distribution determine whether a corporation may incur an additional cost or realize a benefit as the result of distributing treasury shares to cover operating costs.

If a required distribution is a designated number of shares of stock regardless of market price, acquiring the shares hedges the amount of the liability against further fluctuations in the price of the stock. Adjusting both the asset and liability for changes in market value of the stock is unnecessary. If the liability is a fixed dollar amount to be satisfied by the value of stock at the date of distribution, a corporation realizes at the time of distribution the benefits or losses of reacquiring and holding the stock.

Presenting treasury stock held. A corporation may acquire and hold treasury stock to satisfy a specific obligation, but the cost of the stock should not be deducted from the related liability. Two items exist— one is an asset and the other a liability—and they should be shown separately. A ban on offsetting them is comparable to prohibiting the deduction of cash from accounts payable. The number of treasury shares held as an asset should be disclosed in a note referenced to the stockholders' equity section of the balance sheet as well as to the asset.

Even though treasury shares may be designated for an operating plan, the stock should be recorded as retired at the date acquired unless the shares are *required* to be distributed under the plan. As discussed earlier in this section, a corporation did not acquire assets to satisfy a specific obligation.

Dispositions of Treasury Stock for Operating Purposes. Treasury stock acquired and held for an operating purpose is distributed later to satisfy a liability that may be greater, less, or the same as the cost of the shares of treasury stock. A difference represents an adjustment of the costs of operations. The period for which the adjustment is recorded depends on the arrangements and the final determination of effects of the transaction. Distributions for different purposes are analyzed and discussed separately beginning with the most common type of compensation plan.

Compensation plan. The reasonableness of including in net income all effects of treasury stock specifically acquired for operating purposes may be illustrated for deferred compensation under four assumed situations.

A corporation adopts in Year X an additional compensation plan involving distribution of its stock. It awards and accrues additional compensation of $10,000 in Year Y and distributes shares of stock of the corporation as compensation in Year Z.

The market prices of the stock are:

Year X—plan adopted	$ 75
Year Y—compensation awarded	100
Year Z—stock distributed	250

(X, Y, and Z are not consecutive years)

The assumed situations are:

1. Treasury stock held in Year X was acquired at $50 a share and is required to be distributed under the plan. The distribution is based on the market value of the stock at date of award.
2. Treasury stock acquired after the plan is adopted is required to be distributed under the plan. The treasury stock is acquired in Year X+1 at $80 a share. The distribution is based on the market value of the stock at date of award.
3. Treasury stock acquired after the plan is adopted is required to be distributed under the plan. The treasury stock is acquired in Year X+2 at $90 a share. The distribution is based on the market value of the stock at date of distribution.
4. Treasury stock acquired after the plan is adopted is required to be distributed under the plan. The treasury stock is acquired in Year Y+2 at $120 a share. The distribution is based on the market value of the stock at date of award.

Acquiring shares as required by a plan should be the salient factor in determining the charges to net income. In the second, third, and

CHAPTER 11: DECREASES IN EQUITY SECURITIES

fourth situations management was authorized to buy shares of stock for later distribution. If the treasury shares to be distributed are those held at the date the plan is adopted (Situation 1), the transaction is the same as distributing previously unissued shares.

The present income tax laws complicate accounting for deferred compensation payable in shares of stock. The deduction allowable to the corporation for federal tax purposes is determined by the market value of the stock at the date distributed. The following illustration of recommended accounting shows expenses reduced by the additional tax benefit and by the increase in the market price of the treasury stock distributed.

Recommended Accounting

	Situation			
	1	2	3	4
Compensation expense in year of award (Year Y)	$ 10,000	$ 10,000	$ 10,000	$ 10,000
Additional compensation expense representing increase in liability,				
Years Y to Z (Total—$25,000)	15,000			
Years Y+1 and Y+2 (Total—$12,000)				2,000
Additional benefit recorded in year of distribution (Year Z) as reduction of compensation or of financing expenses				
(100 shares at $100 a share less cost of $80 a share)		(2,000)		
(40 shares at $250 a share less cost of $90 a share)			(6,400)	
Tax benefit (assumed tax rate of 50%) of stock distribution	(12,500)	(12,500)	(5,000)	(12,500)
Net expense, Years Y to Z	$ 12,500	$(4,500)	$(1,400)	$(500)
Additional equity recorded in year of distribution (Year Z) as contributed equity	$ 25,000			

The net expense represents the costs incurred for the authorized compensation arrangement. In the third situation, the corporation distributes 40 shares with a market value of $10,000 and holds 60 shares of treasury stock at a cost of $90 a share. The remaining 60 shares are not distributable under the terms of the plan.

257

Present Accounting

	Situation			
	1	2	3	4
Compensation expense in year of award (Year Y)				$10,000
Treasury stock reserved for distribution — 100 shares at $100 each				
(Cost of $50 a share)	$10,000			
(Cost of $80 a share)		$10,000		
(Cost of $90 a share)			$10,000	
Tax benefit (assumed tax rate of 50%)	(5,000)	(5,000)	(5,000)	(5,000)
Net expense	$ 5,000	$ 5,000	$ 5,000	$ 5,000
Changes in equity (Year Z):				
Additional capital recorded in year of distribution (Year Z) of treasury stock				
(100 shares at $100 a share less cost of $50 a share)	$ 5,000			
(100 shares at $100 a share less cost of $80 a share)		$ 2,000		
(40 shares at $250 a share less cost of $90 a share)			$ 6,400	
(100 shares at cost of $120 a share less $100 a share)				$(2,000)*
Additional tax benefit of stock distribution recorded in year of distribution (Year Z) as additional capital				
Tax deduction of $25,000 less compensation liability of $10,000 at assumed tax rate of 50%	7,500	7,500		7,500
Total additional capital, Year Z	12,500	9,500	6,400	5,500
Elimination of cost of treasury shares held in Year X and carried as an unallocated reduction of equity (100 shares at cost of $50 a share)	5,000			
Increase in stockholders' equity, Year Z	$17,500	$ 9,500	$ 6,400	$ 5,500

* Accounting described in APB Opinion 25; the amount might be deducted from retained earnings depending on earlier treasury stock transactions. The prevalent procedure before that Opinion was issued was to record the amount as additional compensation expense representing the increase in the liability from date of award to date the treasury stock was acquired (Years Y+1 and Y+2).

The additional tax benefit from distributing stock that has increased in price after award is shown in the illustration as additional capital to follow the popular view that all effects of treasury stock transactions should be excluded from net income and retained earnings.

Comparison. A comparison of the results of each of the four situations under the recommended and the present accounting shows that after the treasury stock is distributed the resulting total equity is the same. The components of equity—contributed equity and retained earnings—differ. The recommended accounting includes the entire costs and benefits of the compensation plan in retained earnings. Acquiring and distributing treasury stock as required by the plan has no effect on contributed stockholders' equity.

Treasury shares acquired and held for the purpose of a plan are a hedge against fluctuations in the price of the stock. Price fluctuations affect net income and are unrelated to equity transactions. In the third situation, the corporation has a remaining asset of shares of stock not required for distribution. If the remaining stock is sold at the current market price, the excess over cost should be included in net income because the stock was acquired originally to meet an obligation under the operating plan.

Some plans provide that a liability for deferred compensation may be satisfied by distributing stock or its cash equivalent at the option of either the employer or the employee. Neither option changes the basic nature of the transaction. The illustrations of accounting for costs of treasury stock in different situations apply in optional arrangements. For example, if in Situation 2 the employee elects the distribution of cash instead of stock, the corporation would distribute cash of $25,000 to the employee. The corporation could obtain the cash by selling 100 shares of treasury stock. The financial and tax effects for the corporation are the same as those shown in the illustration.

Accounting for newly issued stock. To clarify the differences between the recommended accounting for plans requiring the use of treasury stock and those requiring previously unissued stock (or an option of treasury stock), the accounting is illustrated in the following table. All facts in the four situations remain the same except that treasury stock need not be distributed.

Recommended Accounting for previously unissued stock

	Situation			
	1	2	3	4
Compensation expense in year of award (Year Y)	$ 10,000	$ 10,000	$ 10,000	$ 10,000
Additional compensation expense representing increase in liability, Years Y to Z (Total—$25,000)	15,000	15,000		15,000
Tax benefit (assumed tax rate of 50%) of stock distribution	(12,500)	(12,500)	(5,000)	(12,500)
Net expense, Years Y to Z	$ 12,500	$ 12,500	$ 5,000	$ 12,500
Changes in equity for stock transactions				
Reduction for purchase of treasury stock				
(Cost of 100 shares at $80 a share in Year X + 1)		$(8,000)		
(Cost of 100 shares at $90 a share in Year X + 2)			$(9,000)	
(Cost of 100 shares at $120 a share in Year Y + 2)				$(12,000)
Increase for fair value of stock distributed in Year Z				
100 shares at $250 a share	$ 25,000	25,000		25,000
40 shares at $250 a share			10,000	
Net increase in stockholders' equity	$ 25,000	$ 17,000	$ 1,000	$ 13,000

The combined effects on stockholders' equity are the same as for those plans that require using treasury stock, but the compensation expense included in net income differs if treasury stock is acquired for purposes of the plan. (The corporation retains 60 shares of treasury stock in the third situation illustrated on page 257.) The illustration also shows that unless treasury stock is required and distributed under the terms of a plan the net compensation expense is the same regardless of the date the stock is reacquired or regardless of the purchase price of the treasury stock.

The analysis in this section leads to the conclusion that the benefits or costs of acquiring treasury stock required for a compensation plan relate to the operating costs of compensation for services and should be included in net income. However, the costs or benefits of the treasury stock transactions need not be classified as compensation costs. Arguments for classification as financing expenses as well as compensation expenses are justifiable. The decision probably rests on the terms of a particular plan and the discretion exercised by management in meeting its obligations. The terms, conditions, and discretion of some plans may show that the costs or benefits should be allocated to both compensation and financing expenses.

Stock option and purchase plans. Stock reacquired to be issued under stock option or purchase plans is similarly related to operations, but the circumstances differ from compensation or profitsharing plans. Since stock option or purchase plans entitle employees to purchase shares of stock at designated prices, part of the consideration for the shares issued is the cash the corporation receives. Customarily, outstanding options granted by a corporation are now recognized as a commitment, and stock issued under plans is now accounted for only at the time the options are exercised and only at the cash consideration received.

Chapter 9 on increases in outstanding shares of stock concluded that the consideration for stock issued on the exercise of stock options should be measured by the fair value of the stock at the date of exercise. The estimated compensation should be accrued from the date the option is granted and the accumulated accrual shown as contingent equity financing until the option is exercised. Total compensation plus cash received equals the consideration to be recorded as contributed equity at the date an option is exercised.

Obviously, if treasury stock is acquired for purposes and requirements of option plans, the consideration received for option stock rarely equals the cost unless the corporation purchases the stock on the date the option is exercised. The difference between the cost of treasury shares and the consideration received for the stock are properly costs of operating the plan—either compensation or financing costs. As a part of overall financial planning, a corporation may decide to acquire at advantageous prices the stock to be sold later under stock option and purchase plans. Issuing treasury stock on exercise of the options does not change the contributed equity of the corporation but rather is a cost or benefit of carrying out the required terms of the plan. The cost or benefit should be recognized as a part of operations at the date the option is exercised.

Unless treasury shares are required and have been specifically acquired for a stock option or purchase plan, the fair value of the shares issued on exercise of options should be recorded as equity contributed for newly issued shares.

Other operating costs. Shares of treasury stock that are distributed in payment of operating costs other than compensation and option plans cannot be considered as a part of an operating arrangement. Settlement of pension costs is an illustration and occurs more often than distributing stock for other operating costs. The situation is not comparable to a prearranged compensation plan. Stock rather than cash is distributed to the pension trustees and then only with their consent. The discretion for form of payment does not rest with corporate management; much less is the distribution of stock of the corporation required. The effects of the transaction are the same as if trustees of a pension fund were willing to and did buy shares of stock of the corporation. The corporation should record the issuance of the treasury shares the same as if previously unissued shares had been sold at current fair value.

Treasury stock for multi-purposes. A corporation may reacquire stock and hold it as required for several designated operating purposes, but the stock may not be distributed or sold for a particular designated purpose. For example, employees may not exercise the options granted to them, and the treasury shares held for the option plan may be transferred to another purpose. If the arrangements of another plan require treasury stock to be distributed, the shares should retain their classification as an asset.

Treasury shares that are not required for other specific operating purposes may either be (1) sold or (2) retained as treasury shares for financing purposes. The benefits or costs of selling shares should be included in net income because the corporation reacquired the shares to carry out arrangements of an operating plan. Since the treasury stock was acquired for obligations under a plan, the ensuing costs or benefits relate to the plan, not directly to components of equity.

If treasury stock is not distributed for its original operating purpose and is to be held for a financing purpose instead, the shares should no longer be accounted for as an asset. Costs or benefits of holding the stock for the designated purpose are properly included in operations.

Therefore, the basis of the shares of stock transferred to financing purposes is not cost but the fair value at the time the purpose is changed. The adjustment from cost to fair value of the treasury stock is includable in net income as a part of the expenses of operating a plan. The new basis should be allocated to components of equity as recommended for the constructive retirement of treasury stock acquired for financing purposes.

Results of Recommended Accounting

The accounting for treasury stock recommended in this study results in financial statements showing as a separate amount the cost of those shares held as an asset of the corporation but not of other treasury shares. Only treasury stock acquired to meet the requirements of a specific operating arrangement can meet the tests to be classified as assets. All other shares of treasury stock should be accounted for as a retirement of stock at the date acquired.

The sale, distribution, or retirement of treasury shares held as assets may result in a benefit or additional cost of operations that should be included in net income. The later sale or distribution of other treasury stock results in an increase in equity contributed by stockholders.

12

Adjustments of Equity

This chapter is concerned primarily with major adjustments of equity interests in recapitalizations and reorganizations. Customarily, a corporation adopts an approved plan of recapitalization or reorganization that modifies basic equity interests after incurring continued or sudden large losses. But a corporation may realign the existing equity interests through other changes, for example, by retiring equity securities and by issuing additional equity securities. Those kinds of changes in equity are not unusual in profitable corporations. Adjustments of equity interests other than those through recapitalizations and reorganizations are discussed in earlier chapters of this study.

The last section of this chapter is devoted to transactions with nonstockholders that are often now accounted for as adjustments of stockholders' equity.

Major Adjustments of Capital Structure

Changes in Outstanding Securities. The financial effects of changes in outstanding corporate securities—investments of both creditors and equity owners—may be relatively minor, perhaps to extend the maturity date or to increase the fixed interest rate of a debt security, or they may be extensive, sometimes to reduce existing rights and interests of owners or to eliminate others.

Arthur S. Dewing stated that typical readjustments of the capital structure of corporations fall into four types.

Slight, but nevertheless real, changes in the contract between the corporation and its preference security-holders.

Important, perhaps radical, changes in the provisions pertaining to the stock or funded debt issues.

Readjustments of balance sheet valuations resulting in the revision of the stated value of the capital stock and of the surplus.

Comprehensive readjustments affecting the whole capital structure.[1]

He added that a great number of gradations surround each type of capital readjustment and that it is difficult to catalogue an individual change as one of the four types.

The terms recapitalization and reorganization cover a multitude of changes in and adjustments of outstanding securities and rights but adjustments of equity interests nearly always characterize either event. Some minor changes in securities affect stockholders' equity only indirectly through net income and dividend distributions in future periods.

Proportionate Equity Interests Unchanged. The proportionate interests of existing stockholders are unchanged by a so-called quasi-reorganization. That procedure is unique because an existing corporation obtains a new basis for accounting without a formal reorganization. The changes in equity pertain entirely to the amounts of equity components instead of to the proportionate interests of stockholders. Although a quasi-reorganization does not adjust the relative equity interests, the topic comprises one section of this chapter because the procedure is closely related to corporate reorganizations.

Recapitalizations and Reorganizations

The ability of a corporation to continue operations as a going concern may be in doubt if it is in financial distress or insolvent, and a voluntary reorganization may be the solution. Or, either a bankrupt corporation or its creditors may petition the courts to supervise a reorganization. The origin of plans and the requirements for approval of plans are not a part of this study, which is limited to accounting for adjustments of outstanding securities and equity interests.

Equity Interests Adjusted. Recapitalizations and reorganizations of corporations ordinarily change the rights, claims, limitations, and

---

[1] *The Financial Policy of Corporations,* Volume II, 1953, pp. 1176-1178.

restrictions of security holders in a way that adjusts the interrelation of the respective interests of existing owners. The terms recapitalization and reorganization are not precise and mutually exclusive and are often used interchangeably for some adjustments of securities. A recapitalization differs from a reorganization only in degree, even though one change may be voluntary and the other may require court approval. The interests of owners are altered by either transaction, but a recapitalization may be limited to changing the interests of only some classes of owners and creditors. In contrast, a reorganization can be called a complete recapitalization because all existing interests are affected. Distinctions between the two terms are meaningless for determining the accounting procedures which need to recognize the revisions in equity interests and total equity regardless of the form of the plan. The term reorganization is used in the rest of this chapter to simplify the references.

Retaining sources of equity. The aim in devising a plan of reorganization is to recognize the specified rights and limitations of each class of owners and creditors. The prior rights attaching to some securities take precedence over the rights of residual interests, which are sometimes terminated in a reorganization.

The purposes of the accounting procedures should be to segregate securities with similar rights and limitations and to recognize the adjustments of those interests. At the same time a corporation should maintain the two component sources of resulting stockholders' equity—contributions by remaining stockholders and retained earnings, if any.

Accomplishing the accounting purposes may be simple or difficult depending on the existing financial status and the types of changes in outstanding securities. For instance, accounting for a reorganization is less complex if an existing deficit at least equals the contributions by common stockholders and their ownership interests are eliminated; accounting for a reorganization is more complex if holders of debt securities with interest payments in arrears are offered a selection of equity securities in settlement of their claims.

The effects of different types of adjustments on the component sources of equity are analyzed in this chapter in relation to the principles recommended in this study for recording the origin of and changes in those components.

Types of transactions. The discussion in this chapter is divided by types of changes in existing equity interests. The types of transactions that may be classified as reorganizations are seemingly endless because outstanding securities and equity components vary greatly between individual corporations. However, all of the transactions fit into two general categories—(1) a corporation may exchange outstanding securities for other securities or (2) a corporation may distribute additional but different securities to the holders of outstanding securities. The primary difference in the two categories is whether existing securities remain outstanding or are replaced by other securities. Some transactions in a reorganization combine both categories.

The purpose of the next two sections is to find guides for accounting for the two categories of adjustments of equity but not attempt to cover the recording of every possible type of change. Statutory requirements and the legal consequences in different circumstances are ignored in selecting the preferred accounting procedures.[2]

Exchange of Outstanding Securities

An exchange of outstanding securities for other securities of the same corporation affects stockholders' equity either at the time of the exchange or in future periods. The accounting for immediate changes in equity interests should recognize the consideration distributed to existing security holders and the consideration received for securities issued.

Rank of Equity Interests Unchanged. An exchange of equity securities that has no effect on the priority of classes of securities is the least significant exchange in relation to existing stockholders' equity. Holders of senior securities may agree to accept another senior security with reduced cumulative dividend distributions, deletion of participating features, lower redemption prices, elimination of sinking fund requirements, or waiver of voting rights. Changes of that type modify the rights of the existing stockholders of all classes but the new securities distributed retain a senior rank. A security with new provisions is substituted for a former outstanding security.

Changing outstanding securities of course affects financial results in the future, but the contributions by the stockholders remain the same at the date of the exchange of securities and the transaction neither increases nor decreases retained earnings at that date. The switch in

---

[2] James S. Schindler included a summary of legal factors on pp. 50 and 51 of *Quasi-Reorganization*, 1958.

securities involves neither the receipt nor the distribution of consideration. The change is in the rights and limitations that are often disclosed in financial statements but not recorded in the financial accounts.

Partition of Interests. Holders of common stock may agree to accept in exchange for their securities two classes of common stock, one of which has lesser rights to dividend distributions or some other limitation. That type of an exchange of securities has no effect on retained earnings and no effect on total contributions by common stockholders. The existing interests and rights of the stockholders are divided and the parts are then represented by more and different certificates.

The amount contributed by common stockholders should be allocated to each class of common stock because each class of security now represents different interests. Future transactions may affect one class of stock and not the other. Further, stockholders may dispose of their new securities and new owners may be primarily interested in the equity interest of one security. Each class of new common stock will no doubt sell at a price different from the other class because the rights and limitations conveyed by each security differ. The market price of each class of common stock at the date both are traded may therefore serve as a basis for apportioning the total equity contributed by common stockholders to contributions for each class of the new issues. The contributions for the existing equity interests are thereby allocated to the substituted divided interests.

Common Stock Interests Adjusted. Some reorganizations that adjust the interests of holders of senior securities allow the common stockholders to retain changed but still residual interests in the corporation. Accounting for changes of that type needs to recognize the consideration received and the consideration distributed for exchanges by senior security holders because the proportionate common stock interests are changed.

The principles involved are the same as in conversions and retirements of senior securities, discussed in Chapters 9 and 11. That is, prior claims are settled by the distribution of other securities, and the fair value of those securities measures the consideration. The financial results of the exchange affect net income or equity depending on the type of senior security and the adjustment of existing rights. For instance, the benefits or expenses of exchanging preferred stock for common stock are adjustments of retained earnings (or deficit); the benefits or expenses of retiring debt securities by an exchange for stock reduce or increase costs of creditor financing which are included in net income.

Debt securities exchanged for equity. A distribution of equity securities in exchange for outstanding debt securities is complex because the transaction involves both the claims of creditors and interests of owners. An exchange of that type often accompanies other simultaneous transactions such as eliminating the interests of existing common stockholders and restating equity components to eliminate a deficit. Accounting for those transactions and adjustments is independent of the exchange for debt securities, and the recommended treatment is outlined in later sections of this chapter.

The entire claim of holders of a debt security may be satisfied by an exchange for preferred or common stock. That transaction is in the nature of a conversion of a debt security and accounting for conversions of securities is described in Chapter 9 on increases in equity securities. The exchange of securities should therefore be accounted for as a redemption of a debt security. That is, the fair value of the stock issued measures the consideration received for the equity securities and also the consideration distributed to satisfy the principal and interest claims of the creditors.

The fair value of the stock distributed in settlement of the liabilities usually differs from the recorded amount of the liability for the outstanding debt because the liability was not settled for the required cash payment. Since a difference relates to debt financing, the resulting expense or benefit should be recognized in income for the period. The adjustment of the liability on settlement is thus treated the same as the results of retiring a debt security by a cash payment that differs from the recorded liability. The fair value of the newly issued stock should be recorded as contributions for the new stock.

Preferred stock exchanged for common. A corporation that has issued a noncallable preferred stock may find an advantage in retiring the stock, especially if the dividend rate is higher than the current rate for similar stock. However, preferred stockholders will usually accept an exchange offer only if cash or the value of other securities offered in exchange is greater than the market price of the preferred stock.

The substance of the exchange is the same as a redemption of preferred stock. Thus common stock issued in exchange for outstanding preferred stock should be recorded at its fair value, and the difference between that consideration and the amount contributed by preferred stockholders deducted from retained earnings.

Common Stock Interests Eliminated. The dire financial situation of a corporation may signal the need to reduce the rights of senior security interests for the corporation to continue operations. Exchanging senior equity securities for common stock and eliminating the interests of existing common stockholders often accompanies that step. A consequence of the reorganization is that the equity interests of both existing preferred and common stockholders and the components of equity are transformed immediately.

Senior equity securities exchanged for common stock. A deficit usually exceeds the contributions by common stockholders if a corporation must substitute common stock for senior securities and eliminate existing common stock interests. Accumulated losses incurred before the reorganization have consumed the original investments of common stockholders. The accounting for the reorganization should eliminate the equity contributed by the existing common stockholders as in retirement of stock and should reduce the deficit by the amount of the contributions eliminated.

The amounts contributed originally by the preferred stockholders become in turn contributions applicable to the new outstanding common stock distributed in exchange. Although the corporation received the consideration originally for a senior security, that security is now exchanged for and replaced by a residual equity security with new rights. An exchange of senior securities does not change the amount contributed by those stockholders remaining as owners but their equity interests in the corporation are revised.

A deficit may exceed the equity contributed by the common stockholders whose interests are eliminated and the excess may be deducted from the contributions of former preferred stockholders or the reorganized corporation may continue with a deficit. If equity recognized as contributions for the new common stock is reduced by the remainder of a deficit, retained earnings in later financial statements should be dated to disclose that the earnings are accumulated since a reorganization. In effect, the corporation starts anew at the date the senior equity securities are exchanged for common stock.

Common stock exchanged for warrants. Some corporations have exchanged stock purchase warrants for outstanding common stock as part of a reorganization. The practice is defended by some because by that method the common stockholders are not forced to relinquish all their rights and deprived of potential value. Others state that distributing stock purchase warrants in a reorganization is objectionable in principle.

> The SEC . . . has taken a stand against this practice, contending that if the old stockholders really have no equity they are not even entitled to warrants. This view was followed by the ICC in its action on railroad reorganization plans and was sustained by the United States Supreme Court.[3]

Some distributions of warrants to retire common stock have been permitted, however, and the consideration received for the warrants, if any, may be determined from the equity components applicable to the former common stock. An excess of contributions by common stockholders over a deficit represents the amount to be assigned to the warrants, but if a deficit exceeds the contributions, the warrants issued to former common stockholders should be shown in financial statements as outstanding without a dollar amount. The reorganized corporation received no consideration for the warrants at the date issued.

Stock purchase warrants distributed in a reorganization should be classified as contingent equity financing whether or not an amount is assigned to the securities. Accounting for later exercise or expiration of the warrants should be the same as for warrants sold separately for cash (Chapter 9).

Distribution of Additional Securities

A distribution of either additional securities of outstanding issues or new securities to existing security holders is often a form of reorganization because it usually modifies the interrelationship between existing equity interests. A corporation may for various reasons distribute additional securities to holders of debt securities, senior equity securities, or common stock. The discussion of accounting for distributions is segregated in this section by the types of securities held by the recipients of distributions.

Distributions to Holders of Debt Securities. A corporation may distribute additional securities to satisfy part of the claims of holders of

---

[3] Benjamin Graham, David L. Dodd, and Sidney Cottle, *Security Analysis*, 1962, p. 661.

debt securities. For example, common stock may be distributed as a substitute for cash to pay accrued interest on bonds; the principal amount of the bonds remains an outstanding obligation. Distributions of securities to satisfy the principal amount of debt obligations are considered in the earlier section on exchanges of outstanding securities.

Common stock for accrued interest. A distribution of securities in a reorganization that adjusts the ownership interests in a corporation is typified by the distribution of common stock to satisfy the claim of debt holders for accrued interest. The existing stockholders retain equity interests in the corporation, but the transaction ordinarily reduces their proportionate interests. The principles recommended previously for recording other equity security transactions also recognize the financial effects of a distribution.

The fair value of the securities distributed to holders of debt securities should be recorded as the consideration received for the stock issued. The consideration distributed should be measured by the fair value of the stock distributed because the corporation and the holders of debt securities agree to that settlement. The fair value of the stock issued and the accrued interest are often unequal and the difference between the fair value and the liability satisfied represents an additional expense or benefit applicable to debt financing. The amount of interest accrued is not necessarily a good measure of the consideration received for stock issued because the creditors may be willing to accept a security whose current value is less than a cash settlement which might be further postponed. Or, the creditors may insist that the value of the distribution exceed the recorded interest accrued because interest payments were in default for an extended period. Those factors influence the amount of consideration required to settle a contractual obligation for accrued interest. The consideration distributed should be recorded to recognize the financial effects of the negotiated settlement of a liability.

Distributions to Holders of Preferred Stock. Additional securities are rarely distributed to holders of preferred stock unless the stock is redeemed or exchanged for other securities. However, either preferred or common stock may be distributed pro rata to holders of preferred stock in some circumstances.

Preferred stock in lieu of dividends. The most likely reason for a corporation to distribute preferred stock of a new class or the same class to its preferred stockholders is to distribute securities in lieu of paying cash dividends in arrears. The shares distributed, of course, carry a preference over the common stock in later distributions of dividends and in liquidation. But a corporation distributes no assets to the preferred stockholders at the time the new shares are issued, and the stockholders contribute no additional funds or other assets to the corporation. Instead, the preferred stockholders waive their rights to accumulated dividends in exchange for the rights conveyed by the additional shares of stock.

A corporation expects that retained earnings will be reduced by later dividend payments to the holders of the additional shares and later redemption payments, if any. But retained earnings are not changed at the date additional preferred stock is distributed. The prior rights of the preferred stock may ultimately affect the retained earnings applicable to the shares of common stock. The proportionate interests of the common stockholders remain constant even though the transaction may later reduce the amount of equity applicable to the common stock interests.

Distributing additional preferred shares of the same class of stock changes the interests of preferred stockholders in two respects only: (1) future cumulative dividends are greater and (2) future redemption or liquidation payments are greater. Neither change needs to be recognized at the time additional shares are distributed; the transaction increases the total rights of the existing preferred stockholders in future periods. The number of outstanding shares of preferred stock is increased at the date of distribution but the status of equity is unchanged.

Some authors contend that since preferred stockholders accept additional stock in complete satisfaction of their rights to dividends in arrears, the consideration for the stock issued is the waiver of the preferred right to dividends. Therefore the transaction is in substance a stock subscription settled by preferred dividends.[4] That argument ignores that a stockholder is entitled to receive a dividend after the directors have declared a dividend; even cumulative dividends do not accrue over time as does interest on debt securities. The dividend right of the preferred stockholders is that their limited distributions take precedence over distributions to the common stockholders.

The new shares outstanding should be shown in financial statements with no contribution from stockholders, and the legal aspects of the

---

[4] For example, Thomas York, "Stock Dividends from the Viewpoint of the Declaring Corporation," *The Accounting Review,* March 1941, p. 33.

shares should be disclosed in an explanatory note. Distributions of preferred stock of the same class may be restricted in some states because shares need to be fully paid and nonassessable. Meeting those requirements may be impossible if the stock is assigned a high par value. Since the designation of par value is discretionary, a corporation may avoid the limitation by issuing a new preferred stock with a nominal or no par value.

Common stock distributed. A distribution of shares of common stock to holders of preferred stock changes the existing rights of both the common and preferred stockholders. The corporate laws of some states may permit distributions of that type, and the terms of an issue of preferred stock may provide for common stock to be distributed. For example, a corporation may be required to distribute common stock to holders of a participating preferred stock if it declares a common stock dividend on outstanding common stock. Some preferred stock issued recently provides for regular dividends distributable in common stock in lieu of cash dividends.

Since the common stockholders surrender to the preferred stockholders a part of their existing interests in a corporation, those changes in interests that are permitted and approved should be recognized by accounting for the consideration received for the common stock issued, which is measured by the fair value of the stock. That method shows the effects on the ownership interests of other common stockholders and records the change in proportionate interests due to a transfer to the preferred stockholders.

Distributions to Holders of Common Stock. A distribution of additional shares of common stock to holders of outstanding shares of the same class is discussed in the stock dividend section of Chapter 10. The conclusions of that discussion, however, do not necessarily apply to the distribution of shares of preferred stock to common stockholders.

A corporation may distribute to common stockholders shares of a new issue of preferred stock that does not carry rights taking precedence over the rights of other outstanding senior securities. If so, the present rights and limitations of the common stockholders have been separated into several parts but the total rights of those divided interests are not changed. The common stockholders have received only that which they already held. However, the existing rights attached to a share of common stock have been divided. The amounts of the components of common stockholders' equity—contributions by stockholders and retained earnings—are not changed and the total proportionate interests are the same.

The distribution of preferred stock to common stockholders does reduce the ownership interests conveyed by the shares of common stock and an amount should be assigned to the interest and rights conveyed by the new preferred stock. The original contributions of stockholders now apply to two different outstanding securities. The division may be recognized and sources of equity may remain intact by allocating the total contributions for common stock to the common and preferred stocks based on the fair value of each security. The original contributions are then shown as the contributions by the preferred and common stockholders as revised by the distribution.

Since the new preferred stock carries prior rights, the additional stock could be recorded at its fair value and retained earnings reduced by that amount as though a cash dividend had been distributed. That accounting would be similar to distributing a debt security or incurring an obligation for later distributions to common stockholders. But distributing ownership interests is not comparable with incurring an obligation: retained earnings are not reduced and contributions are not increased. The sources of total stockholders' equity remain the same.

Optional dividends. Sometimes a corporation declares an optional dividend, that is, the dividend is declared as an amount distributable for each share of preferred or common stock, and the stockholders are given the option to receive that amount in either cash or common stock. The number of shares of stock distributed is ordinarily determined by the market price of the stock in relation to the amount of the dividend declared. The arrangement is similar to offering stockholders the right to subscribe to shares of stock. The corporation retains cash that otherwise would be distributed to satisfy the obligation for dividends declared. Therefore, the total dividend should be recorded as a reduction of retained earnings and the portion applicable to shares of common stock distributed should be recorded as consideration received for the additional stock issued.

Quasi-Reorganization

The proportionate interests of the stockholders of a corporation are unchanged by one so-called reorganization—a quasi-reorganization—which is now recognized as an acceptable accounting procedure.

A quasi-reorganization is explained in Chapter 4 as an accounting reorganization without the need for the formal organization of a new corporation or a formal court procedure. The term may be confusing because it implies that the procedure only resembles a reorganization, but a corporation does in effect start anew for financial and accounting purposes. Components of equity may be restated not only by transfers between the existing components but also by revaluations of assets and liabilities.

Accompanying Conditions. Business in general or an entire industry may be depressed because activity declines or the level of prices drops. An individual corporation may incur substantial losses for those reasons or because of specific events such as overproduction, whims of popular demand, and influx of foreign imports. The losses may exceed earnings retained previously, and the prospects of the corporation's recovering the remaining costs of its tangible assets from future operations may be remote. Existing, depressed conditions may lead a corporation to sell its assets to another entity, distribute its funds to stockholders, and liquidate. The decline in value of the corporate assets is reflected in the funds distributed in liquidation and correspondingly in the losses the stockholders customarily realize on their investments. But that solution is not inevitable.

By retaining their interests in a corporation the stockholders may obtain greater benefits from future operations than from an immediate liquidation. The proceeds of a forced sale of corporate assets may be less than fair value to the company. A corporation may assume the role of an arm's-length purchaser of a going concern by adjusting the recorded amounts of net assets to current fair values. The corporation then reports later operating results on the same basis as though the assets as a group had been transferred to another entity at fair market value.

Accounting recognition. If accountants were to insist that a corporation must retain the historical-cost basis indefinitely, stockholders wishing to continue operations and to report on a different basis would be forced to form a new corporation to acquire the existing corporate assets. Forming a new corporation and liquidating a former one would mean incurring additional expenses and time-consuming legal procedures. The alternative method of a quasi-reorganization accomplishes the same adjustment of basis within the same corporate entity with continuing equity interests.

Usually, a corporation that adopts a plan for a quasi-reorganization has accumulated a deficit or the accompanying write-down of assets creates a deficit that is eliminated against other components of stockholders' equity. A corporation that has now recorded the two traditional components of capital stock at par or stated value and of additional capital in excess of par or stated value first reduces the additional capital component. To eliminate a deficit, a corporation may need to reduce the par or stated value of its common stock and transfer a corresponding amount from capital stock to additional capital. The proportionate equity interest of one share of stock remains the same and the total equity amount of one share remains the same.

Formal procedure. Both the AICPA and the SEC have specified conditions that must exist and procedures that must be followed for a corporation to effect a quasi-reorganization.[5] Those specifications make the procedure a substitute for forming a new corporation and prevent it from being a frequent, casual, bookkeeping adjustment.

The existing AICPA and SEC pronouncements sanction a quasi-reorganization only if the revaluations of assets and liabilities result in a net write-down. A net write-up is not approved. The merits of that restriction are not investigated in this study because the basic reasons for seeking to adjust the carrying amounts of net assets differ markedly in each circumstance. Successful corporations may wish to write up assets to recognize their current values, and that purpose is unrelated to financial difficulties leading to reorganization.

Procedure Endorsed. A quasi-reorganization is now and should continue to be a voluntary and not a mandatory corporate procedure. Although a quasi-reorganization interferes with the historical record of sources of stockholders' equity, accounting should not deny a corporation the resort to a fresh basis of accounting if economic conditions warrant adjustments of the carrying amounts of net assets. Acceptance, however, is not an endorsement of general departures from the historical-cost basis of accounting. It is an expedient to recognize a significant decline in value by a practical method. The procedure is unacceptable to record an increase in the value of assets, whether or not a deficit exists.

---

[5] Chapter 7A of *ARB 43* and SEC *Accounting Series Release No. 25* are described on pp. 69-70 of Chapter 4.

The procedure changes the carrying amounts of assets and sometimes liabilities as well as revising equity components. A write-down of assets and elimination of a deficit should first reduce the amounts contributed by common stockholders to retain intact the contributions by preferred stockholders. Stockholders' equity after a quasi-reorganization ordinarily consists of one component only—contributions by stockholders. The remaining amount, however, no longer represents the original consideration received for shares of stock outstanding.

Valuation of assets. Realistic values of all assets and liabilities at the date of adjustment provide the basis for accounting in the future. The expectation is that the results of future operations will be reported as profits based on values at the date of adjustment. Since the tax basis of assets is not changed by the adjustments of a quasi-reorganization, the future tax effects of the changes in book bases need to be recognized in determining the fair values at the date of adjustment. The various types of assets and provisions of tax laws result in numerous expected tax effects. [6]

Adjustments at date of quasi-reorganization. A corporation should explain in its financial statements for the period in which a quasi-reorganization occurs the effects of the reorganization and the adjustments of assets, liabilities, and stockholders' equity. The basis for valuing the adjusted assets and liabilities should be disclosed. The informativeness of later financial statements after departing from the historical-cost basis of assets and sources of equity depends on the adequacy of the disclosure of the adjustments recorded in an earlier period.

Disclosure required. Present requirements to disclose that retained earnings represent the results of operations after the date of a quasi-reorganization emphasize that a corporation in effect made a new start at that date. The history of stockholders' equity begins again.

Proposals for disclosing the effects of a quasi-reorganization in financial statements after the year of the adjustment include:

> showing the reduction of "capital surplus" resulting from a quasi-reorganization,

---

[6] D. J. Erickson discussed varied circumstances in "Quasi-Reorganizations and Related Tax Effects," *The Arthur Andersen Chronicle,* July 1946, pp. 173-189.

describing the basis of the carrying amount of assets, and

"dating" of retained earnings–
permanently
as long as significant (rarely more than ten years)
for a minimum of three years.

Continuing indefinitely to disclose a reduction of capital surplus (the contributed component of equity following the earlier recommendations of this study) is of doubtful value. That procedure would contradict the concept of a new start for a corporation. If a quasi-reorganization is the substitute for a beginning, the amount of earlier reductions in net assets to effect the reorganization are pertinent only for tax reporting purposes. The adjusted amounts of the net assets are comparable with the cost basis as if a new corporation had purchased the net assets at fair value at the date of the quasi-reorganization. The value of the proposed disclosure is no greater if a corporation presents the recommended component of contributed equity instead of the traditional capital stock and "capital surplus" components.

An explanation of the carrying amounts of plant and equipment may be a convenient method of disclosing an earlier quasi-reorganization, especially if it is combined with an explanation of dated retained earnings. Explaining the carrying amounts of assets is not essential because disclosing that earnings have been accumulated since a specified date connotes that the net assets were revalued at that date. Also, a corporation may later sell or retire some of the assets revalued in a reorganization and the earlier adjustments of the remaining assets are unlikely to convey an understanding of the effects of the reorganization or the significance of later results of operations.

Dating earnings significant. Explaining that the retained earnings component of stockholders' equity represents undistributed earnings since a quasi-reorganization is the key to presenting informative financial statements. Some proposals for disclosing that fact seem arbitrary and may be meaningless. Forever is surely not the answer for every corporation. Disclosing that a quasi-reorganization occurred a generation or two earlier in a now profitable corporation can mean little to investors today. To limit disclosure to a specified period, such as three years, may be inadequate unless operations have expanded and become profitable. Therefore, specifying a required period for disclosure by all corporations is impracticable.

Dating retained earnings for as long as the information is significant is the only reasonable solution. Significance depends on amounts—both absolute amounts and the interrelations between amounts, such as contributed equity and retained earnings or retained earnings and deficit written off. As long as the adjustments in a quasi-reorganization or transactions before that event affect later results materially, dating retained earnings is essential. For example, an operating loss carryforward may reduce federal income taxes for later profitable periods and the effects of the loss carryforward on results of operations and equity components would need to be explained by reference to the earlier quasi-reorganization.

Transactions With Nonstockholders

Transactions with nonstockholders are discussed in this chapter because some corporations now account for so-called donations as though they had a direct financial effect on stockholders' equity. Most transactions with nonstockholders in this category involve the receipt of cash or other assets or the reduction of liabilities. But the nature of a transaction usually varies according to the identity of the second party to the transaction. Second parties are primarily governmental units, creditors, and business entities with which a corporation transacts other business. The discussion is divided into those three groups.

Governmental Units. The party most often involved in a so-called donation to a corporation is a governmental unit. A number of state and local governmental units grant various kinds of concessions to business organizations for the purpose of developing industry in their own areas. Although concessions may take several forms, the more typical ones are an abatement or a reduction of income or property taxes of a corporation, a reduced rent for property owned by the governmental unit, and an outright transfer of cash or property to a corporation.

Purpose of concessions. Governmental units grant concessions to corporations to attain specific aims or satisfy planned programs. The general purpose of most concessions is to benefit the overall economy of an area from an expected increase in business activity and employment. A concession granted may be a lump sum transferred immediately, may be a waiver of payments, or may be special rights for a period. Regardless of the form of concession, a government intends to obtain long-term benefits for its area. The concessions are not gratuities.

In return for a concession, a recipient corporation may agree to move to an area, to expand existing operations, or to employ and train inexperienced workers. The recipient corporation in each instance agrees to and accepts responsibility for the specified performance. The responsibilities that a corporation assumes invariably involve additional financial obligations to be incurred immediately or during a long period. For instance, moving to a new area may entail not only moving costs but also may require higher shipping and selling costs in the future. A corporation usually incurs direct training costs to expand operations and to hire inexperienced employees and may incur the indirect costs of less efficient production.

A governmental unit grants a concession to a corporation to compensate for the increased costs the corporation expects to incur. A corporation expects to offset increased costs by the concession received whether it is a periodic abatement or reduction of expenses or an initial receipt of assets.

Accounting for concessions. Corporations have generally distinguished between those concessions that reduce periodic expenses and those that increase resources immediately. Most reductions of expenses have been accounted for as the expenses were incurred while transfers of assets have often been added to stockholders' equity as an increase in capital in excess of par or stated value of capital stock at the date received.

The purposes of a concession granted by a governmental unit and the effects on the operations of a corporation rather than the nature of the concession should govern the accounting. The form of concession is determined by many factors but the financial effects on corporate operations are independent of the form. Therefore, a corporation should account for a concession from a governmental unit on the basis of the nature of the additional expenses that it anticipates will be required to fulfill the responsibilities it assumed in accepting the concession.

The aim should be to match the benefit of the concession granted with the related greater expenses. For example, if property or land is transferred to a corporation because the corporation agrees to move to that location, corporate expenses of moving should be reduced by an amount equal to the value of the property that the corporation received.

If property is transferred to a corporation under an agreement providing that the corporation is to train new workers, the corporation should record an amount equal to the value of the property as a deferred item to be amortized over the training period to reduce the corporate expenses incurred. Unless those procedures are adopted, net income is understated because recorded expenses do not recognize the concession received for the purpose of normalizing the expense.

The recommended accounting emphasizes that concessions of governmental units are not donations to the corporation. The concessions are reflected in stockholders' equity ultimately but only as a reduction of the costs that are otherwise recognized as expenses.

Creditors. Forgiveness of indebtedness is often cited as an example of a donation to stockholders' equity by a nonstockholder. A creditor who is not a stockholder may be forced to relinquish his rights and claims in a bankruptcy proceeding. Distributions of additional securities to reduce or satisfy debt obligations and exchanges of debt securities are discussed in the sections on reorganizations in this chapter. A creditor who is not a stockholder voluntarily accepts a reduction in his existing claims on a going concern only with compensation in some form.

A creditor who is also a significant stockholder may willingly adjust the amount of his debt security investment, but the benefits of reducing his creditor interest flow to his ownership interest. The creditor's willingness to reduce his claim depends on his retaining his stockholder interest. The cancellation of an obligation, therefore, increases contributed stockholders' equity but not as a donation from a nonstockholder. The equity contributions of existing stockholders have been increased voluntarily.

Other Business Entities. Sometimes stockholders of a corporation institute a stockholders derivative action against an individual or entity with which the corporation has arranged business transactions. The action usually is an attempt to recover alleged excessive payments or to obtain alleged adequate compensation for products, services, or securities sold to others.

Corporations now often account for the receipts from successful actions as donations to stockholders' equity by nonstockholders and add the receipts to capital in excess of par or stated value of capital stock. Instead, the amounts received should be treated as a correction of the related amounts recorded previously. The actions are related to specific transactions or events, and the results of later suits should be accounted for the same as the revenue, expense, debt, equity, or other items involved.

Amounts collected should be added to contributions by stockholders only if related to an issue of stock and should be included in retained earnings if related to revenue and expenses of operations of prior periods. A recovery of insider trading profits may be related to contributed equity or to retained earnings depending on the type of securities sold and their derivation. That is, the profits on shares of stock issued under a compensation plan should adjust the compensation expense recorded previously but not change the consideration received for the stock issued.

Absence of Donations. The analyses of the nature of customary transactions between a corporation and the three groups of nonstockholders show that donation is a misleading designation. Both parties to the transaction relinquish resources for the purpose of receiving benefits. However, an obvious exception is a nonprofit organization that receives donations to carry on its operations.

Part IV

Implementation

Chapter 13 — Adopting Recommended Presentation and Accounting

The problems of transition to the recommended presentation of stockholders' equity and accounting principles for transactions are considered in Part IV.

13

Adopting Recommended Presentation and Accounting

Results of Adopting Recommendations

Many practices recommended in this study differ considerably from present accounting for transactions in stockholders' equity, and the recommended presentation of equity in financial statements alters the traditional presentation. Adopting the recommendations will modify the components of equity and will include in net income the financial effects of some transactions that are now either ignored or recorded directly as changes in equity components.

Most potential benefits of adopting the recommendations will be achieved only if the transition from present practices is the same for all corporations. However, the advantages of uniform accounting practices and presentation must be weighed against the practical problems that many corporations may encounter in implementing a transition. Desirable procedures and the potential difficulties are considered in this chapter to find the best manner of adopting new practices.

Uniform Accounting Practices. Individual corporations now account differently for some equity transactions that are similar both in nature and in financial effects. The differences result from expediencies or traditions, both of which are described in earlier chapters of this study. The practices recommended in this study provide that the effects of transactions of a similar nature, regardless of their names, will be accounted for alike.

The recommended presentation of sources of stockholders' equity in financial statements should supersede the many segregations and titles now shown for components of equity.

The preferable procedure for all corporations to obtain uniform accounting for equity transactions and presentation of stockholders' equity is described briefly in this section.

Transactions. Each corporation could adopt the recommendations of this study to account for equity transactions after a specified date. The purpose, of course, would be that all corporations would then account the same for like transactions. The feasibility of corporations accounting alike for equity transactions that occur after the recommendations are adopted depends on whether the transactions increase or decrease outstanding equity securities.

Increases in outstanding equity securities would be accounted for as recommended in this study as long as a corporation records as contributions by stockholders the full amount of the consideration received for stock issued.

The results of accounting for some decreases in outstanding equity securities, which are described in Chapter 11, depend on the components of stockholders' equity existing at the date a transaction occurs. Unless corporations restate the components of equity as of the date the recommendations are adopted, the results of applying the recommended procedures to later decreases in equity securities would not be the same for all corporations.

Classification of equity. Corporations should therefore restate the components of stockholders' equity existing at the date the recommendations are adopted to conform with the presentation of sources recommended in Chapter 7 of this study.

The three traditional components of stockholders' equity should be restated to show the two sources of equity—that is, contributions by stockholders and retained earnings. Components restated completely by source could, of course, be obtained only by analyzing the equity transactions since inception of a corporation to separate the effects of those transactions on contributions by stockholders and on retained earnings.

Reclassifying components would not change total stockholders' equity except that the total may be increased for the cost of some specific shares of treasury stock that was deducted from equity but is reclassified as an asset and

decreased for consideration received for contingent equity financing that is now included in stockholders' equity but is reclassified and presented in a balance sheet as a separate category immediately preceding stockholders' equity.

Practical Aspects of Restating Equity

Available Details of Components of Equity. Nearly every corporation now maintains permanent records that show the derivation of the existing components of equity. Customarily, a corporation has readily available complete historical records of equity transactions since the date of incorporation because of the recurring need to know the composition of capital stock and surplus. A corporation often uses the derivation of components of stockholders' equity in legal and tax matters and therefore compiles the details as transactions occur.

A corporation can readily and with little effort ascertain the sources of the existing amounts of stockholders' equity recorded since the date of incorporation. That procedure requires designating the recorded amounts as contributions by stockholders and as retained earnings.

Business combinations. A corporation that accounted for a business combination by the pooling of interests method would have recorded an increase in stockholders' equity based on the equity components recorded in the accounts of the combining corporation. The combined corporation usually would not have included in its supporting records the derivation of the traditional components; however, that information would be contained in the detailed records of the combining corporation. Since business combinations have been accounted for by the pooling of interests method for several decades, now locating earlier historical records of combining corporations may not be practicable for all corporations.

Results of Accounting for Past Transactions. Accounting for transactions in stockholders' equity according to the accounting pronouncements effective at various earlier dates has modified the original sources of equity. Capital stock and additional capital no longer represent contributions by stockholders. Transfers between retained earnings and the contributed components of equity have further mixed the two sources. The failure to record the entire consideration received for all shares of stock issued has understated existing components of stockholders' equity.

Some earlier changes in equity can be analyzed easily, and the effects on recorded components of equity can be restated in terms of sources of equity. Restating other transactions, such as an increase in outstanding stock recorded at less than the fair value of the consideration received, may appear formidable because corporations lack adequate information.

Limits on revisions of accounting. Many past transactions in equity securities would have had an effect on earlier net income if they had been accounted for according to the procedures recommended in this study. Typical transactions of that type are the exercise of stock options, conversion of debentures, and distribution of common stock for deferred compensation. Differences in net income are now included in retained earnings and are offset by identical differences in other components of equity.

Corporations would find it impracticable to restate the accounting for those transactions as though the recommendations of this study had been effective. The terms of the transactions would not necessarily have been the same; in fact, if the accounting had been different the arrangements are likely to have been different. Assuming that transactions would have been the same, essential information relating to the accounting for each earlier transaction would not always be readily available. Even if the market prices of securities on specific dates are available, the factors necessary to determine the fair value of the securities issued may not be available.

Possible Restatements of Equity

The components of stockholders' equity that exist at the date the recommendations of this study are adopted may be restated in several ways to obtain the sources of equity. The two extremes are for corporations either to restate completely the accounting for earlier transactions or to shuffle the recorded amounts of equity. Various intermediate methods of restatement are also possible. The advantages and weaknesses of the possibilities are described briefly in this section.

Complete Restatement. The most accurate and informative presentation of stockholders' equity would result from a complete restatement from inception of a corporation. That procedure would require analyzing each equity transaction and determining the accounting for a transaction according to the recommendations in this study. Total equity would thereby be divided according to the contributions by stockholders and retained earnings.

Some corporations attempting a complete restatement of equity components would find that recorded information would need to be supplemented by information from other sources to complete the required analyses.

The age of a corporation and the number and types of equity transactions influence the benefits to be derived from completely restating components of equity. A long existence involves changes in price levels, fluctuations in accumulated earnings, and increases in unrealized appreciation and depreciation of resources. The composition of the capital structure of a corporation may have been altered significantly several times through various equity and debt transactions. The restated accounting for many equity transactions would differ depending on the components existing at specific dates. Revised components on the recommended basis would reflect all of those factors, but earlier basic changes in the equity and capital structure of some corporations would reduce the usefulness of the resulting components.

Restatement After Arbitrary Date. One possibility is that each corporation would restate components of equity for transactions occurring after a selected arbitrary date, such as five or ten years earlier. That procedure has little advantage other than to reduce work. The result would be components of equity stated partly on a former basis and partly on the recommended basis of accounting. Therefore, the amounts of the components often would be meaningless or even misleading for those corporations in existence before the selected date. An arbitrary date for modifying accounting practices always carries the objection that it is significant for some entities and meaningless for others.

Estimates of Effects of Transactions. Corporations may estimate the financial effects of various types of equity transactions and restate the component sources as approximate amounts. That procedure cannot be defended as producing reliable results. Nor does it save time unless the estimates are so rough that they would be useless as a basis for presentation in financial statements. Another objection is that supplementary information would need to be obtained as a basis for estimates, the same as for accurate computations.

Recorded Components Restated by Source. The components of stockholders' equity already recorded at the date the recommendations are adopted may be analyzed, and those recorded amounts may be classified as contributions by stockholders and as retained earnings. That procedure would not require recomputing the consideration received for stock issued but would require restating the accounting for some retirements and other decreases in outstanding stock.

A corporation could restate equity on that basis from inception or from a selected arbitrary date. A shorter period of restatement supposedly would be a benefit because a corporation would save time. Ordinarily, the easy access to the details of the amounts of equity recorded since the date of incorporation overcomes the opposition to revisions for a long period. The objections to an arbitrary date for a restatement of recorded amounts are the same as a selected date for complete restatement—the results are not uniformly meaningful for all corporations.

Combined Capital Stock and Additional Capital. Another possible restatement of equity components would be to combine the capital stock and additional capital recorded by a corporation at the date the recommendations of this study are adopted. The combined amount would be assumed to be the contributions by stockholders. That method would require analyzing the additional capital only to the extent of determining the amounts that are applicable to preferred stock and to common stock. Earlier transfers between capital and retained earnings would be ignored and the existing components arbitrarily classified as source. Corporations could follow that procedure easily but the resulting components would have little significance because earlier accounting for transactions, such as stock dividends and retirements of stock, would have mixed the sources of equity.

Treasury stock recorded as an unallocated deduction would need to be accounted for as stock retired at the date of restatement. The cost of the stock would be prorated and deducted from the newly calculated contributed equity and retained earnings. The allocation would be arbitrary because the timing of reacquisitions would be ignored and the restated contributed equity would be inaccurate.

Selected Procedure. Some of the possible restatements seem attractive because a better presentation can be obtained easily. The results of a few methods may be so unreliable that the presentation would be useless. The restatement method recommended in the next section balances the ideal and the practicalities to obtain useful yet uniform components of stockholders' equity.

Recommended Restatement

Aims in Classification. The overall aims in reclassifying stockholders' equity should be to designate the components of total equity by sources—contributions by stockholders and retained earnings—as if the accounting for equity transactions had always recognized those two sources. The practical difficulties of a complete restatement of stockholders' equity since inception of a corporation, particularly for corporations with a long existence, are pointed out in this chapter. The restatement procedure can be curtailed and still most benefits of the ideal presentation can be obtained.

Revision of Total Stockholders' Equity. The most practical solution is to classify by sources the total equity recorded at the time the recommendations of this study are adopted. Restating all transactions since the inception of a corporation to conform to the recommended procedures would involve more work for some corporations than the results would warrant.

Stockholders' equity now presented in financial statements may include some amounts that should be eliminated before the remainder is reclassified. The starting point in the restatement procedure therefore should be to determine the amounts that are not applicable to outstanding equity interests. The major items to be eliminated from equity are contingent equity financing and the costs of treasury stock held that a corporation was required to obtain for operating purposes.

Contingent equity financing. The amounts recorded and included in equity for outstanding convertible debentures, stock purchase warrants, stock options, and deferred compensation should be deducted from stockholders' equity and be classified as contingent equity financing. Related amounts classified as liabilities—for example, the principal amount of convertible debentures outstanding and presented as long-term debt—should also be classified as contingent equity financing.

Many outstanding securities that fall in the contingent category have not been accounted for according to the procedures recommended in this study. Accounting for stock option and deferred compensation plans are notable examples. Corporations need not revise the earlier accounting for outstanding contingent equity financing at the date of restatement. If the recommended accounting procedures are adopted prospectively, corporations will recognize the entire consideration received for stock issued after the date equity is restated.

Treasury stock for operating purposes. Some shares of treasury stock held by corporations at the date the recommendations are adopted should be reclassified as an asset if the conditions described in Chapter 11 are satisfied. Corporations may have allocated the cost of those shares of stock to equity components or may have included the cost in treasury stock shown as an unallocated deduction in equity. The cost of shares that a corporation was required to acquire for operating purposes, such as for a stock option plan or a deferred compensation plan, should be eliminated from total stockholders' equity and classified as an asset.

Remaining shares of treasury stock presented as an unallocated deduction from other equity components should be treated as though the stock had been retired at the dates it was acquired. The cost of the stock should therefore be allocated to the components of equity.

Classification of Remaining Equity. The total equity remaining after adjusting for the recorded amounts of contingent equity financing and the cost of treasury stock shown as an asset should be classified as contributions by stockholders and retained earnings. The detailed historical records of equity transactions ordinarily contain the information necessary to classify each addition or deduction as one of the two components.

Contributions by stockholders. Contributions by stockholders should be compiled for each class of stock outstanding. The reclassification procedure however is substantially the same for each equity security and is outlined in this section as though the only equity security outstanding at the date of restatement and since inception of the corporation is a single class of common stock.

The following items to be included in contributions are divided between additions and deductions.

Additions

Sales of stock –	The cash proceeds the corporation received.
Exercises of options and warrants – Conversions of debentures –	The entire recorded consideration that the corporation received, whether treasury stock or previously unissued stock was distributed. This method assumes that the recorded consideration received represents the fair value of the consideration.
Distributions of stock for acquisition of property, services, or business –	The entire recorded consideration that the corporation received, whether measured by the fair value of the assets acquired or the fair value of stock issued.
Business combinations accounted for by the pooling of interests method –	Contributions by stockholders as a component of equity of the combining corporation determined according to the restatement procedures outlined in this section.

Deductions

Reacquisitions of stock (retired or held as treasury stock) –	Pro rata portion of contributions by stockholders at date the shares of stock were reacquired. Reacquisitions for a period, usually a year, may be totaled unless other transactions during the period change significantly the contributed equity applicable to one share of stock.

The additions and deductions should be compiled chronologically to aid in computing the contributions applicable to one share of stock outstanding at different dates.

The outlined method of determining contributions by stockholders produces the same amount as a complete restatement except that the recorded consideration received would not always equal the fair value of the consideration. The entire consideration received was often not recorded, and contributions would be understated to the extent of a difference between the amounts. Usually, the understated amount would be offset by the same overstatement of retained earnings. Since the transactions would not necessarily have been the same if the accounting had been different, the best presentation is obtained by reclassifying the recorded consideration.

Retained earnings. Retained earnings of a corporation at the date of restatement of stockholders' equity equals the remainder of total revised equity. The amount should be computed, however, based on the undistributed earnings recorded at that date.

Recorded retained earnings, after adjustment for contingent equity financing and treasury stock classified as an asset, should be further adjusted for:

Reacquisitions of stock (retired or held as treasury stock) –	The difference between the cost of reacquired shares of stock less the portion deducted from contributions by stockholders and reductions of retained earnings previously recorded, if any.
Transfers between other equity components –	Earlier transfers from retained earnings to capital for stock dividends, stock splits, etc., should be added to retained earnings. Earlier transfers from capital stock or capital in excess of par or stated value to retained earnings should be deducted from retained earnings.
Business combinations accounted for by the pooling of interests method –	The difference between the retained earnings as a component of equity of the combining corporation determined according to restatement procedures outlined in this section and the recorded additions to retained earnings.
"Donations" to equity –	Receipts from nonstockholders recorded as additional capital should be added to retained earnings.

Retained earnings appropriated for specific purposes should be shown separately in financial statements as a subclassification of retained earnings.

Recognition of Legal Capital. Legal capital should be recognized at the date the recommendations of this study are adopted. The presentation of equity recommended in Chapter 7 provides that legal capital in excess of contributions by stockholders be shown as appropriated retained earnings. The par or stated value of outstanding stock or other legal capital prescribed by the applicable state statutes may be computed and compared with the restated contributions by stockholders. The directors of a corporation may authorize an appropriation of retained earnings to equal legal capital if contributions are less than that amount.

The par or stated value of outstanding stock and other legal capital of a corporation may be disclosed and explained in a note. Appropriate disclosure is illustrated and discussed in Chapter 7.

Revised Equity. The sources of equity obtained through the recommended procedure are not the same as those from a complete restatement. However, each corporation will recognize the sources of the recorded amounts and presentations will be uniform. Presenting the revised components of stockholders' equity in financial statements will facilitate comparisons of different corporations and of a single corporation at later dates.

Future Transactions

Once stockholders' equity is reclassified as of the date the recommendations of this study are adopted, equity transactions after that date should be accounted for as recommended in this study. The general principles described in Chapter 8 recognize the financial effects of equity transactions, even new types that may become prevalent in the future. Recommended accounting for customary increases and decreases in outstanding equity securities are described in Chapters 9, 10, and 11.

Comments by Members of Project Advisory Committee

Comments of William P. Hackney

Miss Melcher's study provides a valuable starting point for any forthcoming pronouncement by the Financial Accounting Standards Board in the area of accounting for stockholders' equity. Her discussion of existing practices and pronouncements is extensive and her analysis and recommendations are thought-provoking.

Unfortunately, I find the study to be replete with general abstractions and unproven assumptions, and many of her recommendations to be unconvincing and of doubtful benefit. Accounting for stockholders' equity is hardly an area in the front lines of controversy surrounding accounting principles today. Nevertheless, Miss Melcher recommends a number of controversial changes from existing practices, some of which I find would be beneficial (although the need for change seems relatively slight), while in my opinion other recommended changes would be confusing, unnecessary and occasionally seriously misleading.

Basic Principles

No one can quarrel with Miss Melcher's overall objective that the proper way to disclose stockholders' equity is to furnish the maximum useful information and to exclude unnecessary details. But "useful" and "unnecessary" are portmanteau phrases that need unpacking, and here I find little help from the study.

Miss Melcher feels that the possible alternative presentations of equity fit generally into three broad groups: (1) classifying equity by its sources; (2) segregating invested capital and retained earnings; and (3) presenting a single amount for total stockholders' equity.

Miss Melcher easily dismisses the "stewpot" approach of presenting the sum of stockholder contributions plus profits retained as a single figure, on the grounds that more information could easily be revealed.

The distinction between the "sources" approach and the "invested capital" approach is not entirely clear, since both initially require a classification by source—the sources being financing (stockholder contributions as invested capital) and operations (retained earnings). The principal distinction apparently is that the "source" presentation of equity demands a permanent purity of concept which bars subsequent transfers from one category to the other. The distinctive features of "source" presentation are:

1. Total equity contributed by each class of stockholders is shown as one amount. Legal distinctions between stated capital and contributions in excess of stated capital are ignored, resulting in the elimination of such accounting concepts as "capital surplus," "paid-in-surplus" or "capital in excess of stated capital."

2. All accumulated retained earnings are so designated whether or not a portion has been "appropriated" for legal capital (i.e., "capitalized" under present practice). In accounting for stock splits, stock dividends and other similar changes, there would be no transfer of retained earnings to capital but rather that portion which under applicable law must be capitalized would be shown as "appropriated for legal capital," and the balance as "unappropriated."

3. Contributions by holders of "contingent equity financing"— convertible debentures, options and warrants—would be excluded from stockholders' equity and accounted for separately until the contingency occurs and the equity security is issued.

Legal Capital: The Relationship Between Law and Accounting

The legal definition of "capital" is not derived from the economic concept of "capital" as opposed to "income," but rather is derived from the early common-law notion that capital is a "trust fund" or safeguard for creditors and investors required by law in return for the privilege of limited liability. Whereas, in a partnership, a partner's "contributed capital" could be withdrawn by him at any time, early state corporation law provided, in effect, that legal capital should be provided for and maintained for the benefit of creditors, while only the excess or "surplus" could be distributed at any time to stockholders. Thus legal capital amounts to a representation as to a fixed number of dollars—"a *quantum,* not a *res*"—which would be contributed to and held by the corporation.

State law proceeded from this notion of legal capital in two directions: (i) the amount paid in by stockholders should not be less than the representation as to minimum capital—i.e., the stock should not be "watered"—and (ii) restrictions of various kinds were then imposed against either reducing the representation as to minimum capital or taking any voluntary action, such as payment of dividends, that would leave the remaining net assets less than the amount represented as minimum capital.

In the earliest days, the law contemplated that the consideration for stock to be issued would be the dollar amount designated as its "capital"—i.e., its par value. When the statutes began authorizing additional shares to be issued in the future at the discretion of the corporation, and such shares might, because of the success of the enterprise, be sold for an amount greater than par, the premium paid by the new shareholder was conceptualized as a payment made to equalize the per-share dividend source with previously outstanding stock—i.e., an amount equivalent to the accumulated undistributed earnings which had been left in the corporation, and in that sense "contributed," by the existing shareholders. Accordingly, such premium, although not specifically contemplated by the early statutes, came to be called "equalization surplus," and was held to be available for distribution to shareholders.

When stock without par value (but with a "stated capital") came to be allowed by law commencing in the early 1900's, it became clear that legal capital might from the very first be considerably less than contributed capital, and some laws then made specific provision for the excess capital contributed, calling it by the self-contradictory phrase, "capital surplus"—"capital" because contributed by stockholders but "surplus" because in excess of legal capital.

Since the principal emphasis of the law has always been to assure the existence and to prohibit the distribution or "impairment" of legal capital, with the balance to be freely distributable, a statute which authorized payment of dividends out of "net profits" or "surplus profits" so that "capital should not be impaired" was generally construed to mean that the amount of assets in excess of liabilities plus legal capital was freely distributable, unless some specific prohibition were set forth as to paid-in or capital surplus.

As Miss Melcher points out, accounting principles have always emphasized the importance of the legal principles relating to "capital" in presentation of the equity section of the balance sheet because of the importance of showing the amount which is free from legal restrictions against the payment of dividends. When the law was primarily stated in terms of a prohibition against impairment of legal capital, it was thus logical and wise to show the amount of legal capital on the balance sheet. When the law imposed other specific limitations upon the distribution or reduction of capital surplus, it likewise became a normal practice to show the amount of capital surplus so limited.

Most modern laws, however, following the lead of the Model Act, separately define the general permissible source of routine dividends in terms of "earned surplus." The change in approach is strikingly evidenced by the fact that the Model Act definition of "earned surplus" is taken almost verbatim from the accounting definition in the AICPA *Accounting Terminology Bulletin No. 1*, at p. 16. While it is probably implicit that there can be no earned surplus if capital is impaired, the amount of legal capital as such is no longer of any material importance in determining the funds available for dividends in most jurisdictions.

The financial provisions of state corporation laws are generally aimed at authorizing, within limits, or imposing restrictions on financial practices such as payment of dividends, purchase and redemption of shares, and reduction of capital. Accounting terms are used and defined for such purposes; but I am aware of no such law which specifically addresses itself to specifying accounting principles to be used in the publication of general purpose financial statements to the shareholders or to the world at large.[1]

Likewise, in the accounting view today, legal principles of state corporation law constitute part of the environment in which accounting

---

[1] I would agree with Miss Melcher's interpretation of Sec. 21.20 of the Michigan General Corporation Act, cited at page 88, note 1, as requiring disclosure by footnote but not governing the presentation of capital and surplus in the net worth section of the balance sheet. The discussion is of course limited to the effects of state corporation laws. The Federal securities laws more or less authorize the Securities and Exchange Commission to set forth the content of financial statements used in prospectuses related to the sale of securities and in proxy statements related to solicitation of proxies, although such authority has been sparingly used to date.

operates, but such law itself does not dictate the accounting principles by which such reports are put together. (See Sprouse and Moonitz, *ARS No. 3* at p. 10.)

As a lawyer, therefore, I find it easy to agree that the fundamental dichotomy in the net worth section of a balance sheet should not be between (i) stated capital, determined in accordance with the varying requirements of inartistic and confusing state laws, and (ii) the rest of net worth (equal to "surplus" under such laws as the Delaware Corporation Law), which is a confusing mixture of stockholder contributions and undistributed earnings. From an economic viewpoint, the two fundamental categories of stockholders' equity to be accounted for are total *contributed capital* and aggregate accumulated, undistributed *retained earnings,* and Miss Melcher seems in my view to be correct in urging that accounting principles should follow economic principles rather than legal concepts.[2] "Capital" as proposed in the study would therefore not be limited to the par value of outstanding shares, or to the various artificial concepts used in the state incorporation statutes such as "stated value" or "stated capital," but would include also what under present-day accounting principles is referred to as "additional capital," or "capital in excess of stated capital," commonly labeled "capital surplus" or "paid-in surplus" in the statutes. Accumulated undistributed earnings would consist of what is labeled in today's accounting terminology as the balance of net profits, income, gains and losses (after deducting distributions and transfers), and commonly referred to as "earned surplus" in the statutes. Miss Melcher is careful throughout her study to indicate that (i) where legal capital is higher than contributed capital, a portion of retained earnings should be shown separately as "appropriated for legal capital"; and (ii) where unappropriated retained earnings are not free to be paid out as dividends, whether because of the provisions of a bond indenture or other private agreement or a restriction imposed by law, a footnote should disclose the amount of the restriction.

In proceeding from the foregoing unobjectionable principles of balance sheet presentation to the particulars of accounting for transactions affecting equity, however, the study proceeds to set forth a number of conclusions and recommendations with which I cannot agree.

---

[2] Miss Melcher seems too often, however, to be asserting that legal principles either control accounting principles or they do not, and since they do not, they are "irrelevant" and may be "ignored." See, e.g., page 136; page 267.

Prohibition Against Transfers Between Components of Equity

Miss Melcher makes the arbitrary but unproven and undemonstrated assumption that one of the most useful (at other times called necessary, relevant, meaningful, fair, logical or essential) facts to be set forth in financial statements is the historical accumulation of undistributed earnings. From this she concludes that it would be erroneous to allow any transfer to be made from retained earnings to capital, whether as a result of stock splits, stock dividends, charter amendments or board action.

In the early decades of this century, accounting principles were aimed primarily at the valuation of assets, with the view that a balance sheet was intended to show the worth-value of assets compared with liabilities and that all increase in net worth (stockholders' equity) was deemed "profits." By 1943, the accounting approach had changed so radically that May could say that since 1900, "perhaps the most significant [accounting] change of all is the shift of emphasis from the balance sheet to the income account, and particularly to the income account as a guide to earning capacity rather than as an indication of accretions to disposable income."[3]

The importance in accounting of correctly stating *earnings*—or rather, because of the overriding accounting principle of conservatism, of *not overstating earnings*—leads as a corollary to one of the earliest of today's fundamental accounting principles: that "Capital surplus, however created, should not be used to relieve the income account of the current or future years of charges which would otherwise fall to be made thereagainst" (*ARB 43*, Chapter 1A, ¶ 2). The stress was entirely in one direction, however: no portion of capital accretions should ever be transferred to retained earnings, either directly or, by relieving the income statement of charges, indirectly.

I see no purpose to be served, however, in establishing a principle that there should be no transfers in the opposite direction. The owners are always free to reinvest dividends in the business, and (aside from tax consequences) the capitalization of retained earnings serves no

---

[3] May, Financial Accounting 5 (1943). See also Study Group on Business Income, Changing Concepts of Business Income 19, 21, 23-25, 27-28 (1952); May, op. cit., 5, 8, 37-39, 79-80, 90-95; Littleton and Zimmerman, Accounting Theory: Continuity and Change 154 (1962); ATB No. 1, at 16-17; ARB No. 43, at 7, ¶ 3; Hackney, Accounting Principles in Corporation Law, 30 Law & Contemp. Probs. 791, 803-4 (1965).

other purpose than an indication that such amount will never be distributed as a dividend.

Therefore I fail to see any evidence of a particular interest in the integrity of the figure of accumulated undistributed earnings. Important historical facts for either an existing investor or a potential investor are the annual earnings for each year over a recent period of years; the earnings per share in such years; and the figures required for a number of ratios such as net income ratios (net income to average total assets, net income to average stockholders' equity, dividends to net income and interest coverage), capital structure ratios (long-term senior securities to total capitalization), liquid asset ratios, turnover ratios, and the like. I am aware of no ratio of importance in financial analysis which is based upon the historical figure of pure accumulated undistributed earnings.

Nor is Miss Melcher's stress upon the purity of the stockholder-contributed capital figure more easily understandable. The *earnings base* is an important figure for analytical purposes, but that concept refers to total assets, or total stockholders' equity, or total long-term debt plus stockholders' equity, at a specific point in time, never to the aggregate of historical stockholder contributions. For a present-day investor, it may be a bit of mildly interesting information, but is of no material consequence, that over the corporation's life the aggregate of today's net worth was derived either in large part or in small part from actual stockholder contributions as opposed to retained earnings.

Even granting Miss Melcher's assumption that investors are apt to have an overwhelming interest in the original historical sources of equity, it would appear to be just as easy and equally informative to divide the capital section of net worth into two components—(1) contributed and (2) derived through capitalization of retained earnings. The formal and overt action taken in distributing stock certificates to shareholders in connection with a stock dividend or split helps to support the idea that the amount capitalized is thereafter more akin to contributed capital than to retained earnings from many points of view, just as though the same amount had been constructively distributed and reinvested.

Miss Melcher's approach here epitomizes, I believe, the principal weakness of her study. I find no survey or other pragmatic evidence of what it is investors are actually most interested in seeing in the equity section. What does "capital" actually signify to the investing public, including the professional analyst? Permanency? Unavailability for dividends? Cushion for a senior security? It is my impression that the SEC's "cap table" required in a prospectus by Form S-1 most often sets forth funded debt in terms of dollars but equity securities solely in terms of numbers of shares, both authorized and issued (plus reserved for issuance). My guess is that a survey would show investors are most interested in such matters as those set forth in the "cap table" plus such items as restrictions on the availability of retained earnings for dividends, the possible existence of dividend arrears, redemption prices in relation to capital set forth, the other basic terms of the security in question (encompassed within the SEC's definition of the "title" of a security), and perhaps the history of equity transactions during the most recent years.

Miss Melcher also asserts that the number of authorized shares of each class of stock need not be presented because the "value" of that information is "doubtful" since such number may so readily be changed. To whom, besides the author, is the value of such information so doubtful? It is a prominent figure in all SEC required presentations and is of obvious significance in appraising future financing and expansion plans. Substantial state taxes are sometimes payable based on authorized shares; a few laws do not authorize the existence of authorized but unissued shares, but require that the procedures for increase be followed each time additional shares are issued; and increases in the number of authorized shares may not really be so easy since they require the solicitation of proxies to get shareholder approval and if a specific use is planned for the increase such proposed use must be fully described.

Likewise dismissed in the study as "not significant financial information" is the par value of each class of shares. Although I personally agree that par value is not significant, in practice I am constantly amazed to see the intense interest in par values (or the fact of being no-par) shown, almost without exception, by clients.

In any event, having come to the rather intuitive conclusion that the historical sources of equity must be shown and that there can be no transfers between the components, Miss Melcher concludes that the only accounting necessary on a stock dividend or stock split is to segregate some retained earnings (to the extent it is required by law to be capitalized) and mark it as "appropriated for legal capital."

Furthermore, on the grounds of strictly logical consistency, since a 5 percent stock dividend and a 100 percent stock split or distribution are alike in that neither results in a change in any of the sources of stockholders' equity, Miss Melcher finds herself unable to see any basis for today's accounting requirement that the small stock dividend be accompanied by the capitalization of earned surplus in an amount equal to the market value of the stock. She supports this conclusion by arguing that the purpose of accounting "is not to police financial and management practices that the public or regulatory agencies believe are undesirable or that companies may have abused" (page 219). Would the author have opposed the issuance of *APB Opinions 16* and *17* on the ground that they were issued as an attempt to eliminate some of the abuses which had arisen in the conglomerate-acquisition period? Does she believe that *APB Opinion 15* on earnings per share had no policing function? Would she not deem it improper as an accounting matter to charge cash dividends to capital surplus when earned surplus exists? (See *In re Coastal Corp.*, Securities Act Release 3775 (1957).)

Some state statutes require no capitalization of surplus when no-par shares are distributed as stock dividends. Would Miss Melcher have no objection as an accounting matter to a regular annual 5 percent stock dividend payment of no-par shares by a corporation with no current earnings and a retained earnings deficit? (Cf. *SEC Accounting Series Release 124* (1972).)

Contingent Equity Financing

Miss Melcher includes in the category of "contingent equity financing" transactions which may result at some future time in the issuance of equity securities at the option of someone other than the corporation, but which to the date of the presentation have not actually resulted yet in the issuance of any capital stock. Included would be such items as convertible debt securities; stock options granted pursuant to employee incentive stock option plans; and warrants issued either to stockholders pursuant to a rights offering, or to underwriters or others as a method of compensation. Miss Melcher's recommended balance-sheet presentation (page 207) is indeed quite informative and could well be a considerable improvement over present-day accounting.

However, her insistence that the issuance of the stock upon exercise or conversion of the contingent equity financing be accounted for on the basis of the *market value of the stock, at the time of issue,* raises a number of serious questions.[4]

---

[4] The difference between present accounting and the recommended new accounting is of great significance, as the examples given by Miss Melcher on pages 207-208 disclose; while both methods of accounting result ultimately in the same aggregate stockholders' equity, in her example, present accounting allows a flow-through of retained earnings of $2,795,000 while her recommended accounting would result in reducing retained earnings to $98,000.

Miss Melcher in my opinion gives no convincing policy argument to support her conclusion that the total cost to the corporation of contingent equity financing is dependent upon the market value of the common stock issued at the date of issuance; rather she relies mainly upon the syllogistic argument that (i) a corporation should record as a part of stockholders' equity the entire consideration received for stock issued, and (ii) in cases of contingent equity financing (as in other cases where the consideration for issuance is other than cash), the best evidence of the consideration received is the fair value of the shares issued at the date of issuance. The excess of the market price of the common stock issued at the time of conversion or exercise over the sum of (a) the consideration received at the time of issuance of the convertible security or the warrant or option and (b) that received upon conversion or exercise is in her view a "financing consideration distributed" and must be recognized by the corporation either as an operating expense or as a cost of equity financing.

I believe that her argument, however, overlooks the nature of the expense or cost involved in the grant of an option or other right the value of which derives primarily from its leverage in a speculation.

Where a right to acquire securities (upon conversion and/or payment of an exercise price) is issued, the underlying securities (whether held in the treasury or authorized and unissued) must be segregated or reserved, and not used for other purposes by the issuer, until expiration or exercise of the right. Such segregation or reservation immediately eliminates the opportunity which the issuer would otherwise have of selling, or holding for future sale, the underlying securities. The *cost* to the corporation of issuance of the right seems to me to be the value of the lost opportunities at the time of issuance.

In theory, if a corporation issues a three-year right to buy, for $25, a security now worth $20, the corporation has incurred an opportunity cost by giving up the following opportunities: (i) to sell the security today for $20; (ii) to wait and sell the security at whatever its value may be during the next three years; and (iii) to refuse to sell the security at all. To say, however, that the cost to the corporation of contingent equity financing is dependent upon the market value of the security at time of exercise is in my view the same as saying that

    (i) if a corporation offers and sells its securities publicly today at $20 per share and such securities have a market price of $25 in six months, the corporation has suffered a "financing expense" of $5 per share; or

    (ii) if a corporation enters into an executory contract to sell a security for a price payable in installments or on call of the board of directors, or by the rendition of future services, and the security appreciates in value during the period until it is fully paid, such appreciation is a "financing expense" to the corporation.

It appears to me Miss Melcher's argument results in looking at the transaction from the point of view of the recipient and holder of the right or option, and concluding that the total economic *gain* to such holder is a measure of the total economic *cost* to the issuer. Such gain to the holder, however, consists of two separate and identifiable (whether or not measurable) components: economic benefit received at the time of receipt of the right, and additional benefit attributable to the holding and subsequent exercise of the right. Consider the following examples:

a. A corporation might purchase and distribute to each of its employees one 50¢ state lottery ticket. The cost to the corporation of such a fringe benefit is not the aggregate value of all such lottery tickets immediately after the winners are announced, but instead seems to be properly determined from the value of the lottery tickets at the time of their purchase and distribution.

b. If a corporation wishes to dispose of a portion of its real estate, and grants an option to a potential purchaser, the gain or loss to the corporation upon exercise of the option is in my opinion dependent upon the relation between the original cost to the corporation (or value at the time the option is given) and the exercise price, not upon the market value of the property in question at the time of exercise of the option.

c. A corporation grants to its employees stock options to acquire a total of 10,000 shares at an exercise price of $100 per share when the market price is $100 per share. The corporation simultaneously purchases 10,000 treasury shares at $100 per share to hold as a hedge against the exercise of the options. The options are exercised at some future time when the stock may be worth $150. Is the economic cost to the corporation of this method of employee incentive compensation $50 or more per share? Or is it just the imputed interest on the cost of the treasury shares while they are held as a hedge against exercise of the options? Is there any difference if authorized but unissued shares are used?

Miss Melcher's syllogistic error is to conclude that total cost to the issuer must be measured by total gain to the holder. Rather, I would conclude that total cost to the issuer is the opportunity cost at time of issuance of the right, perhaps best measurable by equating it to the economic benefit to the recipient upon receipt of the right, but not including the component of gain to the holder attributable to rise or fall in value of the security during the holding period. As stated in ARB 43, Ch. 13B, ¶ 8,

> However, beginning with the time at which the grantee may first exercise the option he is in effect speculating for his own account. His delay has no discernible relation to his status as an employee but reflects only his judgment as an investor.

It is undoubtedly true that the mere arithmetic difference between exercise price and market value at the time the option is granted or becomes exercisable does not fully measure the opportunity cost (or the economic benefit then conferred), since it excludes the speculative element arising from the leverage of being able to exercise the option at any time over a period of years. Such cost is not recognized today on the ground that it is impracticable to do so. See ARB 43, Chapter 13B, ¶ 12; APB Opinion 25, ¶ 10. I would approve of an attempt to cause an employer-corporation to account for such compensation conferred, if measurable, as a required expense, but I cannot agree that the holding gain to the recipient should be charged as a compensation expense to the grantor.

Purchase and Redemption of Stock, and Handling of Treasury Shares

Miss Melcher's recommendations in this area are carefully thought out and deserve the serious consideration of the accounting profession. I find them to be intricate and complicated, but again not persuasive.

Preferred Stock. The only real question with respect to the redemption and retirement of preferred stock arises with respect to the difference between the redemption price and the amount of contributed capital arising from original issuance. Miss Melcher argues that such difference should be accounted for in the same manner as dividends paid on preferred stock since both represent a "cost of financing," and concludes that the entire net cost to the corporation for obtaining equity financing through the issuance of preferred stock should be carried through the retained earnings account. In other words, the difference between the preferred capital contributed and the cost of redemption reduces or increases the effects of preferred dividends paid previously. On retirement of preferred stock, where cost is less than capital contributed, the credit would be to retained earnings, while any excess of cost over contributed capital would be charged to retained earnings.

Several questions arise. Unless prohibited by the terms of the preferred stock issue, it would be possible for a corporation with little or no earnings record and preferred dividend arrears to purchase and retire its preferred stock at a current market price which might be far below its par value, and thereby create a credit to retained earnings. In a system where *source* of equity is stressed and retained earnings are to be derived from *operations* as opposed to *financing*, it seems difficult to justify a creation of retained earnings from the issuance and redemption of preferred stock. She does not specifically discuss the consequences of purchasing or redeeming preferred stock with arrears, nor does she cover the occasion where the corporation may have no retained earnings but redeems the preferred stock with a premium charged to capital in excess of par value contributed by common stockholders.

Common Stock. The recommended accounting for the acquisition, holding and disposition of shares of common stock is initially based on the assumption that since each outstanding individual share of common stock is identical, each holder of common stock acquires a proportionate interest in the equity of the corporation, and therefore each share is identified not with the specific contribution which was made on its original issue, but rather with a pro rata portion of total contributions applicable to the class of stock as well as a pro rata portion of retained earnings.

Miss Melcher next rejects the "unallocated deduction" method of accounting for treasury stock, which is based on the notion that so long as the treasury stock is held, the transaction is incomplete, and a separate "suspense" account is set up as a deduction from total net worth, in the amount of the cost of the treasury stock, pending retirement, resale or redistribution of the shares so held. She asserts that the acquisition of treasury shares (unless purchased and held specifically for an operating purpose requiring the use of treasury stock) is economically the equivalent of the retirement of stock. Having already rejected the idea that the balance sheet should show the legal capital under applicable state law, she feels that the most useful presentation from a financial viewpoint is to have the balance sheet net worth accounts show the contributed capital applicable to the number of shares issued and outstanding and held by stockholders, with the number of treasury shares excluded from such presentation but disclosed in some other fashion, presumably in caption or by footnote. She concludes that it is unnecessary to disclose the total cost of treasury stock. The result is that on a purchase of common stock to be held in the treasury (with an exception noted below), its pro rata portions of contributed capital as well as retained earnings appropriated for legal capital are eliminated, and the balance is charged or credited to unappropriated retained earnings. Since capital is reduced but legal capital may not be, she carefully points out that the appropriation of retained earnings for legal capital may have to be increased; and likewise, if the holding of treasury shares results in a restriction upon the distribution of unappropriated earnings under state law, such restriction in excess of appropriated earnings should be disclosed.

Again, in a system emphasizing that the two sources of equity are financing (contributed capital) and operations (retained earnings), one instinctively rebels (perhaps through prior conditioning) against reflecting a "profit" or "loss" in the purchase of treasury stock in the retained earnings account. Here, as in other areas, one gets the idea that Miss Melcher's "source" thesis is actually to maintain the purity and integrity principally of the "financing" source of equity, contributed capital, and the other source, retained earnings, is actually a catch-all for any transaction which affects equity but does not clearly represent an increase or decrease of contributed capital.

The accounting for dispositions of treasury stock would in Miss Melcher's view be dependent upon a number of factors. First of all, her analysis distinguishes between stock reacquired for "financing purposes" and stock reacquired for "operating purposes." "Financing purposes" would include purchases of treasury stock for such purposes as revising the sources of financing, anticipating conversions of securities or the exercise of warrants, distributing stock dividends, effecting business combinations, or simply utilization of available funds; while "operating purposes" would include the use of treasury stock for the purpose of compensating employees, paying for operating expenses such as commissions to salesmen, or making donations to charities.

Accounting for the disposition of shares held for financing purposes would be identical to that on the issuance of authorized but unissued shares. Miss Melcher argues that from a financial viewpoint, reacquired shares are no longer issued or outstanding, and just as their acquisition is accounted for as a constructive retirement, their disposition should be accounted for in the same manner as an issuance of authorized but previously unissued shares.

Accounting for the disposition of shares reacquired for "operating purposes" is, in Miss Melcher's view, dependent upon whether the use of treasury stock as opposed to authorized but unissued shares is discretionary on the part of management. Unless treasury stock is acquired and held for a specifically designated operating purpose requiring the use of treasury stock, the results of the transaction are not identifiable with a specific operating purpose and its related costs. Where it is thus discretionary with management to use treasury shares or authorized but unissued shares, the decline or increase in the value of treasury shares while so held would be disregarded, and the financial effects of distributing such treasury stock would be the same as if previously unissued shares were utilized.

On the other hand, if management causes shares to be acquired and held for a specific operating purpose requiring the use of treasury stock, the "benefits or costs after the shares are reacquired are directly related to the operating purpose of the transaction and includable in results of operations"—i.e., the treasury shares should be carried as an asset, at cost, and the increase or decrease in value of such shares should result in a profit or loss applicable to the transaction as a whole. Thus, "the reason for the reacquisition of stock determines the accounting for the costs of the stock transactions" (page 254).

I fail to see the importance of the fact that the terms of an employee stock plan or of a resolution relating thereto may specifically require treasury stock rather than leaving an open choice between treasury stock and new stock. If the economic character of the transactions relating to acquisition and disposition of treasury shares is to control, it should be recognized that all shares of the same class are fungible. If the market value increase or decrease of a corporation's outstanding stock is to affect its income in the case where treasury shares are specifically required, then it would appear likewise that the investment of excess funds in treasury shares, or their acquisition for *possible* use in stock dividends or acquisitions, would give rise to the same potential effect on profit and loss. In fact, the adoption by management of an "operating purpose" plan requiring the use of treasury shares, which in effect causes a speculation in the company's own shares resulting in profit or loss which would not be present if the option to use authorized but unissued shares were retained, would raise serious questions in my mind as to the propriety of the initial management decision in adopting such a plan.

The study recommends that if treasury stock is distributed to satisfy a liability fixed in terms of a dollar amount, and through a rise or fall in the market value of the stock fewer or more shares are required than the number at the time the liability is entered into, the corporation should realize at the time of distribution the benefits or costs of reacquiring and holding the shares of stock. To my way of thinking, the distribution of fewer shares in satisfaction of the liability no more gives rise to income (nor reduces or offsets the expense reported by the liability) than would a sale of authorized but unissued stock in the market to raise the cash required to satisfy the liability.

If, on the other hand, treasury shares are acquired as a hedge against a liability fixed in terms of the number of shares, then the study recommends that it is unnecessary to adjust either the asset or the liability for changes in market value of the stock.

Recapitalizations

Exchanges. Where senior security holders (debt or preferred stock) exchange their interests for a junior equity security, the study recommends that the principles applicable to other issuances of equity securities should apply: the fair value of the stock issued measures the consideration, and the difference between such fair value and the recorded amount of the security surrendered is treated (i) as an adjustment of retained earnings where the exchanged security is preferred stock and (ii) as a charge or credit to the income statement where debt securities are retired by an exchange for stock. I have previously commented on my difficulty in seeing any effect in the operating section of stockholders' equity—the income statement and retained earnings—arising from transactions by a corporation in its own shares for a cash consideration, and I see even less justification in the case of exchanges of equity securities.

However, when the financial situation of the corporation is such that the entire existing common stock interests are eliminated, and existing senior equity securities are exchanged for new common stock, the transaction should not according to the study be recorded at the fair value of the stock so issued; rather, the recommendation is that such an exchange "does not change the amount contributed by those stockholders remaining as owners" but the amounts contributed originally by them become in turn contributions applicable to the new outstanding common stock distributed in exchange (page 270).

Stock Distributions. As previously stated, stock dividends, splits, divisions and combinations do not result in any change in the sources of equity—i.e., they do not involve the receipt of any new consideration or the distribution of any assets—and therefore in Miss Melcher's view should not result in the change of any components of equity (except for the possible need to indicate that a new portion of retained earnings is appropriated for legal capital).

Five additional types of stock distributions would be accounted for by Miss Melcher in five different ways:

1. Stock for accrued interest: account for at the fair market value of the stock issued; difference between such amount and amount of accrued interest charged or credited to income.

2. Preferred stock in lieu of preferred dividend arrearages: no change in any component of stockholders' equity; new shares outstanding shown with no dollar amount of contribution indicated.

3. Common stock dividend on preferred stock: account for at fair market value of stock issued; she would charge some account (presumably retained earnings) for the "consideration received" (although I fail to see what consideration has been received).

4. Preferred stock dividend on common stock: in effect a subdivision; common stockholders' contributed equity to be divided and allocated between common and new preferred in proportion to fair value of each security.

5. Optional dividends—giving a stockholder the right to receive cash or stock: account for at the amount of the per share cash dividend; charge to earned surplus.

Miss Melcher favors the continuation of the concept of accounting reorganization called a "quasi-reorganization," under the limitations and restrictions of existing accounting principles, although the writedown of assets and/or elimination of accumulated deficit which ordinarily accompanies a "quasi" of necessity interferes with the historical record of sources of stockholders' equity. Since retained earnings cannot survive a quasi-reorganization, I agree that stockholders' equity after the quasi will ordinarily consist of one component only—contributions by stockholders. Presumably she would require the transfer of any appropriated retained earnings which would otherwise survive to a contributed capital account.

Transactions With Nonstockholders. Miss Melcher denies that it is possible for a corporation actually to receive something for nothing from nonstockholders, whether it be from governmental units, creditors, or other business entities. Invariably, she feels, the corporation assumes other responsibilities which will offset the so-called donation, and she recommends that the amount of the donated property be recorded as a deferred item to be amortized over the expected period of increased related expenses.

Miscellaneous

Strangely enough, Miss Melcher purposely omits discussion of accounting for the declaration and payment of dividends other than stock dividends (page 10). A number of interesting problems exist (some covered by the recent *APB Opinion 29*), such as accounting for dividends declared when there are no retained earnings; dividends declared out of capital surplus when an earned surplus exists; dividends in appreciated property; and distributions in partial liquidation.

In two other areas I feel that the author oversimplifies practical problems raised by her recommendations. She assumes that all stock issued by corporations subject to "g.a.a.p." will have a determinable market value. Many sizeable corporations with a number of shareholders are not listed in the "pink sheets" and it is virtually impossible to ascertain the prices at which sales, if any, have been made. Even those listed in the pink sheets will frequently show only one or a few recent bids or asks, with no facts as to actual sales available. For the accounting profession to assume that a few bid/ask quotations are representative of "fair market value," and to extrapolate such per-share figures so as to quantify large transactions based on large blocks of stock, is to abdicate responsibility entirely.[5]

Finally, in Chapter 13 where she recommends that each corporation be required to reclassify its stockholders' equity section in accordance with the study's recommendations on a simultaneous date for the sake of uniformity, she asserts that "Nearly every corporation now maintains

---

[5] See Hackney, Accounting for Mergers and Acquisitions, 23 Rutgers L. Rev. 689, 705-6 (1969), and particularly the materials of Kripke and Werntz there cited.

permanent records that show the derivation of the existing components of equity." In my experience, many corporations, whether large or small, unless recently formed, are found to have incomplete and inadequate records as to stock issues of many years ago.

Comments of Merle S. Wick

I support publication of this study as it represents a scholarly and thought-provoking effort. However, I have great difficulty envisioning a practical application of its conclusions and recommendations.

Specifically, with regard to recommended accounting for the compensation element in stock options and the issue, exercise and equity financing elements in convertible debt, warrants, etc., the proposal to determine expense at the date stock is issued (or convertible debt or other equity securities are converted) implies that current expense should be determined by future changes in quoted market price for a company's stock. This hypothesis is questionable in that the change in market price of a common stock is the result of investors' reactions to innumerable factors which are not necessarily corollary to either the value of services provided by an optionee or the financing costs which might be expected to result from the financing approach employed. Market price at date of issue is beyond the control of either the company or an affected third party and appears inappropriate as a basis for measuring cost or benefit.

Turning to a second matter, a distinction does exist between a stock dividend and a stock split. In my opinion, the matter should not be viewed in a narrow, bookkeeping context but rather as a sophisticated method of financial reporting and control. Admittedly, each of the terms denotes a change in stockholders' equity resulting from the issuance of common shares to stockholders without consideration. However, the purpose of a stock dividend is generally characterized by the issuer as a means to provide the stockholders with separate evidence of their interest in accumulated earnings, whereas the purpose of a stock split is to increase the number of outstanding shares to effect a reduction in their unit market price in order to obtain a wider distribution and improved marketability of the shares. The proposal to eliminate the distinction ignores this economic reality.

Further, companies frequently describe stock dividends as being made "in lieu of cash dividends." It is basically the characterization of stock dividends and the public's view thereof that have led the New York Stock Exchange and the Securities and Exchange Commission to require the present capitalization concept as a method to prevent abuse of the stock dividend which might otherwise occur if no reduction in retained earnings were required.

In conclusion, while the study has a logical, theoretical basis, I have difficulty envisioning how the application of the proposed concepts would be particularly useful to users of financial statements or would produce more meaningful results than present practice. This does not mean that present practice cannot be improved. Hopefully this study will make a positive contribution in this regard.

Comments of Director of Accounting Research

Accounting Principles v. Practical Expedients

The basic issue of distinguishing between a principle of accounting and an expedient of measurement is the one aspect of the study on which I wish to comment. Unless accountants recognize that distinction, they are likely to generalize a practical procedure that is designed to approximate a specific measurement in specific circumstances into an overall valuation principle that does not fit other circumstances and tends to produce questionable results.

Principle. An accounting principle specifies the attribute of a thing or event that is to be measured and how in concept it should be measured. For example, one of the most firmly established ideas in accounting is that an asset acquired in an exchange transaction should initially be measured at acquisition cost to the acquirer. The first principle of paragraph 67 of *APB Opinion 16*, "Business Combinations," states both the attribute—cost of an asset acquired— and the way cost is to be measured:

> An asset acquired by exchanging cash or other assets is recorded at cost—that is, at the amount of cash disbursed or the fair value of other assets distributed.

Expedient. The attributes specified in accounting principles often are not measurable in practice, however, and accountants are justified in resorting to "surrogates" or "proxy variables" to approximate or estimate the desired, but unmeasurable, attribute. Indeed, they have no alternative short of nonmeasurement.

Using surrogates or proxy variables to approximate other numbers needed for financial statements is a well-established and eminently respectable procedure. But surrogates and proxy variables are useful precisely because they enable accountants to obtain and use reasonable estimates of other numbers that are unavailable; they have no merit in and of themselves. They are measurement expedients.

Perhaps the most oft-quoted of all measurement expedients in accounting is the one related to the principle already quoted from *APB Opinion 16*. Paragraph 67 of the Opinion characterizes it as a "practical rule" stemming from "restraints on measurement" and quotes it from *ARB 24*: ". . . cost may be determined either by the fair value of the consideration given or by the fair value of the property acquired, *whichever is the more clearly evident*" (emphasis added).

The emphasized phrase is probably sufficient to show the accuracy of the characterization in the Opinion—that kind of choice epitomizes practical rules rather than principles. Moreover, the nature of the measurement involved also shows the rule to be an expedient rather than a principle. The acquisition cost of an asset is the fair value of the consideration given to acquire it; cost is a sacrifice—value that is given up or foregone.[1] The fair value of the asset acquired is the value on the other side of the exchange and is not the cost. Measuring the unknown cost of the asset received by using its known fair value is an expedient.

Terminology—Precise and Expedient. The measurement expedient, ". . . cost may be determined either by . . . whichever is the more clearly evident," also includes an expedient of terminology which can be a source of confusion if it is not recognized as an expedient. So far, I have used "cost" to mean a value sacrificed to obtain another value, which is its meaning in general usage.[2] The definitions of cost in paragraph 65 of *APB Statement 4* and paragraph 67 of *APB Opinion 16* use the same precise meaning. Unfortunately, "cost" is also often used in accounting with a broader and less precise meaning—the basis of stating assets in balance sheets. Thus the recorded fair value of an asset received as a gift is often called its cost even though no sacrifice was involved in its acquisition. That terminology is often convenient—for example, we can talk of depreciating cost or allocating cost even if the basis is not actually cost—and both *Opinion 16* and *Statement 4* ac-

---

[1] *APB Opinion 16*, paragraph 67; *APB Statement 4*, "Basic Concepts and Accounting Principles Underlying Financial Statements of Business Enterprises," paragraph 65.

[2] cost—*n*. 1. the price paid to acquire, produce, accomplish, or maintain anything. 2. a sacrifice, loss, or penalty: *to work at the cost of one's health.* 3. outlay or expenditure of money, time, labor, trouble, etc.: *What will the cost be to me? The Random House Dictionary of the English Language*, Unabridged Edition (New York: Random House, 1971).

knowledge that meaning of "cost" and use it. Nevertheless, that expedient also tends to confuse because accountants often talk and act as if cost = sacrifice and cost = basis-of-recording were the same and therefore interchangeable.

Need for Perspective. The issue I raise is not a fanciful one—accountants actually do mistake measurement expedients for principles of accounting. They really have forgotten that it is merely expedient to measure cost by the "fair value of the consideration given or fair value of the property acquired, whichever is the more clearly evident." They have long treated the practical rule as a principle without asking whether the value that is "clearly evident" is or is not a good measure of the attribute specified by the relevant accounting principle.

The evolution from practical rule to principle can be seen in subtle changes in wording from *ARB 24*, "Accounting for Intangible Assets," in 1944, through Chapter 5 of *ARB 43*, "Intangible Assets," in 1953, to *ARB 48*, "Business Combinations," in 1957 (emphasis supplied in each):

> ... cost may be determined *either by* the fair value of the consideration given *or by* the fair value of the property acquired, whichever is the more clearly evident. (1944)

> ... cost may be considered *as being either* the fair value of the consideration given *or* the fair value of the property or right acquired, whichever is the more clearly evident. (1953)

> ... the assets acquired should be recorded ... at cost, measured in money, or, in the event other consideration is given, *at the fair value of such other consideration, or at the fair value of the property acquired,* whichever is more clearly evident. (1957)

The first change was from *cost may be determined by* (measured by, estimated by) to in substance *cost is*. Then, by 1957, *cost* had become the basis of recording assets acquired for cash (and probably debt); the expedient, "either ... or," had become *the basis of recording* assets acquired for other consideration. However, the trend has been reversed; paragraph 67 of *APB Opinion 16* reverts to the 1944 form of the practical rule.

Purpose of Comments

A basic conclusion in the study is that stock issued should invariably, or almost invariably, be recorded at its fair value at the date of issue.

However, using the fair value of stock issued to measure consideration received is an expedient. Fair value of stock issued is not in principle the measure of consideration received for stock. Elevating a measurement expedient to the status of an accounting principle has far-reaching consequences in the study.

I have seriously considered letting the matter pass without comment. The argument in the study is, as far as I can tell, mostly internally consistent. The study contains other matters with which I disagree but on which I have no intention of commenting. And whether the director of accounting research agrees or disagrees with premises, arguments, and conclusions in an accounting research study is not significant.

However, a recent item in the Accounting and Auditing Department of a prominent journal[3] severely chastised the Accounting Principles Board for paragraph 67 of *APB Opinion 16*. According to the contributor, paragraph 67 "can only serve to mislead and confuse the practitioner" (p. 951). The contributor proposed his own general principles, which began: "Independently value the more easily measurable item at its fair market value...." (pp. 950-951).

Since paragraph 67 of *APB Opinion 16* accurately states some basic principles of historical-cost accounting, the argument that those principles are confusing merely confirms that to a significant extent we have already lost the perspective to distinguish accounting principles from measurement expedients. I believe it necessary to reiterate some basic characteristics and principles of historical-cost accounting and to illustrate some of the consequences of using measurement expedients that are not good approximations of the amounts being measured in principle.

Principles of Historical-Cost Accounting

Purchase and Sale Exchanges. Historical-cost accounting depends significantly on transactions with outside parties, and purchase and sale exchanges are the most common and influential of those transactions. Purchase and sale transactions are the sources of costs and revenue, the determinants of net income in historical-cost accounting.

Both purchases and sales are recorded at exchange prices, but the emphasis is different. Cost is recorded in purchase transactions, and cost emphasizes the price paid—"The primary basis of accounting for inventories is cost, which has been defined generally as the price paid

---

[3] Richard E. Flaherty, "Historical Cost and Purchase Combinations," *The CPA Journal*, November 1972, pp. 948-951.

or consideration given to acquire an asset."[4] Revenue is recorded in sale transactions, and revenue emphasizes the price received—"*Revenue* results from the sale of goods and the rendering of services and is measured by the charge made to customers. . . ."[5] With one exception, the principles stated in paragraph 67 of *APB Opinion 16* are principles for purchase exchanges and involve costs. The exception is not a sale, however, and does not involve revenue.

Principles in APB Opinion 16. Paragraph 67 of *APB Opinion 16* states three principles that normally apply "to recording acquisitions of assets and issuances of stock" (paragraph 66):

> 67. *Acquiring assets.* The general principles to apply the historical-cost basis of accounting to an acquisition of an asset depend on the nature of the transaction:
>
>   a. An asset acquired by exchanging cash or other assets is recorded at cost—that is, at the amount of cash disbursed or the fair value of other assets distributed.
>
>   b. An asset acquired by incurring liabilities is recorded at cost—that is, at the present value of the amounts to be paid.
>
>   c. An asset acquired by issuing shares of stock of the acquiring corporation is recorded at the fair value of the asset—that is, shares of stock issued are recorded at the fair value of the consideration received for the stock.

The three principles in substance contain two distinct principles, one pertaining to exchange transactions and one pertaining to issues of stock.

Exchange transactions. Items (a) and (b) of paragraph 67 contain a single principle with three subparts:

> An asset acquired in an exchange transaction is recorded at its acquisition cost which, depending on the nature of the transaction, is
>
>   (1) the amount of cash disbursed,
>   (2) the present value of liabilities incurred, or
>   (3) the fair value of other assets distributed.

---

[4] *ARB 43*, Chapter 4, Statement 3. The same emphasis is in paragraph 70 of *APB Statement 4*.

[5] *Accounting Terminology Bulletin 2*. The same emphasis is in paragraph 181 of *APB Statement 4*: receivables are valued at their face or discounted amount, not at the value of the asset sold.

Disbursing cash or incurring a liability in exchange for an asset acquired—(1) and (2)—are classic examples of a purchase exchange in which the acquisition cost is measured directly by the price paid—the cash disbursed or the present value of the debt incurred. The measurements conform to the principle, and expedients are rarely needed. Sometimes, however, the present value of debt incurred is questionable because no rate of interest is specified or the specified rate is unrealistic. Then an expedient is needed, identified by a tell-tale "whichever is the more clearly determinable," and another expedient is available if the first does not work:

> . . . the cost of the property, goods, or service exchanged for the note should be recorded at the fair value of the property, goods, or service or at an amount that reasonably approximates the market value of the note, whichever is the more clearly determinable. . . . In the absence of established exchange prices for the related property, goods, or service or evidence of the market value of the note . . . the present value . . . should be determined by discounting all future payments on the notes using an imputed rate of interest. . . .[6]

Technically, acquiring an asset by exchanging another asset—(3) above—is not unquestionably a purchase exchange. It might as accurately be called a sale exchange and recorded at the fair value of the asset received. *APB Opinion 16* emphasizes cost in an exchange of nonmonetary assets because the Opinion is concerned with acquiring a business—usually thought of as a purchase exchange. However, a "barter" transaction is an example of an exchange that shows anomalies in the traditional distinction between accounting for purchases and accounting for sales. A barter transaction is also an example of an exchange for which using either the fair value of the asset received or the fair value of the asset given up in exchange is about equally justifiable.

Issues of stock. The principle in paragraph 67(c) is also stated primarily in terms of acquiring an asset—"an asset acquired by issuing shares of stock of the acquiring corporation is recorded at the fair value of the asset." The general principle is stated in the explanatory part of the sentence:

> . . . shares of stock issued are recorded at the fair value of the consideration received for the stock.

---

[6] *APB Opinion 21*, "Interest on Receivables and Payables," paragraph 12. Paragraphs 9, 10, 13, and 14 elaborate on paragraph 12.

The principle in paragraph 67(c) differs significantly from the one in paragraph 67(a) and (b). It emphasizes that which is received rather than that which is given up—cost is not even mentioned in the principle on issuing stock in contrast to its key place as the basis of recording assets acquired by distributing assets or incurring liabilities. However, in accordance with the terminology expedient already noted, the fair value of an asset acquired by issuing stock is usually called a "cost" after it is recorded.

Transactions between a corporation and its stockholders (as owners) are not purchases or sales but are *nonreciprocal transfers*[7] in which items of value to the corporation flow to it or from it but not in both directions at once as in an exchange. That which flows to or from a corporation in a nonreciprocal transfer from or to its stockholders—the consideration it receives on issuing stock or the resources it distributes as dividends—is the value to be measured. Measuring that value by substituting fair value of the stock issued is an expedient, which often works satisfactorily. But if it does not work, the result can be curious or even nonsensical.

Nonworkable Expedient

One kind of transaction for which the expedient almost never works is a deferred compensation arrangement, as illustrated by a so-called qualified stock option. The transaction has a number of characteristics of potential significance to accounting:

> The avowed purpose of granting a stock option is to compensate a key employee of a corporation for services rendered to it, and both grantor and grantee in an option agreement expect the price of the optioned stock to increase during and after the option period.
>
> To "qualify" the transaction for preferential tax treatment for the employee, an option must expire not later than five years from the date of grant, the option price must at least equal the fair market value of the optioned stock at the grant date, and the grantee must hold the stock for at least three years after exercising the option.
>
> The terms of option agreements usually provide that employees cannot exercise them immediately after grant, and up to eight

---

[7] *APB Statement 4*, paragraph 62.

years may elapse between the date of grant and the time an employee can sell the stock without incurring a tax at ordinary income rates.

An option may lapse without being exercised if the stock price fails to rise as anticipated, the employee terminates his employment, or other events occur.

The transaction involves issuing stock to fulfill its purpose and thus comes under the general principle for issuing stock—"shares of stock issued are recorded at the fair value of the consideration received for the stock."

In principle, recording an issue of stock on exercise of an employee's stock option requires determining the fair value of the employee's services that are part of the consideration that the corporation receives for the stock. That value is implicit in the agreement between grantor and grantee. A stock option agreement is, or should be, a bargained transaction based on both parties' perceptions of the situation. Both grantor and grantee have, or should have, in mind estimates of the value of the services and expectations about the future price of the optioned stock. Indeed, a management or directors who granted options without attempting to value the services to be received as part of the consideration or without projecting the market price of the corporation's stock would be derelict in their duty. Therefore, the market prices that appropriately may be used as measurement expedients to approximate the fair value of the services received as consideration are the expected market prices anticipated by the parties at the time of the agreement. Actual market prices at any date will not work except by coincidence.

The traditional measure of the consideration and compensation cost in a stock option transaction is the fair value of the optioned stock at the date of grant, as specified in Chapter 13B of *ARB 43*, and that measure never works. It invariably values the employee's services at zero and therefore understates not only the consideration received for stock issued but also the costs of employees' compensation. The measure completely ignores the substance of a transaction that involves issuing stock for cash *and* services.

Using other market prices produces equally unacceptable results because the fair value of an employee's services to a corporation is unaffected by later fluctuations in the market price of the corporation's stock. In fact, those fluctuations are often largely due to general market factors rather than to factors particular to the corporation. The grantor and grantee value the services on the basis of their expectations at the date of grant, and whether those expectations are realized or unrealized in later events is totally irrelevant to the agreed fair value of the services. Yet the effect of those extraneous price changes is introduced into the measurement by using either of the most widely suggested alternatives to the traditional measure—market value (or fair value) of the stock at the date the option becomes exercisable by the grantee or market value (or fair value) of the stock at the time it is issued on exercise of the option—or any other market value after the date of grant. The market value of the stock at the date of issue has the added defect of introducing into the corporation's measures of the fair value of the employee's services the results of the employee's market-price speculation between exercisable date and exercise date.

The fallacy of attempting to measure the fair value of services by using market prices after the time of the agreement is most clearly shown if the market price of the stock falls below the option price. Market prices then measure, often retroactively, no value (or conceivably a negative value) for the services, despite a bargain between the parties that obviously contemplated a value for the services.

Concluding Observation

The points I raise are not new. They have, however, been largely ignored as accountants have used measurement expedients indiscriminately. Accounting for stock options is a prime example of an area in which arguments about which market value to use have for at least a generation directed attention to the wrong side of a stock issue transaction.

Getting back to principle is no panacea. Measurement problems are often difficult, and determining the fair value of employees' services received in stock option transactions is among the most difficult. Nevertheless, getting back to principle will at least direct our attention to the right problems.

REED K. STOREY

Selected References

Reporting Equity

Pronouncements

AMERICAN INSTITUTE OF CERTIFIED PUBLIC ACCOUNTANTS

Special Bulletin No. 18. 1923. "Surplus," pp. 10-11.
Verification of Financial Statements (Revised). 1929.
Examination of Financial Statements by Independent Public Accountants. 1936.

COMMITTEE ON ACCOUNTING PROCEDURE

Accounting Research Bulletin No. 5, "Depreciation on Appreciation." 1940.
Accounting Research Bulletin No. 9 (Special), "Report of Committee on Terminology." 1941.
Accounting Research Bulletin No. 12 (Special), "Report of Committee on Terminology." 1941.
Accounting Research Bulletin No. 28, "Accounting Treatment of General Purpose Contingency Reserves." 1947.
Accounting Research Bulletin No. 32, "Income and Earned Surplus." 1947.
Accounting Research Bulletin No. 33, "Depreciation and High Costs." 1947.
Accounting Research Bulletin No. 39, "Recommendation of Subcommittee on Terminology—Discontinuance of the Use of the Term 'Surplus'." 1949.
Accounting Research Bulletin No. 43. 1953.
   Chapter 1A, "Rules Adopted By Membership."
   Chapter 6, "Contingency Reserves."
   Chapter 8, "Income and Earned Surplus."
   Chapter 9B, "Depreciation on Appreciation."
Accounting Terminology Bulletin No. 1, "Review and Résumé." 1953.

ACCOUNTING PRINCIPLES BOARD

Opinion No. 6, "Status of Accounting Research Bulletins," par. 17, "Depreciation on Appreciation." 1965.
Opinion No. 9, "*Reporting the Results of Operations,*" par. 28, "Capital transactions." 1966.
Opinion No. 10, "Omnibus Opinion—1966," pars. 10-11, "Liquidation Preference of Preferred Stock." 1966.
Opinion No. 12, "Omnibus Opinion—1967," pars. 9-10, "Capital Changes." 1967.
Opinion No. 15, "Earnings per Share," par. 39, "Non-Recognition of Common Stock Equivalents in Financial Statements." 1969.
Statement No. 4, "Basic Concepts and Accounting Principles Underlying Financial Statements of Business Enterprises." 1970.

AMERICAN ACCOUNTING ASSOCIATION

A Tentative Statement of Accounting Principles Underlying Corporate Financial Statements. 1936
Accounting Principles Underlying Corporate Financial Statements. 1941.
Supplementary Statement No. 1, "Reserves and Retained Income." 1950.
Accounting and Reporting Standards for Corporate Financial Statements —1957 Revision. 1957.

AMERICAN BAR ASSOCIATION

COMMITTEE ON CORPORATE LAWS (SECTION OF CORPORATION, BANKING AND BUSINESS LAW)
Model Business Corporation Act, Incorporating all amendments by the committee including those published in the 1964 Addendum.

CANADIAN INSTITUTE OF CHARTERED ACCOUNTANTS

ACCOUNTING AND AUDITING RESEARCH COMMITTEE

Bulletin No. 20, "Standards of Disclosure in Financial Statements." 1964.
CICA Handbook.
　Section 3240, "Share Capital."
　Section 3250, "Surplus."

UNITED STATES SECURITIES AND EXCHANGE COMMISSION

Accounting Series Release No. 7, "Commonly cited deficiencies in financial statements filed under the Securities Act of 1933 and the Securities Exchange Act of 1934." May 1938.

Accounting Series Release No. 8, "Creation by promotional companies of surplus by appraisal." May 1938.
Accounting Series Release No. 9, "Presentation of stock having preferences on involuntary liquidation in excess of par or stated value." Dec. 1938.
Accounting Series Release No. 35, "Disclosure to be given to certain types of provisions and conditions that limit the availability of surplus for dividend purposes." Sept. 1942.
Accounting Series Release No. 39, "Amendments to Uniform System of Accounts for Public Utility Holding Companies." Dec. 1942.
Accounting Series Release No. 68, "Findings and Opinion of the Commission In the Matter of Proceedings under Rule II(e) of the Rules of Practice to determine whether the privilege of F. G. Masquelette & Co. and J. E. Cassell to practice as accountants before the Securities and Exchange Commission should be denied, temporarily or permanently." July 1949.
Accounting Series Release No. 73, "Findings and Opinion of the Commission In the Matter of Haskins & Sells and Andrew Stewart, File No. 4-66, (Rules of Practice—Rule II(e))." Oct. 1952.
Regulation S-X, Form and Content of Financial Statements.

Books and Articles

AMERICAN INSTITUTE OF ACCOUNTANTS, Report of the Subcommittee on Surplus of the Committee on Accounting Procedure. "Should the Term 'Surplus' Be Eliminated?" *The Journal of Accountancy*, May 1942, pp. 451-457.

AMERICAN INSTITUTE OF ACCOUNTANTS, A Statement by the Research Department. "Corporate Accounting Principles." *The Journal of Accountancy*, Oct. 1945, pp. 259-266.

BALLANTINE, HENRY WINTHROP. *Ballantine on Corporations*, rev. ed. Chicago: Callaghan & Co., 1946.

BEVIS, HERMAN W. *Corporate Financial Reporting in a Competitive Economy.* New York: Macmillan Co., 1965.

BIRNBERG, JACOB G. "An Information Oriented Approach to the Presentation of Common Shareholders' Equity." *The Accounting Review*, Oct. 1964, pp. 963-971.

BLOCK, FRANK E. "The Place of Book Value in Common Stock Evaluation." *Financial Analysts Journal*, Mar.-Apr. 1964, pp. 29-33.

BOTTRILL, G. W. "What Value in the Balance Sheet?" *The Australian Accountant*, Aug. 1967, pp. 419-426.

BRIGGS, L. L. "Dividends from Stock Premiums." *The Journal of Accountancy*, May 1932, pp. 346-353.

CARMAN, LEWIS A. "Primary Accounting Concepts: A Speculation in the Interest of Clarity." *The Journal of Accountancy*, May 1936, pp. 348-375.

CHILDS, JOHN F. "Profit Goals for Management." *Financial Executive*, Feb. 1964, pp. 13-23.

CHOW, Y. C. "The Doctrine of Proprietorship." *The Accounting Review*, Apr. 1942, pp. 157-163.

Conard, Alfred F. "Financial Problems of the Business Enterprise—Getting the Money Out." *University of Illinois Law Forum,* Fall 1954, pp. 427-464.

Dohr, James L. "Capital and Surplus in the Corporate Balance Sheet." *The Accounting Review,* Mar. 1939, pp. 38-42.

Dohr, James L. "Names Wanted—A Problem in Terminology." *The Journal of Accountancy,* Aug. 1942, pp. 133-139.

Fisher, G. R. "Some Factors Influencing Share Prices." *The Economic Journal,* Mar. 1961, pp. 121-141.

Garrett, Ray. "Capital and Surplus Under the New Corporation Statutes." *Law and Contemporary Problems,* Spring 1958, pp. 239-263.

Gibson, George D. "Surplus, So What?—The Model Act Modernized." *The Business Lawyer,* Apr. 1962, pp. 476-499.

Grady, Paul. *Accounting Research Study No. 7,* "Inventory of Generally Accepted Accounting Principles for Business Enterprises." New York: American Institute of Certified Public Accountants, 1965.

Graham, Benjamin; Dodd, David L.; and Cottle, Sidney. *Security Analysis: Principles and Technique,* 4th ed. New York: McGraw-Hill Book Co., 1962.

Hackney, William P. "The Financial Provisions of the Model Business Corporation Act." *Harvard Law Review,* June 1957, pp. 1357-1405.

Hatfield, Henry Rand. "Accounting Principles and the Statutes." *The Journal of Accountancy,* Aug. 1934, pp. 90-97.

Hatfield, Henry Rand. *Surplus and Dividends.* Cambridge, Mass.: Harvard University Press, 1943.

Hayes, Douglas A. "Some Reflections on Techniques for Appraising Growth Rates." *Financial Analysts Journal,* July-Aug. 1964, pp. 96-101.

Heckert, J. B. "Comments on the Definition of Earned Surplus." *The Accounting Review,* June 1930, pp. 168-174.

Hendriksen, Eldon S. *Accounting Theory.* Homewood, Ill.: Richard D. Irwin, 1965.

Hendriksen, Eldon S. *Accounting Theory,* rev. ed. Homewood, Ill.: Richard D. Irwin, 1970.

Hills, George S. *The Law of Accounting and Financial Statements.* Boston: Little, Brown & Co., 1957.

Illinois (University of) Study Group. *A Statement of Basic Accounting Postulates and Principles.* Center for International Education and Research in Accounting, 1964.

Katz, Wilber G. "The Philosophy of Midcentury Corporation Statutes." *Law and Contemporary Problems,* Spring 1958, pp. 177-192.

Knutson, Peter H. "Income Distribution: the Key to Earnings Per Share." *The Accounting Review,* Jan. 1970, pp. 55-68.

Kohler, E. L. "The Concept of Earned Surplus." *The Accounting Review,* Sept. 1931, pp. 206-217.

Kripke, Homer. "Accountants' Financial Statements and Fact-Finding in the Law of Corporate Regulation." *The Yale Law Journal,* May 1941, pp. 1180-1205.

Levy, Harry. "Evaluating and Planning the Corporate Financial Structure." *The Australian Accountant,* June 1970, pp. 229-234.

LITTLETON, A. C. "Capital and Surplus." *The Accounting Review*, Dec. 1932, pp. 290-293.

LITTLETON, A. C. "Creditors' Interest in Surplus." *The Certified Public Accountant*, Apr. 1933, pp. 199-202.

LITTLETON, A. C. "A Substitute for Stated Capital." *Harvard Business Review*, Autumn 1938, pp. 75-84.

MACNEAL, KENNETH. *Truth in Accounting.* Philadelphia: University of Pennsylvania Press, 1939.

MANNE, HENRY G. "Accounting for Share Issues Under Modern Corporation Laws." *Northwestern University Law Review*, July-Aug. 1959, pp. 285-328.

MARPLE, RAYMOND P. "The Balance Sheet—Capital Sources and Composition." *The Journal of Accountancy*, Nov. 1962, pp. 57-60.

MAUTZ, R. K. *An Accounting Technique for Reporting Financial Transactions,* Bureau of Economic and Business Research, Special Bulletin 7. Urbana: University of Illinois, July 1951.

MONTGOMERY, ROBERT H. "Capital Surplus—Help Wanted." *The Journal of Accountancy*, Oct. 1944, pp. 285-287.

NATHO, KERMIT CHARLES, JR. "A Study of the Principles Used in the Classification of the Owners' Equity Section of the Balance Sheet." Ph.D. dissertation, Louisiana State University and Agricultural and Mechanical College, 1970.

PATON, W. A., and LITTLETON, A. C. *An Introduction to Corporate Accounting Standards.* American Accounting Association, 1940.

SPROUSE, ROBERT T., and MOONITZ, MAURICE. *Accounting Research Study No. 3,* "A Tentative Set of Broad Accounting Principles for Business Enterprises." New York: American Institute of Certified Public Accountants, 1962.

STAUBUS, GEORGE J. *A Theory of Accounting to Investors.* Berkeley: University of California Press, 1961.

SYMON, IAIN W. "Business Income: Some Reflections on its Principles and Measurement." *The Accountant's Magazine*, Aug. 1968, pp. 414-426.

VAIR, JAMES W. "Source and Application of Retained Earnings." *The Canadian Chartered Accountant*, July 1959, pp. 24-29.

VATTER, WILLIAM J. "Corporate Stock Equities." *Modern Accounting Theory: A Revision of Handbook of Modern Accounting Theory.* Edited by Morton Backer. Englewood Cliffs, N. J.: Prentice-Hall, 1966, pp. 250-300.

WAKEFIELD, E. E. "When Lawyers and Accountants Disagree." *The Journal of Accountancy*, Aug. 1934, pp. 117-120.

WILDMAN, JOHN R., and POWELL, WELDON. *Capital Stock Without Par Value.* Chicago: A. W. Shaw Co., 1928.

WIXON, RUFUS. "Legal Requirements and Accounting Standards." *The Accounting Review*, Apr. 1945, pp. 139-147.

YORK, THOMAS. "Stock Dividends from the Viewpoint of the Declaring Corporation." *The Accounting Review*, Mar. 1941, pp. 15-33.

Business Combinations

Pronouncements

AMERICAN INSTITUTE OF CERTIFIED PUBLIC ACCOUNTANTS

COMMITTEE ON ACCOUNTING PROCEDURE

Accounting Research Bulletin No. 40, "Business Combinations." 1950.
Accounting Research Bulletin No. 43, Chapter 7C, "Business Combinations." 1953.
Accounting Research Bulletin No. 48, "Business Combinations." 1957.

ACCOUNTING PRINCIPLES BOARD

Opinion No. 6, "Status of Accounting Research Bulletins," par. 22, "Business Combinations." 1965.
Opinion No. 16, "Business Combinations." 1970.

AMERICAN ACCOUNTING ASSOCIATION

A Statement of Basic Accounting Theory. 1966.

Books and Articles

BEYER, ROBERT. "Goodwill and Pooling of Interests: A Re-assessment." *Management Accounting*, Feb. 1969, pp. 9-15.

CATLETT, GEORGE R., and OLSON, NORMAN O. *Accounting Research Study No. 10*, "Accounting for Goodwill." New York: American Institute of Certified Public Accountants, 1968. (Including Selected Bibliography, pp. 176-180.)

GUNTHER, SAMUEL P. "Contingent Pay-Outs in Mergers and Acquisitions." *The Journal of Accountancy*, June 1968, pp. 33-40.

HOLLENDER, JEROME S. "The Fine Art of Valuing and Financing Business Acquisitions." *The New York Certified Public Accountant*, Aug. 1967, pp. 589-594.

KEYES, GERALD E. "Pooling of Interests; a Commentary." *The Ohio CPA*, Autumn 1969, pp. 141-150.

McGILL, JAMES. "Everybody Out Of The Pool(ing)." *Massachusetts CPA Review*, Oct.-Nov. 1969, pp. 127-132.

REUM, W. ROBERT, and STEELE, THOMAS A., III. "Contingent Payouts Cut Acquisition Risks." *Harvard Business Review*, Mar.-Apr. 1970, pp. 83-91.

SUTTLE, WILLIAM C., and MECKLENBURG, WILLIAM G. "Pooling of interests." *World* (Peat, Marwick, Mitchell & Co.), Winter 1968, pp. 53-57 and Spring 1968, pp. 49-55.

WYATT, ARTHUR R. *Accounting Research Study No. 5*, "A Critical Study of Accounting for Business Combinations." New York: American Institute of Certified Public Accountants, 1963. (Including Selected Bibliography, pp. 140-143.)

Conversion of Securities

Pronouncements

AMERICAN INSTITUTE OF CERTIFIED PUBLIC ACCOUNTANTS

ACCOUNTING PRINCIPLES BOARD

Opinion No. 10, "Omnibus Opinion—1966," pars. 8-9, "Convertible Debt and Debt Issued with Stock Warrants." 1966.
Opinion No. 12, "Omnibus Opinion—1967," pars. 11-15, "Convertible Debt and Debt Issued with Stock Warrants." 1967.
Opinion No. 14, "Accounting for Convertible Debt and Debt Issued with Stock Purchase Warrants." 1969.

AMERICAN ACCOUNTING ASSOCIATION

Accounting and Reporting Standards for Corporate Financial Statements— 1957 Revision. 1957.

Books and Articles

CURRY, DUDLEY WALZ. "The Financial Reporting of Convertible Debentures." Ph.D. dissertation, Stanford University, 1969.
ELSAID, HUSSEIN H. "The Function of Preferred Stock in the Corporate Financial Plan." *Financial Analysts Journal,* July-Aug. 1969, pp. 112-117.
HARKINS, EDWIN P., and WALSH, FRANCIS J., JR. "Current Corporate Debt Practices." *The Conference Board Record,* June 1968, pp. 36-42.
HAYES, SAMUEL L., III. "New Interest in Incentive Financing." *Harvard Business Review,* July-Aug. 1966, pp. 99-112.
IMDIEKE, LEROY F., and WEYGANDT, JERRY J. "Classification of Convertible Debt." *The Accounting Review,* Oct. 1969, pp. 798-805.
JOHNSON, RODNEY DEAN. "The Extinguishment of Convertible Bonds: A Theoretical and Empirical Analysis." Ph.D. dissertation, State University of New York at Buffalo, 1970.
KATZ, JAMES L. "A Look at APB No. 10—The Omnibus Opinion." *The Illinois CPA,* Winter 1967, pp. 40-44.
LERNER, EUGENE M., and AUSTER, ROLF. "Does the Market Discount Potential Dilution." *Financial Analysts Journal,* July-Aug. 1969, pp. 118-121.
MAY, GEORGE O. "The Proper Treatment of Premiums and Discounts on Bonds." *The Journal of Accountancy,* July 1906, pp. 174-186.
MCCULLERS, LEVIS DUVAL. "Convertible Securities—Debt or Equity?" Ph.D. dissertation, The University of Florida, 1969.
MOFFETT, H. S. *Accounting for Costs of Financing.* Toronto: Canadian Institute of Chartered Accountants, 1964.

Pilcher, C. James. *Raising Capital With Convertible Securities.* Ann Arbor: Bureau of Business Research, School of Business Administration, University of Michigan, 1955.

Poensgen, Otto H. "The Valuation of Convertible Bonds." *Industrial Management Review,* Fall 1965, pp. 77-92 and Spring 1966, pp. 83-98.

Weil, Roman L., Jr.; Segall, Joel E.; and Green, David, Jr. "Premiums on Convertible Bonds." *The Journal of Finance,* June 1968, pp. 445-463.

Williams, Charles M., and Williams, Howard A. "Incentive Financing—A New Opportunity." *Harvard Business Review,* Mar.-Apr. 1960, pp. 123-134.

Reacquired and Retired Stock

Pronouncements

American Institute of Certified Public Accountants

Committee on Accounting Procedure

Accounting Research Bulletin No. 43. 1953.
Chapter 1A, "Rules Adopted By Membership."
Chapter 1B, "Opinion Issued By Predecessor Committee."

Accounting Principles Board

Opinion No. 6, "Status of Accounting Research Bulletins," pars. 12-13, "Treasury Stock." 1965.

Opinion No. 9, "Reporting the Results of Operations," par. 28, "Capital transactions." 1966.

American Accounting Association

Accounting Concepts and Standards Underlying Corporate Financial Statements—1948 Revision. 1948.

Accounting and Reporting Standards for Corporate Financial Statements—1957 Revision. 1957.

United States Securities and Exchange Commission

Accounting Series Release No. 5, "Treatment of dividends on corporation's own capital stock held in sinking-fund." May 1938.

Accounting Series Release No. 6, "Treatment of excess of proceeds from sale of treasury stock over cost thereof." May 1938.

Accounting Series Release No. 45, "Treatment of premiums paid upon the redemption of preferred stock." June 1943.

Regulation S-X, Form and Content of Financial Statements.

Books and Articles

BALLANTINE, HENRY W. "The Curious Fiction of Treasury Shares." *California Law Review*, Sept. 1946, pp. 536-542.

BIERMAN, HAROLD, JR., and WEST, RICHARD. "The Acquisition of Common Stock by the Corporate Issuer." *The Journal of Finance*, Dec. 1966, pp. 687-696.

BOWLES, H. G. "Treasury Shares on the Balance-sheet." *The Journal of Accountancy*, Aug. 1934, pp. 98-105.

BRIGHAM, EUGENE F. "The Profitability of a Firm's Purchase of Its Own Common Stock." *California Management Review*, Winter 1964, pp. 69-76.

DAHLQUIST, T. W. "Regulation and Civil Liability Under the California Corporate Securities Act: II." *California Law Review*, June 1946, pp. 344-397.

ELLIS, CHARLES D. "Repurchase Stock to Revitalize Equity." *Harvard Business Review*, July-Aug. 1965, pp. 119-128.

ELLIS, CHARLES D., and YOUNG, ALLAN E. *The Repurchase of Common Stock*. New York: Ronald Press Co., 1971.

GARRETT, RAY. "Treasury Shares Under the Model Business Corporation Act." *The Business Lawyer*, July 1960, pp. 916-920.

GUTHART, LEO A. "Why Companies Are Buying Back Their Own Stock." *Financial Analysts Journal*, Mar.-Apr. 1967, pp. 105-110.

HERRICK, ANSON. "Balance Sheet Presentation of Treasury Shares." *The Journal of Accountancy*, Apr. 1963, pp. 74-75.

HUSBAND, GEORGE R. "The Corporate-Entity Fiction and Accounting Theory." *The Accounting Review*, Sept. 1938, pp. 241-253.

"JENKINS REPORT." *Report of the Company Law Committee*, Chapter 5. London: Her Majesty's Stationery Office, 1962.

LERNER, MICHAEL A., and SOLOMON, KENNETH I. "Accounting and the Law Intertwined: A Case Study of the Need for Uniform Accounting Principles." *Georgetown Law Journal*, Apr. 1968, pp. 670-687.

MAY, GEORGE O. "Premiums on Redemptions of Preferred Stock." *The Journal of Accountancy*, Aug. 1941, pp. 127-132.

MAY, GEORGE O. "Losses as a Cause of Gain." *The Journal of Accountancy*, Sept. 1941, pp. 221-228.

MONTGOMERY, ROBERT H. "Dealings in Treasury Stock." *The Journal of Accountancy*, June 1938, pp. 466-479.

MUSSELMAN, D. PAUL. "On the Nature of the Gain on Treasury Stock." *The Journal of Accountancy*, Aug. 1940, pp. 104-116.

PATON, W. A. "Postscript on 'Treasury' Shares." *The Accounting Review*, Apr. 1969, pp. 276-283.

RUDER, DAVID S. "Dangers in a Corporation's Purchases of Its Own Stock." *The Practical Lawyer*, May 1967, pp. 75-91.

RUDOLPH, E. GEORGE. "Accounting for Treasury Shares Under the Model Business Corporation Act." *Harvard Law Review*, Dec. 1959, pp. 323-331.

SCOVILL, H. T. "Premium on Redemption of Preferred-Stock Issues." *The Accounting Review*, June 1940, pp. 205-211.

Sprouse, Robert T. "Accounting for Treasury Stock Transactions: Prevailing Practices and New Statutory Provisions." *Columbia Law Review,* June 1959, pp. 882-900.
Stevenson, Richard Andrew. "The Reacquisition of Corporate Stock." Ph.D. dissertation, Michigan State University, 1965.
Werntz, William W. "Comments on the Capital Principle." *The Accounting Review,* Jan. 1942, pp. 35-41 and p. 57.
Young, Allan. "Financial, Operating and Security Market Parameters of Repurchasing." *Financial Analysts Journal,* July-Aug. 1969, pp. 123-128.
Young, Allan, and Marshall, Wayne. "Controlling Shareholder Servicing Costs." *Harvard Business Review,* Jan.-Feb. 1971, pp. 71-78.

Reorganizations and Adjustments of Equity

Pronouncements

American Institute of Certified Public Accountants

Committee on Accounting Procedure

Accounting Research Bulletin No. 3, "Quasi-Reorganization or Corporate Readjustment—Amplification of Institute Rule No. 2 of 1934." 1939.
Accounting Research Bulletin No. 43, Chapter 7A, "Quasi-Reorganization or Corporate Readjustment (Amplification of Institute Rule No. 2 of 1934)." 1953.
Accounting Research Bulletin No. 46, "Discontinuance of Dating Earned Surplus." 1956.

Accounting Principles Board

Opinion No. 9, "Reporting the Results of Operations," par. 28, "Capital transactions." 1966.
Opinion No. 11, "Accounting for Income Taxes," par. 50, "Operating Losses." 1967.

United States Securities and Exchange Commission

Accounting Series Release No. 1, "Treatment of losses resulting from revaluation of assets." Apr. 1937.
Accounting Series Release No. 15, "Description of surplus accruing subsequent to effective date of quasi-reorganization." Mar. 1940.
Accounting Series Release No. 16, "Disclosure of charge of deficit to capital surplus without approval of stockholders." Mar. 1940.
Accounting Series Release No. 25, "Procedure in Quasi-Reorganization." May 1941.

Books and Articles

AMERICAN INSTITUTE OF ACCOUNTANTS, Committee on Accounting Procedure. Letter to the Executive Committee of the American Institute of Accountants, October 20, 1945. *The Journal of Accountancy,* May 1946, pp. 440-442.

BLOUGH, CARMAN G. "An Occasion for Quasi-Reorganization." *The Journal of Accountancy,* Aug. 1952, pp. 229-230.

BUCHAN, L. J. Transcript of Forum on "Comments on The Capital Principle." *The Accounting Review,* Jan. 1942, pp. 53-56.

DEWING, ARTHUR STONE. *The Financial Policy of Corporations,* 5th ed., vol. 2. New York: Ronald Press Co., 1953.

ERICKSON, D. J. "Quasi-Reorganizations and Related Tax Effects." *The Arthur Andersen Chronicle,* July 1946, pp. 173-189.

RAPPAPORT, LOUIS H. "Quasi-Reorganizations." *The New York Certified Public Accountant,* Jan. 1959, p. 60.

REED, CHARLES H. "Preferred Stock Recapitalizations for Closely-Held Corporations." *The Arthur Andersen Chronicle,* June 1967, pp. 40-47.

SCHINDLER, JAMES S. *Quasi-Reorganization.* Ann Arbor: Bureau of Business Research, School of Business Administration, University of Michigan, 1958.

Restricted Securities

Pronouncements

UNITED STATES SECURITIES AND EXCHANGE COMMISSION

Accounting Series Release No. 113, "Restricted Securities." Oct. 1969.

Accounting Series Release No. 116, "Disclosure Concerning 'Restricted Securities'." Apr. 1970.

Accounting Series Release No. 118, "Accounting For Investment Securities by Registered Investment Companies." Dec. 1970.

Books and Articles

HERSHMAN, ARLENE. "Executive Stock That Can't Be Sold." *Dun's Review,* Apr. 1968, pp. 25-27.

JAENICKE, HENRY R. "Accounting for Restricted Stock Plans and Deferred Stock Plans." *The Accounting Review,* Jan. 1970, pp. 115-128.

MAKELA, BENJAMIN R., Edited by. *How to Use and Invest in Letter Stock.* New York: Presidents Publishing House. 1970.

Stock Dividends and Stock Splits

Pronouncements

AMERICAN INSTITUTE OF CERTIFIED PUBLIC ACCOUNTANTS

Special Bulletin No. 17. 1923. "Stock Dividends," pp. 2-5.
Special Bulletin No. 33. 1929. "Stock Dividends," pp. 1-4.

COMMITTEE ON ACCOUNTING PROCEDURE

Accounting Research Bulletin No. 11, "Corporate Accounting for Ordinary Stock Dividends." 1941.
Accounting Research Bulletin No. 11 (Revised), "Accounting for Stock Dividends and Stock Split-Ups." 1952.
Accounting Research Bulletin No. 43, Chapter 7B, "Stock Dividends and Stock Split-Ups." 1953.

AMERICAN ACCOUNTING ASSOCIATION

Accounting Concepts and Standards Underlying Corporate Financial Statements—1948 Revision. 1948.

NEW YORK STOCK EXCHANGE

Company Manual, Section A 13, "Stock Dividends."

UNITED STATES SECURITIES AND EXCHANGE COMMISSION

Accounting Series Release No. 124, "Pro Rata Stock Distributions to Shareholders." June 1972.

Books and Articles

BAKER, RALPH J. "Dividends of Combined Corporations: Some Problems Under Accounting Research Bulletin No. 48." *Harvard Law Review,* Jan. 1959, pp. 494-502.
BLOUGH, CARMAN G. "Valuing Shares of Stock Issued as a Dividend." *The Journal of Accountancy,* Aug. 1959, p. 76.
EITEMAN, DEAN S. "Are There Two Kinds of Stock Dividends?" *NAA Bulletin,* Oct. 1963, pp. 53-58.
GRAHAM, BENJAMIN. "Stock Dividends." *Barron's,* Aug. 3, 1953, p. 3 and Aug. 10, 1953, pp. 5-6.
HOXSEY, J. M. B. "Accounting for Investors." *The Journal of Accountancy,* Oct. 1930, pp. 251-284.
PUSKER, HENRI C. "Accounting for Capital Stock Distributions." *The New York Certified Public Accountant,* May 1971, pp. 347-352.

Sosnick, Stephen H. "Stock Dividends are Lemons, Not Melons." *California Management Review,* Winter 1961, pp. 61-82.

Sussman, M. Richard. *The Stock Dividend.* Ann Arbor: Bureau of Business Research, School of Business Administration, University of Michigan, 1962.

Whitaker, A. C. "The Stock Dividend Question." *The American Economic Review,* Mar. 1929, pp. 20-42.

York, Thomas. "Stock Dividends from the Viewpoint of the Declaring Corporation." *The Accounting Review,* Mar. 1941, pp. 15-33.

Stock Options and Stock Purchase Warrants

Pronouncements

American Institute of Certified Public Accountants

Committee on Accounting Procedure

Accounting Research Bulletin No. 37, "Accounting for Compensation in the Form of Stock Options." 1948.
Accounting Research Bulletin No. 37 (Revised), "Accounting for Compensation Involved in Stock Option and Stock Purchase Plans." 1953.
Accounting Research Bulletin No. 43, Chapter 13B, "Compensation Involved in Stock Option and Stock Purchase Plans." 1953.

Accounting Principles Board

Opinion No. 10, "Omnibus Opinion—1966," pars. 8-9, "Convertible Debt and Debt Issued with Stock Warrants." 1966.
Opinion No. 12, "Omnibus Opinion—1967," pars. 11-15, "Convertible Debt and Debt Issued with Stock Warrants." 1967.
Opinion No. 14, "Accounting for Convertible Debt and Debt Issued with Stock Purchase Warrants." 1969.
Opinion No. 25, "Accounting for Stock Issued to Employees." 1972.

American Accounting Association

A Statement of Basic Accounting Theory. 1966.

New York Stock Exchange

Listing Agreement, Section I, par. 6.

United States Securities and Exchange Commission

Accounting Series Release No. 76, "Adoption of Rule 3-20(d) of Article 3 of Regulation S-X." Nov. 1953.
Regulation S-X, Form and Content of Financial Statements.

Books and Articles

AMERICAN INSTITUTE OF ACCOUNTANTS, RESEARCH DEPARTMENT. "Accounting for Stock Options: Why Accounting Research Bulletin 37 Was Revised." *The Journal of Accountancy,* Apr. 1953, pp. 436-439.

ARTHUR ANDERSEN & Co. *Accounting and Reporting Problems of the Accounting Profession,* 3d ed., 1969.

BLAINE, R. E. "Accounting for Employee Stock Option Contracts." *The Canadian Chartered Accountant,* Jan. 1967, pp. 68-71.

BOWEN, WILLIAM. "Executive Compensation: the 'New Wave'." *Fortune,* Nov. 1964, p. 176.

CALL, DWIGHT V. "Some Salient Factors Often Overlooked in Stock Options." *The Accounting Review,* Oct. 1969, pp. 711-719.

CAMPBELL, EDWIN D. "Stock Options Should Be Valued." *Harvard Business Review,* July-Aug. 1961, pp. 52-58.

DEAN, ARTHUR H. "Employee Stock Options." *Harvard Law Review,* June 1953, pp. 1403-1449.

DILLAVOU, E. R. "Employee Stock Options." *The Accounting Review,* July 1945, pp. 320-326.

GOLDMAN, DAVID. "Stock options—Where to now?" *Financial Executive,* Mar. 1971, pp. 50-57.

GUTKNECHT, PAUL H. "The Determination of Compensation Under Stock Option Plans." *N.A.A. Bulletin,* Section 1, July 1961, pp. 25-35.

JAENICKE, HENRY R. "Accounting for Restricted Stock Plans and Deferred Stock Plans. *The Accounting Review,* Jan. 1970, pp. 115-128.

JOHNSON, KENNETH P. "Accounting For Sales of Restricted Stock." *The New York Certified Public Accountant* (Accounting and Auditing), Oct. 1968, p. 728.

LADD, DWIGHT R. *Contemporary Corporate Accounting and the Public.* Homewood, Ill.: Richard D. Irwin, 1963.

PEASE, FRED. "The Warrant—Its Powers and Its Hazards." *Financial Analysts Journal,* Jan.-Feb. 1963, pp. 25-32.

PHILLIPS, LAWRENCE C., and STONE, GARY K. "Nonqualified Deferred Compensation Plans for Executives." *Financial Executive,* Nov. 1969, pp. 68-76.

RABY, WILLIAM L. "Accounting for Employee Stock Options." *The Accounting Review,* Jan. 1962, pp. 28-38.

REISS, HARRY F., JR. "Disclosure Requirements With Respect to Stock Option Plans." *The New York Certified Public Accountant,* July 1968, pp. 501-504.

RIGGS, RICHARD C., JR., and WILBUR, E. PACKER. "What Price Stock Options?" *Financial Executive,* Oct. 1968, pp. 34-46.

ROTHSCHILD, V. HENRY. "Financing Stock Purchases by Executives." *Harvard Business Review,* Mar.-Apr. 1957, pp. 136-144.

ROYER, PIERRE. "Long-Term Warrants as Financing Instruments." Ph.D. dissertation, University of Michigan, 1970.

ROYER, PIERRE. "Long-term Warrants." *Canadian Chartered Accountant,* Feb. 1972, pp. 35-39.

SCHWARTZ, WILLIAM. "Warrants: A Form of Equity Capital." *Financial Analysts Journal,* Sept.-Oct. 1970, pp. 87-101.

Sweeney, Daniel L. *Accounting for Stock Options.* Ann Arbor: Bureau of Business Research, School of Business Administration, University of Michigan, 1960.

Washington, George Thomas, and Rothschild, V. Henry, 2nd. *Compensating The Corporate Executive,* 3d ed., vol. 2. New York: Ronald Press Co., 1962.

Index

Accounting Principles
Recommended, 3-4, 133-150
Illustration, 205-209
Implementing, 287-297
Acquisition of Business (*see* **Purchase of Business**)
Acquisition of Stock (*see* **Reacquired Stock**)
Additional Capital
Consideration received, 22-23, 24
Conversions, 26-28, 146
Nonstockholder transactions, 89, 281-283
Presentation, 88-89, 139, 208-209
Reacquired stock, 52-66, 146
Stock purchase warrants, 25-26
Stock rights, 25, 212
Transfers, 67-68
Adjustments of Capital, 264-280
Quasi-Reorganization (*see* **Quasi-Reorganization**)
Allocation of Combined Securities
Fair values, 26, 168
Market prices, 163-164, 168
Allocation of Costs
Reacquired stock, 59-66, 243-244
Retired stock, 52-57, 227-237
Allocation of Sales Proceeds
Fair values, 26
Market prices, 163-164
Appraisal of Assets
Component of equity, 87-88, 119, 135
Concessions, 281-282
Quasi-Reorganization, 68-69, 276-279

Appropriated Earnings, 2, 92-93, 116-117, 119, 148, 212, 220, 236-237, 244-246, 250, 296-297
Articles of Incorporation, 20, 47, 52, 67, 70, 81

Bonus Plans, 175-176, 179-180
Business Combinations
Exclusions from study, 10
Pooling of interests (*see* **Pooling of Interests**)
Present practices, 36-38
Purchase (*see* **Purchase of Business**)

Cancellation of Warrants, 169
Capital
Legal (*see* **Legal Capital**)
Model Act, 18-19
Paid-In, 18, 19, 21, 244-246
Warrants, 26
Permanent, 18, 45, 99, 105, 218
Presentation, 116-119
Stated, 18-19, 104, 106-107
Reacquired stock, 248
Reduction, 47
Surplus (*see* **Surplus**, Capital)
Usage, 20
Capital Stock
Authorized, 20-21, 23, 47
Disclosure, 91, 122-123
Canceled, 47-48

Capital Stock, *cont.*
  Class or series, 2, 80
    Contributed equity, 2, 117, 294
    Distinctions, 232
    Equity, 107-108, 115
    Exchange of stock, 268
    Presentation, 23, 87, 91, 117, 147
  Compensation, 251-261
  Consideration (*see* **Consideration for Stock**)
  Convertible (*see* **Convertible Preferred Stock**)
  Discount, 4, 154-157
  Equity interest, 222
  Fair value (*see* **Fair Value of Stock**)
  Issue costs, 23, 135, 144, 154-155
  Legal regulation (*see* **Legal Regulation**)
  Letter, 4, 154-157
    Fair value, 144, 154-155
  Model Act, 17-18, 47-49, 51
  No par, 18
    Presentation, 23
    Regulation, 18
  Nonredeemable, 47-48
  Outstanding, 48, 246
  Par value
    Change, 67
    Disclosure, 117, 122-123
    Pooling of interests, 37
    Preferred, 227-232, 273-274
    Presentation, 23, 104, 297
    Regulation, 17-18, 21
    Stock dividends, 42-43, 44, 214-215
    Stock splits, 44, 214-215, 219-220
  Preferred (*see* **Preferred Stock** *and* **Convertible Preferred Stock**)
  Premium, 17-18
  Presentation, 87-94, 113-115
  Reacquired (*see* **Reacquired Stock**)
  Redeemable, 47
  Regulation (*see* **Legal Regulation**)
  Residual ownership, 119, 222, 232
  Restated, 288-289
  Restricted, 4, 154-157
    Employees, 28
    Fair value, 144, 154-155
  Retired, 50-51, 52-55, 57, 222-223, 232-237

Capital Stock, *cont.*
  Splits (*see* **Stock Splits**)
  Stated value, 18
    Change, 67
    Presentation, 297
    Regulation, 21
  Stock dividends (*see* **Stock Dividends**)
  Stock splits (*see* **Stock Splits**)
  Transferable, 99
  Treasury (*see* **Reacquired Stock**)

Capital Surplus (*see* **Surplus, Capital**)

Cash Consideration, 22-23, 74, 76, 152-153, 210

Charter of Corporation, 20, 47, 52, 67, 70, 81

Closely Held Corporation, 11
  Acquisition
    Contingent consideration, 199-205
  Issuance of stock, 24
  Retirement of stock, 223
  Stock dividends, 43-44

Combinations
  Exclusions from study, 10
  Pooling of interests (*see* **Pooling of Interests**)
  Present practices, 36-38
  Purchase (*see* **Purchase of Business**)

Combined Securities, 25-26, 163-165, 166-167, 168

Common Stock (*see* **Capital Stock**)

Compensation
  Bonus plans, 175-176, 179-180
  Cash, 173
  Contingent, 173-176
  Deferred, 176, 186-187, 251-261
    Reacquired stock, 250-251, 256-261
    Reclassified, 293-294
  Liability, 154, 252-255, 256-261
  Phantom stock, 175-176
  Reacquired stock, 251-261
  Stock options, 29, 30-31, 34-35, 170-173, 175-180, 182-188
    Illustration, 205-209
  Variable plans, 34

Components of Equity, 97-130
  Adjustments, 67-71

Components of Equity, *cont.*
Alternatives, 100-116
Appraisal of assets, 87-88, 119, 135
Changes
　Decreases in securities, 221-263
　Quasi-Reorganization, 265
　Reorganization, 270-271, 274
Legal, 9, 18-20
Model Act, 18-19
Pooling of interests, 36-37
Presentation
　Recommended, 115-119, 287-297
　Traditional, 87-94
Reacquired stock (*see* **Reacquired Stock**)
Recommended change, 2-3, 115-123
Restated, 289-293
Sources, 100-103, 115-123, 134-136, 146-148
　Advantages, 127-130
Transfers, 85, 112-113, 148
　Quasi-Reorganization, 277-279
Treasury stock (*see* **Reacquired Stock**)

Consideration for Stock, 73-77, 139-144
Accounting recommended, 137, 151
Additional
　Purchase of business, 201-205
Adequate, 17-18, 139-141, 152-153, 167, 172, 173-174, 198
Allocated, 21-22
Cash, 22-23, 74, 76, 152-153, 210
Contingent, 199-205
Convertible debt, 5, 190, 192-194, 195-196, 295
Convertible preferred, 5, 190, 196-197
Fair value of stock (*see* **Fair Value of Stock**)
Illustration, 205-209
Issue costs, 23, 135, 144, 154-155
Noncash, 23-24, 76, 139-144
Presentation, 115-119
Property, 23-24, 152-153
Purchase of business, 37-38, 198-205
Recommended changes, 4-5
Reorganization, 268-271, 272
Required, 17
Services, 23-24, 29, 153
　Financing, 143
Stock options, 169-188

Consideration for Stock, *cont.*
Stock purchase warrants, 157-169
Stock rights, 79-80, 210-213

Consolidated Financial Statements, 6
Stock dividends, 43

Constructive Retirement, 49-51, 59-64, 241-242, 263

Contingent Compensation, 173-176

Contingent Equity Financing, 123-127
Convertible debt, 190-196, 293-294
Deferred compensation, 293-294
Expenses, 125
Illustration, 205-209
Presentation, 3
Reclassified, 288-289, 293-294
Stock options, 169-188, 261-262, 293-294
Stock purchase warrants, 157-169, 212-213, 271, 293-294

Contingent Issues of Stock
Purchase of business, 199-205
Recommended change, 5

Contraction of Capital, 49-51, 59-64, 241-242, 263

Contributed Equity
Allocated, 268
Classes of stock, 2, 117, 294
Contingent, 199-205
Convertible debt, 192-194
Convertible preferred stock, 196-197
Creditors, 282
Debt forgiven, 282
Derivative action, 282-283
Exchange of securities, 68, 267-271
Illustration, 205-209
Nonstockholders, 89, 280-283
Pooling of interests, 36-37, 148-149, 295-296
Presentation, 2, 87, 106, 115-119, 127-130, 139
Purchase of business, 198, 199-205
Recapitalization, 68
Reduction, 52-57, 58-66
　Reorganization, 69-71, 270-271
Restatement, 289-290, 295
Retirement of stock
　Common, 233-235
　Preferred, 226, 227-232

345

Contributed Equity, *cont.*
  Sale of stock, 152-157, 247-248
  Stock options, 169-188
  Stock purchase warrants, 159-169
  Stock rights, 212-213
  Stockholder derivative action, 282-283

Convertible Debt
  Consideration for stock, 5, 190, 192-194, 195-196, 295
  Classification, 123-127, 191-192, 195, 293-294
  Contingent equity, 123-127, 191-192, 195, 293-294
  Discount, 27
  Exchange right, 188-190
  Fair value of stock, 190, 192-195
  Financing expenses, 192-194, 195-196, 205-209
  Illustration, 205-209
  Interest expense, 192, 194
  Obligations assumed, 190-192, 195-196
  Present practices, 26-27
  Presentation, 3, 123-127, 191-192, 195, 205-209, 293-294
  Privilege, 188-190, 191-192
  Proceeds
    Allocated, 27
  Reacquired stock, 238-239, 249
  Recommended change, 5
  Redemption, 124-125, 189, 190-192, 194
  Treasury stock, 238-239, 249
  Warrants attached, 191, 195

Convertible Preferred Stock
  Consideration for common stock, 5, 190, 196-197
  Contributed equity, 196-197
  Exchange right, 188-190
  Fair value of stock, 190, 196-197
  Financing costs, 196-197
  Present practices, 26, 27-28, 146
  Privilege, 188-190
  Reacquired stock, 238-239, 249
  Recommended change, 5
  Redemption, 189, 197
  Retirement, 225-226
  Treasury stock, 238-239, 249

Corporate Charter, 20, 47, 52, 67, 70, 81

Corporations
  Entity, 98-99
  Laws, 8-9
  Legal entity, 98-99
  Limited liability, 99, 102, 107
  Regulation (*see* **Legal Regulation**)

Costs
  Allocation
    Reacquired stock, 59-66, 244
    Retired stock, 52-57, 227-237
  Debt financing (*see* **Financing Costs,** Debt)
  Equity financing (*see* **Financing Costs,** Equity)
  Financing (*see* **Financing Costs**)
  Issuing stock, 23, 135, 144, 154-155

Creditor Financing
  Adjustments, 264-266
  Exchange for stock, 68, 268-269
  Expenses, 144-146, 268-269
    Convertible debt, 192-196
    Warrants, 165-166, 169
  Interest arrears, 271-272
  Nonstockholders, 282

Date of Transaction, 73-74, 136, 137, 138
  Effective date, 137, 138

Debt
  Combined with warrants, 25-26, 163-165, 166-167, 168
  Convertible (*see* **Convertible Debt**)
  Exchange for stock, 68, 268-269
  Expenses, 144-146, 165-166, 268-269, 271-272
  Forgiven, 282
  Surrendered for warrants, 165

Decreases in Securities, 45-66, 221-263
  Recommended changes, 5

Deferred Charges
  Financing costs, 156-157
  Issue costs, 23

Deferred Compensation, 176, 186-187, 251-261
  Reacquired stock, 250-251, 256-261
  Reclassified, 293-294

Deferred Grants, 282

Deferred Equity (*see* **Contingent Equity Financing**)

Deficit
Eliminated, 69-71, 269, 271, 276-280
Pooling of interests, 37
Presentation, 128
Quasi-Reorganization, 69-71, 276-280
Reduction of capital, 111
Reorganization, 270-271
Stock issue costs, 23

Derivative Action, 282-283

Disclosure
Capital stock, 91-92, 117, 122-123
Capital surplus, 88-89
Classes of stock, 87, 91
Components of equity, 9, 88-89, 97-130
Contingent consideration, 205
Contingent equity, 124-125
Convertible debt, 191, 195
Legal capital, 111, 112, 120-121, 147-148, 236-237, 244-246, 297
Paid-In surplus, 88-89
Preferred stock, 91-92, 147
Purchase of business
  Contingent consideration, 205
Quasi-Reorganization, 70-71, 278-280
Reacquired stock, 90-91, 246, 255
Reorganization, 70-71
Restrictions, 91-93, 122, 246
Retained earnings, 88-89, 116-117
  Dated, 70-71, 90, 270, 278-280
Stock options, 35-36
Stock purchase warrants, 163, 165, 213
Treasury stock, 90-91, 246, 255
Surplus, 88-89

Discount on Stock, 4, 28-30, 154-157
Par value, 18, 22

Distributions of Stock, 267, 271-275
Compensation, 251-261
Dividends (*see* **Stock Dividends**)
Liabilities, 154
Reacquired, 58-61, 222
  Financing purpose, 246-250
  Operating purpose, 255-263
  Present practices, 64-66
Required, 224
Splits, 38-41, 44, 213-220

Distributions to Stockholders
Authorization, 99
Common distributed, 274-275
Deficit, 111
Dividends, 10, 46, 275
Liquidation, 21, 45
Optional dividends, 275
Preferred, 226-227, 227-232, 272-274
Preferred distributed, 272-275
Pro rata, 214-220
Reacquired stock, 49-51, 240-244
Regulation, 22
Restrictions, 45, 46-49, 92, 111-112, 122, 148, 273-274
Retirement of stock, 233-235
Stock dividends, 38-44, 213-220
Stock purchase warrants, 211, 212-213
Stock splits, 38-41, 44, 213-220
Stock rights, 24-25, 210-213
Treasury stock, 49-51, 240-244

Dividends
Financing costs, 144-146
In kind, 46
Optional, 275
Preferred, 226-227, 227-232
  Arrears, 92, 272-274
Reacquired stock, 48
Restrictions, 92, 122, 148
Scope of study, 10, 46
Stock (*see* **Stock Dividends**)
Treasury stock, 48

Donations
Misnomer, 280-283
Present practices, 89, 280-283
Restated, 296

Earned Surplus (*see* **Surplus, Earned;** *see also* **Retained Earnings**)

Earnings (*see* **Retained Earnings**)

Equity Financing Costs (*see* **Financing Costs,** Equity)

Exchange of Securities, 68, 267-271
Change of rights, 267-268
Common stock, 268, 270-271
Contingent equity, 124-125

Exchange of Securities, *cont.*
　Contributed equity
　　Allocated, 268
　　Unchanged, 267-268
　Conversions (*see* **Convertible Debt** *and* **Convertible Preferred Stock**)
　　Debt, 269
　　Preferred stock, 269-270
　　Warrants, 270-271

Fair Value of Securities
　Allocation basis, 26, 168
Fair Value of Stock
　Consideration, 4-5, 74-77, 137, 139-144, 151
　Contingent, 199-205
　Convertible debt, 190, 192-195
　Convertible preferred, 190, 196-197
　Discount, 154-157
　Distributions, 274-275
　Issue costs, 144, 154-155
　Letter stock, 4, 144
　Liability satisfied, 154
　Market price, 137, 143-144
　Measure of consideration, 24, 38, 74-77, 152-153, 295
　Measurement date, 75
　Purchase of business, 38, 75, 198-205
　Reacquired stock, 262-263
　Reorganization, 268-270, 272
　Restricted stock, 4, 144
　Stock dividend, 41-42, 75-77, 214-219
　Stock options, 75, 173-174, 178-181
　Stock purchase warrants, 157-169
　Treasury stock, 262-263
Financing Costs
　Contingent equity, 125
　Convertible preferred, 196-197
　Debt, 144-146, 165-166, 192-194, 195-196, 268-269, 271-272
　　Warrants, 165-166, 169
　Deferred, 156-157
　Equity, 135, 137, 138, 143, 144-146, 201-202, 205-209
　　Contingent consideration, 201-202
　　Convertible preferred, 196-197

Financing Costs, *cont.*
　Equity, *cont.*
　　Dividends, 144-146
　　Illustration, 205-209
　　Preferred, 196-197, 226-227, 227-232, 268, 269-270
　　Price discount, 156-157
　　Restricted stock, 156-157
　　Stock purchase warrants, 159-163, 164-165, 167, 168-169
　Illustration, 205-209
　Preferred stock, 196-197, 226-227, 227-232, 268, 269-270
　Purchase of business, 201-202
　Restricted stock, 156-157
　Stock purchase warrants, 159-163, 164-165, 165-166, 167, 168-169
Forgiveness of Debt, 282

Hybrid Securities, 123-124, 222

Implementing Recommendations, 287-297
　Contingent equity financing, 288-289, 293-294
　Convertible debt, 295
　Deferred compensation, 293-294
　Legal capital, 297
　Liabilities, 293-294
　Pooling of interests, 289, 295-296
　Reacquired stock, 288-289, 294-296
　Recommended restatement, 293-297
　Restatements of equity, 289-293
　Retained earnings, 296
　Revised accounting, 294
　Sources of equity, 289, 293
　Stock dividends, 296
　Stock options, 293-295
　Stock purchase warrants, 293-295
　Stock splits, 296
　Treasury stock, 288-289, 294-296
Increases in Securities, 17-44, 151-220
　Illustration, 205-209
　Interests unchanged, 210-220
　Recommended changes, 4-5
　Reduction of interests, 151-209
Insider Trading, 283

348

Invested Capital, 103-104
  Legal influence, 112-113
  Presentation, 100, 112-113

Issuing Stock, 17-44
  Consideration (*see* **Consideration for Stock**)
  Costs, 23, 135, 144, 154-155
  Fair value (*see* **Fair Value of Stock**)
  Interests reduced, 4-5
  Interests unchanged, 5

Lapsed Options, 34-35, 187-188

Lapsed Warrants, 162, 168-169

Laws
  Corporation, 8-9
  Influence on accounting, 81-84, 97-98, 109-111
  Issuing stock, 17, 21-22
  Model Act, 8-9, 17-19, 47-49, 51, 58, 88
  Reacquiring stock, 46-49, 224-225
  Stock dividends, 216
  Treasury stock, 46-49, 224-225

Legal Capital
  Changes, 20-21, 94
  Disclosure, 111, 112, 120-121, 147-148, 297
  Illustration, 236-237, 244-246
  Pooling of interests, 36-37, 148-149
  Presentation, 93, 101-102, 108-112, 113, 115, 116-119, 147-148, 236-237, 244-246, 297
  Reacquired stock, 47-48, 51, 224-225, 241-243, 244-246, 248, 250
  Status, 109-112
  Stock dividends, 42-43, 220
  Stock rights, 212-213
  Treasury stock, 47-48, 51, 224-225, 241-243, 244-246, 248, 250
  Trust fund theory, 47-48, 241-243

Legal Regulation, 8-9, 100-101, 103-104, 115
  Accounting, 21-22, 57-58, 109-113
  Capital stock, 17-22
    Adjustments, 67-68
  Consideration for stock, 17-18
  Corporate charter, 20
  Disclosure, 120-121

Legal Regulation, *cont.*
  Issue costs, 23
  Issuing stock, 17-22
  Presentation of equity, 88, 97-98, 103-104, 108-112
  Reacquired stock, 57-58, 224-225, 248
  Redemption of stock, 47-48
  Retirement of stock, 52, 224-225
  Stock dividends, 41, 42-43, 44, 220
  Stock splits, 44
  Surplus, 19, 21-22
  Transactions, 81-84, 136
  Transfer of components, 67-68
  Treasury stock, 57-58, 224-225, 248

Legal Restrictions
  Distributions to stockholders, 45-51, 92, 273-274
  Dividends
    Disclosure, 92, 148
    Presentation, 148
  Reacquired stock
    Dispositions, 57-58
  Reacquiring stock, 46-49, 51, 224-225, 242-243
  Treasury stock
    Dispositions, 57-58

Letter Stock, 4, 154-157
  Fair value, 144, 154-155

Liabilities
  Compensation, 154, 252-255, 256-261
  Convertible debt, 190-192, 195-196
  Debt, 269
    Interest arrears, 266, 271-272
  Distributions of stock, 154
  Purchase of business, 198-199
  Stock options, 187-188

Market Price of Stock
  Adjustments, 143-144
  Allocation basis, 163-164, 168
  Contingent consideration, 202-205
  Fluctuations, 142
  Measure of compensation, 31, 34-35
  Measure of consideration, 24, 38, 160-161
  Measure of fair value, 75-77, 137, 141-142, 143-144

Market Price of Stock, *cont.*
  Optional dividends, 275
  Stock distributions, 215-216
  Stock dividends, 41-42
Model Act
  Capital stock, 17-18, 47-49, 51
  Capital surplus, 18-19
  Components of equity, 18-19
  Presentation of equity, 88
  Provisions, 8-9
  Reacquired stock, 47-49, 51, 58
  Stated capital, 18-19
  Surplus, 18-19
  Treasury stock, 47-49, 51, 58

Noncash Consideration, 23-24, 76, 139-144, 163, 197-205
Nonequity Securities, 3, 123-127
Nonstockholder Contributions, 89, 280-283
  Creditors, 282
  Government concessions, 280-282
  Individuals, 282-283
  Restated, 296

Options (*see* **Stock Options**)

Paid-In Capital, 18, 19, 21, 26, 244-246
Partnership, 98-99
Phantom Stock, 175-176
Pooling of Interests
  Components of equity, 36-37, 148-149, 295-296
  Legal capital, 36-37, 148-149
  Reacquired stock, 60
  Restated, 289, 295-296
  Retained earnings, 37, 148-149, 296
  Stock issued, 24
  Treasury stock, 60
Potential Equity (*See* **Contingent Equity Financing**)
Preferred Stock
  Combined with warrants, 25-26, 163-165, 166-167

Preferred Stock, *cont.*
  Contributed equity, 226, 227-232
  Convertible (*see* **Convertible Preferred Stock**)
  Disclosure, 91-92, 147
  Distributed to common stockholders, 274-275
  Dividends, 226-227, 227-232
    Arrears, 92, 272-274
  Exchange, 68, 268-269, 269-270, 270
  Features, 225
  Financing costs, 196-197, 226-227, 227-232, 268, 269-270
  Liquidating preference, 91-92, 121
  Nonredeemable, 225-226, 269-270
  Par value, 227-232, 273-274
  Premium, 226-227, 227-232
    Amortization, 228
  Presentation, 107-108, 115, 116-117, 121
  Reacquired, 52-57, 91
  Redeemable, 225-226
  Redemption, 146
  Retired, 52-57, 222-223, 227-232
  Treasury, 52-57, 91
  Warrants combined, 25-26, 163-165, 166-167
Presentation of Contingent Equity, 3, 123-127, 191-192, 195, 293-294
  Illustration, 205-209
Presentation of Equity, 97-130
  Alternatives, 100-116
  Capital stock, 22-23
  Components, 87-94, 117, 134-136, 146-148
  Contributed, 2, 87, 106, 115-119, 127-130
  Current, 87-94
  Illustration, 116-117, 205-209, 236-237, 244-246
  Invested capital, 103-104
  Legal capital, 93, 115, 116-119, 147-148, 297
  Legal requirements, 88, 97-98, 103-104, 108-112
  Preferred stock, 116-117, 121
  Reacquired stock, 46, 52, 59-60, 87, 90-91, 246
  Recommended, 108-130
    Adoption, 287-297
    Illustration, 116-117

Presentation of Equity, *cont.*
  Retained earnings, 2, 88-89, 100-103,
      103-104, 115-123, 127-130
    Dated, 70-71, 90, 270, 278-280
    Retired stock, 236-237
    Single amount, 104-108, 113-115
    Sources, 2-3, 100-103, 115-119,
        146-148
      Advantages, 127-130
    Surplus, 88
    Total, 104-108, 113-115
    Traditional, 87-94, 108-112
    Treasury stock, 46, 52, 59-60, 87,
        90-91, 246

Proprietorship, 98-99

Purchase of Business, 197-205
  Combined securities, 168
  Consideration for stock, 37-38,
      198-199
    Additional, 201-205
  Contingent consideration, 199-205
  Contributed equity, 198, 199-205
  Disclosure
    Contingent consideration, 205
    Escrow agreement, 205
  Fair value of stock, 38, 75, 198
    Contingent consideration, 199-205
  Financing costs, 201-202
  Liability, 198-199
  Present practices, 36, 37-38
  Reacquired stock, 38, 240, 248-249
  Warrants issued, 168

Qualified Stock Options, 28, 34-35

Quasi-Reorganization, 68-71, 265,
    275-280
  Appraisal of assets, 68-69, 276-279
  Components of equity, 277-279
  Dating retained earnings, 278-280
  Deficit, 69-71, 276-280
  Disclosure, 70-71, 278-280
  Procedures, 276-277
  Revaluation of assets, 68-69, 276-279
  Sources of equity, 277-280

Reacquired Stock, 45-66, 221-263
  Allocation of costs, 59-66, 243-244
  Assets, 46, 60, 247-248, 254-255, 263
    Presentation, 91
    Reclassified, 288-289

Reacquired Stock, *cont.*
  Canceled, 47-48
  Compensation deferred, 250-261
  Contraction of capital, 49-51, 59-64,
      241-242, 263
  Conversions, 238-239, 249
  Decrease in equity, 221, 233
  Disclosure, 90-91, 246, 255
  Dispositions, 57-61, 222, 224
    Financing, 246-250
    Operating, 255-263
    Present practices, 50-51, 64-66
  Dividends, 48
  Exchange for investment, 46
  Financing purposes, 237-250, 262
    Conversions, 238-239, 249
    Exercise of warrants, 238-239, 249
    Purchase of business, 240, 248-249
    Recommended change, 5
    Stock dividends, 219, 239, 249-250
  Legal capital, 47-48, 51, 224-225,
      241-243, 244-246, 248, 250
  Legal regulation, 224-225, 248
  Legal restrictions, 46-49, 51, 57-58,
      224-225, 242-243
  Limitations, 46-49
  Operating purposes, 250-263
    Recommended change, 5
    Stock options, 250, 261-262
    Stock purchase plans, 250, 261-262
  Optional acquisition, 222
  Optional distribution, 222, 224,
      251-261
  Outstanding status, 48, 246
  Pooling of interests, 60
  Preferred, 52-57, 91
  Present practices, 46-52, 58-66, 73,
      75, 80, 90
  Presentation, 46, 49-52, 87, 90-91,
      246, 255
  Purchase of business, 38, 240,
      248-249
  Purposes, 222
    Financing, 223-224
    Operating, 223-224
  Reclassified, 288-289, 292, 294
  Recommended change, 5
  Required acquisition, 222, 252-254
    Reclassified, 294
  Required distribution, 222, 224,
      251-261
  Regulation, 224-225, 248

351

Reacquired Stock, *cont.*
Restrictions, 46-49, 51, 57-58, 122
Retained earnings restricted, 47-49, 51
Retirement, 49-51, 222-223
  Common, 233-235
  Preferred, 226, 227-232
Sales, 57-61
Status, 48
Stock dividends, 219, 239, 249-250
Stock options, 35, 250, 261-262
Stock purchase plans, 250, 261-262
Stock purchase warrants, 238-239, 249
Surplus restricted, 47-49, 51
Suspense (*see* Unallocated deduction)
Timing of transaction, 73
Unallocated deduction, 49-52, 58-59, 61-65, 241-243
  Presentation, 90-91
  Reclassified, 292, 294-296
Warrants, 238-239, 249

Recapitalization, 68, 264-275 (*see also* **Reorganization**)

Recommendations in Study
Adoption, 287-297
Summary, 2-6
Transactions, 133-150

Redemption of Stock
Optional, 227
Permitted, 224-225
Preferred, 146
Regulation, 47-48
Required, 226-227
Restrictions, 224-225

Regulation (*see* **Legal Regulation**)

Reorganization, 68-71, 264-275
Common stock interests, 268-271, 274-275
Debt, 269, 271-272
Disclosure, 70-71
Distributions of securities, 271-275
Preferred stock, 269-270, 270, 272-274
Quasi (*see* **Quasi-Reorganization**)
Stock purchase warrants, 270-271

Reporting (*see* **Disclosure** and **Presentation of Equity**)

Residual Equity, 119, 222, 232

Restatement of Equity
Classifying components, 288-293
Contingent equity financing, 288-289, 293-294
Contributed equity, 289-290, 295
Limitations, 290
Pooling of interests, 289, 295-296
Reacquired stock, 288-289, 292, 294
Recommended, 293-297
Retained earnings, 296
Treasury stock, 288-289, 292, 294

Restatements
Reorganization, 69-71

Restricted Stock, 4, 154-157
Employees, 28
Fair value, 144, 154-155

Retained Earnings (*see also* **Surplus, Earned**)
Appropriated, 2, 92-93, 116-117, 119, 148, 212, 220, 236-237, 244-246, 250, 296-297
Changes, 135, 137
Component of equity, 100-103, 104-107, 115-120
Dated, 70-71, 90, 270, 278-280
Deficit (*see* **Deficit**)
Definition, 19
Distributions, 93-94, 233
Dividends (*see* **Dividends**)
Financing costs (*see* **Financing Costs,** Equity)
Increases, 135
Pooling of interests, 37, 148-149, 296
Presentation, 2, 88-89, 100-103, 103-104, 107-108
  Recommended, 115-123, 127-130
Reductions, 52-57, 58-66, 135
  Disclosure, 90
  Illustration, 205-209
  Reorganizations, 68-71
  Stock options, 181-182
Regulation, 18-19, 22
Reorganizations, 68-71
Restated, 296
Restrictions, 47-49, 117, 122, 148, 246
  Reacquired stock, 47-49, 51
  Retirement of stock, 52-57, 227-237
  Stock dividends, 41-44, 214-218
  Stock splits, 214-215

Retained Earnings, *cont.*
   Transfers, 67-68, 103-104, 148
     Disclosure, 90
     Restated, 296
     Retirement of stock, 227-232, 233-237
     Stock dividends, 214-215
     Stock splits, 214-215
     Unappropriated, 2, 92-93, 116-117, 212, 236-237, 244-246, 250

Retirement of Stock, 50-51, 52-57, 222-223, 227-237
   Allocation of costs, 52-57, 227-237
   Common, 232-237
   Constructive, 49-51, 59-64, 241-242, 263
   Effective, 241-242
   Illustration, 236-237
   Preferred, 222-223, 227-232
   Present practices, 52-57, 61-64
   Reacquired stock, 49-51
     Pooling of interests, 60
   Recommended change, 5
   Regulation, 52, 224-225
   Treasury stock, 49-51
     Pooling of interests, 60

Revaluation of Assets
   Component of equity, 87-88, 119, 135
   Quasi-Reorganization, 68-69, 276-279

Rights (*see* **Stock Subscription Rights**)

Sale of Stock
   Cash proceeds, 22-23, 152-153
   Legal regulation, 17-18

Scope of Study, 6-11
   Exclusions, 9-11
   Recurring transactions, 6-8

Shadow Stock, 176

Sources of Equity, 100-103
   Contributions, 2, 115-119, 139
   Earnings, 2, 100-103, 115-120
   Features, 134-136
   Financing, 100-103
   Maintained, 146-148, 266

Sources of Equity, *cont.*
   Presentation, 2-3, 100-103, 115-119, 127-130, 146-148
   Recommended, 115-123, 287-297
   Retained earnings, 2, 100-103, 115-120
   Revised Quasi-Reorganization, 277-280
   Transfers, 93

Splits (*see* **Stock Splits**)

Stated Capital, 18-19, 104, 106-107
   Reacquired stock, 248
   Reduction, 47

Statutes (*see* **Laws, Legal Regulation,** *and* **Legal Restrictions**)

Stock Dividends, 213-220
   Closely held corporation, 43-44
   Definition, 39
   Fair value of stock, 41-42, 75-77, 214-219
   Legal capital, 41, 42-43, 220
   Limitations, 218-219
   Par value of stock, 42-43, 44
   Present practices, 38-44
   Reacquired stock, 48, 219, 239, 249-250
   Recipient, 216
   Recommended change, 5
   Regulation, 219
   Restated, 296
   Subsidiary's, 43
   Treasury stock, 48, 219, 239, 249-250

Stock Options, 169-188
   Compensation, 29, 30-31, 34-35, 170-173, 175-180, 182-188
     Allocation, 183-186
     Deferred charge, 186-187
     Illustration, 205-209
     Liability, 186-187
     Measurement date, 31-34
     Period, 183-184
     Present value, 186
   Consideration for stock, 4-5, 79-80, 170-174, 177-181, 185-188
   Reclassified, 294-295
   Contingency, 173-176
   Contingent equity, 123-127, 187, 261-262, 293-294
   Contributed equity, 171-172, 187

Stock Options, *cont.*
Date of transactions, 178-180
Dilution, 181-182
Disclosure, 35-36
Discount price, 28-30
Disposition of stock, 183-184
Disqualifying disposition, 187
Exercisable date, 31, 32, 35-36, 179, 184-185
Exercise date, 31, 33, 35-36, 178-181, 183-184
Fair value of stock, 75, 173-174, 178-181
Grant date, 31-32, 34-35, 35-36, 179-180, 183-184, 186
Illustration, 205-209
Lapsed, 34-35, 187-188
Measurement date, 31-34
Noncompensatory, 29-30, 171
Nonqualified, 28
Opportunity cost, 182
Option price, 170, 176
Present practices, 28-36
Presentation, 123-127
Property right, 33
Qualified, 28
  Compensation, 34-35
Reacquired stock, 35, 250, 261-262
Receipts of optionees, 180
Recommended change, 4-5
Restated, 293-295
Risks, 174-175, 182-183
Services of employees, 172-178
Stock purchase warrants, 170
Terminated, 187
Timing of transactions, 73, 178-180
Treasury stock, 35, 250, 261-262
Value of services, 172-173, 174-175, 176-180
Variable plans, 34

Stock Purchase Plans (*see* **Stock Options**)

Stock Purchase Warrants, 157-169
Allocation of proceeds, 26, 163-164, 168
Business combination, 168
Canceled, 169
Cash sale, 158-163
Combined with other securities, 25-26, 163-165, 166-167, 168
Consideration for stock, 4
Reclassified, 295

Stock Purchase Warrants, *cont.*
Consideration received, 158-161
  Noncash, 163, 168
Contingent equity, 123-127, 157-169, 212-213, 271, 293-294
Creditor financing, 165-166, 169
Date of transactions, 159-160, 167
Description, 24-25
Detachable, 26, 163-165, 191
Distributed to stockholders, 212-213
Exercise, 159-161
Fair value of stock, 157-169
Financing costs, 159-163, 164-165, 165-166, 167, 168-169, 205-209
Illustration, 205-209
Lapsed, 162, 168-169
Market price of stock, 160-161
Nondetachable, 26, 166, 195
Perpetual, 158
Present practices, 25-26
Presentation, 123-127, 205-209
Proceeds, 158-161
  Allocation, 26, 163-164, 168
Purchase of business, 168
Reacquired stock, 238-239, 249
Recommended change, 4
Redeemed, 169
Reorganization, 270-271
Restated, 293-295
Stock options, 170
Stock rights, 211
Timing of transactions, 73-74, 159-160, 167
Treasury stock, 238-239, 249

Stock Splits, 213-220
Description, 38-40
Legal capital, 44
  Illustration, 236-237, 244-246
Par value of stock, 44
Present practices, 38-41, 44
Recommended change, 5
Regulation, 220
Restated, 296

Stock Subscription Rights, 24-25, 210-213
Consideration for stock, 79-80, 210-213
Contributed equity, 212-213
Description, 24-25
Interests of stockholders, 210-212
Legal capital, 212-213

Stock Subscription Rights, *cont.*
  Present practices, 24-25
  Stock purchase warrants, 211, 212-213
Stockholder Derivative Action, 282-283
Surplus
  Capital
    Disclosure, 88-89
    Model Act, 18-19
    Presentation, 105-106
    Quasi-Reorganization, 278-279
    Reduction, 51, 52-57, 69-70
    Regulation, 18, 21
    Stock dividends, 41-42
  Earned (*see also* **Retained Earnings**)
    Disclosure, 88-89
    Model Act, 19
    Reduction, 52-57, 58-66, 69-71
    Regulation, 19
    Restrictions, 47-49, 51
    Stock dividends, 41-42
  Meanings, 20
  Paid-In
    Disclosure, 88-89
    Distribution, 49
    Regulation, 18, 19, 21
  Presentation, 88
  Restated, 289-290
  Restrictions, 47-49, 51
  Terminology, 89

Tender Solicitation
  Retirement of stock, 52, 226

Terminology
  Additional capital, 89
  Capital, 18-20
  Contingent equity financing, 123-127
  Earned surplus, 19
  Equity, 118-119
  Nonequity securities, 126-127
  Reacquired stock, 46
  Retained earnings, 19, 89
  Stock dividends, 38-41
  Stock splits, 39-41
  Stockholders' equity, 118-119
  Surplus, 20, 89
  Treasury stock, 46
Total Equity, 104-108, 113-115
Transaction Date, 73-74, 136, 137, 138
  Effective date, 137, 138
Treasury Stock (*see* **Reacquired Stock**)
Trust Fund Theory, 47-48, 241-243

Unappropriated Earnings, 2, 92-93, 116-117, 212, 236-237, 244-246, 250
Undistributed Earnings (*see* **Retained Earnings**)

Warrants (*see* **Stock Purchase Warrants**)